*The SDLP: the Struggle for Agreement
in Northern Ireland, 1970–2000*

The SDLP

The Struggle for Agreement in Northern Ireland, 1970–2000

SEÁN FARREN

FOUR COURTS PRESS

This book was set in 11 on 14pt Adobe Garamond
by Mark Heslington, Scarborough, North Yorkshire for
FOUR COURTS PRESS LTD
7 Malpas Street, Dublin 8, Ireland
www.fourcourtspress.ie
and in the United States for
FOUR COURTS PRESS
c/o ISBS, 920 N.E. 58th Avenue, Suite 300, Portland, OR 97213.

© Seán Farren and Four Courts Press 2010

A catalogue record for this title is available from the British Library.

ISBN 978–1–84682–238–4

Printed in Great Britain by
MPG Books Ltd, Bodmin, Cornwall

To Nora, Anna & Oona

Contents

Illustrations

(Illustrations appear between p. 256 and p. 257)

1 John Hume addresses demonstrators at a civil rights protest in Derry, 1969.
2 An early SDLP press conference.
3 A sit-down anti-internment protest in Derry, 1971.
4 Michael Canavan at an anti-internment demonstration in Derry, 1971.
5 Hugh Logue, John Hume and Ivan Cooper under army escort.
6 John Hume calming demonstrators at an anti-internment protest.
7 John Hume being frisked by a British soldier in Derry.
8 SDLP assembly members with Paul O'Dwyer at Stormont, 1973.
9 SDLP chairman Denis Haughey addressing the media, 1974.
10 Gerry Fitt making the leader's address at an SDLP annual conference, 1975.
11 Paddy Devlin and Denis Haughey at a conference of social democratic and labour parties.
12 John Hume accompanied by his wife and party colleagues, 1979.
13 John Hume, John Taylor and Ian Paisley, 1979.
14 John Hume views damage caused by a fire-bomb attack, 1983.
15 John Hume, Séamus Mallon, Eddie McGrady, Joe Hendron and Austin Currie, 1983–4.
16 John Hume accompanies Tip O'Neill on a walk-about in Derry, 1982.
17 Séamus Mallon canvassing in Newry, 1986.
18 Séamus Mallon carried in triumph after his victory in the 1986 by-election.
19 Eddie McGrady greets news of his election, 1987.
20 Joe Hendron and Alasdair McDonnell, 1992.
21 Eddie McGrady, Joe Hendron, John Hume and Séamus Mallon.
22 Gerry Adams, Albert Reynolds and John Hume shake hands, Dublin, 1994.
23 Mark Durkan, Denis Haughey, Bríd Rodgers and Seán Farren with Nelson Mandela, 1997.
24 Bríd Rodgers under police escort at Drumcree.

Abbreviations and acronymns

ANC	African National Congress
APNI	Alliance Party of Northern Ireland
CDU	Campaign for Democracy in Ulster
DFA	Department of foreign affairs
DUP	Democratic Unionist Party
EC	European Community
ECHR	European Court of Human Rights
EEC	European Economic Community
GAA	Gaelic Athletic Association
HC	House of Commons
IICD	Independent International Commission on Decommissioning
IIP	Irish Independence Party
INC	Irish National Caucus
INLA	Irish National Liberation Army
IRA	Irish Republican Army
LAW	Loyalist Association of Workers
NAI	National Archives of Ireland
NAUK	National Archives of the UK
NDP	National Democratic Party
NIA	Northern Ireland Assembly
NIC-ICTU	Northern Ireland Committee of the Irish Congress of Trade Unions
NICRA	Northern Ireland Civil Rights Association
NIF	New Ireland Forum
NIHC	Northern Ireland House of Commons
NILP	Northern Ireland Labour Party
NIO	Northern Ireland Office
NUM	New Ulster Movement
PES	Party of European Socialists
PIRA	Provisional IRA

PR	Proportional representation
PRONI	Public Records Office of Northern Ireland
PSNI	Police Service of Northern Ireland
PUP	Progressive Unionist Party
RAF	Royal Air Force
RUC	Royal Ulster Constabulary
SAS	Special Air Service
SDLP	Social Democratic and Labour Party
UDA	Ulster Defence Association
UDP	Ulster Democratic Party
UFF	Ulster Freedom Fighters
ULC	Ulster Loyalist Council
ULCCC	United Loyalist Central Coordinating Committee
UN	United Nations
UPUP	Ulster Popular Unionist Party
UUC	Ulster Unionist Council
UUP	Ulster Unionist Party
UUUC	United Ulster Unionist Council
UVF	Ulster Volunteer Force
UWC	Ulster Workers' Council

Acknowledgments

In the course of writing this book many people provided invaluable assistance and to all of them I owe an enormous debt of gratitude. First, I wish to express my thanks to those dedicated professionals who assisted me locate the many primary and other sources I consulted. To the librarians at the University of Ulster, the Newspaper Library in the Belfast City Library, and at Belfast's Linenhall Library, as well as to the archivists at the National Archives of Ireland, the Public Record Office of Northern Ireland and the UK National Archives, I offer sincere thanks.

Among many individuals who offered assistance and advice, I am particularly indebted to my SDLP colleague and friend, Denis Haughey, who read an early version of the text and drew on his vast experience of the party from its foundation to offer extremely helpful information and advice. To the many other SDLP members who discussed their own involvement and who are named elsewhere, I am also deeply indebted. Along with them are the many hundreds of other members not mentioned, but whose dedication to democratic politics in the most challenging of circumstances inspired me to undertake this work.

Finally, I offer the most heartfelt thanks and appreciation to my loving wife and soulmate Patricia, and to our children, Orla, Ciara, Niamh and Ronan, without whose support and encouragement through the years, this book would not have been possible.

Portstewart
May 2010

Introduction: 'Your trouble, you've no guns'

'Your trouble, you've no guns' was a remark British Prime Minister Tony Blair made to members of an SDLP delegation during the tortuous negotiations over decommissioning that followed the breakdown of Northern Ireland's power-sharing executive in October 2002. His remark indicated why the party had been marginalized by the British and Irish governments as they focused their efforts on persuading Sinn Féin and the Provisional IRA (PIRA) that time was running out, and unless a credible decommissioning of PIRA weapons took place soon, the 1998 Good Friday agreement was in danger of becoming a dead letter.

While the SDLP resented its marginalization and its consequent loss of influence, ironically, Blair's remark summed up an essential and fundamental element of the party's philosophy ever since its foundation in 1970. Founded as a social democratic party committed to working peacefully for Irish unity, and emerging from the cauldron of the civil rights agitation in the late nineteen-sixties, the SDLP was convinced that violence in the cause of unity was a tragic and disastrous contradiction. The party believed that violence would undermine the very cause itself, not least because its targets included the people a united Ireland must embrace. In effect, the SDLP believed that the PIRA and all of the other so-called republican paramilitaries were waging war on Irish men and women and, not, as their propaganda suggested, just on British forces and British interests. The number of violent deaths for whom the combined forces of these paramilitaries was responsible starkly bears out this judgment. Of the 3,636 people killed in the period 1966–99, they were responsible for 2,139, the vast majority of whom were civilians, many from a Protestant-Unionist background. To these deaths must be added the hundreds more injured and the many millions of pounds worth of property damaged and destroyed, businesses ruined and businesses lost. It was a heavy price for a goal unachievable using their methods.

For the SDLP, a united Ireland meant first and foremost an *agreed* Ireland, on the premise that unity could only persist in an agreement supported by a majority in the North sufficient to guarantee constitutional stability. This approach directly challenged as outmoded and simplistic traditional Nationalist arguments that Britain alone had been responsible for the partition of Ireland, that the British 'presence' in the North was purely in defence of British interests, and that Britain should, therefore, either withdraw voluntarily or be forced to withdraw. In the SDLP's analysis, the political and religious divisions that had caused partition long pre-dated 1920, and while British involvement in Ireland had shaped those divisions, they would not be overcome by attempts to force Britain's withdrawal against the wishes of a majority in the North. In effect, as SDLP leader (1979–2001), John Hume frequently argued it was the *people* of Ireland, and, in particular, the people of Northern Ireland who were divided, not the territory, and that attempts to force Unionists into a united Ireland against their will were doomed to failure.

However, if Unionists could not be coerced into a united Ireland, Nationalists had been obliged to live in a state to which they had not given their consent, much less their allegiance. Since partition in 1920, the Nationalist community had, for the most part, withdrawn from full participation in the North's political and civic life. Unsure of their place in a divided Ireland, Nationalists sought refuge in the strength and vibrancy of their own community. It was a withdrawal reinforced by the various forms of discrimination practised against them by successive Unionist-controlled administrations – discrimination in employment, particularly in the public service, in the gerrymandering of electoral boundaries, in the allocation of public housing and in the demonstrably British ethos of public life. It was not until the 1960s when the civil rights movement raised fundamental questions about the nature of the state, and when the SDLP provided the means whereby those questions were forced onto the political agenda, that politicians began grappling with the task of defining and agreeing a new constitutional and political framework for the North. For the SDLP, that framework had to be based on respect for the allegiances and aspirations of both Nationalists and Unionists, and had to allow the two communities and their representatives to work together for the mutual benefit of all of the people of the North, doing so in close cooperation with the rest of Ireland.

In essence, the challenge was to devise acceptable constitutional and political arrangements that would embrace the sense of Irishness and Britishness held by each community, and would enable the people of the North to move from their confrontational relationship to one of mutual respect and cooperation. The

SDLP's founders insisted, therefore, that the *principle of consent*, that is to say, that a majority of the people of Northern Ireland would have to *agree* to Irish unity, was at the centre of the party's constitution and that a partnership approach would inform its relationships with Unionist representatives. In other words, the party would work for unity, not wage war for it.

While most people of the Nationalist tradition in the North, as in the south of Ireland, shared that conviction, and supported the SDLP's approach, it was not a message welcomed by those who saw in the turmoil of 1968–9 an opportunity to force a British withdrawal. Tragic and impractical as that attempt was, it was directed by men and women who did not lack determination, and who branded the SDLP as British lackeys and as traitors because of their efforts to reach out to Unionists, and to create political institutions North and South that would facilitate reconciliation between the country's divided traditions.

The SDLP's approach was also a new and more daunting challenge to Unionists than the challenge hitherto offered by northern Nationalists. By offering Unionists a partnership approach to governing Northern Ireland, both in local and regional government, and by doing so on a basis of equality, and parity of esteem for both traditions, the SDLP challenged Unionists' claims to govern by virtue of numerical superiority, and forced a long, slow rethink about community relationships.

This study tells the story of SDLP's role in Ireland, North and South, over the turbulent period from the party's foundation in 1970 until the first post-Good Friday Agreement power-sharing executive took office in December 1999. It is a story of persistence with the message that only on a basis of democratic principles, partnership and respect for human rights could a solution be found to the North's problems. A combination of republican and loyalist violence together with Unionist unwillingness to accept partnership politics within the North and between North and South, tragically delayed the ultimate triumph of the SDLP's brand of constitutional politics.

The story is traced through four phases, the first of which embraces the early efforts by the SDLP to negotiate and establish a new political relationship with Unionists, and covers the period from 1970 to 1976. The second phase traces the years 1977–85, when the SDLP's focus switched to promoting a joint British-Irish approach to the North's problems that led to the 1985 Anglo-Irish Agreement. The third phase, 1986–94, discusses the party's role in efforts to engage with the parties linked to and supporting the paramilitary campaigns to persuade them to declare a ceasefire. The fourth phase, 1995–2000, traces the

SDLP's involvement in the negotiations that followed the 1994 ceasefires, to the early stages of implementing the 1998 Good Friday Agreement.

The author was a prominent member of the party for much of this period, serving as a public representative and as a member of several negotiating teams, as well as a minister in the power-sharing executive, 1999–2002. It is not his personal story. Rather it is the story of a party whose leaders and ordinary members were people of great dedication, and commitment, pledged to work for the unity of the people of Ireland, Catholic, Protestant and dissenter, in a spirit of mutual respect and partnership. These leaders and members were convinced that their approach was the only basis for an honourable settlement, and were also convinced that it would ultimately triumph, as indeed it did in the agreement reached on 10 April 1998. This book bears testimony to their convictions.

PART I

Years of hope (1970–1976)

Chapter 1

Foundation and early challenges

After the turmoil of the preceding two years, 1970 opened with considerable hope that an accommodation between Northern Ireland's divided communities was a possibility. Writing in the *Irish Times* at the beginning of the New Year, political correspondent Michael McInerney listed sixteen reforms of greater or lesser significance that had been announced by the Northern Ireland government in face of demands from the civil rights movement, and under pressure from the British and Irish governments.[1] McInerney lyrically surmised that 'it should now be possible to knit again this scattered corn into one mutual sheaf, those broken limbs into one body'. Tragically, this hope would not to be realized. As the year advanced, it was not an accommodation that emerged, but a quickening pace towards almost three decades of political instability and intercommunal violence. By the year's end, the gulf between the communities had widened considerably and political divisions were becoming more sharply marked than ever before.

In effect, 1970 was to witness significant political upheaval and, more ominously, paramilitary organizations from the Nationalist and Unionist communities launch their campaigns of terror. The brief calm after two years of upheaval was about to be shattered with terrible consequences. Those two years had been marked by street demonstrations demanding, or opposing, civil rights reform culminating in the siege of Derry's Bogside in August 1969, and in violent repercussions elsewhere.[2] An extremely volatile public order situation had been created, resulting in British troops patrolling the streets of Northern Ireland, and the emergence of so-called paramilitary defenders in both communities. The toll of deaths and injuries was still low in early 1970, but bombings and shootings were to increase over the year, presaging a worsening situation the following year.[3] At the other end of the spectrum, new political parties formed, while others reformed or fragmented as forces within each community reacted to the wider situation.

PARTIES IN DISARRAY

The relative calm at the beginning of the year suggested, as McInerney's assessment indicated, that the initiative might still lie with the politicians. Within the
Unionist community, Prime Minister Terence O'Neill's reform programme,
though under pressure from colleagues opposed to reform, still retained majority
support in the administration led by his successor James Chichester-Clarke. But
the political calm was deceptive. The long-dominant and apparently monolithic
Ulster Unionist Party (UUP)[4] continued its internecine pro- and anti-reform
battles. The party was fragmenting, as elements opposed to the civil rights reform
programme gathered strength and stridently challenged the need for and the pace
of change. To them, reforms were unjustified concessions to people committed
to the destruction of the northern state. In their attacks on the government, anti-
reformers found common cause with extreme figures outside the party, like the
anti-ecumenist Protestant cleric Ian Paisley, whose uncompromising resistance to
reform was also attracting growing support.

Some progressive Unionists who believed the party incapable of delivering
sufficient reform were contemplating other options. A number would resign
from the party; others would find a home in one of the new parties about to be
established. One of those parties would come from the New Ulster Movement
(NUM), a political pressure group established in 1967, where moderate
Unionists and others of no party affiliation were discussing the possibility of a
new cross-community party. NUM members were appalled at the persistence
of Northern Ireland's sectarian divisions, which they claimed were reinforced by
a political system so markedly linked to religious affiliation. Their aim was to
establish a party that would accept Northern Ireland's constitutional relationship within the UK but, by appealing to Protestants and Roman Catholics
alike, would also be a party that would work to heal divisions between them.
Plans to form such a party intensified in the early months of 1970.

Outside unionism, the political landscape was more complex. The Northern
Ireland Labour Party (NILP) had experienced mixed fortunes with the electorate. In the 1969 Northern Ireland parliamentary elections, two of its Belfast
candidates had been successful. Pro-reform, but also pro-UK, the party's
membership was drawn from both the Protestant and the Catholic communities, and in 1970 was anticipating becoming an integral part of the British
Labour Party. A majority of its members had endorsed proposals for such a
move and the expectation was that the merger would take place early in 1970.

But, despite that endorsement, divisions existed between those who favoured such a merger and those opposed, fearing that it would alienate the party's Catholic, or Nationalist support.

If in 1970 the fragmentation of the UUP was imminent, fragmentation had long been the reality as far as the Nationalist community was concerned. Several parties and several independent members represented the community at council and parliamentary levels. These included the Nationalist Party, Republican Labour, Irish Labour, the National Democratic Party and Sinn Féin, plus a number of independent MPs first elected at the 1969 Northern Ireland parliamentary elections.

Of these, only the Nationalist and Republican Labour parties had representation in parliament. The former had the largest representation – six MPs and four senators, all of whom represented constituencies outside of Belfast. Republican Labour had two MPs and one senator, all three Belfast-based, as was most of the party's membership. One of Republican Labour's MPs was Gerry Fitt, since 1966 also an MP at Westminster. There he had become prominent helping to organize the Campaign for Democracy in Ulster (CDU),[5] which highlighted civil rights abuses in the North, and urged British government intervention to address those abuses. Of the other parties drawing support from the Nationalist community, Irish Labour and the recently founded National Democratic Party (NDP) each had a small number of council representatives. The NDP was the majority party on two town councils, Downpatrick and Strabane. There were also three independent MPs – Ivan Cooper, John Hume and Paddy O'Hanlon, all prominent in the civil rights movement. By entering parliament they had signalled their belief that street protests had reached the limit of their effectiveness in terms of achieving reform, and that the time for concerted political action had come.

The other party of significance in the Nationalist community was Sinn Féin, a party with extremely close links to the IRA. Sinn Féin's policy was not to contest elections to what it regarded as Ireland's 'partitionist' northern and southern parliaments and, although it had previously contested and won seats at Westminster elections, in 1970 it did not hold any. Sinn Féin's close links with the IRA, and the latter's dominance of the party, put it outside the realm of normal constitutional politics. Furthermore, in 1969 Sinn Féin had been racked by internal dissension that gripped both it and the IRA. As a result, two distinct Sinn Féin parties and two distinct IRAs emerged, the Official IRA and the Provisionals of Provos (PIRA), of which, the PIRA was to become the stronger.[6]

NEW NATIONALIST VOICES

Faced with the disarray and perceived ineffectiveness of Nationalist politicians, pressure for more cohesive political representation had been growing within the wider Nationalist community over several years. Up until 1970, that pressure had been mainly directed at the Nationalist Party. As a party it only existed in a parliamentary sense offering MPs representing the Nationalist community an umbrella under which they could convey an impression of cohesion. However, that cohesion was paper-thin, since it was really only a consensus on the constitutional issue that united the MPs, that is, opposition to unionism and to the partition of Ireland. Otherwise, the party consisted of a number of constituency-based fiefdoms controlled by their MPs, several of whom were often returned to parliament unopposed. The MPs lacked a coherent organizational structure, and had only recently begun to convene annual conferences and to create such a structure. But the party also lacked energy, and with its political focus firmly on the wrongs of Ireland's partition, it seldom concerned itself with a wider social and economic agenda, except on matters such as education, when Nationalist MPs usually acted as political spokespersons for the Catholic Church.

This lack of cohesion and political organization had attracted considerable criticism over the previous decade. Writing in *Hibernia*, as early as 1959, Michael McKeown, a young teacher, and later a leading figure in the NDP, claimed that if the 'nationally minded people of the North organized themselves in a properly structured political party, they might hope to secure some reforms within the Northern system'.[7] For McKeown, the unification of Ireland on its own should no longer be the sole aim and objective of Nationalist politics. Other, more immediate priorities, particularly housing, education, employment and, above all, civil rights, demanded action that should not be deferred until unity had been achieved.

Austin Currie, the Nationalist Party's youngest MP, elected to the northern parliament at the age of 23 in 1964, frequently stressed the need for a coherent party structure and was one of the few among his colleagues pressing for party reform. In his manifesto for selection as a parliamentary candidate, Currie argued the necessity of a new approach through the creation of a properly organized party that would 'enable new thinking ... on the national and social problems of the present time'.[8] These policies, he argued, should address and offer solutions for everyday 'bread and butter issues', such as economic development, unemployment, housing, health etc., as well as advancing the civil rights reform agenda.

Another emerging Nationalist voice was that of Derry teacher John Hume, who had come to prominence through the credit union movement and his leading role in organizing opposition to the government's decision to reject Derry as the location for Northern Ireland's second university.[9] Hume, like McKeown and Currie, had been arguing the case for a modern political party to represent the Nationalist community. In one of two highly prescient articles written for the *Irish Times* in 1964, Hume had strongly criticized the Nationalist Party because 'in forty years of opposition, they have not produced one constructive contribution on either the social or economic plane to the development of Northern Ireland'.[10] He argued that the need for 'a fully organized democratic party which can freely attract and draw upon the talents of the nationally minded community was obvious'. Hume was also a committed Europhile who was deeply impressed by post-Second World War efforts at reconciliation through the development of the European Economic Community (EEC),[11] the institutions of which he believed were examples of what could be achieved democratically to overcome the legacy of conflict in Ireland. The party he envisaged was one in the European social democratic tradition, rather than the class-based approach of the British Labour Party.

National Unity, a movement that provided a platform for debate among all shades of Nationalist opinion, had been established in 1959 and became a strong advocate of the need for a well-organized political party with a strong social justice agenda committed to a non-violent approach to ending partition. From it emerged the National Party in 1965, which aimed 'to promote the cause of Irish unity; to promote the economic, social and cultural welfare of the Irish people; to promote the creation of a society in the community in which social justice prevails'.[12] At its inaugural meeting, party chair Gerry Quigley stated that the 'overwhelming conviction among the various groups represented was the tremendous necessity to secure unity'.[13] The National Party planned to link up with the Nationalist Party, which had been making efforts to modernize, but despite early signs that this would happen, no link was established and the name National Democratic Party was adopted. Electorally, the NDP had only limited success, but its high profile, its socio-economic agenda and its modern outlook pointed to what was needed, in terms of policy, structure and organization.

STREET POLITICS

Adding to the political pressure for Nationalist unity were events on the streets; events that dramatically highlighted the glaring absence of a cohesive political organization to represent that community. The civil rights agitation that had gathered momentum over the previous five years focused on allegations of discrimination against Catholics and Nationalists, particularly in public authority housing allocations, in employment opportunities, especially in the public sector, and in voting rights caused by the restricted local government franchise. Street protests and demonstrations organized by civil rights groups such as the Dungannon-based Campaign for Social Justice, the Derry Housing Action Group and, later, the Northern Ireland Civil Rights Association (NICRA), pushed reform to the forefront of political life and for a while gave these organizations greater significance than the political parties and their public representatives within the Nationalist community and beyond.

Despite the fact that the civil rights movement explicitly avoided any position on the constitutional issue, many Unionist politicians claimed that it was a Nationalist, even an IRA or communist conspiracy aimed at undermining the North's relationship with Britain. Civil rights protest marches were met with counter-demonstrations by right-wing Unionists led most notably by Ian Paisley. Paisley was seen as responsible for inciting strong loyalist opposition to civil rights demonstrations, and for organizing large counter-demonstrations at which serious rioting had occurred. Within the UUP, William (Bill) Craig, a former minister who had been dismissed by O'Neill, had made no secret of his opposition to reform, and, by 1970, was the leader of growing internal party dissent.

Age-old sectarian animosities had once again come to the surface, threatening the North's very existence. The result was that British troops had been brought onto the streets in support of an over-stretched Royal Ulster Constabulary (RUC), the North's police force, and, more significantly, had obliged the British government to intervene directly in Northern Irish affairs. These security moves, together with a forced quickening of the reform programme, had helped produce the calm that had descended on the North at the close of 1969.

Twelve months previously, O'Neill had attempted to forestall the increasing pressure within the UUP by calling an early general election for February 1969. O'Neill's intention was to face down his opponents as well as to garner support for his reform programme. Unfortunately for O'Neill, the election results had the opposite effect. Unionism emerged even more seriously divided between those supporting reform and those opposed to it. Within two months, his cousin, James Chichester-Clark, a man more anxious to heal divisions within unionism than to pursue the reform programme, had replaced O'Neill as prime minister and leader of the party. As far as Nationalist politics were concerned, the election marked the beginning of the end for the Nationalist Party. Ivan Cooper, John Hume and Paddy O'Hanlon, defeated three of its leading MPs, Hume taking the Derry seat of party leader Eddie McAteer. Another civil rights campaigner, Paddy Devlin, a member of the NILP and a former IRA activist, who had served a period of detention in the 1940s, defeated the veteran labour and republican politician, Harry Diamond, for the West Belfast seat. The stage was being set for new political alignments.

COHERENT OPPOSITION

In his election manifesto, Hume had pledged himself to work for the 'the formation of a new political movement based on social democratic principles, with open membership, and an elected executive to allow people full involvement in the process of decision-making'.[14] He also committed himself to ensure that 'the movement must be completely non-sectarian and must root out a fundamental evil in our society – sectarian division'.[15] On the constitutional question Hume stated that the party he wanted to see established 'must be committed to the ideal that the future of Northern Ireland should be decided by its people, and no constitutional changes accepted except by the consent of its people'.[16] On this issue, Hume was also resolutely opposed to violence in order to effect constitutional change. Cooper and O'Hanlon, the other two civil rights activists, shared Hume's commitment to create a new political alignment and had included similar commitments in their own manifestoes,[17] while Austin Currie was re-elected pledged to pursue the same objective.

Following his election, Hume set about creating the conditions whereby such a party could be established. Together with the two other civil rights MPs, he persuaded several members of the opposition to hold regular meetings to plan parliamentary tactics in order to maximize their impact. Those who joined them included Gerry Fitt, Austin Currie and Paddy Devlin. According to Hume, the initial purpose behind the group was 'not so much party unity as efficiency in parliament'.[18] However, it was soon clear that a new party was in gestation.

Regular parliamentary meetings produced a degree of cohesion among these opposition members, evidence of which was to be seen in the vigour they brought to debates and to the questioning of ministers, notably on proposed legislation to deal with the growing problem of street disturbances, rioting and the general security situation. Group members lost no opportunity to argue the inadequacies of the government's emphasis on security. As Paddy O'Hanlon stated sarcastically when debating the criminal justice bill in June 1970, 'If laws were an indication of a just, democratic and orderly society, Northern Ireland would rank as one of the most orderly places in the world'.[19]

For the first time ever, an effective opposition, formally called the Opposition Alliance, was holding the government to account, and bringing its leading figures to the attention of wider audiences in Ireland and Britain. The next logical step was to formally establish a properly organized political party, and a major step towards that goal was taken at a meeting in Toomebridge, Co. Antrim, in February 1970. In his autobiography, Austin Currie describes how the meeting, which was held under the cover of discussing the local eel fishing industry, agreed that a new party should be formed and that it should be called the Social Democratic and Labour Party (SDLP). It was also agreed that since there was more preparatory work to be done, the party would not be publicly launched immediately. However, the Irish government was informed of developments when two days later Hume told Eamonn Gallagher of the Irish department of external affairs (later the department of foreign affairs) that plans were going ahead for the creation of a new opposition party in the North. Critically, Hume asked that Gallagher convey to the Taoiseach that 'notwithstanding the necessary inclusion of the word Labour in the name of the party, there will be no connection between it and the British, Irish and Northern Ireland Labour parties'.[20] Hume was obviously anxious to counter any suggestion that the new party would not work with Fianna Fáil, or with whatever party might be in government in the South. Hume himself had favoured the simple Social Democratic title, a view shared by Currie. It was out of deference to Fitt's and Devlin's strong socialist views that 'Labour' was included in the new party's title. Despite this flurry of activity in February, it was to be another six months before the party would be officially launched.

SDLP LAUNCHED

In April 1970, the long anticipated move to establish a new centre party from within the NUM happened, when the formation of the Alliance Party of Northern Ireland (APNI) was announced. The same month, meetings organized by the NDP brought together representatives from the Nationalist Party, Republican Labour and the NILP as well as the independent civil rights MPs, to formulate a common 'strategy for the seventies'.[21] However, such meetings proved to be mere talking shops and the leaders of the embryonic SDLP separately continued their preparatory work. Discussions, interrupted by the Westminster elections in June, were resumed shortly afterwards, several taking place away from the glare of publicity in the West Donegal holiday resort of Bunbeg. In July, at one of these meetings, the basic document stating what had been agreed about the nature of the party was signed by the founding fathers of the SDLP. All that now remained was to decide when the formal announcement of the party's establishment would be made. A further month was to pass before that was to happen, a month during which the already worsening situation on the streets threatened to seriously destabilize Northern Ireland.

From April onwards, fresh outbreaks of street violence in Belfast, Derry and elsewhere, the emergence of the PIRA, the expulsion of Catholic workers from the Harland and Wolff shipyard and the infamous three-day Falls Road curfew in July,[22] had considerably heightened inter-communal tensions threatening increased support for paramilitarism with an inevitable further crackdown by the RUC and British army. Democratic politics was under growing pressure, especially within the Nationalist community. Finally, on 21 August at a press conference in Belfast, the formation of the SDLP was publicly announced. Currie explains the six-month delay following the Toomebridge meeting as being due to the pressure of events, especially the June elections, but also the need to ensure that Gerry Fitt would commit to leading the party. Fitt's hesitation had to do with those elections, his membership of Republican Labour and his hopes that his colleague Paddy Kennedy MP would join him. With the elections over, and when it was clear that neither Kennedy nor many Republican Labour colleagues would join the new party, Fitt finally committed to do so (pl. 2).[23]

The founding members were six MPs and one senator: Gerry Fitt, John Hume, Austin Currie, Paddy Devlin, Paddy O'Hanlon, Ivan Cooper and Senator Paddy Wilson. Most were still in their early thirties; Wilson at thirty-seven and Fitt at forty-four, being the oldest. Wilson had been a colleague of

Fitt's in the Republican Labour Party and like him also a member of Belfast City Corporation. A second senator, Claude Wilton from Derry joined soon after the SDLP was founded. Wilton was a Protestant and a former member of the Liberal Party. While there had been some speculation that John Hume might have become the party's leader, the group unanimously chose Fitt, their most experienced politician. At the launch, Hume made his position on the leadership clear, saying 'I have worked for the creation of a left-of-centre, democratically organized movement. If that can be created then Gerry Fitt is acceptable to me as leader'.[24]

The SDLP's founders were determined that the party would pursue the civil rights agenda, that it would be 'based on radical left-of-centre principles',[25] and that it would present a socio-economic programme in keeping with those principles and endorsed at annual party conferences. At the press conference launch, Fitt stated that the party would 'support the maintenance of Stormont at the present time, as it is the only institution which can bring about the reforms we desire'.[26] Constitutionally, the SDLP stressed its commitment to working for a united Ireland, but only through peaceful means and with the consent of the people of Northern Ireland, and by promoting 'cooperation, friendship and understanding between North and South'.[27] In making this commitment, the party became the first from the Irish Nationalist tradition, North or South, to make a formal statement in its constitution that unity should only be achieved through peaceful means, thus establishing the 'consent' principle many years before it was formally adopted by other parties.[28]

Although the founding members of the party were all public representatives from the Nationalist community, other significant voices from that community had not joined. Initially, it was hoped that all Nationalist Party MPs and senators, as well as independents Bernadette Devlin and Frank McManus, both Westminster MPs, might join. Gerry Fitt stressed the importance of uniting all those opposed to unionism, saying he intended 'to engage in further discussion with my Parliamentary colleagues and to do all in my power to give real expression to the real hopes, fears and aspirations of those opposed to unionism'.[29] But hopes that Devlin and McManus would join the SDLP proved groundless. They never joined, and over the next few years they were among the party's fiercest critics for not being 'Nationalist' enough.

Hopes that the party would attract support from progressive elements within the Protestant community also proved to be in vain. Ivan Cooper, a Protestant and a former member of the UUP, claimed that 'with the Unionist Party veering to the right, the community badly needed a real alternative', and expressed the hope that the SDLP would embrace progressive voices from the Protestant community.[30] This was another hope not to be realized to any significant degree, and Claude Wilton was the only other prominent member of the Protestant community to join the party at this stage.

Nationalist comment on the formation of the new party was mixed. The *Irish News*, the main voice of northern Nationalists, welcomed the formation of the SDLP commenting that 'obviously a lot of hard organizational work lies before the new party, but if it can supply that desired united voice, it will be work well done'.[31] The NDP's welcome foreshadowed its own demise, claiming that it 'had striven for the emergence of a large political movement capable of a radical alternative to unionism',[32] and saw in the new party the potential for such a movement.

The same was not the case for the Nationalist Party, which accused the leaders of the SDLP of wanting to absorb rather than amalgamate with other groups serving the Nationalist community. They also warned that the SDLP's contacts with the Labour Party in the Republic would lead to a loss of the Nationalist identity.[33] Gerry Fitt's old party, Republican Labour, responded to the SDLP's foundation by immediately expelling him and Paddy Wilson, and by accusing the new party of being funded by the South's governing party, Fianna Fáil. The NILP, whose attempt to merge with British Labour was faltering, attacked the SDLP for not consulting with them before its launch[34] as did the Liberal Party.[35] Both also claimed that the SDLP would never attract significant Protestant support.

Political commentators were generally sceptical of the new party's chances. The SDLP's founders were perceived as an odd grouping of strong-minded individuals whose fate would be similar to those who had previously attempted, unsuccessfully, to create a party with cross-community appeal as well as attempting to straddle Nationalist and socialist philosophies. Andy Boyd, writing in the *Irish Press*,[36] and Barry White in the *Belfast Telegraph* dismissed the new party's chances of survival, with the latter claiming that 'opposition unity has been as hard to achieve as Unionist unity, for obvious personality reasons, and the chances of the magnificent seven agreeing for any length of time on strategy and tactics are almost nil'.[37]

MEMBERS – POLICIES – STRUCTURES

Nonetheless, despite scepticism and the pressures of the ongoing political and security situation, the SDLP's founding members pushed ahead as quickly as possible with the organization and development of party structures. A headquarters office was acquired close to the centre of Belfast, staff were recruited,[38] and the first steps were taken towards creating the party's organizational structure. An interim executive chaired by former NDP member Paddy Fox was established with each of the party's MPs nominating two people from their constituency organizations. The executive was charged with developing a comprehensive set of policies, as well as with establishing the party's structures, with undertaking a membership drive and with organizing the party's first annual conference. The party was assisted in these very early days by Séamus Scally, a full-time official with the Irish Labour Party, who was seconded for several weeks to help organize the operation at headquarters.

The membership drive was launched in early September with a large newspaper advertisement that emphasized the new party's commitments to economic development, social justice and Irish unity. The advertisement also stated that the SDLP 'will look for a just and adequate distribution of wealth, the promotion of cooperatives, a minimum wage, equal pay for equal work and civil rights for all'.[39] The advertisement stressed that on the question of North-South relations, the SDLP's aim was 'to promote cooperation, friendship and understanding between North and South with a view to the eventual reunification of Ireland through the consent of the majority of the people in the North and in the South'.[40]

This initial appeal for members was boosted when John Hume's constituency organization in Derry decided to give its full support to the new party. Members of the constituency organizations of the other MPs as well as many civil rights activists also added numbers to the fledgling membership. At the same time, the resignation of prominent members of the Nationalist Party in Derry, organizationally its strongest base, together with their expressions of support for the new party, strengthened its initial growth. A further boost to membership was given when, in October, the NDP's executive decided to dissolve and advised its members to join the SDLP. Among NDP members who would play significant roles in the SDLP's formative years were Eddie McGrady, already a councillor in Downpatrick and a future MP, Ben Caraher, who was to become a key policy adviser, John Duffy, who would serve as general-secretary, and Alasdair McDonnell, also a future MP and a deputy leader of the party. Significant civil rights activists Michael Canavan, Miriam Daly, Arthur Doherty, Denis Haughey and Hugh Logue also joined at this early stage. The expanding membership lent an air of excitement to the whole enterprise, and Haughey recalls being 'totally seized of the challenge of building a strong coherent party'.[41] The party's arrival seemed to answer the hopes of many Nationalists.

While the first formal meeting of the party's organization committee did not take place until February 1971, it is obvious from reports of meetings over the following months that considerable effort was devoted to establishing basic structures. Four regional committees covering the whole of the North were established, each charged with organizing public meetings to publicize the new party and to attract new members. Such meetings attracted large attendances – one at Camlough in Co. Armagh was reported as attracting over four hundred, with over one hundred new members being enrolled. Holding public meetings to publicize the SDLP was not without risk in some areas. Shots were fired through the windows of a hall in Magherafelt, Co. Derry, where one such meeting was being held, while in other places word of mouth let it be known that meetings to be addressed by party leaders would be unwelcome, and so were cancelled. Nevertheless, many meetings did proceed and the immediate objective was to have at least twenty branches in operation before the first annual conference was summoned. That objective was achieved by the summer of 1971.

The SDLP founders' determination that the party would pursue a civil rights agenda, that it would be left-of-centre, and that it would present a fully worked-out socio-economic programme, was given early expression in one of the party's first policy statements in October 1970.[42] The party called for an increase in publicly owned industries, the break-up of large estates, the redistribution of their land, and the repeal of the Northern Ireland Special Powers Act, which gave wide powers to the RUC and was seen as directed primarily against the Nationalist community. The party's stress on Irish unity being only possible with the consent of a majority in the North meant it recognized that, to gain that consent, significant constitutional and legal change would be required in the South. Hume and Cooper frequently argued that, prior to the current unrest, the South had virtually ignored the North and had made no genuine moves towards accommodating its Protestant people. Hence the party argued not for the traditional approach to unity – a demand for British withdrawal –

but for a 'new Ireland' that would accommodate, recognize and respect all of the country's traditions.

These early statements of aims and objectives were intended to mark the SDLP as a principled, policy driven party, with respect to its position on social and economic issues as well as on its approach to unity. This was in marked contrast to the policy of most previous parties representing the Nationalist community. For such parties, the 'evil' of Ireland's partition in 1921 and, by contrast, the 'benefits' that would immediately flow from Irish unity, had been the almost exclusive basis to their politics. It was also an approach that contrasted with the views of those Nationalists who saw in the North's turmoil an opportunity for promoting unity as the *only* solution, notwithstanding the determined opposition of the overwhelming majority of the North's million Unionists. An early decision was the establishment of a policy committee, charged with developing detailed positions on all of these issues and, from early 1971, discussion papers were being drafted, outlining possible positions in several areas. These early documents discussed the background to the civil unrest, as well as outlining possible negotiating positions and proposals for economic development. All were evidence of the party's determination to ground its policies in clear principles and a sound evidential basis.

SOUTHERN RELATIONS

From the outset, the SDLP was also anxious to develop good working relations with the Irish government, but this was not easily achieved. In 1970, the Fianna Fáil party, generally seen as a centre-right party favouring big business, had been in government for the previous twelve years. Critically, that same year, Fianna Fáil was riven by the 'arms scandal', when allegations were made that leading members of the party had attempted to smuggle arms into the country for use by the PIRA in the North. While the majority of Fianna Fáil members did not support the use of violence, the scandal had revealed ambivalence towards PIRA violence by some, reflecting the 'slightly constitutional' characteristic often attributed to that party, and, consequently, scepticism as to what the SDLP could achieve.

In contrast to Fianna Fáil, the SDLP had not only declared itself to be strongly opposed to the use of violence, but also to be 'left-of-centre', keen to join the Socialist International and, notwithstanding the anxiety of some members to avoid formal links with parties in the South, to associate with the recently formed all-Ireland Council of Labour, a loose umbrella organization aimed at fostering co-operation between the Irish Labour Party and labour voices in the North.[43] Furthermore, the SDLP's two Belfast-based MPs, Gerry Fitt and Paddy Devlin prided themselves on upholding traditional socialist values. Neither lost opportunities to attack parties like Fianna Fáil, which they judged to be extremely right wing and profoundly ignorant of how Unionists felt. Not surprisingly, such attacks did not make for easy relationships with the southern government. An early example was Devlin's comment on the Taoiseach Jack Lynch's speech to the UN, less than a month after the party's foundation. Lynch claimed that the Dublin government was the Nationalist community's 'second guarantor' as far as civil rights was concerned. Devlin took grave exception to the claim, saying that it had been made without any consultation with the SDLP and dismissed it as meaningless.[44] However, the claim to be a 'guarantor' was rooted in the reality that the southern government was looked to by many Nationalists as a source of support and assistance in troubled times, as events since 1968 had demonstrated.[45] Furthermore, if they were to succeed, any new arrangements for the North would inevitably require at least acceptance by the South and preferably its active involvement in shaping those arrangements. Hence, a critical need for the SDLP was to develop good working relations with whatever party was in government in the South, or was likely to be in that position, and to avoid open conflict as far as possible. This was the view that John Hume espoused and sought to impress on his colleagues, though not one that Fitt and Devlin ever easily embraced.

INTERNATIONAL RELATIONS

Uniquely for parties in Northern Ireland, the SDLP sought, from its inception, to develop international relationships. Hume's emphasis on the party adopting European social democratic traditions together with Paddy Devlin's strongly declared socialism meant that little time was lost in applying for membership of the Socialist International, the main umbrella organization that brought together socialist, labour and social democratic parties across the world. The initiative in making the application was taken by Devlin, who was also anxious to clearly establish the party's left-wing credentials and who believed that relationships with the Socialist International would publicly demonstrate those credentials. In response to a letter from Devlin, the party was granted 'associate' status in February 1971, and it was left to the party executive, mainly in the person of Denis Haughey, to pursue relationships with the International and to ensure that full membership was eventually achieved. However, membership of the Socialist International never meant a great deal in practical terms to the SDLP. The International would be represented at the party's annual conferences, but attendance at meetings of the International had to be funded by participating parties themselves, and the SDLP was seldom able to afford representation. Far more significant for the SDLP would be membership of the European social democratic grouping, later the Party of European Socialists (PES), bringing together left-of-centre parties with members in the European Parliament. This development was several years away and would coincide with the party's participation in the elections to that parliament in 1979.

Initially, it was also hoped that the party could establish formal links with the trade union movement in the North, but this never materialized. The trade union movement's umbrella group, the Northern Ireland Committee of the Irish Congress of Trade Unions (NIC-ICTU), had only been formally recognized by the Unionist government in 1963 and was anxious to maintain a distance from local politics. As a result, close relationships with the SDLP were never possible. Nevertheless, the party regularly invited NIC-ICTU to be represented at its annual conferences and frequently met with its officers to discuss social and economic matters.

STRONG OPPOSITION

Organization and policy development were not the only, or indeed the main, considerations facing the new party. Established in the midst of a gathering storm, the SDLP faced formidable political challenges from its inception. As parliamentarians, the party's founders' first responsibility was to use their role as the largest opposition party to advance their objectives as effectively as possible. Building on their earlier experience in parliament, they were soon earning for themselves a reputation as very effective performers, leading one commentator to write 'Small as the SDLP opposition in Stormont is, there is probably more talent on its side than on the whole of the government benches, and strategically the SDLP is better placed'.[46]

Among issues that the SDLP addressed in these early months were local government reform, proposals for a new housing executive and ongoing street violence. Local government had been a particular focus for civil rights protesters for several reasons: the local government franchise was still based on property rights rather than being universal; discriminatory practices in many authorities had frequently denied Catholics jobs; electoral boundaries had been gerrymandered to ensure Unionist majorities; and the allocation of public housing in many areas had overwhelmingly favoured Protestants. Derry city's corporation was the most blatant example of gerrymandering. There, Unionists had controlled the corporation despite the city having a clear Nationalist majority. Such practices could no longer be tolerated and, under pressure from the civil rights movement and the British government, O'Neill's and Chichester-Clarke's administrations had been moving slowly towards the comprehensive package of reforms outlined by McInerney. A government report proposing significant reform to local government was welcomed by the SDLP.[47] Hume complimented the government for bringing it forward and expressed the hope that, when implemented, all sides of the community would be able 'to feel they are playing a part in moulding society in Northern Ireland'.[48] This was a theme that he would return to frequently with respect to central government reform. A particularly notable feature of the proposed reforms was that plural voting was to be abolished, a measure that SDLP MPs all heartily endorsed.

One of the debates that underscored the focus and vitality the new party brought to politics was on the report of the inquiry into the police assault suffered by Samuel Devenny and members of his family when their house was raided during street disturbances in Derry in 1969. Forty-six-year-old Devenny received twenty-two stitches in the head, and he died several months later. In the debate, Hume excoriated the RUC officers involved for their conspiracy of silence in not cooperating with the inquiry,[49] highlighting as he did what would become a central political theme in the years ahead – the need for a police service that would have the support, confidence and allegiance of all sections of society in the North.

PARAMILITARY CHALLENGE

However, the biggest challenge facing the SDLP was not in parliament, but on the streets, where violence continued to escalate, notably in Belfast. The IRA, both the Official IRA and the Provos, conscious of their inactivity during the preceding two years of street demonstrations, had begun to demonstrate their military capacity, engaging in gun-fights with the British army, especially after the Falls Road curfew, and in bomb attacks on Unionist owned business premises. The Conservative government that had assumed office in June supported the army's increasingly aggressive tactics which, in turn, provoked further reaction from the paramilitaries. What had initially been justified as defensive action to protect 'defenceless' Catholic communities, was gradually losing that justification as paramilitary groups like the PIRA launched attacks in circumstances where no Catholic community was under threat from loyalists, and no British army operation was taking place. In effect, both IRAs had declared 'war', with the aim of forcing a British withdrawal from Northern Ireland while maintaining the pretence of defensive action. The immediate effect of IRA activity was increased surveillance of Nationalist areas and frequent raids for arms and suspects by the British army, which by now had assumed the primary role in security operations. Not surprisingly, army operations were seldom undertaken with a light touch and relationships with local Nationalist communities cooled rapidly. By the end of 1970, those relationships were mutually poisonous, a situation that paramilitaries were only too ready to exploit. Confrontation with the army became more frequent and more violent.

Given its opposition to the use of force to achieve unity, the SDLP was not slow to condemn the activities of both IRAs. However, many in the Catholic-Nationalist community believed that the paramilitaries still provided some element of defence, particularly in Belfast, where loyalist mobs could attack their areas with ease and had done so, as during the turmoil of August 1969.[50] Consequently, SDLP representatives found it expedient to temper their condemnations of the IRA. Paddy Devlin reflected this 'defender' view of its role, and while he condemned 'offensive' action, he argued the IRA should maintain a defensive role. Devlin, who lived in West Belfast, where army and police activity was at its most aggressive, regularly bombarded the authorities with letters of complaint about security force behaviour, building up large files of affidavits and statements from people claiming that they had been unjustly arrested and ill-treated.[51] Fitt also frequently condemned troop behaviour, claiming that the army was 'adopting tactics to bring about a confrontation in these areas'.[52] He spoke at Westminster about 'Catholics being disarmed while Protestant areas were not being raided',[53] and expressed a widely held Nationalist fear regarding the number of licensed gun clubs operating in predominantly loyalist areas – thirty new clubs had been formed since 1968. The SDLP argued that these clubs put thousands of extra arms into the hands of Unionists and frequently, but vainly, called for tighter controls.

CIVIL WAR THREATENS

Increased IRA activity and street riots put serious pressure on UUP ministers, and especially on Chichester-Clarke. Bill Craig and other opponents of reform pilloried the prime minister for not adopting a more robust security policy. They demanded internment without trial for suspected IRA paramilitaries, and threatened to take matters into their own hands if a vigorous security policy was not pursued. In February 1971, Craig boasted that 'an organized body of loyalists trained and ready to attack at the drop of a hat' was already in existence.[54] His words had a chilling effect on the Nationalist community, and intensified its sense of being under siege. But as IRA attacks increased, so too did loyalist anger and the possibility of widespread retaliation became a very dangerous threat. In March, following the murder of three young Scottish soldiers lured to their deaths by the PIRA, thousands of loyalist workers in Belfast docks downed tools and marched into the centre of the city demanding internment without trial for known IRA activists.

Community tensions reached such a level in the early months of 1971 that some SDLP representatives feared all-out civil war. Speaking after a weekend of riots in Belfast and Derry, and expressing concern about imminent Orange Order parades, Ivan Cooper warned that 'I can only see a bloodbath which can only lead ... to a civil war and sectarian confrontation the like of which this island has not seen'.[55] The situation was so ominous that, a week later, the Catholic archbishop of Armagh, Cardinal William Conway, a man not known for alarmist statements and who did not believe that civil war was imminent, claimed that 'the possibility of untold suffering to innocent people was less remote than it had been'.[56]

More loyalist demonstrations calling for tougher 'law and order', more street clashes between loyalists and Nationalists, and a threat from the SDLP that it would withdraw from Stormont if internment was introduced, added further pressure on the government. In March, talks between Chichester-Clarke and Prime Minister Heath produced little in terms of stronger security measures. Consequently, Chichester-Clarke, whom many suspected of having argued for internment, felt that he had no alternative but to resign, which he did on 19 March. The choice of Brian Faulkner as his successor provided a breathing space, and a slight lowering of the temperature. Many, including some within the SDLP, saw Faulkner, despite his support for internment, as a modernizer and a man who might quicken the pace of change. There was, therefore, a willingness to allow him time to prove himself. With a keen sense of the challenges ahead, Fitt declared that if Faulkner and his government were to renege on the reform programme, 'I have no hesitation in saying that the prime minister will be the last prime minister in this six-county state'.[57]

REFORMING MOVES

An early move suggestive of positive possibilities was Faulkner's appointment of David Bleakley of the NILP as minister for community relations, the first non-Unionist to be appointed to a cabinet post in Northern Ireland. In June came the announcement of Faulkner's plans to strengthen the committee system within parliament, and to offer at least two committee chairs to members of the opposition.[58] These proposals were Faulkner's response to demands from the SDLP for direct opposition involvement in decision-making. In the preceding months, the party's MPs had been advocating a root-and-branch reform of government. Hume called for the 1920 Government of Ireland Act, effectively Northern Ireland's constitution, to be replaced, saying 'it is time the whole constitutional framework of Northern Ireland was re-examined so that the sections of the community who had not been given a voice in the past could be given an opportunity to express themselves'.[59]

In effect, Hume was arguing for a form of cross-community coalition, later to be known more popularly as power-sharing. Such views were extremely radical at the time, and were anathema to most Unionists for whom the 1920 act was almost sacred text. Like his fellow Unionists, Faulkner believed in the Westminster-style of majoritarian government, arguing that 'it may not be a perfect system, but I have yet to learn of a better one'.[60] He was firmly opposed to its replacement by a cross-community coalition, especially as it would mean allocating cabinet seats to representatives whom he believed were intent on undermining the North's political institutions because of their commitment to Irish unity. However, going some way towards recognizing Northern Ireland's special circumstances, Faulkner also argued that 'within the context of our democratic system, we must try to provide the means for all responsible elements in our community to play a constructive part in its institutions'.[61]

The prime minister's offer was acknowledged as positive by the SDLP, but no commitment was made to accept it. Replying to the offer, Gerry Fitt said that Faulkner had shown that 'he is at least prepared to try new projects and to take a different line of action from that taken by his predecessors over the past fifty years'.[62] Fitt promised that the proposals would be carefully studied by the SDLP, saying 'we hope to cooperate with him (Faulkner) in the new departures he has announced, provided that these new avenues of approach will be to the benefit of the whole community'.[63] Hume also complimented Faulkner, but stressed that government required the consent of the minority, and stated that the SDLP was willing to enter into talks on the offer, provided that the agenda was open to other proposals as well.[64] More bluntly, Austin Currie pointed out that the SDLP had been arguing for a fundamentally new approach to government, and that Faulkner's offer represented 'only a tinkering with a system that is not relevant to the exceptional conditions of political life in Northern Ireland'.[65] In effect, the SDLP regarded Faulkner's suggestions as opening the door for at least an initial discussion on new possibilities, and, as democrats, they were willing to explore those possibilities, among which would be their own much more radical proposals for reform.

SDLP WITHDRAWS

For what turned out to be a brief moment, the prospect that something might be built on Faulkner's offer existed. A preliminary meeting between Faulkner and the SDLP took place the next week, talks that widened out to include the NILP and the Nationalist Party. However, by the end of that same week, the offer was overtaken by events on the street. Two young Derry men, Desmond Beattie and Séamus Cusack, were killed by British troops in controversial circumstances, and Hume called on Faulkner to ensure that a public inquiry would be held. At a hastily convened meeting of party leaders held in Derry and attended by, among others, Hume, Cooper and Currie, but not Devlin or Fitt, a statement was prepared and issued, in which the SDLP threatened that if, within a week, there was no decision to hold such an inquiry, the party would withdraw from Stormont and establish a rival assembly 'to deal with the problems of the people we represent and to become the authoritative voice to negotiate a political solution on their behalf.'[66] With no such commitment forthcoming, the SDLP fulfilled its threat and within the week had withdrawn from Stormont.

It has been suggested that not all of the SDLP leadership, Fitt and Devlin in particular, were happy with the decision to withdraw. In his biography of Fitt, Ryder quotes him as saying 'Although I chaired the press conference announcing the move, I was far from satisfied with the hook upon which we had now impaled ourselves'.[67] In his autobiography, Devlin talks about himself and Fitt being 'livid with anger' at the decision,[68] but at the time both he and Fitt expressed full agreement with the decision and vehemently argued that there would be no return to parliament. Fitt claimed that Stormont had 'been nothing but an assembly for the benefit of the Protestant majority ... and the situation following the Derry shootings has proved that once again'.[69] Some months later, Devlin talked about being forced to withdraw by 'the vicious, repressive policies being pursued by Faulkner'.[70] At the time, the full leadership put their names to a lengthy statement outlining their reasons for withdrawal, and calling for talks of a fundamental kind to resolve the crisis. According to Ivan Cooper, tensions within the Nationalist community following the killings were such that when added to a growing feeling that Faulkner was about to introduce internment, the party felt obliged to take a strong stand. The threat of withdrawal was judged the strongest card the party could play, notwithstanding the risk of isolation it involved.[71]

INTERNMENT

Two weeks later, the crisis was compounded a hundred-fold when, on 9 August, Faulkner, with the agreement of the British government, finally introduced internment without trial for those suspected of involvement in terrorist activity. July had witnessed a significant intensification of IRA, official and provisional, activity, with over ninety bomb explosions. Unionist demands for internment were incessant. The SDLP strongly warned against its introduction, with Fitt pleading that it was political reform, not 'extra-legal' action that was required. He had further warned that internment 'would lead to ultimate disaster with the terrible cost of human life'.[72] But Faulkner was convinced that internment was essential if his government was to defeat terrorism. He believed it had worked in the 1950s and had convinced the British government that it would work again.[73]

In dawn swoops, several hundred alleged PIRA and Official IRA activists and sympathizers across the North were arrested. Nationalist outrage was profound, not least because many of those detained had no paramilitary involvement whatsoever and also because no loyalist suspects were detained, despite clear evidence of loyalist paramilitary activity. IRA retaliation was swift and several gun battles in Belfast over the following days left a death toll of twenty-three, some at the hands of the IRA, and others at the hands of the British army. More generally, as fear and intimidation gripped the city, thousands of Catholics and Protestants abandoned homes in mixed areas to seek safety in their respective ghettoes, many setting fire to their houses lest they fall into the hands of the 'other side'. Hundreds of other Catholics sought refuge in the South, where they were given emergency accommodation in hastily prepared army camps. Not only was internment proving a disastrous blunder, but in its wake, the North teetered on the brink of widespread sectarian conflict.

PROTEST RALLIES (pls 3–7)

Internment presented a huge leadership challenge within the Nationalist community. Only a year in existence, the SDLP had not yet gained sufficient standing within that community to do so on its own and, as yet, there were several competing voices. Gradually, however, the SDLP emerged as the most credible voice and the one to which outsiders, particularly the Irish government, referred to most. Two days after its introduction, John Hume declared internment to be 'wrong in principle and ... a policy which has already failed and has produced massive reaction from the people'.[74] The party called for the immediate release of those detained, but words alone could not match the gravity of the situation. Something more was required. A meeting of representatives from the SDLP, the Nationalist Party, Republican Labour and the Civil Rights Association took place in Dungannon and called on all Nationalist public representatives to withdraw from their positions, and on all Nationalists nominated to public bodies to do likewise. A majority in both categories responded positively. The meeting also urged the general public to withhold payment of rents and rates,[75] a protest that only met with support from the Nationalist community, and then mainly in Nationalist strongholds. Furthermore, the meeting called for Northern Ireland's parliament to be suspended and for talks to be convened to achieve a new political and constitutional settlement. SDLP leaders who had previously urged Nationalists to join the recently formed Ulster Defence Regiment (UDR) promptly reversed their position, declaring that because of the British army's behaviour, they could no longer advise supporters to do so.[76] Internment also dashed any prospect of an SDLP return to Stormont without a substantial reform to its institution having been agreed first.

Soon after the Dungannon meeting, in a very public demonstration of their opposition to internment, Hume and Cooper undertook a sit-down protest in Derry during which they and two other prominent SDLP members, Michael Canavan and Hugh Logue, were arrested and charged with 'failing to move on command of a member of HM forces'.[77] Besides highlighting Nationalist reaction to internment, their protest and arrest became a legal *cause celèbre* when the High Court ruled that the British army was not empowered to arrest civilians. In a more concerted effort to mobilize democratic Nationalist opinion, the SDLP and the Nationalist Party convened a meeting of their MPs and councillors to coordinate their protests. Both parties announced that they would soon establish the alternative assembly promised by the SDLP at the time of the Derry killings.[78] Cross-party Nationalist delegations met with the Dublin government and southern parties to discuss a crisis that was having strong repercussions on public opinion in the South as well. Rallies were held across the North to denounce internment and to strengthen community opposition. Leading members of the SDLP spoke at several rallies. At a rally in Keady, Austin Currie stressed that the SDLP would not participate in any negotiations until internment had ended, and then 'only on the basis of the suspension of Stormont; ... and four-party talks embracing Westminster, Dublin, Unionists and non-Unionists in order to establish a long-term solution to the Northern Ireland problem'.[79]

Then, as evidence of the ill-treatment of detainees began to filter out into the public, the call was for determined diplomatic pressure to shame the British government into ending internment immediately. To help publicize what had transpired, the party joined with the Northern Ireland Civil Rights Association in commissioning a report from two sociologists at the University of Leeds. Their report, *Belfast, August 1971: a case to be answered*, was published in December and became a very useful propaganda tool in campaigning against internment, especially abroad.[80]

Conscious of the deteriorating public situation, the growing gulf between the Catholic and Protestant communities, and the danger of widespread inter-communal conflict, Hume attempted to allay fears, saying that 'we have no quarrel with people as Protestants and we want to live with them in a situation that will provide peace, justice and stability. We will not raise our hands against Protestants. If there is any suggestion of intimidation in any street against Protestants it is our duty to protect our Protestant neighbours'.[81] At the same time, the SDLP also strongly condemned recourse to violence as a means of ending interment, emphasizing that 'we stand on civil disobedience, non-violence and passive resistance'.[82] While such messages failed to prevent the rapid deterioration in community relations that followed internment, at least they showed that there were Nationalist voices totally opposed to violence calling for a political, not a military solution.

For the SDLP and Nationalists generally, internment was a major watershed. It was no longer a question of simply reforming Stormont, but one of whether Northern Ireland itself could or should be reformed at all. But, as violence escalated and as extreme Nationalists heaped scorn on the SDLP for its determined anti-violence stand, it was also a contest between those who espoused democratic means and those who believed that violence would produce a solution.

Chapter 2

New ways forward

Following its withdrawal from Stormont and the imposition of internment, three major challenges faced the SDLP. The most immediate were to have internment ended and to end the violence. The third was to find a political way forward that would command widespread consent across Northern Ireland, and would be endorsed by the South. All three were to severely test the new party's capacity for leadership over the next three years.

At a stroke, internment had cemented division between Northern Ireland's communities. The Nationalist community saw internment as directed exclusively at them since no loyalist paramilitaries had been arrested, notwithstanding considerable evidence of their involvement in violence against Nationalists and the security forces. This perception became more acute as knowledge of the severe interrogation techniques being applied against internees spread. Thirdly, instead of putting an end to violence, internment had only made the security situation worse. In the weeks following 9 August, violent deaths, injuries and the destruction of property dramatically increased, and Northern Ireland seemed to be moving almost inexorably towards the civil war that some had been predicting.[1]

Key to the SDLP's anti-internment campaign was the decision to publicize as widely as possible the party's view of events and its determination to play a central role in the campaign against internment. Armed with a dossier that included accounts of the ill-treatment of internees,[2] meetings were held with British and Irish ministers and with British and Irish political parties. The Dublin government assisted in organizing a visit by Gerry Fitt to the US. There he held meetings with high profile Irish-American politicians and UN Secretary-General U Thant, to whom the ill-treatment of internees was highlighted. The SDLP demanded an impartial investigation into the treatment of internees and suggested the Dublin government bring a case to the European Court of Human Rights (ECHR) alleging torture by the British government. To highlight the crisis, Currie, Hume and O'Hanlon undertook a forty-eight-hour hunger strike protest outside 10 Downing Street, the prime minister's

London residence. Conscious of the absence of a democratic forum in which they could operate, the SDLP was also anxious to expedite plans to convene the alternative assembly. With PIRA activity escalating and directed not just against the security forces, but increasingly against civilian targets in Protestant areas, all-out sectarian conflict was a real possibility. One attack, on the Four Step Inn in the Protestant Shankill area of Belfast, killed two men and was described by SDLP MPs as 'a criminal outrage and clearly a callous murderous attempt to stir up sectarian strife in Belfast'.[3] Ruairí Ó Brádaigh, Provisional Sinn Féin's president, menacingly added to people's fears of greater conflagration when he called for the 'North to be made ungovernable as the first step in achieving a united Ireland'.[4]

Faced with the urgent need for a democratic forum in which to voice Nationalist concerns and to offer an alternative to the paramilitaries, the SDLP and the Nationalist Party agreed that the Assembly of the Northern Irish people, as the new forum was to be called, would meet as soon as a suitable venue could be found. The venue eventually chosen was Dungiven Castle in Co. Derry, and a date at the end of October was set for the assembly's first meeting.

FIRST ANNUAL CONFERENCE

Meantime, the SDLP held its first annual conference at the same venue on 23 October, attended by over three hundred delegates. It was an historic occasion, but one overshadowed by the deepening political and security crisis. The conference conveyed a deep seriousness of purpose, with thirty-five motions down for discussion, covering a wide range of social and economic issues as well as one endorsing the stand taken by the party's MPs in their refusal 'to negotiate with anyone in government while internment without trial lasts'.[5] The same motion called for the replacement of the present system of government by one 'in which the minority participates as of right'.[6] Notwithstanding the mayhem outside, the conference found time to debate such issues as the abolition of the so-called '11-plus' selection procedure for second-level schooling, the nationalization of fishing rights on lakes and inland waterways, an issue that had strong left-wing appeal at the time, as well as the repeal of the Special Powers Act. Gerry Fitt's address condemned paramilitary and British army violence, and attacked British policy in the North, especially its sanctioning of internment. He also appealed to liberal-minded Unionists to join the SDLP, emphasizing the non-sectarian nature of the party, and demanded that the southern government amend the state's constitution to make it more acceptable to Protestants.

The conference provided the party with its first elected executive and among those chosen were Eddie McGrady as chair, and Denis Haughey as vice-chair. To mark the SDLP's desire to link with the Socialist International and its relationship with the Irish Labour Party, Roddy Connolly, son of executed 1916 leader, James Connolly, and chair of the Labour Party, was invited to address the conference on behalf of the Socialist International. Organizationally, the party decided to strengthen its headquarters by employing a full-time general secretary, and by developing as far as resources would allow its research, publicity and training capacities. Steps were soon to be taken with respect to the first item, and early in 1972 the position of general-secretary was advertised, leading to the appointment of an Englishman, Julian Jacotet. Satisfied that the proceedings had demonstrated the capacity to organize a large annual conference to determine policy, Fitt sent delegates away, proclaiming that 'we leave here a party'.[7]

ALTERNATIVE ASSEMBLY

A few days after the annual conference, the first meeting of the Assembly of the Northern Irish People took place. Over one hundred Nationalist MPs and councillors attended what Eddie McGrady described as a 'heady' occasion full of expectation that a new political order was about to take shape.[8] However, the assembly was not fully representative of the Nationalist community in the North. Notable absentees included MPs Frank McManus and Bernadette Devlin, who, together with both Sinn Féin parties, were highly critical of the initiative. Some of the latter had been planning another alternative assembly, Dáil Uladh, to represent the nine historic counties of Ulster as part of a Sinn Féin plan that envisaged the establishment of a four province federal state for the whole of Ireland.

John Hume had already been nominated as president of the assembly and, in its main motion, members endorsed the withdrawal of Nationalist representatives from Stormont and from local authorities. In his address, Hume struck a defiant note, saying 'today we do not recognize the authority of the Stormont Parliament and we do not care two pence if it's treason or not'.[9] The assembly then committed itself, as stated in its draft constitution, to 'work towards the objective of obtaining equality for everyone in Northern Ireland, irrespective of political views or religion'.[10] Rhetoric apart, and despite claims by some that the assembly could become more than an expression of opposition to Stormont, it had little prospect of sustaining itself. The assembly lacked authority and resources. Initially, there were expectations that the Dublin government would provide some financial assistance. Taoiseach Jack Lynch wished the assembly well, saying that it 'can provide a focal point for all non-Unionists in Northern Ireland who seek to make real and lasting political, economic and social progress'.[11] Indeed, officials from the Irish government's special interdepartmental unit on the North had helped draft the assembly's constitution and standing orders, and gave some consideration to a grant-in-aid to cover members' expenses, but no funding ever materialized. Suggestions that the assembly might provide a policing service in Nationalist areas were discussed, but was never a realistic proposition. The assembly only met twice and, despite its grand ambitions, it was a minor sideshow, essentially a short-term safety valve for Nationalist anger caused by internment and its aftermath.

For Unionists, however, the assembly was evidence of the SDLP's negative approach; a further retreat from engaging with them in Stormont, and the logical outcome to the abstensionist tendency so prevalent among Nationalist politicians since partition. Even for some Nationalists, it was a meaningless charade; an attempt by the SDLP to play an unwarranted leadership role for the whole Nationalist community. An internal SDLP critique of the assembly prepared by Denis Haughey spelled out possible options, but honestly acknowledged the formidable difficulties the assembly would face in becoming a meaningful representative institution.[12] While the assembly did not convene again after its second meeting, its executive committee did, making plans to open a number of offices, and to recruit a full-time researcher.[13] However, further consideration of these options was brushed aside in the aftermath of the most dramatic, tragic and traumatic event of the time, the Bloody Sunday killings in Derry on 30 January 1972. Direct rule was imposed soon afterwards, and, in the new context it created, addressing the crisis in more fundamental ways became the pressing necessity.

BLOODY SUNDAY

If internment marked a clear watershed for Nationalists in terms of their relationships with existing political arrangements, then Bloody Sunday became another watershed, this time for British relationships with both unionism and nationalism, and, consequently, for Northern Ireland as a whole. The killing of thirteen, later fourteen,[14] unarmed civilians by British troops on the streets of Derry during a civil rights march sent shock-waves through the political establishments in the North, Britain and the South, and had severe international implications as well. Society in the North became even more polarized; recruitment to the PIRA was almost unstoppable; the British embassy in Dublin was attacked and destroyed by fire; British ships were boycotted in US ports; and demonstrations against British interests were mounted in many cities across the world.

The Derry march on the 30 January was one of a series of demonstrations planned for the early weeks of 1972 to express continuing opposition to internment, and to any talks before internment had ended. On the first weekend of the year, a rally in Belfast heard Ivan Cooper, Paddy Devlin and Austin Currie reiterate the pledge that there would be no talks 'until the last man and woman was released from internment'.[15] Fitt repeated this message at Westminster and called again for Stormont to be suspended to allow for inter-party talks.

Coincidentally, the British government was planning all-party talks for Westminster in February, and Faulkner appealed to the SDLP to 'help achieve progress in Northern Ireland'.[16] The Dublin government was also extremely anxious that the SDLP should take part, and Taoiseach Jack Lynch again provoked the anger of Paddy Devlin when he suggested that a formula would be found to enable that to happen.[17] For Devlin, this was unwarranted and unhelpful interference and he accused Lynch of trying to manoeuvre the SDLP 'to give the impression that we are subservient to your directions in the North'.[18] Ending internment had become an absolute precondition and Devlin, many of whose constituents had been interned, was adamant that it would remain so. However, it was also becoming clear that it was no longer a unanimous commitment within the party leadership. Fitt and Hume in particular were anxious to find a way out of the dilemma and the latter had been in touch with Lynch on the question of all-party talks. Within the party at large, however, sensitivities on internment were still raw, and Fitt's brief appearance at a meeting of Belfast Corporation to ensure that his seat would not be forfeit to a Unionist, was regarded as a breach of the party's boycott of public bodies. Both men were rebuked by Devlin,[19] though the latter was not above exploring the possibility of SDLP returning to Stormont when, some weeks later, he held secret talks with Unionist MP, Desmond Boal.

ALL'S CHANGED

By then, however, Bloody Sunday had changed everything and had underlined more dramatically than internment the absolute need for fundamental reform in the North. The SDLP's immediate response to the killings reflected the anger and outrage of the people in Derry. Hume compared the killings to the notorious 1960 Sharpeville massacre in South Africa.[20] Pointing to Derry's Bogside, where the killings had occurred, he said that such was the revulsion at what the British troops had done, that people were now saying they would settle for nothing less than a united Ireland. While Unionists were quick to use his response as further evidence of his extremism, Hume was accurately reflecting the now total alienation from the northern state felt by Nationalists, and their determination that radically new constitutional and political arrangements would have to be achieved if any semblance of a state was to survive. At Westminster, a few days later, Gerry Fitt reinforced Hume's assertions saying that 'what happened last Sunday has dramatically changed the whole political outlook [and] a political solution which may have applied last Saturday would no longer be acceptable'.[21] The following week, a civil rights rally in Newry in protest against the killings in Derry attracted over 20,000 people. At it, Fitt repeated his call for Stormont to be suspended, and rejected any suggestion of talks while internment lasted.

Northern Ireland was now in a crisis of considerable magnitude, and one demanding decisive intervention from Edward Heath's government, not least because of its damaging effects on Britain's international standing. Heath's immediate response was to establish a judicial inquiry, a move condemned by the SDLP, which had called for an independent inquiry headed by an international lawyer, not Lord Widgery, the UK lawyer appointed by Heath. But on a new political initiative, Heath delayed several weeks.

Not surprisingly, in the immediate aftermath of Bloody Sunday, speculation was rife as to Northern Ireland's political destiny: should it continue to exist; should Irish unity now be the immediate goal; should the North be fully integrated into the rest of the UK, or should it become an entity completely independent of Britain and of the rest of Ireland. The debate raged, raising unrealistic expectations and fears on all sides. Witnessing the disarray among Unionists and the scale of the crisis facing the British government, many Nationalists believed that unity was at last attainable. Provisional Sinn Féin was not alone in proclaiming Irish unity as the immediate answer. Within all major parties in the South, the proposition was being raised, with greater or lesser conviction. Liam Cosgrave, leader of Fine Gael, a party not renowned for empty rhetoric on unity, argued that 'a United Ireland is the only way to bring about a permanent and peaceful settlement'.[22] Even that renowned pillar of liberal moderation, the *Irish Times*, urged Faulkner to spell out his opposition to unity as if to suggest it could be easily overcome. Another surprising voice in support of unity was Harold Wilson, British Labour Party leader, who proposed that unity be prepared for over a fifteen-year period.[23] For some Unionists like Bill Craig, an independent Northern Ireland was proving attractive, for others under the influence of the conservative MP Enoch Powell, who was beginning to take an active interest in the North's situation, complete 'integration' within the UK was the answer. More realistically, the British government's special cabinet committee on Northern Ireland had been considering suspending devolution and imposing direct rule from London as the prelude to talks leading to new arrangements. Heath had hesitated in the vain hope that Faulkner might have been able to achieve some progress. After Bloody Sunday, the initiative was unquestionably with the British government and with absolutely no prospect of the SDLP returning to Stormont, suspension became inevitable.

Faulkner, who refused to acknowledge that direct rule was even being contemplated, still hoped that the SDLP would return to Stormont and join him in addressing the crisis. Ignoring the sea-change brought about by internment and Bloody Sunday, Faulkner also continued to dismiss SDLP calls for a 'meaningful participation' in decision-making. As Hume pointed out, internment had proved disastrous from whatever perspective it was viewed and had profoundly altered the political landscape. The security situation had deteriorated, not improved as Faulkner had hoped. Eighty-eight people had died from violence in the weeks since internment, compared with twenty-eight during the preceding months; community divisions were wider, while Bloody Sunday had greatly intensified the crisis. The SDLP ignored Faulkner's appeals and reiterated its demands for the immediate suspension of the northern parliament, and for negotiations leading to a new form of cross-community government. The party proposed that, once parliament was suspended, an interim commission should take control of government functions, while negotiations 'to provide a long term solution to the Northern Ireland problem' took place.[24]

SDLP PROPOSALS

The party's policy committee had already prepared detailed proposals for what-ever negotiations might transpire.[25] A draft policy paper argued that the 1920–1 arrangements had institutionalized interdenominational tensions, and had made it temptingly easy for Unionists to find ways of keeping themselves permanently in power, not just in parliament, where they had a built-in majority anyway, but in many local councils where they did not. The paper accepted that instant unity would provide no cure. Instead, it proposed: a bill of rights; a fair representation act to include the revision of electoral arrange-ments and ensure fairer representation on local authorities and in parliament; the abandonment of the Westminster model of government in favour of a government elected from an assembly on a proportional basis, that is, a cross-community government; a council of Ireland to deal with matters of mutual interest North and South; the deletion from the South's constitution of its claims to jurisdiction over Northern Ireland (Articles 2 and 3), and the right of northerners to vote in the South's presidential elections.

Along with these proposals, the party's policy committee drew up a detailed commentary entitled *Background to the present condition of civil unrest*, to be used in briefing the media and in meetings with other parties and the two governments and in the party's international contacts, especially in the US.[26] This paper outlined the reasons for Catholic-Nationalist alienation, the commu-nity's experience of discrimination by public authorities, and of hostility at the hands of the security forces. In its conclusion, the paper stressed the need for reassurances for both communities, claiming that any change must be directed at guaranteeing the civil rights of Catholics and at removing from Protestants their apprehension at being coerced into an all-Ireland sovereign state.[27]

DIRECT RULE

Throughout February and early March 1972, pressure grew for a government initiative. Direct rule from London was openly anticipated; just when and under what conditions it would happen was in question. Defying the evidence, Faulkner remained determined that his administration and Northern Ireland's parliament should retain their integrity and continue with all functions intact, especially those related to law and order. In his desperation to retain some credibility, he suggested, contrary to his long-held position, that people in Northern Ireland, 'whatever their ultimate aspirations to some long-term future may be, should be given a part to play in the community'.[28] In an oblique way, he seemed at last to be considering a greater role for the opposition than that envisaged in his earlier offer of committee chairs. But any suggestion that such a role might amount to a place in government was still anathema to most Unionists. One of Faulkner's leading UUP critics, Desmond Boal, denounced the idea of Catholics in government 'as a complete negation of democracy and ... totally impracticable'.[29] Bill Craig dismissed any such prospect as 'fatuous and only an incentive to those who sought to destroy the constitution'.[30] But it was precisely on such a prospect that much of the speculation about any future government for the North was now focused.

The backdrop to the British government's initiative was complicated by the ongoing violence that in turn required a high level of security activity. The early months of 1972 were marked by forty-eight violent deaths, including those killed on Bloody Sunday, with several hundred more injured and bomb attacks on property a daily occurrence. Bill Craig was further fuelling apprehension, addressing large rallies organized by his recently formed Vanguard movement, threatening reprisal action against 'enemies of the country' and warning of a holocaust should the British government introduce what he termed 'an Irish package', meaning Nationalists in government.[31]

As speculation about future developments mounted, the SDLP was again anxious to have its case heard not only in Ireland and Britain, but also in the US. There, the IRA campaigns had been attracting considerable support and, for the Irish government and the SDLP, the need to offset the appeal to many Irish-Americans of an apparently anti-British 'war of liberation' was an imperative. To highlight the SDLP's approach, John Hume undertook a week-long visit to the US in mid-March. During the visit he met with senior officials in the administration and leading Irish-American politicians, as well as speaking at several Irish-American functions. His message was that violence was only exacerbating a bad situation and making it worse. The SDLP's constitutional, non-violent approach was the only way to avoid an outright civil war, while the party's demand for fundamental reform of how Northern Ireland was governed was essential if peace was to be restored. Thirdly, Hume emphasized that Irish unity, if it was to be real unity, had to be worked for, not fought for. This was the message that Hume would return to on many subsequent visits over the following two-and-a-half decades, during which time he would become the most familiar Irish politician in Washington. When he arrived home, it was virtually on the eve of the first step being taken towards achieving the fundamental change sought by the SDLP.

That step was taken on the 24 March when Heath informed Faulkner that the Northern Ireland parliament could only continue functioning if responsibility for security was transferred to Westminster. Faulkner and his cabinet colleagues were committed to reject any such proposition and when they did so, Heath suspended the parliament and declared 'direct rule' over Northern Ireland. William Whitelaw MP was appointed secretary of state with full authority over all of the functions for which the parliament and government had previously exercised responsibility. Fifty years of Unionist rule in Northern Ireland was ended, and a new chapter in Northern Ireland's history began. It was to be a much longer chapter than anyone at the time imagined.

TERMS FOR NEGOTIATING

The SDLP welcomed Heath's moves and offered 'full cooperation to their implementation'.[32] In a detailed statement, the party leadership stressed that internment remained an obstacle to talks, and that the SDLP expected it would soon be phased out, and it reiterated its commitment to not engaging in talks until that had happened. Once again, the party sought to reassure a Protestant community fearful as to what further initiatives the British government might be planning, by emphasizing that the party genuinely wanted to work with its leaders. As for the IRA campaigns, Hume said that it would be a disaster for the whole country if they were to continue in the new circumstances. Yet, by also arguing that those campaigns were inhibiting an early end to internment, Hume and his colleagues were, probably unconsciously, handing a veto to the paramilitaries over when, or indeed whether talks could take place.

For the SDLP, the suspension of Stormont had, in the words of Paddy O'Hanlon, 'created a situation fraught with possibilities'.[33] Suspension was precisely what the party had been demanding as the first step towards a new start for Northern Ireland. Now the question was how to ensure a key role for the party and, secondly, how to ensure that its proposals would be part of the agenda leading to that new start. However, the precondition that internment must end before the party would engage in negotiations was proving a significant hurdle. Despite its public statements, differences on the precondition persisted within the leadership and now became more evident. Hume and Devlin were described as heading rival groups, with Devlin's 'group' reported as being opposed to any dilution of the 'no negotiations until internment had ended' condition, while Hume was said to have a more flexible approach. Complicating internal relationships were attitudes on other matters such as membership of the EEC, a matter of considerable public debate at the time, and towards the southern government. Devlin's well-known antagonism towards the Lynch administration, always anxious that the SDLP enter talks, and his own pronounced anti-EEC views put him at odds with Hume, for whom positive relations with the Dublin government remained a priority, and who had never concealed his decidedly pro-EEC views. A party statement in early March suggested that efforts were being made to smooth internal relationships and denied any division. The statement again stressed that there would be no return to Stormont, and that Devlin's criticism of Lynch was an expression of his personal, not party, views.[34]

Concern that the SDLP might have been out of touch with its electorate was allayed when Gerry Fitt's wife, Anne, won a council by-election in Belfast's Dock Ward at this time. Her victory was rendered more important because of the heavy pressure from militant republicans, who openly attempted to intimidate her supporters from voting. In her campaign, Fitt strongly condemned IRA violence, and her victory was a boost for the SDLP and a vindication of its strong stand against violence. In the immediate aftermath of direct rule, considerable pressure was being directed on both IRA movements, especially the Provos (who were fast becoming the more militant), to at least call a truce in order to allow for political negotiations. Ivan Cooper and Paddy Devlin, both of whom had long favoured talks with the PIRA, met with its leader Seán Mac Stíofáin in a vain attempt to argue the case for a truce. Cardinal Conway added his voice, calling on the two IRAs to end their campaigns and saying that the demand within the Catholic community was 'loud and clear for peace'.[35] The PIRA's response was blunt and was given by one of its prominent activists in Derry, Martin McGuinness, who proclaimed that, 'We fight on. We're not stopping until we get a united Ireland'.[36] To emphasize this determination, April witnessed an intense period of violence with twenty-three IRA explosions on one day alone.

Adding to the SDLP's difficulties in deciding how it might meaningfully engage with the British government was the publication of Lord Widgery's report on the Bloody Sunday killings.[37] The report claimed justification for the soldiers who had opened fire, saying that evidence existed that at least some of those killed had been handling explosives and shots had been fired at the troops first. Reflecting Nationalist outrage and disbelief, the SDLP dismissed the findings as 'whitewash', saying 'we regret that our recommendations for an international investigation into the events coupled with an independent examination of the forensic evidence was not acted upon'.[38] Trust among Nationalists that Britain could act impartially was extremely low, if not non-existent. Unless politics could regain and sustain the initiative, violence seemed likely to escalate. Consequently, the Irish government maintained its pressure on the SDLP to engage with Whitelaw, and expressed some irritation that the party was not moving more rapidly to embrace the opportunities that had been presented. In a conversation with John Peck, British ambassador in Dublin, the minister for foreign affairs, Patrick Hillery, expressed this irritation, saying that 'the time had come when the SDLP should be induced off their horse about internment and get down to talks, if not with Mr Whitelaw, at least with his officials'.[39] But Peck added that in Hillery's view, 'the Dublin government had no formal control over the SDLP ... Paddy Devlin, for example, hated Lynch's guts'.

Despite the mistrust and suspicion, British moves towards creating a climate for progress were gradually changing the general atmosphere. Within his first month, Secretary of State Whitelaw released over sixty internees, closed the prison ship *Maidstone*, which had held several hundred detainees, and the internment centre at Magilligan prison in Co. Derry, lifted the ban that had been imposed on public parades, and began a process of private discussions with individuals and groups from across the whole community. Whitelaw also moved to establish an advisory commission, though not the representative kind proposed by the SDLP. These moves signalled that the party's ideas for interim arrangements had been heard and acted upon, to some extent at least, even if the party itself stated that it would not work with Whitelaw's commission.

EDGING TOWARDS TALKS

The first major move by the SDLP towards political re-engagement with the British government and with Unionists came at the end of May, when the party called on Nationalists who had withdrawn from public office in opposition to internment to resume their duties. In its statement, the SDLP acknowledged the changes that had been taking place since direct rule saying 'now is the time to demonstrate our determination to create community reconciliation. It is time for a positive response to Mr Whitelaw as a gesture of our confidence that meaningful peaceful progress is now possible'.[40] Again, the statement sought to reassure the Protestant community 'that our strong and determined campaign for political change in no way represents a desire for sectarian conflict ... it has been our consistent view that the political changes that we seek are necessary for the removal of the sectarian barriers that disfigure our society'.[41] The statement also indicated that the party would be taking steps to enter into dialogue with the Protestant community. It had already done so on a limited scale when, a few days earlier, a delegation led by Gerry Fitt had met with Protestant leaders in the Shankill area of Belfast to try to defuse sectarian tensions. Hume engaged in a television discussion with a masked representative of the UDA, during which he sought to persuade the latter that the SDLP was genuine in its desire for peace and a positive relationship with the Unionist community.

The SDLP's approach was not universally welcomed within the Nationalist community. James Doris, chairman of the NICRA, accused the party of 'arrogance' in making the call to public representatives, and advised that no one should return to the offices from which they had withdrawn until the complete ending of internment.[42] Michael Farrell of the student movement, People's Democracy, which had been active in civil rights protests, described the SDLP's statement as 'a despicable attempt to sell the liberty of over 500 men and buy the favour of William Whitelaw and the British political establishment'.[43] The PIRA greeted the statement with a bomb attack in Belfast that killed one woman and injured over forty other people.

While the SDLP's call for a return to public office was welcomed by the British and Irish governments and, more significantly, was responded to by many of those to whom it had been directed, the condition for entering into direct talks with the British remained. Devlin reinforced the party's commitment to that condition, saying that the call to engage in talks 'should not be seen as undermining the civil disobedience campaign'.[44] But as the climate changed, attempts were made to replace violence with discussion and efforts were increasingly made to encourage political dialogue. An important move was made when the Official IRA declared a ceasefire on 29 May. With that, further pressure mounted on the Provisionals to do likewise. Devlin again urged the PIRA to adopt a purely defensive role. In his view, 'no responsible person having regard to nightly attacks on Catholics by mobile assassination squads operating from behind Unionist barricades could ask republicans to leave Catholic enclaves'.[45] Eventually, the sustained pressure began to have some effect, and the PIRA invited Whitelaw to meet them to discuss a way forward. He refused, but crucially there had been no reference in the PIRA invitation to any precondition regarding internment. The SDLP regarded the absence of such a precondition as an opportunity for them to also seek a meeting with the secretary of state, though strictly confined to discussing terms for a ceasefire, which Hume and Devlin had been exploring with the PIRA leadership. The importance of the request was that the taboo on such meetings had been broken, although it is now clear, as government papers reveal, that the SDLP had maintained a degree of contact through officials ever since its withdrawal from Stormont; contacts that became more frequent following the suspension of Stormont. Hume and Devlin undertook to convey the PIRA's preconditions for talks with the British to Whitelaw, with whom a meeting had been arranged.[46] The ceasefire conditions included granting 'political status' to paramilitary prisoners, that any meeting not be at Stormont and that there be no restriction on who would represent the PIRA. The latter condition effectively meant releasing leading PIRA representative Gerry Adams from detention so that he could take part. Whitelaw acceded to all preconditions, and soon afterwards the Provisionals declared a ceasefire to allow for 'meaningful talks between the major parties in the conflict'.[47]

The talks and ceasefire were short-lived. A meeting in London between a PIRA delegation and Whitelaw was, in the latter's words, a 'non-event'. The PIRA's representatives demanded a British withdrawal from Northern Ireland by 1975, a demand totally unacceptable to the British. The delegation returned home with nothing to show but a determination to pursue their campaign, and pursue it they did, with devastating effects. Within a week Belfast experienced one of the city's darkest days when, on 21 July (ever since called Bloody Friday), twenty-six bombs were exploded, leaving eleven civilians dead and over 130 injured. With little prospect of another PIRA ceasefire, the SDLP now had to shoulder almost full responsibility for political leadership within the Nationalist community. The PIRA had sidelined itself, while politicians like McManus and Bernadette Devlin as well as what remained of the Nationalist Party, lacked cohesion and the breadth of representation enjoyed by the SDLP. Furthermore, the party was being credited with its efforts, albeit unsuccessful, to end PIRA violence, and with a clear commitment to seeking a new and comprehensive solution.

How the party would meet the challenges of its leadership role was soon to be tested when, on 20 July, Whitelaw announced that, following consultations with all the constitutional political parties, he would convene a conference to establish how much common ground existed between them. Austin Currie, one of those who had been most adamant on not speaking while internment lasted, argued that the SDLP would be fully justified in meeting Whitelaw, even if it meant breaking its bond.[48] Others stressed that it was the party's duty to do so. The most doubtful was Paddy Devlin, but even he relented when, after a weekend of discussions involving the party's public representatives and executive members, the SDLP announced that it would enter talks with Whitelaw. Significantly, no commitment was made regarding the proposed conference. Instead, in its statement the party addressed the internment precondition making a strong attack on the PIRA, saying 'these men don't care for human life, don't care for democracy, don't care for the internees who would have all been released if the truce had not been broken'.[49] The implication was that since the PIRA had failed to achieve any progress with the British, and had decided to pursue what the SDLP regarded as a vicious, unjustified and immoral campaign of violence, the party had an obligation to explore other approaches to political progress. The SDLP also pointed out that PIRA leaders had been flown to London in an RAF aircraft to hold discussions with Whitelaw, without any concessions whatsoever being promised on internment. The SDLP stressed that its immediate objective would be 'to secure all-round agreement for quadripartite talks involving the British and Irish governments as well as representatives of both communities in the North, at which a political settlement will be worked out'.[50]

OPERATION MOTORMAN

Whitelaw had one further major hurdle to overcome before he would proceed with his political agenda. He viewed as no longer tolerable the so-called 'no-go' areas in Derry and Belfast where paramilitaries (loyalist as well as republican) openly exercised a degree of control and where public authorities could only provide services with their consent. In Derry, meetings had already taken place under John Hume's auspices between local community leaders and civil servants to find ways to end the city's 'no-go' areas, but these had not produced any immediate results. Following the failed talks with the PIRA and, in particular, after Bloody Friday, Whitelaw decided that it was time to act.

Whitelaw ordered a large-scale military operation to assert control over the areas in question. Called Operation Motorman, the British army's biggest operation since Suez in 1956 took place on 31 July. Barricades were dismantled with hardly any resistance and with the active cooperation of civilians in both cities. Despite fears of widespread resistance, particularly in Derry, only sporadic incidents occurred, during which troops fatally shot two youths. The PIRA had, apparently, instructed its activists to withdraw from the city. So, notwithstanding its public warnings predicting mayhem, SDLP reaction was muted. Ivan Cooper was a lone voice in saying that the operation had 'precluded talks with Whitelaw',[51] a comment for which he was severely rebuked by Taoiseach Jack Lynch, who said that elected leaders should not say that talks were unlikely. A party statement accused Whitelaw of 'imposing an iron-fisted military regime on the Catholic minority',[52] but in more measured terms, Hume argued that the military action had changed nothing, since 'it's one thing to end no-go areas physically, but they are still no-go areas in the mind'.[53] While the SDLP was concerned that British army behaviour was not creating an atmosphere conducive to talks, continued PIRA action only emphasized the urgent need to break the circle of violence by injecting some hope for a political solution. Emphasizing that urgency was a PIRA operation on the same day as Operation Motorman, when bombs were exploded with callous disregard for the consequences in Claudy, a denominationally mixed village in Co. Derry. Eight civilians were killed, and many more severely injured.

TALKING TO PRIME MINISTERS

The Irish government's anxiety that the SDLP should not forgo the opportunity to engage with Mr Whitelaw was dramatically underlined by the late-night meeting it convened with several of the SDLP's MPs on the day after Operation Motorman. An Irish Army helicopter flew Hume, Devlin and Cooper from Donegal to Dublin, where they were joined by Currie and O'Hanlon – Fitt was in London and unable to travel – for the first of several meetings over the following days with the Taoiseach and leading members of his government.[54] At these meetings, the Taoiseach and his colleagues stressed their conviction that talks with the British government

> were now number one priority if peace was to be saved (and that) …
> it would be tragic if one more opportunity should be missed and if

the Provisional IRA would be again given breathing space to recoup, recover and blow more people to bits, returning once more to square one.[55]

They were clearly telling the SDLP leadership not to delay in becoming involved in meaningful discussions.

A few days later, an SDLP delegation met with Whitelaw in Belfast in the first of two lengthy meetings within a week. According to the delegation's own notes of the meeting, concern was expressed about the presence of troops in Catholic areas, their occupation of Catholic-owned premises and their behaviour when conducting searches and manning roadblocks, the number of licensed weapons still held mainly by individuals from a Unionist background, and alleged inaction against Protestant paramilitaries. However, the main issue raised was internment and the party's demand that it be ended forthwith.[56] To emphasize its determination to see progress on this issue, the party requested a meeting with Prime Minister Heath. Whitelaw listened, thanked the SDLP for its support during Operation Motorman – neither side detailed what that support had amounted to – and stressed the importance of the conference that he would be convening in the near future, and his hope that all parties would attend.[57] The second meeting repeated many of the points made at the first, with SDLP delegates emphasizing that they needed to see results quickly if they were to retain credibility within their own community. As yet, apart from the release of forty-seven more internees, and the promise of action to control army behaviour, there was little of substance to show for the party's efforts.

The meeting with Heath, the first ever between a British prime minister and representatives of the North's Nationalist community, took place at Chequers on 12 September. The delegation seems to have impressed Heath with their arguments, but his failure to give any assurance on an early end to internment, or to indicate that talks would be widened to include the Irish government, strengthened the view within the SDLP that the party should not attend Whitelaw's forthcoming inter-party conference.[58] The pressure on the SDLP to maintain a robust stand in its dealings with the British government can be gauged from the reaction that these initial meetings provoked within sections of the Nationalist community. Soon after the first meeting with Whitelaw, effigies of both Fitt and Devlin appeared in West Belfast proclaiming them as traitors because they had engaged in talks while internment continued. Frank McManus described the party as 'an unexpected ally of Mr Whitelaw',[59] and the party was roundly denounced at anti-internment rallies. However, there was consolation for the SDLP in an opinion poll that showed John Hume receiving strong endorsement among Catholics, while support for the PIRA was recorded as extremely weak.

TOWARDS A NEW IRELAND

Whatever about its initial hesitancy in engaging with the British government, or its decision not to participate in Whitelaw's conference, the SDLP had now set itself firmly on the path of political dialogue and prepared to become fully involved in wider talks that it now believed to be inevitable. Faced with that prospect, the party had to determine what it would negotiate for and, ultimately, what it would settle for. By now, the party's policy committee had completed its deliberations, and after several weeks of intense internal discussions that included consultations with experts in various fields of constitutional law, government and politics, a decision was taken at another Donegal 'think-in' to publish its recommendations.

Entitled *Towards a new Ireland*, the policy document based its proposals on the claim that Northern Ireland was inherently unstable, that civil strife had been a feature of its fifty-year existence and that fundamental constitutional as well as institutional changes were required. The thrust of the proposals was that only unity could provide the optimal context for peace and harmony on the island. This conclusion led to the demand that that the British government make a declaration that 'it would be in the best interests of all sections of the communities in both islands, if Ireland were to become united on terms which would be acceptable to all of the people of Ireland'.[60]

However, realizing that unity could not be achieved in the immediate future, the SDLP proposed that for an interim period Northern Ireland would become the joint responsibility of the British and Irish governments; that the government of the region consist of representatives of the whole community; and that a national senate with significant executive powers of an all-Ireland nature be established with equal representation from North and South. Critically, the SDLP proposed that responsibility for security should be exercised jointly by the British and Irish governments and not returned to a Northern Ireland government. Furthermore, the party proposed 'a new unarmed police force or forces jointly recruited by both governments'.[61]

In effect, the SDLP was proposing that Northern Ireland become a British-Irish condominium for a period during which new institutions of government would prepare for unity. *Towards a new Ireland* was an unashamedly united Ireland document that significantly diluted the consent principle as previously articulated by the SDLP.[62] It was a proposal to which the British government with its commitment to upholding the will of the majority was never likely to agree. Furthermore, Unionists, should they ever agree to what the SDLP was proposing, would have accepted that unity would be the clear objective for any new government in Northern Ireland. Within its terms, consent was only applicable to the form that unity would take, not to whether or not Ireland should be united. It was a proposition that Unionists were never likely to accept. Critically, however, the SDLP document recognized the dual allegiances of the two communities in the North, and argued that while it had its own preferred solution, progress towards a mutually acceptable settlement could only be made by taking those allegiances into account as fundamental realities. Such recognition was the essential novelty of the SDLP's proposals, and, in that respect, it marked a clear break with previous thinking within Nationalist political circles.

Towards a new Ireland was given a positive response by most Nationalists, North and South, but, not surprisingly, it evoked strong criticism from Unionists, who dismissed it as totally unacceptable, with the paramilitary UDA threatening civil war if its implementation was ever attempted. It is unlikely that the SDLP leadership believed it could negotiate full acceptance of all its proposals. It is more likely that the party was putting forward a maximum position and, in doing so, protecting itself against any criticism that it had abandoned ultimate Nationalist aspirations. What the party was essentially saying was that the Northern Ireland crisis could not be resolved within Northern Ireland itself. Instead, it required a joint approach by Britain and Ireland as well as local political parties. This would entail a new constitutional framework; one that recognized the Britishness of Unionists and the Irishness of Nationalists; one that also created political institutions that would equally and equitably reflect those identities and ensure fairness for all. Furthermore, despite the qualifications on the principle of consent implied by *Towards a new Ireland*, the general understanding was that the party's real position was closer to that stated in its own constitution, which upheld the right of a majority in Northern Ireland to determine the region's constitutional future. These fundamental principles were in line with what the party had been saying since its foundation and would remain the bedrock of its position in all negotiations over the next thirty years. Indeed, in his autobiography, Austin Currie confirms that the declaration sought in *Towards a new Ireland* was of 'tactical importance to cover our backs against possible criticism within and without our own ranks that we were concerned only with a stop-gap interim solution'.[63] Hume was also to acknowledge that *Towards a new Ireland* was essentially the party's opening bid, and that it never expected to achieve all that it proposed,[64] but he did believe that the British would have to introduce 'something along the lines of the SDLP plan'.[65]

SOUTHERN CRITICISM

One source from which the SDLP's document evoked the strongest criticism was not any shade of unionism, but rather its sister party in the South, the Irish Labour Party. More precisely, the criticism came from Labour's Northern Ireland spokesperson, Conor Cruise O'Brien. O'Brien was a former Irish and UN diplomat, and academic, who had recently been elected to the Dáil, where his questioning voice about southern attitudes and policies towards the North had made him a national figure. Vehemently opposed to violence and, in partic- ular to the PIRA, O'Brien's approach virtually eschewed any mention of Irish unity, fearing that it only provoked the kind of reaction threatened by the UDA. Instead, he advocated power-sharing as the primary focus in any negoti- ations, together with changes in the South's constitution to remove those articles that claimed jurisdiction over the North. Unity, he believed, was best left aside as a matter for active discussion until considerable progress on economic and social reconstruction had been achieved in the South coupled with reconciliation within the North.

O'Brien's reservations about the SDLP's proposals centred on the demand for a British declaration in favour of Irish unity, a demand he found extremely unhelpful. Highlighting the point, *Irish Times* correspondent Dick Walsh wrote that 'a declaration by Britain would run counter to Dr O'Brien's view that only when a majority of the people in Northern Ireland decide should there be any suggestion of Irish unity'.[66] Other Labour reservations centred on the very nature of 'joint sovereignty', which would require Dublin to contribute to the cost of public services in the North at a time when social benefits, for example, were more favourable there than in the South. However, there was considerable reluctance within the Irish Labour Party to criticize the SDLP, with the result that while the parliamentary party would not initially endorse *Towards a new Ireland*, the party's administrative council did. The controversy that followed was one that not only affected SDLP-Irish Labour relationships but also convulsed the Labour Party itself for a period throughout the early autumn of 1972. At the annual conference of the British Labour Party, the differences between the two parties produced sharp exchanges between O'Brien and Austin Currie at a fringe meeting organized by the CDU. O'Brien insisted that 'it would be better to have no talk of Irish unity until first the Republic had proved its good faith, and, second, there had been reconciliation between the two communities in Northern Ireland and the idea of unity was no longer productive of divisive violence'.[67] Currie, on the other hand, 'insisted that a solution must be sought within the context of the whole of Ireland and that the Dublin government must be involved immediately'.[68] The climax to this controversy was a television debate between Hume and O'Brien on RTE's *Late Late Show*, when Hume challenged O'Brien on the latter's assertion that even mentioning Irish unity was to risk civil war.[69] Hume accused O'Brien of offering a more subtle and effective defence of unionism than any that had come from any Unionist quarter and denied that talking about Irish unity should be seen as inherently provocative. He agreed with O'Brien that partnership and reconciliation were essential in order to stabilize the situation and that those aims were at the heart of SDLP policy.

The controversy was sidelined as attention began focusing on how Whitelaw would assess the prospects for progress following the publication of the SDLP's proposals and his inter-party conference to be held at Darlington in England at the end of September. Despite pressure from the Irish government, and despite Whitelaw's establishment of a commission to consider alternatives to internment, the party still refused to participate in the conference.[70] The party maintained its commitment to no participation in talks while internment continued, and the Darlington conference became very much a one-sided affair.[71] By now, however, Whitelaw had a good sense of the main parties' positions and it was time to indicate what the British government planned for the future government of Northern Ireland.

Chapter 3

A brave new world

In a discussion paper *The future of Northern Ireland*, published at the end of October 1972, Whitelaw set out broad principles for agreeing a new political framework.[1] From an SDLP perspective, two principles were of critical concern. First, for the return of devolved government to Northern Ireland, the paper stated that 'there are strong arguments that the objective should be achieved by giving minority interests a share in the exercise of executive power'.[2] In other words, the paper endorsed the SDLP's demand for cross-community government. Secondly, on the question of North-South relationships, in a section entitled 'The Irish Dimension', the paper argued that 'a settlement must recognize Northern Ireland's position within Ireland as a whole'.[3] The phrase 'Irish dimension', which now entered political discourse, was an acknowledgment of the SDLP's insistence that a political solution must, in some meaningful way, take account of the wider Irish context, possibly through the creation of a council of Ireland. As for the declaration on unity sought by the SDLP, the discussion paper merely reiterated the traditional British approach that it had no wish 'to impede the realization of Irish unity, if it were to come about by genuine and freely given mutual agreement and on conditions acceptable to the distinctive communities'.[4] To test current opinion on unity, the British recommended that a plebiscite be held.[5] Dubbed a 'border poll', this proposal was greeted with strong opposition from all shades of Nationalist opinion, because of its inevitable result and the potential for heightening tensions during the run up to polling day. On policing, the discussion paper offered no suggestion that further reform was needed,[6] and completely ignored the party's proposal that policing should become a responsibility of an all-Ireland body.

BASIS FOR DISCUSSION

While much would have to be negotiated, key principles that the SDLP had been advocating were now enshrined as fundamental to the British government's thinking about the future form of government in Northern Ireland, and about relationships with the South. This was a significant achievement, given Heath's previously stated opposition to any direct role for the Irish in talks on a way forward, and his belief that the principle of majority rule should be upheld in forming a devolved government.[7] Despite enshrining power-sharing and an Irish dimension, the SDLP's immediate response to the discussion paper was mixed. Paddy Devlin described it as 'too limited in scope to produce a formula that will give the North a chance for permanent peace and stability'.[8] He criticized the paper for failing to provide firm directions on Irish unity, arguing that it does not propose 'anything that will create new political alignments or new sets of political issues. What it does do is to institutionalize the religious alignments ... and [it] makes the conditions for a final settlement more difficult to obtain'. In line with *Towards a new Ireland*, Devlin called for interim arrangements that would pave the way 'inexorably towards a united Ireland'. Austin Currie struck a slightly less negative note, saying that while Whitelaw's document only tinkered with the 1920 settlement, the acknowledgment of the Irish dimension was a positive step.[9] Fitt was more fulsome in his welcome when the paper was debated in the House of Commons two weeks later, though he was careful to direct his welcome at the section which referred to the 'Irish dimension'. For Fitt, 'the inclusion of this paragraph tells us for the first time that a Conservative government, with the support of the Labour opposition, recognize that Ulster is in Ireland, that Ulster people are Irish, and that sooner or later, the Irish people will have to be given the opportunity to determine their own destiny'.[10]

In its more considered response, the party acknowledged that by ruling out a number of Unionist-preferred options – a return to majority rule, independence and full integration into the UK – and by pointing firmly in the direction of power-sharing and an Irish dimension, Whitelaw had opened up some positive opportunities.[11] Effectively, the party was saying 'good, but not good enough'. So, while the party's statement repeated its call for a British declaration in favour of Irish unity as the long term solution, Whitelaw's discussion paper afforded the SDLP a sufficient basis for negotiations, and indicated its willingness to engage. The party's response was very much in line with the approach the Irish government had announced a few days earlier. Taoiseach Jack Lynch had welcomed the paper, stressing its references to the Irish dimension. For Lynch, the Irish dimension could mean a strong council of Ireland with significant responsibilities that would be 'an important bridge towards greater understanding and mutual respect among all people, and hence towards true

Irish unity'.[12] London was pleased with these responses. Whitelaw had been sending strong messages to Dublin appealing for a supportive approach, urging that the SDLP be encouraged to enter talks and in particular to commit to participating in the elections to the new local authorities scheduled to take office in 1973.[13]

The SDLP lost little time in re-engaging with Whitelaw. While the party discussed its main concerns with the secretary of state – internment, prospects for political progress and security force behaviour in Nationalist areas – what was surprising was the range of other matters also addressed. These included representation on public bodies, especially on the new area boards to be established as a result of local government reform, discrimination against Catholics within the public service and in the allocation of public housing. Such a comprehensive agenda indicated that the SDLP now accepted that there had to be a regular relationship with Whitelaw if the party was to effectively represent its supporters' concerns and needs. Politics seemed to be assuming some of its normal functions again.

SECOND ANNUAL CONFERENCE

At the party's second annual conference in November, there was an obvious anxiety to answer O'Brien's accusation that *Towards a new Ireland* had not paid sufficient attention to reconciliation. With O'Brien in the audience representing the Irish Labour Party, party chair Eddie McGrady argued that 'North and South must be radically changed in many ways. These changes will require time and, of the three Rs, reunification comes last. It is preceded, as it must, by reconciliation and reconstruction'.[14] John Hume also referred to O'Brien's accusation, saying 'what we have done is to be much more realistic about the framework necessary for reconciliation ... we believe that reconciliation can only be achieved by recognizing initially the differences that exist and allowing for free expression of these. That is why we have proposed joint sovereignty...'[15] Not only was the party anxious to underline its commitment to reconciliation, in the main motion to the conference it also stressed its left-of-centre credentials. The motion read:[16]

> That the SDLP commits itself to working whole-heartedly for the unity of the working people of Northern Ireland and eventually of all Ireland;

that it should make every effort to talk with and establish common ground with the comrades from whom we have been separated by the artificial barriers of religious sectarianism and capitalist exploitation but with whom we have a common bond of solidarity in the class struggle.

Paddy Devlin proposed it to the conference, saying that it provided the basis for the party's plans for social and economic development.

In light of ongoing political developments, the motion proposed by Ivan Cooper calling on the party 'to enter into immediate discussions with the British secretary of state and all interested political parties' was of greater immediate significance. Cooper underlined the party's obligation to provide vision, leadership and hope and, therefore it had to talk to all who would listen. The motion passed without serious opposition, and this freed the party from the existing inhibition of not talking to the government until internment had ended.

Relationships with Fianna Fáil were again raised by Fitt in his address, when he referred to controversial remarks that he had made at a recent meeting in Co. Galway. There, he had accused Fianna Fáil of never having done anything for the North. He described it and the UUP as 'political Siamese twins – both know what power is and how to hold on to it'.[17] Members of the SDLP's main fund-raising group in the South, which was representative of all parties and none, took exception to the remarks, claiming not only that they were unwarranted, but also that they would have adverse effects on the group's activities. These concerns were also echoed within the party's executive, where it was reported that financial support from the South was lower than expected as a result of the remarks. In his address, Fitt stood by his comments, saying 'I am a socialist and I have absolutely no connection with anyone who is a member of, or pays lip service to any conservative party'.[18] What impact his remarks actually ever had on fund-raising is impossible to measure, but the reality was that financial support from the South was crucial to sustaining the party, as were positive relationships with all of the parties there to achieving its political goals. Remarks like Fitt's did not help either objective, and the party had to work hard to mend bridges.

MEMBERS UNDER ATTACK

As the party grew in confidence and strength, so did its threat to others, among them paramilitaries from both communities, who singled out some of its leading members for violent attention. Targeted several times was Austin Currie, whose home and family were subject to a number of attacks, one particularly brutal attack occurred in mid-November 1972. Two armed men forced their way into his home demanding to speak to Austin and when they discovered he was not at home – he was in Cork on party business – they assaulted his wife Annita in the presence of their children, cutting the initials UVF onto her chest. It was not the first time that the Currie house had been attacked by loyalist and PIRA gangs, nor was it to be the last. Among other SDLP members attacked during these early years, either personally or through family members or their property, were Ivan Cooper, Paddy Devlin, Gerry Fitt, John Hume, Hugh News and, most tragic of all, Senator Paddy Wilson, who was brutally murdered by a UFF gang in June 1973.

1972 proved to be the worst year of the Troubles to date, with 496 deaths through violence and over ten thousand bombs being exploded. Reflecting on the year, and despite his own family's trauma, Austin Currie took some consolation from what he perceived to be changing attitudes: 'I detect among the population generally a greater willingness to accept that the other fellow has a different point of view and that his view has as good a right to be accommodated as one's own'.[19] He hoped that the SDLP's proposals would be seen as a contribution to making accommodation a reality, and that 1973 would see considerable progress towards achieving that reality. His words would turn out to be both right and wrong.

PRESSING RADICAL CHANGE

At further meetings with Whitelaw, the SDLP detailed their *Towards a new Ireland* proposals, emphasizing the futility of seeking a mere 'interim' solution, and arguing that a system that would command the allegiance of the entire community had to be found if Northern Ireland was to avoid future outbreaks of violence. The party seemed to ignore the fact that its own joint-sovereignty proposals were for institutions that would be interim, pending the creation of a united Ireland, and so were unacceptable to Unionists. On policing, the SDLP argued that 'our joint sovereignty proposals for the recruitment of a new police service under London and Dublin are the only ones which appear to face up to the reality of the situation'.[20] While self-evident to the SDLP, it was not just Whitelaw who had to be convinced. Critically, Unionists would also have to accept the argument for new policing arrangements. Given that joint authority was not simply about ensuring a police service that would command cross-community support, but was centrally aimed at preparing for a united Ireland, it too was not a proposal that Unionists were likely to accept. Furthermore, it was also becoming clear that the Dublin government would not be easily persuaded to transfer significant responsibility for policing to an untried all-Ireland body.

BORDER POLL OPPOSED

As 1973 opened, and as a British white paper detailing the government's proposals for a settlement was being anticipated, the prospect for political progress seemed to improve, but it was against the backdrop of a still very menacing situation. Some Unionist leaders were beginning to acknowledge that any future government for Northern Ireland would require support from both communities, although they were careful to stress that having Nationalists in the cabinet would not be acceptable. Whitelaw's decision that the plebiscite on Northern Ireland's future would take place in March provided some reassurance to Unionists, if not to Nationalists. The SDLP and the Irish government still strongly opposed the poll, arguing that its outcome would not contribute anything new or positive to the search for a way forward. The SDLP advised that the referendum was 'a futile exercise with a result that can be readily forecast ... so we call on our supporters to ignore completely the referendum and reject this extremely irresponsible decision by the British government'.[21] It was wise advice given the violence of the time.

Loyalist murders of Catholics and attacks on Catholic areas – most of the 106 murders by loyalist paramilitaries in 1972 had been random killings of Catholics – continued to cause serious concern. When the Loyalist Association of Workers (LAW), closely associated with the UDA, called a general strike on 7 February to protest against security forces' operations in Protestant areas and alleged inaction against republicans, tensions rose considerably. During the strike, several Catholic premises, including a church and a home for mentally impaired children, were attacked. In London, an SDLP delegation emphasized to the government and opposition the scale and urgency of the situation, highlighting UDA bombings, North and South; the use of licensed weapons by loyalist paramilitaries and the party's belief that the security forces and the courts were not dealing effectively with threats from the UDA, which was still legal despite its obvious paramilitary nature.[22]

ENGAGING UNIONISTS

The Nationalist boycott of the border poll contributed significantly to the relatively peaceful circumstances in which it was eventually held. With only the Unionist parties campaigning, the outcome, as predicted, was overwhelmingly in favour of retaining Northern Ireland within the UK.[23] Apart from whatever reassurance the result gave Unionists, it had no bearing on political developments where, despite a climate of suspicion, dialogue of a sort between the SDLP and some Unionists was beginning. In early February, it was revealed that John Hume, Ivan Cooper and Paddy Devlin had met with Unionist politicians Bill Craig and John Taylor at the latter's request.[24] Discussions focused on what Craig and Taylor had been saying publicly about the case for an independent Northern Ireland, should Britain decide to withdraw from the North. According to Taylor, if independence were to work, it would require the support of the two communities both for internal stability and so that Northern Ireland could deal with the Irish and British governments on a basis of equality. Craig had hinted at a similar position, while some extreme loyalist groups who were deeply suspicious of British government intentions also found independence attractive.

To most Nationalists, independence held little appeal but, since it would entail breaking the link with Britain, some believed it could be a transition to unity. Within the SDLP, independence was not taken very seriously, except in so far as Taylor's and Craig's interest seemed to represent some fresh Unionist thinking that, in an independent North, they would be prepared to recognize the different loyalties of Northern Ireland's two communities. Hume suggested that they had based their proposals on the same premise on which the SDLP had based its 'joint sovereignty' conclusions, that is, the twin allegiances of the North's communities. The party invited Craig in his capacity as leader of the United Loyalist Council (ULC) to hold further meetings. The invitation was eventually declined, to the disappointment of the SDLP. Fitt regretted that an opportunity to establish links between the SDLP and working-class Protestants had not been taken up. However, in an attempt to reach out more widely to the Unionist community, the party launched a campaign for peace, a feature of which was a full-page advertisement setting out its policy placed in both the Unionist *News Letter* and the Nationalist *Irish News*. It was a bold initiative aimed at highlighting the SDLP's commitment to an inclusive, partnership vision of the future. The commitment to dialogue was further reinforced when the party advised branches to establish contact with local loyalist organizations, but there is no record of such dialogue having taken place. As to independence, the issue that had sparked the SDLP initiative, an opinion poll at the time revealed that only 3 per cent of Catholics and Protestants believed it could be a viable option.

Entitled *A policy for partnership*, the party's advertisement sought to promote cross-community dialogue aimed at gaining acceptance for partnership government, and the vision of people working together 'to end forever the sectarian conflict that has caused so much bitterness and suffering throughout our long history'.[25] In it, the SDLP set out its *Towards a new Ireland* proposals, arguing that 'the people of Northern Ireland need each other. They need partnership, rather than polarization'.[26] The advertisement outlined proposals for an assembly and a partnership executive together with a North-South body dealing with a wide range of issues of common concern. The advertisement produced no immediate results, but all parties and the whole of the North would soon be tested on whether its people wanted to live in partnership or not.

WHITELAW PROPOSES

The British government's white paper was published at the end of March; elections to the twenty-six new district councils were announced for 30 May, with those to a new assembly for the end of June. From April until June, parties were preoccupied with reacting to the white paper and preparing for what would be the first electoral tests of public opinion since direct rule. For the SDLP, these elections would also be the first tests of its claims to offer a coherent leadership and policies to address the immense problems besetting the people of Northern Ireland.

The white paper's proposals for new political institutions again stressed the principle of power-sharing between representatives of both communities as essential for the creation of an executive.[27] However, as far as North-South arrangements were concerned, the form and functions of any new body or council were left to be negotiated at a conference of the main parties and the two governments that would follow the elections. In a detailed commentary on the proposals, the SDLP welcomed the entrenchment of power-sharing and the return to a proportional voting system, but was highly critical of the absence of clarity on North-South arrangements, and quite scathing of the failure to acknowledge the need for police reform, or to address economic and social issues.[28] The absence of any indication of an end to internment was also strongly criticized. However, the party did welcome the proposal for a charter of rights, hoping that it would signal an end to emergency legislation, and the commitment to deal with discrimination in all its forms. Crucially, the party indicated that it would negotiate within the institutional framework proposed, and that it would take its seats in the proposed assembly.

FIRST MAJOR ELECTORAL TESTS

At the launch of the party's manifesto for the local government elections, party vice-chair Denis Haughey emphasized that the SDLP was not going to make the same mistake Nationalists had made following the 1920–1 settlements; the party would not abstain from the new institutions. There had been considerable pressure from other Nationalist groupings to do so, but invoking the experience of Unionist-controlled councils, Haughey argued that

> those who either refuse to fight these elections or who have declared their intention not to take their seats if elected must bear the responsibility of making it easy for the old Unionist establishment to maintain and even accentuate the familiar, vicious discriminatory practices.[29]

Many councillors, some formerly independent and others from one or other of the pre-existing parties representing the Nationalist community, had joined the SDLP. Now they had their first opportunity to seek support as SDLP members, alongside many others new to local government. One-hundred-and-sixty-six candidates were nominated, of whom over one hundred were predicted to win seats and the manifesto committed SDLP councillors to work with their Unionist colleagues for the good of their local communities.

During the election campaign, the SDLP was the target of criticisms from both extreme Nationalists and Unionists. Nationalist critics accused the party of treachery because it was participating in elections while internment continued. A widely publicized letter from a group of internees described the SDLP as 'traitors who sold out on the internees'.[30] The Nationalist Party, still smarting over its displacement within the Nationalist community by the SDLP, accused it of 'a crude bid for political power' by nominating so many candidates, especially in Derry.[31] Unionists, who were beginning to realize the threat posed by a party of determination and ability, denounced the SDLP as inexperienced novices.

The outcome of the elections fell far short of the more than one hundred seats predicted. SDLP candidates won eighty-two seats but, with almost 14 per cent of the vote, the party was the second largest after the UUP and, more significantly, had established itself as the main party representing the Nationalist community. The Nationalist Party and the various other groups won only a handful of seats, mainly on western councils. While the SDLP failed to win overall control of any council, it came close to winning control in Derry. There it became the largest party and the new mayor was SDLP councillor Raymond McClean, the first from the Nationalist community since the early 1920s. Derry council was also one of the very few in which the SDLP was able to ensure a cross-community division of civic offices. Councillor Jack Allen, a Unionist, was nominated deputy mayor with SDLP support, thus inaugurating a form of cross-community power-sharing never before practised in the North. Elsewhere, the party emerged as a significant presence in such traditionally Nationalist areas as Down, Fermanagh, Newry and Mourne and Omagh. On those councils also the party was able to ensure a cross-community sharing of civic offices.

With the local elections over, attention now focused on the assembly elections to be held at the end of June. Twenty-nine candidates were selected to contest seats in all twelve constituencies, a first for a party from the Nationalist community and a demonstration of the SDLP's determination to appeal for support throughout the North. The party also brought a new discipline and organization to the conduct of elections. In most constituencies, candidates were selected at special party conventions, a manifesto was published and a central committee took charge of the overall conduct of the campaign. The manifesto, *New North – new Ireland*, spelled out the SDLP's overall programme and committed the party to 'create a fair and just system of administration in the North which will be the basis of a just, peaceful and stable society, and we shall work to create an all-Ireland institution.' [32] The manifesto outlined the party's position on such matters as policing, human rights, the economy, the Irish language and unity. On unity, the manifesto stated that the SDLP was 'committed to the unity of Ireland ... (but) ... on the basic logic of the present Irish situation does not seek instant unity.' [33] However, the council of Ireland would be the means whereby trust and confidence would be built between the people of the island, thus 'providing the opportunity to achieve that objective by planned and agreed steps'.[34] The manifesto also reiterated the party's commitment to ending internment and its forthright condemnation of political violence.

During the short month-long campaign, the SDLP again came under severe attack from within the Nationalist community by the PIRA and Frank McManus' 'Unity' movement, as well as from all shades of unionism. To McManus and colleagues, the SDLP was selfishly collaborating with Whitelaw's plans to gain the spoils of office. The PIRA vowed that it would destroy any attempt to establish new political institutions and its leader in Derry, Martin McGuinness, described the SDLP as 'cringing and crawling' in its approach to the British and promised no end to the war until 'the murderous British army was withdrawn'.[35] The SDLP's most likely partner in any future power-sharing administration, Brian Faulkner, described the party as wanting to 'revert to their traditional policy of abstention and boycott'.[36] Defying the criticism, throughout the campaign the SDLP's over-riding message was that a power-sharing administration together with a council of Ireland would be essential if peace and stability were to be achieved.

PADDY WILSON MURDERED

Against a background of continuing violence, the party stressed the futility of that violence, and challenged its perpetrators to demonstrate otherwise. Tragically, highlighting that futility was the brutal murder of Senator Paddy Wilson, election agent for Gerry Fitt, in the final days of the campaign. A loyalist gang from the Ulster Freedom Fighters (UFF) murdered Wilson and a woman friend, Irene Andrews, and dumped their bodies in an isolated quarry in North Belfast. One of the gang, John White, who was later to become prominent in the Ulster Democratic Party (UDP), was convicted of Wilson's murder.

Sadly, Paddy Wilson's murder was yet one more in what was to be another very bloody year in the campaigns of terror. Earlier in June, a PIRA bomb had killed six pensioners in Coleraine and, later that month, the PIRA murdered a mentally impaired Protestant boy in West Belfast and a Pakistani civilian who supplied tea and sandwiches to British soldiers in Derry. Alongside their sectarian killing of Catholics, loyalists pursued a bloody internecine vendetta that resulted in several killings within their own ranks. On election day, bombs exploded in several areas, and voters were attacked outside a number of polling stations.

SDLP DOMINANT

Turnout on 28 June was an impressive 72 per cent and, for the SDLP, the elections were a significant triumph. While slightly disappointed at not winning extra seats in some constituencies, the party was very pleased with the outcome, with more than 159,000 first preference votes, an increase of 67,000 over the local government results four weeks earlier, and nineteen seats. The SDLP also emerged as the only party representing the Nationalist community, all other Nationalist parties failing to win a single seat. In addition to the party's founding members, the elections brought many new faces into public life, among them several who would become prominent over the coming years – Tom Daly in Fermanagh, Paddy Duffy in Mid-Ulster, Frank Feely and Paddy O'Donoghue in South Down, and Séamus Mallon in Armagh. Women had been a glaring absence in the list of candidates, a characteristic not exclusive to the SDLP, and so there was not one woman in the party's assembly group.

At first sight, the overall results suggested victory for candidates who favoured the white paper's proposals. The SDLP's nineteen seats, together with twenty-four for pro-white paper Unionists, eight for the APNI and the single NILP seat, against the twenty-six anti-white paper Unionists, held out the prospect that progress could be made towards a cross-community resolution. The following months were to see intensive efforts to achieve such a resolution and equally intensive efforts to prevent its achievement. In order to avoid heightening tensions during the climax of the loyal orders' marching season in July and August, serious inter-party negotiations did not begin until early autumn. The formal opening of the Assembly took place on 31 July, however, but the proceedings did not augur well for its future. Disruptive behaviour by anti-white paper Unionists gave notice of the strong opposition they would mount to any attempt to implement Whitelaw's proposals.

PREPARING FOR NEGOTIATIONS

For the SDLP, these months were a period of detailed preparation for the negotiations that lay ahead. The new assembly group and the party's executive met together on several occasions and identified five priorities: agreement on a power-sharing executive; agreement on a council of Ireland; reform of the policing service; ending internment; and, in keeping with its social justice agenda, the party determined to achieve agreement on a significant socio-economic package.[37] Conscious of its socio-economic commitments, the party had established a number of working groups to prepare policy proposals on issues such as the economy, education and cultural matters.[38]

While pro-white paper parties and both governments had accepted that there should be some form of all-Ireland council, its composition and, more so, its functions revealed a considerable divergence of opinion. For the SDLP, giving meaningful expression to the 'Irish dimension' was critical in any search for a resolution. Firstly, a council of Ireland would allow the North and, in particular, the North's Nationalist community to participate in an all-Ireland political institution, a key step towards undoing the exclusion from the rest of Ireland imposed by partition. Secondly, a council of Ireland would clearly demonstrate that the SDLP could achieve more in terms of creating the conditions necessary for Irish unity than PIRA violence ever could. The party's *Towards a new Ireland* document had argued for a strong council with significant powers over policing and socio-economic issues. By contrast, Unionists who were prepared to acknowledge the need for such a council envisaged an institution with a very modest advisory role. The British and Irish governments' approaches were somewhere in between, with the British more inclined to the Unionist view and the Irish to the SDLP view.

POLICE REFORM

Alongside new political institutions, police reform was regarded as a fundamental requirement by the SDLP. The party pointed to the very obvious facts that, despite recent reforms, few Nationalists had joined the RUC, the RUC received little spontaneous cooperation from the Nationalist community, especially on politically related crime, and in several Nationalist areas like West Belfast and the Creggan in Derry, the RUC could not freely and openly operate and, significantly, no police officers lived in those areas. The events of recent years held vivid memories of a police force out of control, and operating in what most Nationalists judged to be a highly discriminatory and biased manner against their communities. Hume frequently argued that political stability required cross-community acceptance of the agencies of law and order, and, conversely, that where such acceptance was absent there could be no effective law and order. Hence the case for significant structural and cultural reform in policing, and for control to be vested in acceptable institutions. The SDLP believed that if some degree of control could be given to a council of Ireland, the Nationalist community would support the police service. Most Unionists regarded the RUC as 'their' police force, however, and no Unionist leader was prepared to accept the kind of fundamental change implied in the SDLP's proposals. Moreover, Whitelaw's proposals had scarcely mentioned policing as an issue, let alone more police reform and much less the possibility that an all-Ireland body could have any significant policing functions. The British government assumed that reforms introduced following the Hunt Report in 1969 had adequately addressed the matter, and that further reform would only be minor. In so far as Whitelaw did mention policing, he stressed that the RUC would remain as Northern Ireland's police service.

To reinforce its case for police reform and, in particular, to emphasize the sense of Nationalist alienation from the security forces, the party presented the NIO with a dossier entitled *Loyalist violence and the result of it: the failure of the security forces to deal with it*.[39] Prepared by assembly member Paddy Duffy, the dossier detailed over 200 murders committed since January 1972, of which the PIRA had been responsible for 30, the rest having been carried out by loyalists. The dossier pointed out that only 20 loyalists had been belatedly interned, compared with over 600 alleged PIRA and other republican activists. Duffy also cited several murders of innocent Catholics and attacks on Catholic-owned businesses and churches in the Armagh-Tyrone area, for which no one had been apprehended, let alone charged. Quite apart from the immediate need to address the party's complaints about policing failures, the clear message for the future of policing was that significant reform to enable Nationalists to support and enrol in the service was absolutely essential.

DUBLIN RELATIONSHIPS

Anxious that it would have Irish government support, the SDLP used the period following the assembly elections to develop relationships with the recently elected Taoiseach, Liam Cosgrave, and his cabinet. Some within the party were concerned that a number of Cosgrave's ministers, in particular Garret FitzGerald and Conor Cruise O'Brien, were unduly sympathetic to Unionists and would not favour the party's ambitious plans for a council of Ireland and for police reform. At a meeting of the party's assembly members in July, annoyance was expressed about 'the present government's statements on national unity which indicated a clear drift away from the stance of the last government ... Equivocation similar to that emanating from the coalition government could be damaging to us at a time when we appear to be on the verge of a breakthrough'.[40] At a subsequent meeting with the Irish government, Hume reflected this concern and argued that the SDLP expected full support for a meaningful Irish dimension as well as for radical changes to policing.[41] The party also reassured the government that, after a long and bitter struggle, it was 'prepared to work very hard indeed to make the new assembly in the North a worthwhile institution'.[42]

The SDLP published details of its council of Ireland proposals just prior to a meeting between the British and Irish prime ministers in mid-September, with the obvious intent of influencing both governments.[43] The party proposed a council with equal representation from North and South exercising executive, harmonizing and consultative functions over such matters as tourism, energy, regional planning and development, as well as having a significant role in policing, North and South. The party also proposed that the council establish a court of human rights, with judges from each jurisdiction to hear cases of alleged denial of human rights in any part of Ireland. Most of these recommendations would appear in the Irish government's proposals published some time later.[44] While there was general support for the framework and broad functions of the council, the Irish government did not fully share the SDLP's suggestion for joint Irish-British responsibility for policing in the North. A department of foreign affairs briefing paper bluntly acknowledged the 'reluctance of some ministers to envisage any role for the council in relation to the Gardaí'.[45] Garret FitzGerald, alone of southern ministers, remained sympathetic to the SDLP's proposal, and suggested that a joint police authority accountable to the council of Ireland could have a role in policing on both sides of the border.[46]

INTER-PARTY NEGOTIATIONS

Inter-party negotiations were slow to get underway. Faulkner was still adamant that power-sharing at cabinet level was not possible, and remained unwilling to embrace Whitelaw's proposals on the formation of an executive. At a meeting in Chequers with Heath and Cosgrave, he tried to convince both of his position, arguing that the SDLP could not be nominated to the cabinet 'as the SDLP differ from the majority on fundamentals (acceptance of Northern Ireland's constitutional position)'.[47] Faulkner was still considering enhanced roles for parliamentary committees chaired by the opposition as the means by which the SDLP could become more closely involved in decision making. His case fell on deaf ears, and he was obliged to face the reality that talks would only be successful if a power-sharing arrangement was agreed. As a way out of his dilemma, Faulkner now insisted that the SDLP accept Northern Ireland's constitutional position.

Tired of the delay in getting talks underway, the SDLP forced the pace by calling for a conference of assembly parties willing to discuss the formation of a power-sharing executive. It was then announced that negotiations would finally get underway at Stormont on 5 October.[48] Unionist insistence that the SDLP recognize Northern Ireland's constitutional position as a precondition for substantive negotiations was met when the party indicated at the opening session of the talks that it accepted the 1973 Northern Ireland Constitution Act. The act defined Northern Ireland's place in the UK, as well as the terms under which that might change.[49] Attending the talks along with the SDLP were representatives of the pro-white paper Unionists and the APNI.[50]

Chaired by Whitelaw, the talks lasted nearly seven weeks. During the initial stages, considerable discussion was devoted to an economic and social programme, essentially based on SDLP proposals. Despite some significant differences between the SDLP and Unionist negotiators when the latter objected to the SDLP's proposals as too left wing, agreement was eventually reached on a common programme,[51] and gave hope that progress could be made on more fundamental issues. Inevitably, the latter proved more difficult. Key sticking points included the formation of an executive, the council of Ireland, policing and internment. Faulkner insisted on a Unionist majority on the executive, saying that he would not otherwise be able to gain party support.[52] The SDLP argued for equal representation of both parties, together with two seats for the APNI. On a council of Ireland, the SDLP presented its proposals for a strong council with a role in policing, and demanded that internment be brought to an end and all detainees released. Internment was an issue on which the party felt particularly vulnerable, to the point where Hume claimed that 'their position would be undermined from the start if they were seen to acquiesce in the continued detention of members of the minority who had been arrested before the executive was formed and in many cases before direct rule'.[53] The British answer went no further than repeating that internment would be phased out as and when the security situation allowed.

Despite several threats of collapse, the talks produced an unexpected break-through when, on 21 November, the three parties announced that they were prepared to form a power-sharing executive.[54] While the SDLP had sought simultaneous agreement on the council of Ireland and on the creation of the executive, the party agreed that negotiations on the former would follow the latter. The SDLP did obtain a commitment that the council would have executive powers, however, and so it would be more significant than the consultative body envisaged by Faulkner. The compromise make-up of the executive was to be seven UUP members, six SDLP and two from the APNI, but with voting rights at executive meetings restricted to six, four and one respectively, the others being the equivalent of junior ministers. On policing, the SDLP had to defer the matter to the negotiations on the council of Ireland, now due in two weeks, and to hope that the Irish government would provide added weight to their case for radical change. Two days later, on 23 November, Whitelaw notified his cabinet colleagues that an agreed 'package' was likely and that it would include a power-sharing executive in which Unionists would have a majority, together with a council of Ireland. Also envisaged was a statement on internment that would contain 'small steps to mollify SDLP' (the release of some prisoners before Christmas), but no firm commitment as to when it would end.[55]

OPPOSITION INTENSIFIES

While progress was being recorded among the negotiators, those opposed to a power-sharing agreement were, ominously, intensifying efforts to undermine a positive outcome. These efforts were at their most intense among Unionists, with Faulkner's supporters under strong pressure, both within the party and, especially, in the assembly. Although the UUP's standing committee narrowly supported a motion on participation in a power-sharing executive, 132–105,[56]

Craig vowed that he would 'physically and visibly ... make clear that there was not widespread acceptance of the executive'.[57] In assembly meetings, Craig and Paisley were among the anti-Faulknerites who disrupted proceedings, shouting down pro-agreement colleagues, describing them as 'traitors', physically attacking them and forcing adjournments.

Opposition was not confined to anti-agreement Unionists. If Faulkner was subjected to vilification and threats from hard-line Unionists, the SDLP was subjected to similar abuse from extreme Nationalists. Bernadette McAliskey (Devlin) denounced the party for siding with British 'imperialism', saying 'I do not believe it [the executive] will work, should not [sic] be allowed to work and should not be allowed to start to work'.[58] Using more colourful language, the PIRA attacked the SDLP for grovelling 'in the mire to show Mr Whitelaw that they are willing servants of the British Crown', seeking 'plum executive positions'.[59] They predicted that the SDLP would be swept away, and that the PIRA's campaign would render both the party and the new political arrangements inoperable.

PREPARING FOR GOVERNMENT

Undeterred, the SDLP announced its nominees for ministerial positions and prepared for negotiations on a council of Ireland, now scheduled for early December at Sunningdale in England. The SDLP ministerial team was, as many had anticipated: Gerry Fitt to be deputy to Faulkner, who would be chief minister; Austin Currie to be minister for housing, local government and planning, Paddy Devlin to be minister for health and social services and John Hume to be minister for commerce. In addition, two non-executive ministers were nominated: Eddie McGrady with a brief for economic planning and coordination, and Ivan Cooper in charge of community relations.

Not surprisingly, there was considerable satisfaction within the SDLP when it met for its third annual conference at the end of November, the first three-day conference of any party in the North. For the first time ever, a conference of a party from the North's Nationalist tradition was taking place on the threshold of it entering government to share power with Unionists, and likely to play a major role in an all-Ireland political institution. While only three years old, there was a deep sense of achievement and growing self-confidence, especially after the two recent election campaigns had firmly established the party as the leading voice of northern nationalism. More significantly, two major planks of the party's policy for a new beginning in Northern Ireland, a power-sharing executive and a council of Ireland, were now about to become realities. Emphasizing the historic nature of what had been agreed, Fitt said that he had not found it easy to negotiate with Brian Faulkner, and he was certain that Faulkner had not found it easy to negotiate with him, but 'the dramatic developments which have taken place since the June elections in Northern Ireland show there is a desperate yearning for peace and an end to violence by the majority of people'.[60] Fitt claimed that the efforts of the party's founders only three years previously 'had now been crowned with success'.[61]

Given very recent developments, several conference motions were overtaken by events and had to be sidelined, among them a motion condemning Faulkner as totally unacceptable for leadership of the executive, and one rejecting an executive that would contain a Unionist majority. On internment, motions reiterated the call that the party not enter an executive until it had been ended. They were the only motions to cause disquiet. In his address, party chair, Eddie McGrady, called on the PIRA to declare a ceasefire so that internment could be brought to an end, while John Hume promised that the party would exert 'intolerable' political pressure to end internment and that the council of Ireland would ensure 'adequate policing'.[62] Fitt said that 'he could not see any circumstances in which an executive worked (sic) in close cooperation while the obscenity of internment lasted'.[63] It was clear that the party intended to lobby as hard as possible on internment, but it was also clear that the SDLP now firmly believed that PIRA activity would dictate the pace at which internment would end. With momentum behind the prospect of an overall agreement, the SDLP eagerly looked forward to the negotiations about to take place at Sunningdale.

SUNNINGDALE

Negotiations on the council and other all-island matters were held at the Civil Service College in Sunningdale, outside London. These negotiations were the first ever comprehensive British-Irish negotiations, consisting of the parties about to form Northern Ireland's first power-sharing administration, as well as the British and Irish governments. The party's original six-person negotiating team was supplemented by assembly members Michael Canavan, Paddy Duffy and Paddy O'Hanlon, and also benefited from the specialist advice of Kadar Asmal[64] and former attorney-general of Ghana and political commentator, Geoffrey Bing. Talks commenced on 6 December and, in his opening remarks, Fitt set out the SDLP's position, referring to already agreed principles regarding the nature of a council of Ireland. On policing, he acknowledged that the SDLP wanted to give 'full support to the enforcement of law and order', but stressed that this could only happen 'if the police service is acceptable throughout Northern Ireland and if all sections can identify with it'.[65] It was for this reason that the SDLP believed a council of Ireland should have 'a positive role in policy, common law enforcement and the defence of human rights in both parts of Ireland'.[66]

Agreement was quickly reached on such matters as the form and composition of a council. Seven ministers from each jurisdiction would compose the council of ministers, with consensus being required for all decisions. A consultative body of 60 members, 30 from the Oireachtas (Irish parliament) and 30 from the North's assembly would also be established. Agreement was quite quickly reached on another difficult issue, the South's recognition of the status of Northern Ireland. Unionists pressed for the deletion of Articles 2 and 3 from the Irish constitution. However, recognizing the difficulties that would pose, not least the need for a constitutional referendum, Faulkner accepted a formal declaration by the Irish government to be lodged at the UN that no change in Northern Ireland's status could happen without the consent of its people.

Intended to last only three days, negotiations were forced into a fourth by two critical issues. These were policing and, to a lesser extent, judicial procedures to deal with fugitive offenders in the South. Given British and Unionist unwillingness to concede any further significant reform of the RUC, not least any change in its name and symbols, the SDLP argued as imperative that the Council of Ireland have a role in policing. Otherwise, support for the police would be difficult, if not impossible for its supporters, and support for whatever might be agreed would be jeopardized. In principle, the SDLP had the support of the Irish government for its proposals, but, in practice, this support was not wholehearted. As anticipated, Irish justice minister, Patrick Cooney, one of the South's negotiators, still viewed as very problematic any significant responsibility for policing being conceded to an untested council. Indeed, control over policing with the prospect of significant disagreement on critical issues, was not something either government found possible to concede, though Garret FitzGerald, conscious of the SDLP's predicament, still strongly believed that a significant role was possible.[67] Searching for a resolution left the talks deadlocked for many hours.

From an SDLP perspective, the agreement finally reached on policing was far short of the party's expectations. A standing committee consisting of Northern Ireland's chief constable and the South's Garda commissioner, would consider matters of mutual interest, but would not in any way be directly answerable to the Council of Ireland. The council's role would be limited to nominating up to one-third of the North's policing authority and, likewise, of a similar authority yet to be established in the South. Means by which policing might become more acceptable throughout the North would be studied by an all-party assembly committee which, given its likely composition of Unionists opposed to significant reform and Nationalists in favour, would be unlikely to recommend radical change. The one important SDLP gain on policing was that an independent police complaints body would be established. But no changes to the name or symbols were agreed, nor were any particular measures aimed at increasing recruitment from the Nationalist community. The new beginning for policing was to be more a hope based on changing political circumstances than anything practical. As a result, the party was unable to call for full support for the police, a call it had hoped it could have made at the close of the negotiations.

The best that could be said for these arrangements was that they conceded a very minimal role for the council over policing. For the SDLP, the hope was that in time this role could be developed into something more substantial. On the functions for which the council would be responsible, eight areas were agreed, though the detailed arrangements were left until discussions had taken place at official level. On internment, the SDLP had to be content with a promise from the British that it would be phased out 'as soon as the security situation permits'. The declaration sought from the British on Irish unity did not contain the SDLP's demand for a commitment to encourage unity. Like earlier statements on constitutional change, the declaration merely repeated the longstanding position that, in the event of a majority indicating a wish to become part of a united Ireland, the British government would support that wish. On judicial matters such as extradition, common law enforcement, and an all-Ireland court, it was agreed that legal experts who would report to both governments and to the council, would undertake detailed studies.

Despite falling short of what the party had sought, the Sunningdale agreement, taken together with the earlier power-sharing agreement, represented an historic step forward for Nationalists. The agreement gave their representatives a role in the government of Northern Ireland and in an all-Ireland forum that offered opportunities to develop and intensify all-Ireland relationships. Furthermore, the agreement strengthened the Irish government's role as a guar-antor of the Nationalist community's position. So, despite the limitations of the agreement, there was considerable cause for rejoicing within the SDLP when its delegates returned home. In John Hume's words, 'The agreement reached has proved a means whereby the conflicting aspirations of the people of this country can be accommodated and where all aspirations can now be fully and freely pursued by peaceful means'.[68]

There was a warm welcome for the agreement from a majority of commen-tators in the South. Bishop Cahal Daly of Ardagh and Clonmacnoise, a leading spokesperson for the Catholic Church on northern matters, said that 'the great mass of people in both parts of this island and in both communities in the North who long for peace will feel a real sense of relief at the new prospects for peace opened up by Sunningdale'.[69] His views were echoed by leaders of the other churches, with the Church of Ireland bishops expressing their 'deep appreciation of the courage and integrity of all who took part in the Sunningdale talks. Their communiqué can provide a basis for building a fair and peaceful society, both in Northern Ireland and in the Republic'.[70]

CRITICS' ANGER

This was not how everyone from a Nationalist background viewed the agree-ment, however. MPs McAliskey and McManus condemned the agreement, with the latter accusing the SDLP of gaining nothing and, together with the Dublin government, of consenting to British control over Northern Ireland.[71] The Republican Clubs (Official Sinn Féin) commented that 'the world had witnessed the utter humiliation and degradation of the Irish nation by its politi-cians'.[72] In the South, where some Nationalists were also unhappy with the formal declaration on Northern Ireland's status, anger was directed against the government. Others, like the independent Donegal TD Neil Blaney, vehe-mently attacked the SDLP, strongly denouncing the party, saying 'I am ashamed of them now as I have never been ashamed of "Irish" representatives before. They have sold out while they are participating in this sham assembly.'[73] The NICRA, with which many SDLP members had close associations, attacked the agreement, saying that it let the British government 'off the hook' once again on the issue of human rights in Northern Ireland.[74]

Hume's challenge to those critics was to ask if they 'were really saying they did not trust the other side. If they are right, then is there any solution to the problem other than total conflict between the different sections of the community?' [75] His challenge was met with PIRA bombs in London, PIRA killings in Northern Ireland and a PIRA announcement that it would not observe a Christmas truce. Conscious of its leadership role and of what the party saw as a new beginning, the SDLP issued a statement after Christmas, once more calling on the PIRA to end its violence and, more significantly, calling for an end to the 'rent and rates' strike 'in view of the major advances made ... in establishing institutions which can remove the injustices which this society has endured for so long'.[76] The party justified the call, arguing that the human rights provisions in the Sunningdale agreement would mean the early phasing out of internment and, although a greater number had been expected, it pointed to the pre-Christmas release of sixty-five internees and the promise of more releases as the security situation improved.

Like the SDLP leadership, Faulkner and his colleagues were quite pleased as they left Sunningdale, believing they had achieved a good deal for Unionists, particularly on the divisive issue of the Council of Ireland, where the unanimity requirement protected Unionist interests. More important, in Faulkner's view, was the formal statement to be lodged at the UN that the Irish government respected Northern Ireland's constitutional status. As he recorded himself

> All the delegates were in optimistic mood, happy that the long hours of argument has produced an agreement which could mark a significant step forward in the relationships between Northern Ireland, the Irish Republic, and Great Britain.[77]

Faulkner had not reckoned on the determination of his Unionist opponents to undermine the whole package of agreements that had emerged over recent months. Anti-agreement Unionists intensified plans to wreck the new institutions, and loyalist paramilitaries established the Ulster Army Council as an umbrella organization for loyalist 'armies', saying they would support politicians opposed to the agreement.[78] In the assembly, amid scenes of disruption and fisticuffs on the Unionist benches, the agreement was bitterly and loudly denounced by all of Faulkner's opponents. Paisley described the agreement as 'the machinery to force the pace towards a united Ireland' and accused Faulkner of blatant treachery.[79] Calling for extra-parliamentary action, he said that 'the time for speeches was almost past and the time for action had come. They would fight in the assembly but he needed support of grass-root protests throughout the province'.[80] The Grand Orange Lodge of Ireland denounced the agreement as 'an obvious preparation for a united Ireland'.[81] Few Unionists outside Faulkner's own immediate followers and the leadership of the Protestant churches were prepared to express any support.

In this atmosphere of political pressure and continuing violence, the pre-Christmas optimism of 1973 was soon to dissipate in the cold winds of the first half of 1974, and while most of the pressure would be on Faulkner, the SDLP would be forced to bear its share as well.

Chapter 4

False dawn

Three days after taking office, the new executive published *Sunningdale's twenty points to peace*, a summary statement of the benefits that would soon flow from the agreement.[1] But as the New Year advanced, it was a not promise of a peaceful future that beckoned, rather menacing clouds threatening more uncertainty and instability. No sooner had he assumed office as the chief executive than Brian Faulkner experienced a significant setback. The ruling body of his party, the Ulster Unionist Council (UUC), voted, 454–374, to reject the Sunningdale agreement, and he resigned as leader and formed the Unionist Party of Northern Ireland (UPNI). Severely weakened, Faulkner now only had the pro-Sunningdale assembly majority to rely on, plus the hope that, with time, the executive that he and Gerry Fitt led, would gradually earn widespread support.

DAUNTING CHALLENGES

While the SDLP's assembly group was by no means always unanimous in its decisions, and was to experience considerable backbench and party unease over internment and over the pace at which the Sunningdale agreement was being implemented, Fitt did not face the same intense problems, nor had he any assembly-based Nationalist opposition to deal with. However, together with his party colleagues, he had formidable challenges to meet, given the SDLP's commitments on internment, policing and the Council of Ireland, as well as the huge security problems posed by the PIRA's campaign and British army tactics. In government, but without any responsibility for, or much influence over, security policy, and with no sign that internment would be quickly phased out, the SDLP, like Faulkner, hoped that the executive would soon demonstrate that power-sharing could deliver at least realistic prospects of a new and more positive era for the North. Ignoring these difficulties, Hume expressed this hope, saying that 'partnership ... has replaced conflict as the basis of our politics and constitutional thinking … It is for us to use those institutions and the powers they give us to improve the quality of life of our people'.[2]

An early indication of problems ahead was former Fianna Fáil minister Kevin Boland's high court challenge to the constitutionality of the Sunningdale agreement, in particular to the Dublin government's declaration on the status of Northern Ireland. In its defence, the Irish government successfully argued that formal recognition had not been granted to Northern Ireland, but rather recognition of the status quo. This argument was immediately interpreted by anti-agreement Unionists and, more worryingly, by some pro-agreement Unionists, as Dublin minimizing the declaration's significance. Boland appealed the judgment and, although the Supreme Court eventually determined that the Sunningdale agreement was not repugnant to the constitution, the challenge dented confidence in the agreement and only added to Faulkner's woes. The challenge also delayed the assembly and Dáil's ratification of the agreement, causing considerable unease within the SDLP. Early indications of the challenges ahead came both from within and without the party. Mock New Year greetings to SDLP ministers from PIRA internees at Long Kesh appeared in the final edition of the *Irish News* for 1973 to remind Fitt and his colleagues how some Nationalists regarded their 'treachery'.[3] Within the party, a number of members formed the 'Motion Number 1' group, to maintain pressure on the leadership on the need to have internment brought to a quick end.[4] Although the group posed no serious threat to the leadership, it was another signal that internment remained a very sensitive issue within the Nationalist community.

AMBITIOUS MINISTERS

It was against the background of this uncertainty that SDLP ministers took office alongside their Unionist colleagues. They were determined to demonstrate that they could deliver, but they were also very conscious of the pressures mounting against the power-sharing institutions. The policy framework within which the executive set about its work was the SDLP-inspired programme agreed at the outset of negotiations. Within three weeks of taking office, the executive published *Steps to a better tomorrow*,[5] detailing how the new administration was going about making a difference. Key to achieving the objectives set out in this document would be the SDLP-controlled ministries: commerce; housing; health; and community relations.

As deputy to Faulkner, Fitt exercised no direct executive responsibilities. Rather, he became the SDLP's daily link with the chief executive minister with whom he developed a very positive and personal relationship. Publicly, he exercised almost an ambassadorial role for the new arrangements, attending functions in Ireland and Britain. Not a man for the formalities of office, Fitt, as Chris Ryder points out, became quite adept at co-hosting with Brian Faulkner receptions and dinners for leading industrialists and business people, impressing on them the advantages of investing in Northern Ireland.[6]

As minister for commerce, John Hume launched himself into a hectic schedule to secure new investment. At an early stage, he also found himself addressing with British ministers the implications for the North of the UK's growing fuel and energy crisis. Then, with his keen interest in and support for the EEC, Hume began making his presence felt in Brussels, where he presided over the opening of a Northern Ireland office. His fluent command of French impressed the media and officials, while his contacts with Irish-American politicians proved a positive asset when he visited the US to encourage investment in the North. Hume combined his drive for investment with further appeals to Irish-Americans not to provide financial support for PIRA terrorism. As a result of his visit, several US companies expressed interest in locating plants in Northern Ireland,[7] but it was an uphill challenge given ongoing violence and, in particular, the PIRA's failure to release Hans Neidermayer, the Belfast head of the German company, Grundig, whom they had abducted in December.[8] Hume was convinced that the abduction was responsible for Grundig's decision not to invest in a new multi-million-pound project that it had been planning for Newry, an employment black-spot. As well as trying to attract new investment, Hume also worked to protect existing jobs, notably in the Harland and Wolff shipyard, which was then under considerable financial pressure. Notwithstanding the intense loyalist affiliations of much of its huge workforce, Hume successfully lobbied Whitelaw for additional funds to support the enterprise.[9]

Paddy Devlin was determined to use his position as minister for health and social services to address poverty and to raise standards in both services. His style was very informal, insisting that he be addressed as 'Paddy'. To tackle the poverty that afflicted so many, Devlin established a commission to report on how best his department should respond to the challenge, and, together with Bob Cooper, APNI's minister of manpower, he initiated a scheme to provide work for the disabled.

Austin Currie, in housing, local government and planning, faced several challenges: the large deficit in social housing provision; the introduction of local
government reform; and the problems caused by the SDLP's decision to call for
an end to the 'rent and rates' strike, and the question as to whether or not
payment for arrears would be required from those who had engaged in that
strike. To meet the need for social housing, Currie committed the government
to an ambitious annual house-building target of 20,000, and mobilized the
construction industry's assistance by establishing the Construction Industry
Council to liaise with government.[10] As the minister responsible for local
government, Currie was anxious to observe the operation of the new councils,
and undertook a number of visits to meet councillors. It was a daunting undertaking since, on several visits, he received a hostile reception when
anti-agreement Unionist demonstrators gathered to vent their anger against a
politician whose civil rights activities had focused attention on the abuses
of Unionist controlled councils. At Magherafelt council, Revd William
McCrea greeted him, saying that he should 'go back to the rebel scum in
Coalisland',[11] and at other locations police protection was essential to ensure
him safe passage.

However, it was Nationalist, not Unionist anger that was to mark Currie's
few months in office. As minister for housing, Currie believed he had no option
but to determine not only that rent and rates payments should recommence,
but, more controversially, that arrears would have to be paid despite there being
no immediate end in sight to internment. In light of the SDLP's original
pledge, a pledge that Currie himself had underlined on several occasions, that
the strike would last until internment had ended, and the last internee had been
freed, his decisions appeared to be a complete *volte-face*. Defending his decision,
Currie pointed out that of the 26,000 who had originally been on strike, only
11,000 continued to withhold payments. He went on to argue that, taking into
account the political changes that had occurred, together with the commitments on internment, his decision was correct, otherwise those who continued
to withhold payments would be subsidized by those who paid. For those who
encountered difficulties in meeting their repayments, Currie promised that
while 'those who can afford to pay should repay immediately, those who cannot
afford it will be allowed to do so over a reasonable period of time'.[12]

While support for the rent and rates strike had waned considerably, Currie's
decisions became a political millstone around his neck, about which he would
be repeatedly reminded in the years ahead. Conscious of the hostile reaction

within the Nationalist community, SDLP backbenchers demanded evidence that internment would very rapidly be phased out. Leading backbencher Paddy Duffy denounced what he termed the failure of the British government to honour its commitment, declaring that 'it would be better to have joint British-Irish rule with a commitment from the British to get out in a ten- to fifteen-year period' than the new arrangements.[13] The unease spread to SDLP members of the executive, and Paddy Devlin submitted his resignation – almost immediately frozen because of the wider political crisis – arguing that, as minister for health and social services, he would not take responsibility for deducting any levy from benefit payments in order to recoup rent arrears, given the continuation of internment.[14]

Ivan Cooper, in charge of community relations, had responsibility for an area of considerable importance in terms of developing policy and initiatives to address sectarianism and to promote better relationships between the North's communities. A public agency, the Community Relations Commission, independent of the department but reliant on it for funding, had been established several years previously, and the creation of a government department with responsibilities in the same area soon gave rise to tension. The commission enjoyed considerable support among community organizations, while the department was viewed with some suspicion, not least when Cooper decided to fundamentally change the commission's role and transfer most of its functions to the department.

During the inter-party talks, the SDLP had argued against a separate department because 'community relations were a matter for all departments and it would be wrong to try to handle community relations problems from one specific department'.[15] Not having won that argument, the SDLP believed that with a power-sharing executive giving the lead on community relations, a separate agency was no longer required. Cooper decided, therefore, that 'executive decisions would lie with the government' and that a reconstructed commission would be only advisory.[16] His decision was greeted with considerable opposition from community activists and from public opinion more generally. According to Maurice Hayes, a former chairman of the commission, Cooper's decision 'played into the hands of the civil servants in the department of community relations, which had been jealous of the commission'.[17] Defending his decision, Cooper claims that his period in office was marked by several initiatives intended to promote positive community relations, among them joint constituency visits in the company of Unionist minister Basil McIvor, and meetings with sporting and community organizations in both Nationalist and Unionist areas.[18]

As if to underline the SDLP's point for not having a separate department, one of the executive's more significant community relations initiatives was UUP minister for education, Basil McIvor's 'shared schools' (interdenominational schools), proposal. With the majority of pupils receiving their education in schools segregated by religious affiliation, the suggestion was frequently made that schools be organized on an inter-denominational basis. This was what McIvor proposed. Despite the Catholic Church's strong reservations, several SDLP members welcomed the proposal. Séamus Mallon said that 'as a teacher he welcomed the concept of shared schools', adding that he believed 'they are the best proposals that the minister could have come up with'.[19] The gathering political crisis made it impossible for the executive to progress the proposal, though it would receive legislative support some years later under direct rule.

The SDLP's sixth minister, Eddie McGrady, was in charge of economic planning and co-ordination, a very amorphous office, and one that had no direct public profile. The minister's responsibilities were intended to ensure that executive business would be coordinated according to the agreed programme, a very necessary role in such a disparate coalition. McGrady's own view of his responsibility was that 'the total harmonization of all administration action is essential for the most efficient use of the assets of this community'.[20] This required each minister to prioritize his programme according the executive's manifesto, *Towards a better tomorrow*, though, as Maurice Hayes, the civil servant assigned as McGrady's assistant, recalled, 'getting ministers to cooperate was not an easy task'.[21] Essentially, it was a managerial task that would have developed had the assembly continued, but in the short period during which the institutions existed, McGrady had little scope to demonstrate its potential.

ELECTION DISASTER

No matter how earnest, committed or enthusiastic SDLP ministers and assembly members were, the new institutions had little time to take root. Faulkner's setback with the UUC was followed by Heath's decision to call an early general election in February in the hope that he would strengthen his mandate to deal with growing pressure from disputes with the coalminers' unions. The SDLP recognized the danger such an election would pose to the Sunningdale and power-sharing agreements and tried to persuade Heath against his decision, but to no avail. In Northern Ireland, where the British miners' disputes had little impact, anti-agreement forces seized upon the election as an opportunity to rally Unionist opinion to its side. This is precisely what happened, and with the slogan 'Dublin is just a Sunningdale away', those forces mounted an all-out campaign aimed at undermining Faulkner and the power-sharing executive.

The election was scheduled for the last day of February. The SDLP nominated candidates in all twelve constituencies to give voters everywhere another opportunity to vote for the party and its policies of partnership, of social and economic progress and of North-South cooperation. The manifesto, *Another step forward with SDLP*, placed considerable emphasis on the capacity of the power-sharing administration to achieve 'rising living standards, sustained full employment and the greatest possible measure of equality of opportunity and social and economic justice' (pl. 9).[22] With respect to the Council of Ireland, the party appealed to Unionists 'to drop the defensive mentality that has stultified their political thinking for too long to recognize in these steps the only reasonable way forward for the people of Ireland, North and South'.[23] On internment, the party stated that its 'stand on this question is undiminished and we are telling the people the honest and blunt truth as we see it – the only way to end internment now is through a political settlement',[24] and that it had obtained a commitment from the British government to phase it out. Addressing the thorny issue of policing, the party claimed that the appointment of new police authorities, North and South, with representation from both sides of the community on the northern authority, together with an independent complaints procedure, amounted to significant reforms.

Although there had been some talk of a common approach by the three pro-agreement parties, each contested the elections separately.[25] Consequently, in all but two constituencies, Derry and South Down, where the SDLP provided the only pro-agreement candidates, the anti-agreement coalition was faced with a divided opposition. Not surprisingly, in the first-past-the-post electoral system, anti-agreement Unionists won eleven of the twelve parliamentary seats, even though they won just over 50 per cent of the votes cast. SDLP leader Gerry Fitt retained his West Belfast seat in a very tough campaign marked by widespread intimidation on the part of supporters of one of his opponents, Albert Price, father of two sisters jailed for planting bombs in London.[26] The party's decision to contest all twelve seats resulted in a split Nationalist vote in the constituencies of Mid-Ulster and Fermanagh-South Tyrone, and the consequent loss of Bernadette McAliskey's and Frank McManus' seats. In the tense circumstances of the elections, the SDLP did remarkably well. The party's overall vote, at 22 percent and an increase of 24,000 votes over the previous June, was viewed as a strong endorsement of its approach. The results strengthened the party's conviction that its policies were, by and large, the correct ones. In Britain, the election returned Labour to power, with Harold Wilson again prime minister, and Merlyn Rees secretary of state for Northern Ireland.

While the SDLP's vote held up, pro-agreement Unionists suffered a serious decline in electoral support – only 23 per cent of the vote in the few constituencies contested. The Unionist pendulum had swung decidedly against Faulkner and, despite the best efforts of the executive, it was now becoming clear that the new dawn could be very short-lived. Not surprisingly, anti-agreement Unionists claimed that Faulkner and his colleagues could no longer claim a mandate, and that the assembly should be dissolved and fresh elections called.

STRUGGLING TO SURVIVE

Continuing paramilitary activity added considerably to pressure on the agreement. In the first four months of the year, seventy-four people were killed and hundreds more were injured, while massive PIRA bomb-attacks in predominantly Unionist towns like Bangor and Lisburn intensified anger within the Unionist community and threatened more widespread violence. The PIRA declared that executive ministers were to be considered 'legitimate' targets. Shots were fired into the home of SDLP general-secretary John Duffy,[27] a bomb was thrown at the home of Belfast councillor Tom Donnelly, while a bomb planted at the Dunowen Inn in Dungannon, where leading members of the SDLP were gathered for a meeting, was only discovered in time to enable them escape what otherwise could have been a massacre.[28] As Gerry Fitt pointed out in the House of Commons, 'the PIRA and the UDA were out to defeat Sunningdale'.[29]

Faulkner believed that it was the Council of Ireland rather than power-sharing with the SDLP that had antagonized Unionists, and had turned them against the agreement. He pointed to remarks like those by Hugh Logue during a debate at Trinity College, Dublin, that 'the Council of Ireland is the vehicle that would trundle Unionists into a united Ireland',[30] as having reinforced Unionist suspicions as to the council's true purpose. Faulkner thought that those fears and suspicions could be allayed if the council's full implementation could be delayed, claiming that 'the executive would not be able to continue if Sunningdale was to be ratified as it stood at present'.[31] Faulkner proposed a two-phase implementation, whereby the Council of Ireland would only exercise a consultative role until after the second assembly elections, when full implementation would be achieved.[32] Adding to Faulkner's woes was the inability of the Anglo-Irish Law Enforcement Commission, established at Sunningdale, to agree that extradition should be used in cases where fugitives from justice, mainly PIRA terrorists who crossed into the South, claimed their actions to be 'political', and so avoided prosecution. The issue had been a running sore with Unionists who regarded the South a 'safe' haven for such fugitives. Many Unionists saw court decisions not to extradite as saying that the South was not serious in combating terrorism, and concluded that it was covertly on the side of the PIRA.[33] This only served to increase hostility to the Sunningdale agreement, with the result that Faulkner was anxious to slow down the speed at which the new arrangements would be implemented.

Concerned that such a delay ran the risk of the council never moving to the second phase, the SDLP resisted Faulkner's proposal for several weeks. Backbench SDLP members, already uneasy about internment, were particularly opposed to any concession on setting up the council, and some threatened resignation. Expressing their unease with Faulkner's suggestion, Séamus Mallon, chair of the assembly group, warned as early as March that the Sunningdale agreement had to be implemented 'in toto, or we quit'. To the SDLP, the Council of Ireland was not an optional extra, but rather the party's best defence against allegations that they had 'sold out', or had merely settled for the temptations of office.[34] According to Eddie McGrady, the Council of Ireland was the SDLP's price for a restoration of devolved government, and it had to be fully established in accordance with the terms of the agreement.[35] Furthermore, Nationalists would see any concession as surrender to threats from anti-agreement Unionists, and so, it had to be resisted.

But as those threats grew, so too did Nationalist anger, especially over the failure to end internment. While the campaigns of violence were the overriding reason for not ending internment, the slow pace of releases caused deep annoyance within the SDLP. To the backbenchers' frustration was added unease within the party generally, as evidenced by the Motion Number 1 group.

Branches and local councillors in several areas demanded that all of the commitments on the Council of Ireland and internment be met, and many members signed petitions addressed to the leadership to this effect.

Nevertheless, faced with the growing threat to the institutions by anti-agreement Unionists, John Hume and Paddy Devlin agreed to participate in an executive working group to examine how the different aspects of the Council of Ireland might be timetabled.[36] The group quickly produced proposals for staggering its implementation over the assembly's first term, with the aim of achieving full implementation at the beginning of the second. In the meantime, the Council of Ministers would meet on a regular basis to address areas for cooperation and to deal with North-South policing arrangements.[37] However, a joint meeting of the SDLP assembly group and the party's executive only agreed that a phased introduction of the 'procedures' relating to the council's establishment would be accepted, provided full implementation would be achieved by the following December, a mere ten months away.[38] Since this did not satisfy Faulkner's demands, the SDLP was asked to think again. At further meetings of the assembly group, attempts were made to agree a more compromised position, but to no avail. It was not until an unprecedented intervention by Stan Orme MP, a minister of state at the Northern Ireland Office (NIO) and generally supportive of the SDLP, who pleaded with members not to allow themselves be blamed for bringing down the executive, that they endorsed by 14–5 a phased introduction of the council's operation, closely modelled on what the working party had proposed.[39] The executive itself was then able to formally agree that, until the assembly's second session (following elections in 1977), the council would consist only of the designated ministers from both jurisdictions, and its functions would be restricted to coordinating action on matters of common interest to both parts of the island.[40] The formal ratification of the agreement was then planned to take place on 3 June.[41]

It was too late. The final act in the power-sharing executive's short life was already underway, and there was barely a week to its dénouement.

UNIONISTS REBEL

The final act commenced in the assembly when the pro-agreement parties entered an amendment to a motion by anti-agreement Unionists that called for the rejection of all of the recently agreed arrangements, the power-sharing executive and the Council of Ireland.[42] After a protracted and bitter debate, and before the amendment was voted on, a hitherto virtually unknown loyalist umbrella group, the Ulster Workers' Council (UWC),[43] issued a statement warning

> the Unionist assembly members at Stormont to vote cautiously in the crucial issue of Sunningdale. Assemblymen must remember that they were returned to Stormont to represent the views of the electorate and, as such, they should vote in line with the majority views within their constituencies.[44]

The UWC had already threatened a general strike in opposition to Sunningdale, and had delayed calling it pending the outcome of the debate. Pro-agreement Unionists ignored the 'advice' and voted for the amendment, as did SDLP and APNI members. Consequently, on 14 May, when the amendment was passed (44–28), the defeated anti-agreement Unionists greeted their defeat with threats to resort to other means of achieving their goal.

Those means became apparent when the UWC called its threatened general strike as soon as the assembly vote was announced. The strike was slow to gain momentum, but gain momentum it eventually did, particularly when loyalist paramilitary groups like the UDA declared their support. The UDA then began mobilizing groups of young men to erect barricades in Unionist areas, and at strategic locations such as road bridges. Businesses were ordered to close and violence threatened against anyone who dared refuse. Catholic workers were assaulted at several locations, among them large plants like Courtaulds' in Carrickfergus and Michelin's in Ballymena. In Dublin and Monaghan, loyalist paramilitaries exploded several car-bombs, killing thirty-three men, women and children in what was to be the greatest loss of life in any one day throughout the whole of the Troubles.[45] Prominent Unionist politicians like Bill Craig and Ian Paisley eventually gave the strike their support, and gradually its effects were being widely felt. Workers in the electricity generating plants in the greater Belfast area, a majority of whom were sympathetic to the strike, reduced energy output, and held Northern Ireland to virtual ransom. The same was true at fuel depots, where delivery trucks were prevented from distributing oil and gas. Adding to the sense of crisis were regular BBC bulletins that carried statements from the strikers, and especially from the power plants about impending power-cuts.

EXECUTIVE COLLAPSE

At a meeting between Prime Minister Wilson and several of his leading ministers, including Merlyn Rees, with Faulkner, Fitt and APNI leader Oliver Napier,
it was agreed there would be no negotiation with strike leaders, who were
described as 'extremists' trying 'to establish an unacceptable form of neo-fascist
government'.[46] Full support was pledged for the executive, together with 'some
action on the ground to show that Her Majesty's government and executive
retain credibility and the will to govern, and are capable of influencing events'.[47]
Heartened by these pledges, ministers attempted to counter the strike's effects
but, since it was practical assistance from the army that was sought, the 'action'
that was promised turned out to be much less than required. John Hume,
whose department of commerce was responsible for energy, planned to requisi-
tion fuel depots and ensure supplies to essential users. He needed army support
to do so, and had to threaten resignation before troops were moved into some
fuel depots and petrol stations, and limited supplies began moving again. It was
too late and too little. The strike had gained considerable support within the
Unionist community, and had begun to impose hardships. With fuel and
energy supplies reduced, essential services like hospitals, water and sewerage
were being seriously affected, while UDA intimidation of businesses had the
intended effect of closing them down. The authority of the executive and of the
NIO was fast ebbing away.

Faulkner's support evaporated and, despite the fact that he had described the
strike leaders as 'insurrectionists',[48] he eventually accepted that talks with them
would have to take place. Already one of his ministers, Roy Bradford, was
secretly in touch with some strike leaders. When the secretary of state ruled out
this option, Faulkner and his ministerial colleagues resigned on 28 May. Since
they were totally opposed to any contacts with the strikers, the SDLP ministers
would not resign. Instead, they argued that the strikers should be confronted
for attempting a coup against the legitimate authorities. However, with
Faulkner's resignation there was no possibility of a new power-sharing executive
being formed, and the SDLP ministers' appointments were terminated the next
day by the secretary of state. It would be twenty-five years before another
power-sharing executive would be formed.

Chapter 5

Another experiment

The fall of the North's executive sent shock-waves through the body politic in Britain and Ireland. The British government had shown itself to be unwilling to confront a strike mounted by a group holding no popular mandate. Tapping into the anti-agreement mood of the majority of the Unionist community, the UWC had succeeded in defying the British government in a manner strongly reminiscent of the anti-home rule movement of 1912–14. On this occasion, if unionism was not too clear about what it wanted, it clearly knew what it would not settle for – 'no' to power-sharing with Nationalists, and 'no' to a Council of Ireland. Faced with such strong resistance to what had painstakingly been devised as an answer to the crisis in Northern Ireland, and to what had been worked out with the Irish government and the SDLP, the British were unsure in which direction to turn, though in principle they had little option but to remain committed to the essentials of what had been agreed.

The immediate decision was to hand the problem back to local politicians. In a white paper, *The Northern Ireland Constitution*, published a few weeks after the fall of the executive, Secretary of State Merlyn Rees proposed that a constitutional convention be elected to consider the future government of the region.[1] The white paper reiterated that power-sharing in some form, and an Irish dimension would have to remain basic to whatever might be agreed, but it would be for the convention to decide the form that both would take. Following the dramatic events of May, however, the political atmosphere was once again rife with speculation about all kinds of eventualities, not least the possibilities that the British would withdraw and that Northern Ireland would become some kind of independent state, or be united with the rest of Ireland. In such an atmosphere, an early election to a convention was not feasible.

INDEPENDENCE AGAIN

The independence debate was most lively among loyalists, and was being encouraged from several sources, among them, surprisingly, Merlyn Rees, who spoke about 'a strong feeling of Ulster nationalism growing, which will have to be taken into account and which it would be foolish to ignore'.[2] When loyalist paramilitaries held a three-day conference in June and endorsed 'negotiated independence',[3] they received support from an unexpected quarter when the PIRA welcomed the move, claiming that it would precipitate a British withdrawal.[4] As before, the SDLP attempted to engage with some Unionists proposing the independence option in order to explore their thinking, among them members of the UDA. The attempt came to nothing when, after one meeting, dissent within the UDA's ranks about talking to the SDLP prevented further meetings taking place.[5] However, while independence was not party policy, not even as an option, it began to attract support from some leading SDLP members over the next two years.

SDLP FRUSTRATION

For the SDLP, the fall of the executive was a bitter demonstration of the power of the Unionist veto, though in some respects the party may well have been spared difficult situations and decisions that could have had divisive effects had the executive not fallen. Considerable risks had been taken in entering the power-sharing arrangements with Brian Faulkner, a leader under considerable pressure not just within his own party, but within the wider Unionist community as well. The SDLP's most important achievement, the Council of Ireland, had also proved to be the most vulnerable element in the whole agreement. Not only did it become the rallying point for anti-agreement Unionists, but the party had been obliged to make significant concessions on its phasing. Secondly, on the party's other major demands, reform of policing and a role for the council in supervising the service, little had been gained. Furthermore, the decision to call for an end to the rent and rates strike, and Austin Currie's ministerial decision to recover arrears, had attracted considerable criticism from within the Nationalist community, criticism exacerbated by the fact that internment remained in force.[6] Furthermore, a not altogether united approach by leading party members to these issues had exposed stresses and strains that may have quickly come to surface with significantly divisive effects.[7] However, the manner in which the executive had collapsed meant that most blame fell on anti-agreement Unionists and their paramilitary allies. Within the Nationalist community, the PIRA's persistence with its campaign of violence and its determination to destroy the new institutions meant that it too was seen as having contributed significantly to the collapse. So, with blame directed elsewhere, the SDLP escaped responsibility for what had happened. In fact, the SDLP was extremely proud of its contribution, a contribution that had brought Nationalists and Unionists together in government for the first time ever, and produced some genuinely warm cross-party friendships. The party's ministers and their Unionist colleagues had shown that cooperation between them was possible, and the party remained convinced that, had time permitted, the risks would have been vindicated. Consequently, the SDLP remained convinced that such an arrangement would have to be central to any new agreement.

Politically, what to do next was the dilemma facing the SDLP. Power-sharing with Unionists together with a Council of Ireland were at the core of the party's approach to resolving the North's political stalemate. Now there were no Unionists with either the mandate or the capacity to partner in achieving these objectives. So, having managed to realize its goals, for however short a time, an understandable sense of abandonment and betrayal pervaded the party as it reflected on a situation that contained few signs of hope. Not surprisingly, the months immediately following the executive's fall revealed more the frustration, anger and apprehension over what had transpired than clear thinking as to what to do next. The SDLP was deeply angry with the British government for not confronting the UWC strike more robustly, and it was no surprise that some members believed that a British withdrawal should now become party policy and, while not rejecting the proposed convention, did not believe it would produce agreement. In its frustration, the party accused the British and Irish governments of covertly retreating from the Sunningdale arrangements, while Unionists were accused of wanting to return to 'ascendancy' rule and of openly recruiting a 'third force' to assert that rule.[8] Many in the Nationalist community feared that militant Unionists would precipitate further community upheaval, and that intervention from the South would be required. At a meeting with Irish government ministers in August, Hume spoke of 'the desperate sense of isolation and alarm throughout the Nationalist community'[9] and at a weekend meeting in Donegal, assembly and party executive members discussed the possible need for joint British-Irish military intervention to protect vulnerable communities should the worst happen.[10]

TAKING STOCK

Eventually, the SDLP began to address the realities of the situation in a more focused manner. Following a series of meetings with political parties and both governments in London and Dublin, its detailed analysis of the situation was issued in early September.[11] The party restated its conviction that Northern Ireland's divided society required a partnership government to give all of its people a sense of participation in decision making, while a Council of Ireland was essential to express the North's 'Irish dimension'. The SDLP expressed deep scepticism about the proposed convention and accused the British government of diluting commitments to power-sharing and the Irish dimension. The party criticized the proposed convention because it would be allowed to decide for itself the form of government, saying that it 'seriously undermines the possibility of achieving a solution'.[12] In light of recent experience, the party believed that Unionists, with their inevitable majority, would use that majority to prevent cross-community agreement on power-sharing and a Council of Ireland. Faced with this prospect, the party demanded the withdrawal of the British guarantee of no change in Northern Ireland's constitutional position within the UK without majority consent. In its place, the party argued for an initiative led by the British government, in full cooperation with the Irish government

> to bring about a situation in which Irish people of different traditions can build institutions of government to provide for lasting peace and stability on this island and for new and harmonious relations with Britain itself.[13]

In effect, the SDLP was saying that if power-sharing and an Irish dimension continued to be rejected, the British should leave the Irish to determine their own future.

While this statement was seen by many Unionists as a call for immediate withdrawal, representing a hardening of the SDLP's Nationalist position, it was hardly a surprising demand given the widespread view, also held and, indeed, feared by many Unionists, that withdrawal was being actively considered. If so, the SDLP wanted to ensure that withdrawal would only happen in circumstances where the risk of violence would be minimized, and opportunities for a peaceful situation maximized. To create such circumstances, a prolonged process of negotiation would be required. However, a more imminent sense of withdrawal seemed to be on other agendas when, later in the year, prominent Protestant churchmen engaged in talks with the PIRA's leadership.[14] These talks were followed by a PIRA ceasefire and, more significantly, by talks between British officials and the PIRA. Both developments inevitably heightened ongoing speculation that withdrawal was being seriously contemplated by London, but without the immediate involvement of politicians with a popular mandate.

FERMANAGH-SOUTH TYRONE MILLSTONE

Democratic politics forced Northern Ireland into a second general election in October, when Wilson decided he needed to strengthen his parliamentary majority. The SDLP first declared that, as in February, it would contest all twelve seats. Since this would inevitably mean again splitting the Nationalist vote in the Fermanagh-South Tyrone and Mid-Ulster constituencies, the party found itself coming under intense pressure both internally and externally not to contest those seats. The pressure was more severe in Fermanagh-South Tyrone, where Frank McManus announced that he would contest to regain the seat he had lost to Unionist MP Harry West in February. Recognizing feelings among Nationalists, Austin Currie, the SDLP's candidate, stated that he would not contest if McManus would do likewise. McManus withdrew and, after a period of confusion, Frank Maguire, a man with Sinn Féin sympathies, was nominated. In Mid-Ulster, Bernadette McAliskey announced that she would not be contesting the seat and so pressure on the SDLP's Ivan Cooper was less and his candidacy stood. Elsewhere, SDLP hopes of gaining an extra seat lay in South Down, where Newry councillor, Seán Hollywood, was judged to have a good chance of winning against Enoch Powell. Powell had recently resigned his Wolverhampton seat to enter Unionist politics on an 'integrationist' ticket, a move that earned him the title the 'Wolverhampton Wanderer' from Paddy O'Hanlon.

The party's manifesto, *One strong voice* (pl. 10), stressed that SDLP's policy continued to be based on two principles that all sections of the Northern people should have access, by right, to the decision-making process at all levels, and that the two national identities must be recognized in Northern Ireland's relations with Great Britain and the Republic of Ireland ... these principles are expressed in power-sharing in Government and an Irish dimension expressed through agreed North/South institutions.[15]

However, if the Unionist population continued to reject these principles, the manifesto stated that

it would be inevitable then that the fundamental basis of British policy towards Northern Ireland since 1920 would have to be re-examined ... (and) we shall call on the British Government ... to declare that it will remain in Northern Ireland until such time as agreed institutions of government are established which will allow the people of Ireland, North and South, to live together in harmony, peace and independence.[16]

To strengthen its case for a new inclusive system of government, the manifesto also highlighted the social and economic consequences of political instability and violence – the lack of investment, growing unemployment and a deterioration in public services. On internment, the manifesto quoted from its submission to the recently appointed Gardiner committee investigating how to judicially deal with terrorism, saying that

the SDLP believes that internment without trial is a totally repugnant instrument of policy ... Politically speaking, it intensifies the alienation of whole communities from government and sustains sympathy for violent men and acquiescence in their activities.[17]

Despite a very vigorous campaign, Hollywood did not succeed in winning South Down, although he won a commendable 45 per cent of the vote, against Powell's 50 per cent. In Mid-Ulster, where a Republican Clubs candidate also contested, the split Nationalist vote denied Cooper his chance of taking the seat. Gerry Fitt, again elected for West Belfast, remained the sole SDLP MP. Frank Maguire was also elected, but his victory was to prove a thorn in the SDLP's side locally, with unhappy consequences several years later. Overall, the SDLP retained its 22 per cent electoral support despite its actual vote declining slightly. With elections for the new convention planned for late spring 1975, the SDLP's attention during the closing months of 1974 was on whether or not to contest these elections and, if so, how it should use whatever opportunities a convention would provide to advance its policies. The party viewed those opportunities with two minds. On the one hand, the SDLP determined that if it contested the elections it would do so with a firm commitment to power-sharing and an Irish dimension as agreed in the 1974 negotiations, but, on the other hand, it would oppose the convention if these requirements were not met.[18]

The UUP had reinforced SDLP scepticism about the convention, when it made clear that it would not be considering either power-sharing or an Irish dimension in the convention. In a manifesto issued in June 1974, the UUP, now part of a coalition of Unionist parties termed the United Ulster Unionist Council (UUUC), declared that while the SDLP would be offered places on parliamentary committees, such committees 'would not be allowed to muffle or frustrate the decisive role of government at the top'.[19] Such a clear rejection of what the SDLP regarded as essential indicated that any convention would be doomed from the outset. No Nationalist party, however anxious for an agreement, was now ever likely to negotiate within such parameters.

Anxious to ensure that it still had Irish government support, but worried about signs of slippage in the Irish government's position, the SDLP leadership used a meeting in November 1974 to insist that the Irish maintain a full commitment to power-sharing and the Irish dimension.[20] Party concerns had been raised some time previously, when Taoiseach Liam Cosgrave spoke in disparaging terms about the people of the North, making no distinction between either community, saying that the Republic did not desire 'unity or close association with a people so deeply imbued with violence and its effects'.[21] To the SDLP, this had implied a weakening of the Dublin government's resolve on the Irish dimension and that the most it would do would be to offer support for power-sharing.[22] Expressing their fears about a British withdrawal, the SDLP delegation claimed that withdrawal would be followed by a Unionist attempt to seize power that would provoke resistance from the Nationalist community, leading to 'outright confrontation' that would involve the South.[23] The Irish government sought to reassure the SDLP that its resolve had not weakened and that it was fully aware of the dangers posed by the existing situation.

TENUOUS TRUCE

The PIRA and loyalist campaigns only added to the sense of crisis. Both campaigns had been maintained with considerable ferocity throughout the autumn and early winter of 1974. Two prominent legal figures, Judge Rory Conaghan and Magistrate Martin McBirney, both Catholics, had been murdered by the PIRA in September, while bombs in London and Birmingham claimed over twenty lives, as well as several hundred injuries. There was some respite from the violence when a PIRA Christmas ceasefire was extended into mid-January and, although it was called off, the following month brought renewed hope when a truce was declared.[24] Since from the PIRA's perspective, the truce only applied to attacks on security forces, it did nothing to inhibit PIRA attacks on other republicans, on loyalists and on Unionist businesses, nor did it inhibit some of its members who chose to ignore the truce and continued attacking security personnel.

Rees hoped that the truce would encourage Sinn Féin to fully participate in the political process, and he indicated that if the truce held, the army would gradually withdraw into barracks and its numbers would be reduced to peacetime levels. As a signal of its seriousness, the British government allowed a number of 'incident' centres to be established, manned by local Sinn Féin representatives working in liaison with NIO officials.[25] Equipped at government expense with telex machines, telephones and typewriters, the purpose of these centres was to monitor the ceasefire and to prevent any incidents from escalating into a crisis. While welcoming the truce and the prospect of a complete end to PIRA violence, the SDLP was unhappy at the degree of recognition now being afforded to paramilitaries, several of whom seemed to have preferential access to government, and also because in some areas they were representing themselves as providing a police service. Fitt raised the issue at Westminster where he sought assurances from Rees that 'in any talks about policing or law and order in the areas concerned, the elected representatives will be listened to before the Provisional Sinn Féin'.[26] Rees' reply was essentially evasive and not reassuring.

By early April the truce existed in name only and, while it persisted nominally until the end of the year, it served no useful purpose except to keep open channels of communication with Sinn Féin and to provide some cover for the secretary of state as he released internees and eventually brought internment without trial to an end.[27] During the period of the so-called truce, the PIRA was responsible for over ninety deaths as well as several bomb attacks in Britain and in the North, including an attack that destroyed the incident centre in Derry. Throughout 1975, loyalists also continued their campaigns of randomly assassinating Catholics. Among their atrocities was the murder of three members of the Dublin-based Miami Showband in July, and in the 'murder triangle' around east Tyrone and north Armagh, the killing of several Catholics, among them chair of the local SDLP branch Denis Mullan gunned down by loyalists outside his home at Moy.

MAINTAINING A DEMOCRATIC AGENDA

During the 1974 Christmas ceasefire, the SDLP had pressed for convention elections to be postponed to allow for consultation, whereby paramilitaries could be represented in the political process. The truce gave further impetus to this demand, but neither happened and preparations for the elections went ahead. Meanwhile, the SDLP's fourth annual conference took place in January. In his opening address, party chair Denis Haughey said that the SDLP was engaged in a noble and fundamental struggle to demonstrate that politics alone could work in bringing about a solution to the problems in Northern Ireland.

Two critical policy areas, policing and the Irish dimension, underlined key aspects of that struggle and caused heated debate. On policing, the conference voted 61–53, despite opposition from prominent members like John Hume and justice spokesperson Michael Canavan, to refer back an executive paper which had simply reiterated the principle of qualified support for the RUC and contained no detail regarding particular reforms. One delegate said that he had expected 'an in-depth study of the central structure of the present RUC and, if, why and where it was unacceptable'.[28] Another delegate described the paper as consisting of 'woolly-minded generalities . . . (and) a series of truisms' because it had failed to detail the precise reforms that should be sought by the party.[29] The debate was evidence of internal tensions and differences on the extent to which the party should cooperate with the RUC, a debate that would eventually come to a head at the next annual conference. The approach advanced by John Hume, and the one that gained majority support within the party was that the SDLP would cooperate with the RUC in the course of normal policing, and that it would encourage its supporters to do likewise. However, since the party was not in government, nor even in an assembly where it would share some responsibility for policing, the SDLP would not call on supporters to join. There were some in the party, however, who believed that the policy should go further and be more supportive of the RUC, among them Gerry Fitt.

On the Irish dimension, a motion from the North Belfast branch became the focus for considerable public attention because it urged that 'in view of the ever increasing bitterness and hostility among people, the party must face up to the reality of the present situation, that there is no prospect of peace until more emphasis is placed on local cooperation, and less on the Irish dimension'.[30] The motion reflected the view widely held in some sections of Unionist opinion that without the Council of Ireland the power-sharing executive would have survived. Indeed, prior to the conference, the motion had been welcomed by the UUP, which described it as a move 'to drop the backward looking SDLP insistence on a Council of Ireland'.[31] However, since the Irish dimension was central to the party's policy, the motion was heavily defeated. Several leading members of the party, including Hume, Currie and Mallon, spoke against the motion to remove any doubt about the SDLP's continued commitment to an Irish dimension, and on its insistence that it be an essential agenda issue for any talks at the convention. In Hume's words, the SDLP 'would be abandoning our total approach if we abandoned the Irish dimension'.[32] The party was making it clear that what Séamus Mallon called a 'cornerstone' of its policy should not be weakened.[33]

Demonstrating that party concerns went beyond the high-profile issues of power-sharing, the Irish dimension and policing, one of the liveliest debates at the conference was generated by a policy document on education.[34] Among its recommendations were proposals along similar lines to those of Basil McIvor's 'shared schools' concept, for experiments in interdenominational schooling as well as calls for the abolition of selection at eleven, and parental representation on school management boards.[35] Interestingly, for a party that was frequently described as 'the mainly Catholic SDLP', several delegates levelled strong criticism at church authorities for not agreeing to parent and teacher representation on school boards. One delegate accused the church of preserving 'a dictatorship within its schools'.[36]

The harsh world of real politics, however, offered little immediate prospect of the party being able to implement its main policies of partnership, let alone those for education. The convention elections were now anticipated before the summer. But with Unionists still determined to oppose both power-sharing and the Irish dimension, the party harboured grave doubts as to the convention's value, and delayed its formal decision on participation in the elections until mid-February.[37] A further British paper on the future government of Northern Ireland published in early 1975 did little to allay its fears that a dilution of the 1973 agreements faced them.[38] Nowhere did the paper make any explicit reference to either power-sharing or the Irish dimension. Only in its oblique comment that 'there must be genuine and widespread participation in the business of government so that there may be government by consent' did the SDLP find any support for its approach.

QUESTIONABLE CONVENTION

Despite its misgivings, the party eventually decided that it had no option but to contest the elections. To do otherwise would have left the party open to the criticism that it was following in the abstensionist tradition of the Nationalist Party and effectively passing the initiative to the men of violence. Once again, the SDLP decided to nominate candidates in all twelve constituencies and, buoyed up by its October vote, had high hopes of at least retaining its nineteen assembly seats and of adding one or two more. The manifesto, *Speak with strength*, outlined the SDLP's organizational and electoral achievements over the four years since its foundation, as well as the party's commitment to partnership within the North and between North and South.[39] Considerable stress was placed on the SDLP's belief that 'the prejudices, the bitterness, the hatred and fears can only be eradicated by both traditions working together and demonstrating their joint concern for all of the people'. In other words, a partnership government was essential if community relations were ever to become harmonious. On the sensitive issue of support for the RUC, the party outlined the kind of reforms it believed to be essential, and indicated that if these were achieved and a power-sharing executive established, it would offer 'full support and loyalty to the police service of a fully agreed system of government'. Until then, the party would confine its support for the RUC in 'impartially upholding the law', but would not call on its electorate to join.

Thirty candidates contested the elections for the SDLP, again all of them male. In many areas the election campaign was marked by intimidation, violence and attempts to persuade Nationalist voters to boycott the elections. Prominent in the call to boycott the elections were Fr Denis Faul and Fr Brian Brady, both priests well known for their stand against human rights abuses and for their opposition to internment. They believed that a boycott would add considerable pressure towards ending internment. The SDLP denounced the boycott, however, saying that it was 'against all the best interests of the minority in Northern Ireland', that it would 'make a mockery of the efforts of those who struggled to win for us our democratic right to "one man one vote"', and that it would have no effect on the campaign to end internment.[40] Despite these pressures, the SDLP increased its share of the vote to over 23 per cent, but hopes of winning extra seats were dashed when Paddy O'Hanlon in Armagh and Aidan Larkin in Mid-Ulster were not re-elected and there were no break-throughs elsewhere. O'Hanlon's loss was directly attributed to PIRA intimidation and the boycott call, both of which seriously impacted on his constituency. The UUUC had campaigned on a manifesto of opposition to power-sharing and an Irish dimension, and overall, the results gave them a comfortable majority, with forty-seven of the seventy-eight seats; the SDLP won seventeen and other parties, APNI and UPNI, likely to support the 1973 agreements, fourteen. The political dice was heavily weighted against any form of partnership government and all-Ireland institutions.

SDLP feelings were quite bitter over its losses. Séamus Mallon criticized the Irish government for not giving the party more support, saying that 'there is no fence left for the Dublin government to sit upon – they must take up a posi-tion in which they can persuade the British government that there is no alternative in the North to power-sharing'.[41] Almost by way of response, minister Conor Cruise O'Brien said that he saw no possibility of agreement on either a power-sharing executive, or an institutionalized Irish dimension.[42] These remarks fuelled SDLP suspicions that, despite earlier assurances of support for the party contesting the elections, the Irish government might not support their approach in the convention. In his typical swash-buckling fashion, Paddy Devlin accused O'Brien of stabbing the SDLP in the back, describing the minister as 'the deadly enemy of the Catholic population of Northern Ireland'.[43] Relationships between the SDLP and the Dublin govern-ment were again damaged, but it was not until August that the party had an opportunity to discuss the situation in detail with Cosgrave and his colleagues.[44] By then, the Convention had met and, surprisingly, some progress seemed possible.

SHORT-LIVED HOPES

A week after the elections, the Northern Ireland Constitutional Convention held its first meeting, chaired by Chief Justice Sir Robert Lowry. Lowry's brief was to assist the parties to agree 'the provision for the government of Northern Ireland that is likely to command the most widespread acceptance throughout the community' and to report his findings to the British parliament.[45] For the SDLP, 'widespread acceptance' meant that both communities would have to participate in government through some form of power-sharing. However, that was not how members of the UUUC saw the purpose of the convention. For the UUUC, the normal practices of British democracy should be observed, the majority party in parliament governs, and minority parties could hold committee places, and might even chair some of those committees. Given these mutually incompatible positions, the convention appeared set for impasse from the very outset. Nevertheless, a positive atmosphere was created in some of the early exchanges. Along with Unionists of all shades, SDLP speakers emphasized the need for, and the value of, an acceptable form of devolution. John Hume called on all sides to reconsider their traditional attitudes and, addressing Unionist convention members, stated that 'The real security your tradition has rests in your own strength and numbers and in nothing else'.[46] He then called for a partnership between Unionists and Nationalists in which 'the government, the political parties and the people ... have to ask themselves where their political dogma or political commandments have led them or led us in the North'.[47] On policing, Austin Currie indicated that, given an agreement, there would be no difficulty in setting up an acceptable police service with support from both communities.[48] Neither hopes would be realized.

Before the summer break, informal talks commenced between the SDLP and the UUUC, and the parties agreed that these should continue during the recess. However, not much progress was achieved until towards the end of August when the parties exchanged papers setting out their basic proposals. Not surprisingly, the SDLP proposed maximum devolved power to an administration with 'all sections of the community represented at governmental level'.[49] The party also proposed North-South institutions, devolved policing powers, and referenda in both jurisdictions in support of the new institutions.

However, it was the UUUC paper that evoked most interest. In it, the Unionist coalition referred to the possibility of a coalition government being formed 'where an emergency or crisis situation exists'.[50] What became known as 'voluntary coalition' drew on the cross-party form of government that had existed in the UK during the Second World War. In other words, a coalition consisting of the main parties in parliament was formed to last for the duration of the national emergency in which the state had then found itself. Applied to Northern Ireland, this could mean a role for the SDLP and other parties in government for as long as the emergency that gripped the region persisted. Coming from the UUUC that had bitterly opposed the 1973 agreements, it was a suggestion that the SDLP believed should be investigated and, in its comments on the UUUC paper, asked for further information.[51] While interested in the UUUC's suggestion, the SDLP had serious reservations about voluntary coalition, not least because the UUUC suggestion envisaged the party's participation in government being by invitation of the Unionist parties, rather than as of right, and therefore could be terminated by the Unionists as and when they pleased. But the party was willing to explore the possibilities further. By early September, both sides had considered the suggestion sufficiently to invite Robert Lowry to determine what further progress could be made. But before this could happen, the possibility for progress suddenly vanished. Not all parties within the UUUC were equally attracted to the proposition, especially not Paisley's DUP, whose delegates successfully tabled a motion rejecting power-sharing, and effectively brought the negotiations to a halt.[52] Surprisingly, Bill Craig, a leading opponent of the 1973 agreements, had favoured further negotiations, but was the only member of the UUUC negotiating team, to vote against the motion, which passed, 37–1, with two abstentions.[53]

The decision sent a clear message to the SDLP that power-sharing was the issue to which Unionists most objected, not the Council of Ireland. In its formal submission to the convention, the party argued that

> We have no doubt that loyalist admiration for the Westminster model of government is sincerely held. But, in fact, when that model would indicate an all-party government such as at present, the loyalists shy away from it. This shows that the loyalist objection to power-sharing is not based on power-sharing being a departure from the Westminster model. It is based on something much deeper in Northern Ireland society.[54]

The clear implication was that Unionists could not tolerate the idea of Nationalists in government, and so 'the matter to be decided is whether

Northern Ireland is to be governed by a Protestant ascendancy regime or whether it is to become a modern society, the government of which will cherish all the citizens equally'.[55]

The Unionist majority ensured the passing of the convention report, which called for a return to 'majority rule' in an assembly where the 'opposition' would be invited to join a number of scrutiny committees.[56] The report explicitly rejected power-sharing, and on North-South matters simply called for 'good neighbourly' relations with the Republic of Ireland, effectively ruling out any joint institutional arrangements. In other words, there was no agreed report. Despite no agreement, however, Rees did not immediately dissolve the convention, and in January he decided to have it reconvened to consider a number of specific matters: power-sharing; finance; and law and order.

RESTATING POLICIES

In the interval, the SDLP held its fifth annual conference at the end of November, but, with little political progress in sight, the mood was subdued. The most notable debate was on a policing document slightly revised from that of the previous year. The speaker most in favour of changing party policy was Belfast councillor, Tom Donnelly. Before the conference, Donnelly issued a detailed statement outlining the reasons why he believed the RUC was a much reformed police force. In particular, he cited reforms introduced in the wake of the Hunt Report and the recruitment of many new personnel.[57] Donnelly called on the party to move from its qualified support for the RUC to full support, and declared that he would resign if that did not happen. While the debate was intense, most of those who spoke agreed with the party's existing line of support for the police in the impartial discharge of its duties. As John Hume stated, 'what we cannot do is give unequivocal and blanket support to security forces for which we have no responsibility'.[58] The existing line was overwhelmingly endorsed and Donnelly resigned. Gerry Fitt later claimed that he shared Donnelly's view, but he did not participate in the debate, nor did he otherwise express any serious reservations about the party's policy.[59] Unionists immediately accused the SDLP of losing an opportunity to reassure them of their sincerity in seeking agreement on the lines indicated during the inter-party talks. To answer this criticism, the party took another advertisement in the *News Letter* to explain its position, both on policing and on the constitutional status

of Northern Ireland.[60] Entitled *An open letter to the Loyalist people*, the advertisement stressed the principle of consent for constitutional change, and the
SDLP's anxiety to have a police service that Nationalists would be willing to
support and join, but insisted that this required a political agreement acceptable
to the two communities.

Overshadowing the conference debate on the convention was the controversy caused when, a few weeks previously, Gerry Fitt had, with greater
justification this time, sharply criticized Fianna Fáil for demanding a British
declaration that it intended to withdraw from Northern Ireland and to agree a
timetable for an orderly departure,[61] a position he believed was close to that of
the PIRA and Sinn Féin.[62] Fianna Fáil's new emphasis on withdrawal marked
a move away from the position Lynch had espoused when in government, and
it caused serious difficulties for the SDLP, given the party's own strains on the
issue. John Hume advised parties in the South to change their policies from the
negative approach of the past, saying that over 1,300 deaths represented the
failure of all parties; they all had to rethink their positions and not 'revert to the
comfort of our traditional trenches'.[63] Writing in the first edition of the party's
new monthly, the *Social Democrat*, Hume spelled out the SDLP's approach,
saying that

> Ireland is not a romantic dream, it is not a flag, it is not just a piece of
> earth. It is four and a half million people divided into two powerful
> traditions and its problems can only be solved, if the solution is to be
> lasting and permanent, not on the basis of victory for either, but on the
> basis of agreement and partnership between both. The real division of
> Ireland is not a line on a map but is in the minds and hearts of its
> people.[64]

His words amounted to a strong rebuke to Nationalists, North and South, who
believed that a British withdrawal could solve the North's problems. Although
Hume himself believed withdrawal to be a real possibility at the time, it was not
his preference, and he never urged it. Instead, he stood firmly by the party's
proposals for power-sharing and an Irish dimension.

The party's *News Letter* advertisement coincided with the beginning of the
second round of convention negotiations, but its effect seemed to be nil,
judging by the outcome to those negotiations. The SDLP continued to maintain that only a power-sharing arrangement could justify a return of devolved

government, and with the UUUC refusing to countenance even an 'emergency' or 'voluntary' coalition, no agreement was possible. The talks ended with the SDLP accusing the UUUC of not seriously attempting to 'to meet the partnership conditions' set down by the British government.

After the convention was dissolved in early March 1975, discussions continued over the next few months between John Hume and Paddy Devlin for the SDLP, and the Revd Martin Smyth and Austin Ardill of the UUP. Papers were exchanged between both sides and for a while the possibility existed that proposals for some form of coalition government might emerge. However, there was little ground for real optimism. With a sense of resignation, an NIO official commented that 'it is unlikely that the coalition proposed ... would attract sufficiently widespread consent in Northern Ireland in the near future to be workable'.[65] Paisley and his supporters within the UUUC were again opposed to the talks, and at a meeting of the UUUC in June a motion forbidding further contact with the SDLP was adopted.[66] Notwithstanding this motion, the four politicians continued meeting occasionally until early September. A joint statement issued at the end of July indicated a number of areas of agreement, but there was none on how an executive might be formed.[67] The UUP would not concede power-sharing, and its representatives ended the talks when, on 6 September, they announced there would be no further contact with the SDLP. Hume and Devlin then issued a statement expressing regret at this decision, and revealed the proposals they had put to the UUP. These included a considerably stronger form of devolution than contained in the 1973 act, including control over policing, a power-sharing executive, a freely negotiated agreement with Dublin on matters of common concern, and provision for a review of the new arrangements after two assembly sessions.[68]

HOPE FADES

The UUP decision to call off the talks, together with the earlier UUUC vote, marked a halt to a process that had commenced with the assembly elections in June 1973 and had made partnership government in the North and an Irish dimension essential, if new arrangements were to attract the support of the SDLP. While a majority of Unionists had rejected both, a few had begun to realize that a form of partnership with the SDLP was inevitable if devolved government was to be returned to Northern Ireland. As yet, they were too few;

for the majority of Unionists, power-sharing and the Irish dimension remained steps too far. Over the following years, attempts would be made to minimize the significance of the Irish dimension, or even to suggest that it was not really necessary, and to find some formula to replace power-sharing. Neither would be acceptable to the SDLP, and the North was to remain in a state of political crisis for the next twenty years.

The scale of the crisis was emphasized by PIRA and loyalist campaigns of murder and destruction, intensified by a deepening economic recession. 1976 witnessed some of the most horrific events of the Troubles to date: in January, loyalist murders of Catholics in north Armagh and east Tyrone were followed by the horrific massacre of ten Protestant workers by the PIRA at Kingsmills in Co. Armagh;[69] a pro-PIRA mob attacked Gerry Fitt's home in August; and there were widespread bombings and a rise in unemployment to 11 per cent of the workforce. In total, 308 individuals were killed in violent incidents during the year, an increase of forty-one over the previous year.

PART II

Party in waiting (1977–1985)

Chapter 6

Seeking a new focus

With no prospect of negotiating a new power-sharing agreement with Unionists the party was faced not just with a political impasse, but with organizational problems as well. The former convention members no longer had any forum in which they could represent their electorate, and with one MP at Westminster, the party's only other public representatives were its councillors. The challenge for the SDLP was how, in these circumstances, it could maintain a significant political profile. John Hume, Austin Currie, Paddy Devlin and their colleagues were now redundant as full-time politicians and the party lacked the financial resources to contribute any meaningful support.[1] Nonetheless, the convention group decided to maintain organizational cohesion, to continue playing a political role and to provide, to the best of their ability, a service to constituents, notwithstanding the personal difficulties many of its leading members were to experience. The group now described itself as the SDLP's 'constituency representatives'. Expressing their determination to maintain their leadership role, Currie declared that 'there will be no flight of the earls this time', a reference to the sixteenth-century Irish leaders who sought refuge in Europe following their defeat in the wars against Queen Elizabeth I.[2]

INDEPENDENCE APPEALS

Following the convention, a number of leading party members were again attracted to the idea of an independent Northern Ireland, Paddy Devlin being the most prominent. At a meeting in Dublin at the same time as the talks with Smyth and Ardill, Devlin claimed that loyalist ties with the UK were weakening and that the British were preparing to withdraw.[3] In evidence, he pointed to the economic downturn in the North, and claimed that British investment was declining. Withdrawal, he argued, would mean growing support among Unionists for power-sharing in an independent Northern Ireland. A few weeks later, he claimed the independence bandwagon was rolling and that 'the proposition could no longer be ignored or dismissed'.[4] Others in the SDLP leadership to support his argument included Ivan Cooper and Joe Hendron. Cooper argued that independence was the 'only means of finding an acceptable political solution in Northern Ireland'.[5] The general disillusionment with the British government probably had as much, if not more, to do with the attraction of this option, than any deep conviction as to its viability. Nevertheless, as the party's chief whip, Austin Currie authorized branches to discuss independence, saying that one of its advantages 'would be that it would switch off the Provisional IRA who wanted to drive out the British but were unable to do so'.[6]

While the debate generated some public interest, and the high profile of those party members who seemed to support it gave it credibility, independence received a frosty response from the SDLP's leadership as a whole. A weekend conference of executive and former convention members in June 'totally rejected any concept of negotiated independence'.[7] However, this was not to be the end of the debate. The issue would re-emerge at the party's annual conference later in the year, when another leading member, Paddy Duffy, would table a paper advocating independence. By then, however, the SDLP had issued its considered assessment of the general political situation, one that did not include any mention of independence. In a joint statement in September, the constituency representatives and the party's executive reviewed efforts to reach agreement with Unionists.[8] Their review concluded that the party had to face the reality that since agreement had not proved possible, 'inter-party talks are not a vehicle for agreement', since such talks 'can only lead to deadlock and continuation of the deadly political vacuum'.[9] The assessment concluded that henceforth the focus would be on clarifying British intentions.

BRITISH INTENTIONS

For the SDLP, the Unionist position was one of open defiance of the expressed will of the British government, and begged the question whether that government was 'willing and determined to implement its own policy, democratically approved by virtually the entire British parliament, as to the fairest method of governing Northern Ireland'.[10] The statement went on to argue that 'to do so would be to accept what is their sovereign responsibility. To refuse is to abandon those responsibilities, with fundamental consequences for everyone. What is the British position?'[11] However, the SDLP's analysis did not suggest how, in light of Unionist intransigence, the British could exercise those responsibilities. The implication was that, if they could not ensure power-sharing and an Irish dimension, they should withdraw, a case the SDLP was wary of putting explicitly because of its dangerous implications. The alternative was to maintain regular pressure on Unionists in order to persuade them that power-sharing and an Irish dimension were essential. That was a task that required not just action by the British, but continued action by the SDLP itself and the Dublin government, together with some sense that the PIRA campaign would end in order to create a more viable context for democratic politics. As a counter to Unionist claims that partnership politics would not work, the party's statement argued that partnership was clearly working in district councils like Derry, Newry and Mourne and Down, where SDLP's strength ensured that major council offices like the chair and mayoralties rotated between Nationalists and Unionists and that council committees were proportionately representative. While Unionists were happy and indeed eager to accept office in such councils, there was no reciprocation in councils they controlled, nor an acknowledgment that power-sharing worked.

PEACE MOVEMENT CHALLENGES

Overshadowing the political stalemate was the continuing violence of loyalist and republican paramilitaries. As far as the PIRA was concerned, there was little sign that its campaign would come to an early end. By now, they seemed locked into a campaign with no objectives other than the completely unattainable British declaration to withdraw. Consequently, its violence had a totally nihilistic quality, reflected in the words of Sinn Féin vice-president Máire Drumm, who threatened that 'if it is necessary (Belfast) will come down stone by stone, and if it is necessary other towns will come down, and some in England too.' [12] Immune to appeals from politicians and churchmen, the only direct public pressure on the PIRA and other paramilitaries was to emerge through the Peace People movement.[13] Founded in the autumn of 1976 in reaction to the violence, the movement organized a series of very large rallies across Northern Ireland, the South and in London. However, despite large attendances and considerable publicity, and the award of the Nobel peace prize to its leaders, Mairéad Corrigan and Betty Williams, the movement did not persuade the paramilitaries to cease their campaigns, and it gradually lost support. While many SDLP members participated in the peace rallies, the party leadership had an ambivalent attitude towards the movement, suspecting it of political ambitions, and of offering a distraction from the key issues that had to be addressed. Paddy Devlin was particularly critical of this possibility and openly warned the movement against 'going political'.

SECURITY DIVIDES

In September 1976, Roy Mason replaced Merlyn Rees as secretary of state and with his appointment came a stronger emphasis on combating terrorism through the 'Ulsterization' of security, which meant giving the RUC and the UDR a greater role and de-emphasizing that of the British army. The process was already well advanced under Rees, but Mason was determined that it be intensified.[14] An obvious effect of this policy was that RUC and UDR personnel, retired as well as serving, increasingly became PIRA targets, deepening local tensions and driving communities further and further apart.

As the Ulsterization policy developed, the position of the SDLP vis-à-vis the security forces, especially the RUC, once again came under particular pressure. While recognizing that the party was unlikely to change its position of not fully endorsing the RUC, efforts were made at NIO level to encourage party councillors to join local security and local police liaison committees in the hope that they would become more sympathetic to what the police and army were trying to do. Security committees had operated for a number of years to provide a channel of communication between the security forces and local communities, addressing complaints and other concerns about the forces' behaviour. Despite having made clear its opposition to members participating in such committees, to the party's embarrassment, a small minority of councillors, some of them quite prominent, did not abide by the decision.[15] In the Newry and Mourne, and the Craigavon council areas, for example, several SDLP councillors regularly attended such committees, giving rise to a hope within the NIO that more might do so.[16] That hope was not realized, and most councillors abided by party policy. The continuing participation of some councillors, not only on the local security committees, but also on the more public police liaison committees, remained an embarrassment. Their presence was a reminder that divisions over policing continued to exist within the party.

Along with such pressure on councillors came more pressure on the party generally to fully support the RUC, and it came not just from the NIO and Unionist parties. In the aftermath of Ian Paisley's unsuccessful attempt to organize a general strike in early May 1977,[17] and when the RUC was seen to have played a decisive role in maintaining freedom of travel, there were many calls on the party to be more supportive of the police. Garret FitzGerald was among those who sought to persuade the SDLP that it would be in the party's interests to publicly offer more support. He had several conversations with John Hume on the matter,[18] but Hume resisted all attempts to change the party's position. Within the party, Fitt and Devlin had long favoured more support for the RUC. Fitt praised the manner in which the RUC had handled the abortive strike, but was realistic enough to recognize that there would be no early change in the way Nationalists regarded the force.[19] Devlin was more positive, believing that the RUC could operate more openly in places like West Belfast and that its officers would be welcomed.[20] A special meeting of the party's executive and constituency representatives acknowledged that there had been 'an improvement in the RUC's impartiality in some areas', and expressed the party's intention to be 'positive and constructive' in its dealings with the police, but was also highly critical of many aspects of the force's security operations.[21] The statement was an obvious attempt to balance the views of those who favoured giving more support against the views of those who still regarded the RUC with considerable suspicion and hostility.

ECONOMIC AND POLITICAL INITIATIVES

Alongside his security initiatives, Mason also gave economic development a greater priority in the belief that less unemployment would act as a deterrent to terrorism. Attracting the De Lorean sports car investment proved to be his most high profile, most controversial and most disastrous economic initiative.[22] But as far as political initiatives were concerned, apart from a few desultory attempts to encourage inter-party talks aimed at agreeing a gradualist approach to devolution, he had no success.[23] At a meeting with an SDLP delegation in January 1977, Mason claimed that some Unionists like James Molyneaux, MP for South Antrim, were beginning to move away from the convention report, and that the SDLP should encourage them.[24] He instanced a speech in which Molyneaux had advocated a form of administrative devolution in which parties 'should participate in an assembly in proportion to their elected representation' to scrutinize government business.[25] Mason's argument did not impress the SDLP, for whom administrative devolution held no attraction. The party pointed to other Unionist leaders who remained deeply opposed to power-sharing, and who were becoming increasingly integrationist. The SDLP resisted all attempts to persuade it to abandon power-sharing and an Irish dimension. Even initiatives outside the immediate political domain, such as proposals for a separate bill of rights, were resisted because, the party argued, on their own they 'could not be regarded as a substitute for a widely acceptable constitutional settlement involving both communities in the government of the province'.[26]

The only significant measure the party supported at this time was the bill proposing the establishment of a fair employment agency to oversee employment practices and to ensure the elimination of employment discrimination on religious grounds.[27] Equality of job opportunity had been one of the key demands of the civil rights movement and, with continuing evidence of significant disparities in the occupational profiles of Catholics compared with Protestants of similar education and skills, the need to adopt a pro-active approach was critical if equality of job opportunity was to be assured.

WIDER HORIZONS

In the political vacuum, SDLP leaders took the opportunity to develop overseas relationships, in the US with significant Irish-American politicians, and in Europe with the Confederation of European Socialist Parties. In the autumn of 1976, John Hume spent two months at Harvard University, during which time he strengthened his acquaintance with leading politicians like Tip O'Neill, Ted Kennedy, Hugh Carey and Daniel Moynihan, who became known as the 'Four Horsemen' and who led the Friends of Ireland group in the US Congress.[28] Influenced by Hume and the Irish department of foreign affairs, and commencing on St Patrick's Day 1977, the Four Horsemen issued an annual statement on Northern Ireland that generally reflected the SDLP's assessment of the situation, and acted as a strong counter to the more militant statements from pro-PIRA support groups in the US, such as NORAID (Northern Ireland Aid). The group's first statement asked that Americans, especially Irish-Americans, 'renounce any action that promotes the current violence or provides support or encouragement for organizations engaged in violence'.[29] With its anti-violence credentials, the group would gradually exercise significant influence over successive US administrations, and become an effective pressure group on British policy in Northern Ireland.[30]

Strengthening relationships within the European Community (EC) became important as the prospect of direct elections to the European Parliament loomed. John Hume, with his decidedly pro-EC views, was particularly enthusiastic in championing the benefits of the community. When the British referendum on continued membership of the community took place in June 1975, the party supported the call for a 'yes' vote. Later, in 1977, Hume accepted an invitation to join the cabinet of Irish commissioner Richard Burke, an appointment that was to give him invaluable first-hand experience of European institutions, as well introducing him to leading community politicians. It was also an opportunity for the party to develop relationships with the Confederation of European Socialist Parties in preparing for the first direct parliamentary elections. On the matter of Northern Ireland's representation in the European Parliament, the SDLP was anxious that the region should be allocated three seats in order to ensure a Nationalist representative, and that the seats be contested in a single constituency on a proportional basis. On this demand, the party had the strong support of the Irish government, whose foreign minister, Garret FitzGerald, lobbied extremely hard to ensure that this would be the situation.[31]

WITHDRAWAL THREATENS PARTY UNITY

The political failures of 1974–6 dominated political discussion at the SDLP's 1976 annual conference. Motions from several branches directed blame towards the British and Irish governments, with several demanding the British government declare its intentions for the government of Northern Ireland, or else withdraw. The fact that Fianna Fáil had moved in the same direction had only encouraged similar thinking within sections of the SDLP. On withdrawal, the composite motion before conference demanded that 'the British government ... declare its intention of withdrawing to give the divided people of Northern Ireland the opportunity to negotiate a final political solution and a lasting peace in Northern Ireland'.[32] Proposed by Paddy Duffy, the motion provoked a very intense debate that saw the leadership of the party quite divided. Among those supporting the motion were Paddy Devlin, Ivan Cooper, Eddie McGrady, Séamus Mallon, Joe Hendron and several other former convention members.

Those who opposed the motion included Gerry Fitt, John Hume, Austin Currie and Hugh Logue. Fitt had privately made it known that support for a withdrawal policy would lead to his resignation from the party.[33]

Séamus Mallon, who had prepared his own paper on future strategy for the party, argued quite a subtle approach that contained the seeds of future developments.[34] Mallon suggested the SDLP and the Irish government should establish 'a political forum for the purpose of agreeing to proposals . . . on which power-sharing and a meaningful Irish dimension will be formed'. Should the British reject the idea, he proposed that the SDLP together with the Irish government conclude that 'the British dimension is standing in the way of political agreement (which), therefore, must be subsequently sought in an Irish context'. Such a situation would, he believed, oblige the British government to declare whether or not it intended to withdraw from Northern Ireland. If the option was withdrawal, the SDLP would, in Mallon's opinion, be credited with having achieved it by political means. Opposing the motion, John Hume argued that the risks were too high, describing talk of withdrawal as extremely dangerous and advocating instead the longer-term strategy of persuading the British to support the party's policy of power-sharing with an Irish dimension. While the motion was defeated by forty-two votes, 153–111, the debate had revealed serious divisions within the party on a fundamental issue, not least at leadership level.

INDEPENDENCE AGAIN

The debate on the independence motion took place in a context of renewed public discussion of the issue. In advance of the conference, a paper entitled *Negotiated independence: a way forward*, submitted by the Cookstown branch, was already receiving considerable attention. The paper was largely the work of Paddy Duffy who, along with Devlin, had become one of the party's most ardent advocates of independence and of a British withdrawal. Adding to the focus on independence was the publication, shortly before the party conference, of the Ulster Loyalist Central Coordinating Committee's (ULCCC) document, *Ulster can survive unfettered*, detailing the case for independence from a loyalist perspective. John McKeague, a loyalist paramilitary connected with the paramilitary Red Hand Commandos, and a leader of the ULCCC,[35] met several members of the SDLP, among them Paddy Duffy, Paddy Devlin and Séamus

Mallon, to discuss his ideas, much to the annoyance of Gerry Fitt, who was scathing about McKeague in his leader's address. Fitt's opposition to independence was shared by several colleagues, among them Hugh Logue, who described the proposals as 'poorly propounded, jingoistic, contradictory, glib and superficial', and called for support for current SDLP policies, i.e. partnership and an Irish dimension.[36]

At the conference, Paddy Duffy strongly argued the case for independence, saying that 'negotiated independence from Britain offers the most hopeful solution'.[37] He claimed that independence would address deep-rooted fears of each other held by both sides of Northern Ireland's community. As to the form of government in an independent Northern Ireland, Duffy argued that power-sharing would be essential, as would a council of Ireland, to deal with all-Ireland matters. While conference did not vote directly on Duffy's paper, which was referred to the incoming executive for further discussion, the vote allowing that to happen was supported by a significant majority, 147–51, indicating that perhaps there were more members prepared to consider the independence option than had previously been thought.

What the debates on withdrawal and independence revealed was a degree of confused thinking allied to an anxiety lest the party lose the leadership of the Nationalist community and the feeling that, to avoid doing so, it had to find a new way forward. The attraction of a withdrawal policy supported by the Irish government was, as Mallon had argued, that it 'would be favourable to our party position'.[38] Independence was similarly attractive, because it too would entail a British withdrawal, and had the added attraction that a number of prominent Unionists were already espousing the idea. In other words, nationalism and unionism might, for the first time, find common cause through both policies. Both policies were, as Hume had argued, high risk, requiring, if they were to be peacefully achieved, much greater levels of agreement between Unionists and Nationalists than seemed realistically possible. Withdrawal without Unionist consent would be likely to precipitate widespread violence in which many Nationalist communities would be extremely vulnerable. Independence, despite the high profile of some of its champions, was proving to have limited popular appeal, and was generally quite unacceptable to southern parties that were all still committed to achieving Irish unity.

Adding to the different messages coming from the conference, in a separate debate, a short policy document, *Partnership in Ireland*, was endorsed. This paper reiterated the party's commitment to the principle of partnership between both communities in Northern Ireland, and between Northern Ireland and the Republic on one hand, and the UK on the other, as the only basis on which to make political progress and guarantee stability. The document ruled out any attempt at a purely internal solution, arguing that

> Partnership between the British and Irish traditions in Northern Ireland can only take place if each tradition recognizes and respects the identity of the other; partnership must, therefore, make provision for the British identity of some of the people of Northern Ireland and the Irish tradition of others.[39]

So, while withdrawal and independence were eventually rejected by the SDLP, a significant shift in focus was, nonetheless, taking place in how the party believed partnership could be achieved. As Séamus Mallon's paper stated, the party had reached 'a dead-end with pan-unionism' and needed 'to kick the ball into the courts of the only people who can solve the problem – the Irish and British governments'.[40] The new focus was, therefore, on developing the wider British-Irish context, and over the next few years the SDLP was to painstakingly devote considerable energy to developing that approach.

RETURN TO BASICS

In the immediate aftermath of the conference, Hume was quite apprehensive about the party's future, given the number of senior colleagues who had supported the withdrawal motion.[41] It was a fear shared by the British and Irish governments. As early as September 1976, NIO officials feared that the SDLP would adopt a more extreme Nationalist line, and that 'new faces might emerge in the leadership who would almost certainly look to more orthodox republicans for support'.[42] After the conference, another NIO report commented that 'rarely if ever since the SDLP's foundation ... has ideological disharmony within the party been so apparent'.[43] Garret FitzGerald believed that 'the SDLP was on the brink of reverting to the uncompromising nationalism of the minority pre-1968 and had almost lost hope of ever achieving anything by constitutional politics'.[44]

Determined to counter the withdrawal tendency, and to restore a clear sense of purpose to the party, Hume prepared a discussion paper outlining the options it faced.[45] The first option, referred to as course A in the paper, suggested ways whereby existing policy should be strengthened and how the party should campaign to achieve its objectives. Hume recommended that the intransigent opposition of loyalists to partnership should be constantly exposed, as well as the British failure to properly confront that intransigence; that every effort should be made to convince the British of the need to persuade the wider community of the value of partnership and of North-South cooperation; and that the party should stress that the problem of Northern Ireland could not be solved by the people of Northern Ireland alone, and that a solution had to include both London and Dublin. The more radical option, referred to as course B, was for the party to change its policy and to call for a British withdrawal as a significant number had attempted to do at the annual conference. But if such was to be the policy, Hume indicated that the party would have to consider carefully the steps to be taken to maintain order in the immediate aftermath of a British declaration, or of an actual British withdrawal; what long-term government structures the party should propose and, crucially, the means to be used to achieve agreement on such structures by the different representative groups in Ireland. It was quite clear from his paper that Hume was advocating the first option, since the second contained far too many unknown and dangerous risks, all likely to have grave consequences for the people of Northern Ireland, if not for the people of the whole of Ireland. His sober assessment helped ensure that the party did not opt for course B, though this was by no means the end of the debate within the party.

POLICE OUT OF CONTROL

Meantime, there were fresh allegations of the ill-treatment of paramilitary suspects in police custody to be investigated, and a proposal to increase the number of Northern Ireland MPs at Westminster to be addressed, elections to be contested, and ongoing organizational challenges to be tackled. No assembly and no executive did not mean an end to politics for the SDLP. Nor did the absence of an assembly mean that the SDLP ceased developing its policy portfolio. In addition to the key political debates, the 1976 annual conference considered a number of policy papers, among them *Local government 1977, Poverty in Northern Ireland, Economic analysis and strategy* and *An examination of land use*. Responding to the current debate on education reform and proposals to abolish the selection tests for transfer to second level, the party executive tabled a detailed set of recommendations under the title *An opportunity for excellence*, advocating a system of non-selective secondary schools. The preparation of these papers had all demanded time, effort and expertise and amounted to an ongoing commitment to an agenda wider than constitutional matters, no matter how limited the opportunities to implement any of their recommendations.

The lull that gripped the Northern Ireland political scene from the end of 1976 allowed Roy Mason full scope to pursue the much more aggressive security policy he relished. His decision to use the Special Air Services (SAS) in south Armagh and, more disturbingly, the use of extreme interrogation techniques on suspected terrorists were notable features of the policy. Reports of the ill-treatment of suspects in police and army centres, especially at Castlereagh and Armagh, began to reach public attention in early 1977 and in March the SDLP issued a detailed statement outlining its concerns at these reports. The fact that the allegations were supported by medical evidence, in particular the testimony of police doctors, several of whom were from a Unionist background, meant that they were credible. The party called upon the secretary of state and Chief Constable Kenneth Newman to intervene and have the reports investigated.[46] Over the next year, law and order spokesperson Michael Canavan and health spokesperson Joe Hendron, a medical practitioner, led the party's campaign demanding an end to the ill-treatment of suspects and calling for an inquiry. Receiving no response to its initial call, Gerry Fitt raised the issue in the House of Commons in June,[47] where he reiterated the party's demand for a special inquiry. With still no response, the party raised the matter in meetings with the Dublin government and opposition, and in early October it accused the RUC of 'illegal, inhuman and obscene' behaviour. Canavan claimed the chief constable to be 'unwilling or unable to control those elements in the RUC' who were responsible for the maltreatment,[48] and a motion condemning police treatment of suspects was unanimously carried at the party's annual conference in November. Hendron, who had been approached by the families of some of those arrested, claimed that 'brutality was going on, especially at Castlereagh holding centre', and that the chief constable and perhaps even the government knew and condoned the practice.[49] Pressure was maintained and, following a critical report by Amnesty International in 1978,[50] the British government was forced to establish a special committee to investigate the situation, the results of which were very damming of police procedures.[51]

LOCAL GOVERNMENT ELECTIONS

In the absence of an assembly, local government assumed considerable significance for all parties, but especially for the SDLP, and the party prepared
enthusiastically for the North's second district council elections, to be held in
May 1977. Organizationally, the SDLP was much stronger than in 1973. Dan
McAreavy,[52] who had succeeded John Duffy as the party's general-secretary in
1975, proved to be a dynamic organizer, and by 1977 over one hundred branches
had been established, thus widening the pool of potential candidates and giving
the party opportunities to contest seats not previously fought. The manifesto,
Know where you stand, expressed the party's opposition to the return of significant functions to local authorities as suggested by some Unionists, and endorsed
the SDLP's commitment to power-sharing at council level. The manifesto
argued that 'both main traditions should participate in the decision-making
process in councils and their committees, and should be given a fair share of
appointments to those committees which formulate and execute policy'.[53] It
was important for the party to maintain this position, not just because it was
right, but also because it was a practical example of the workability and effectiveness of power-sharing.

Election results gave the party 113 councillors, an increase of 31 over 1973, and
again the SDLP emerged as the dominant party within the Nationalist community.[54] With a greater number of councillors, the party was able to put its local
government partnership policy into practice much more effectively than in
1973. Consequently, in councils where the SDLP had a majority, the policy of
rotating the main public offices was again implemented and reinforced.

MASON TRIES AGAIN

The abortive Paisley-led strike in May, and the poor showing by the DUP in
the local elections, encouraged Mason to commence fresh discussions with the
parties on the possibilities for a new political initiative. From early summer
until the end of the year, his officials undertook a series of meetings, which, at
one stage, seemed to suggest that a very modest form of interim devolution might
be feasible.[55] Mason's plans ruled out majority rule and a power-sharing executive, and offered little more than a consultative assembly with scrutiny powers
over government departments by proportionally representative committees,

with the possibility of moving to legislative powers provided there was sufficient agreement.[56] Significantly, there was no mention of an Irish dimension. For the SDLP, the proposals had no appeal, though the party did consider the possibility of a new constitutional assembly that would become a fully fledged legislative body with a power-sharing executive once consensus would be reached.[57] However, the party was not prepared to countenance any form of devolution that would not guarantee eventual full power-sharing, especially not administrative devolution. Notwithstanding these considerations, the party in general was convinced that unionism had turned its back on power-sharing, and that the British government had lost the will to insist that this was the only viable form of devolution for a society as deeply divided as that in Northern Ireland. Furthermore, the UUP was no longer prepared to even consider a voluntary coalition,[58] and was now very much under the influence of Enoch Powell's integrationist views. Although the Irish government, once again with Jack Lynch as Taoiseach, was anxious that the SDLP should adopt a positive approach towards Mason's proposals,[59] the party eventually bluntly rejected what Hume described as 'cosmetic politics'.

Despite the fact that Mason and his officials continued discussions with the party throughout 1977 on a possible initiative, their efforts came to nothing. For Unionists, the immediate focus was on gaining more seats at Westminster for Northern Ireland and, as for devolution, they would only contemplate a reform of local government that would establish three or four regional councils with control of such functions as planning, health and education. Mindful of past and current abuses at council level, the SDLP was totally opposed to such a proposal and it was not seriously pursued. While extra seats at Westminster were justified on a population basis, in the context of direct rule, Unionists regarded them as essential if the region was to be treated on a par with the rest of the UK, and, secondly, extra seats would strengthen the integration of Northern Ireland into the UK. But it was precisely for this latter reason that the SDLP opposed the move, although, ironically, the party was likely to gain three, and possibly more of the extra seats. However, with eleven Unionist seats far outweighing Gerry Fitt, on whom Labour could usually count anyway, and with Labour holding only a very slim majority in the House of Commons, Unionists were in a strong position to strike a bargain. This they did, and in return for the setting up of a speaker's conference to consider extra seats, Unionist MPs agreed not to oppose the government in key votes.[60]

DEVLIN DEPARTS

While the SDLP had participated in the discussions on Mason's proposals, its real focus was moving elsewhere. A fundamental review of the party' position followed from discussions on John Hume's options paper, and commenced after the local government elections. Those involved included Hume, Currie, Duffy, Denis Haughey, Hugh Logue and Séamus Mallon. Despite the fact that the 1976 conference had mandated further study of the independence option, there was little appetite for doing so within the leadership, Paddy Devlin and Paddy Duffy apart, and the working group did not seriously address the issue. The review focused instead on the British-Irish context and a paper, *Facing reality*, was prepared for submission to the annual conference.[61] *Facing reality* summarized the party's unsuccessful efforts to reach an accommodation with Unionists and was bitterly critical of the British government for entering into voting pacts with Unionists at Westminster. The document restated the party's firm belief that there was 'a clear need for the British government to spell out its long-term strategy for the future of Northern Ireland and for its relationship with the rest of Ireland'. The document claimed that for as long as the British declined to do so, 'it leaves as its only long-term statement, its continually renewed Unionist pledge', which meant that Unionists would 'find no willingness to budge from their present intransigent stance'. The central demand in the document was that, for as long as the British remained in Northern Ireland, they 'should promote reconciliation and an end to division between all Irish people, leading to the establishment of structures of government which allow both traditions in Ireland to flourish freely together in unity and harmony'. The paper concluded with a call for the British and Irish governments to work together towards that end and, in the meantime, to cooperate on social and economic projects that would be to the benefit of both parts of Ireland.

Facing reality was essentially a restatement of existing SDLP policy, but given the prevailing anti-power-sharing and anti-Irish dimension mood within unionism, the greater emphasis on a British-Irish initiative implied going over the heads of Unionists in the first instance. Also implied was a British withdrawal, but now only as a long-term outcome. Nevertheless, party critics seized on the implications as further evidence that the SDLP was adopting an increasingly extreme Nationalist position, and turning its back on Unionists.

While the document was being prepared, the SDLP experienced its first leadership defection, when Paddy Devlin unexpectedly announced his resignation as chair of the constituency representatives, though he did not immediately resign from the party. Devlin's disaffection arose from what he regarded to be the mistaken policy direction taken by the review group, claiming that *Facing reality* was 'a hastily drafted piece of froth' that represented a drift towards a more Nationalist stance and a move away from efforts to attract Unionists.[62] It was a curious argument for a leading member who, at the previous annual conference of the party, had supported British withdrawal and, on many public occasions, had also endorsed the case for an independent Northern Ireland. A hint of Devlin's disaffection was contained in an article that had appeared in the *Irish Times* just a few weeks before the review group completed its work.[63] In it, Devlin questioned whether, in light of Unionist opposition to power-sharing, the SDLP should persist with its commitment to the same principle. Instead, he argued that voting trends suggested that an SDLP-APNI coalition would win considerable support, and that it would be much more progressive than a coalition with Unionists. It was a highly debatable claim, but it was a sign that Devlin was moving away from core SDLP policies and was searching for something new, but in a different direction from most of his colleagues. His very public criticism of the work of the policy review group, to which he had not contributed, accompanied by criticisms of the party's leadership, led the constituency representatives group to recommend that Devlin be relieved of his executive membership, that he be suspended from all party spokesperson roles and that he attend its next meeting to defend his criticisms, an invitation he declined.[64] The meeting also unanimously elected Séamus Mallon as the new chair of the group. At a joint meeting of the constituency representatives and the party's executive on 31 August, the whip was removed from Paddy Devlin and the group's recommendations on Devlin were endorsed.[65] Subsequently, he was expelled from the party he had help found, and to which he had contributed in many significant ways over the seven years since then.[66]

Given the different policy options that Devlin had supported over the years, it is doubtful if policy was the only, or main, reason he parted company with the SDLP. Austin Currie has suggested that Devlin's attack on the party may have had more to do with the likely candidature of John Hume for the forthcoming European elections.[67] In contrast to Hume, Devlin had never made a secret of his anti-EC views, a decidedly minority position within the party. So, despite his own ambition, it was very unlikely that he would have gained a place on the party's ticket. His subsequent independent candidature in the 1979 European elections suggests that he would have wanted to at least share that ticket with John Hume, if not to be the sole candidate himself. The personal nature of Devlin's disaffection with the SDLP was underlined by the fact that his departure caused few ripples within the party; even his own branch in West Belfast expressed no concern at his expulsion. In his biography, Devlin admits that he was not entirely blameless in the whole affair, saying that his dispute with the SDLP was 'a most unworthy squabble in which I was not the innocent party'.[68] However, Paddy Devlin's contributions to the party were significant. He had helped develop the social democratic policy orientation of the party, and had been instrumental in establishing links with the international socialist movement (pl. 11). His departure deprived the party of one of its more colourful and fearless members, but it hardly signalled, as many of the party's critics claimed, that the SDLP had abandoned its founding principles.

BRITISH-IRISH FRAMEWORK

Facing reality became the party's basic document from the autumn of 1977, and its recommendations were the basis for discussions with the Irish and British governments that took place over the following months. In a meeting with the new Fianna Fáil government in Dublin in September, an SDLP delegation stressed the danger of a simple withdrawal policy, and emphasized instead the need for the Irish government to be fully involved in the search for a solution, as it had been in 1972–4.[69] At the same meeting, the party recommended a new initiative on North-South economic development, and at a later meeting in November devoted solely to this issue, outlined some of its detailed thinking, elaborated in a document prepared by a special working group of the party's policy committee.[70] The party's plans covered such areas as energy, industrial development, agriculture, tourism, roads and the redevelopment of the Shannon-Erne waterway. While the opportunities to take many of its recommendations forward were limited, they again underlined the party's determination to pursue a broad and progressive approach to all-Ireland issues.

At the party's seventh annual conference in November, *Facing reality* was endorsed, with Gerry Fitt describing it as 'not just right, but the only policy which gave hope of progress in Northern Ireland'.[71] Denis Haughey spelled out once again the SDLP's demand that all sections of the community had a right to be involved in government with adequate guarantees for all, and he called on both communities to engage in dialogue and to make a 'realistic effort to grasp

the fears and misgivings of the other side in a spirit of generosity and toler-
ance'.[72] To demonstrate its good faith, the party agreed to consider participating
in Mason's proposal for inter-party talks.[73] But, as discussed earlier, when the
UUP ruled out the secretary of state's ideas for a transitional approach to power-
sharing and reiterated its belief that district councils should be reformed and
given greater powers, the proposal became moribund. The SDLP had made
clear that with Unionists also opposed to power-sharing at council level, the
UUP proposal had no appeal whatsoever. Mason's belief that opinions had been
changing within unionism was proved baseless, as would be his belief that the
tide was turning in the battle against terrorism.[74]

Chapter 7

Democratic politics sidelined

The political frustrations of the preceding two years persisted into 1978, with no signs of any imminent breakthrough to relieve them. When the Conservative party's Northern Ireland spokesperson, Airey Neave, announced that power-sharing was no longer practical politics, and that his party was abandoning its bipartisan approach with Labour to Northern Ireland and, instead, would support James Molyneaux's demand for reform of local government, Unionists sensed that their case was gaining ground.[1] To the SDLP, both the Labour government and the Tory opposition now appeared to have totally succumbed to Unionist influence. The former was dependent on Unionist MPs to stay in power, and the latter had abandoned the central tenet of its Northern Ireland policy, a policy developed by their own former secretary of state William Whitelaw. No wonder the SDLP felt its political fortunes to be at low ebb.

WITHDRAWAL AGAIN

Compounding a feeling within SDLP ranks of being left behind was a statement from Taoiseach Jack Lynch,[2] quickly followed by one from the recently appointed archbishop of Armagh, Tomás Ó Fiaich,[3] both calling for a British statement of intent to withdraw from Ireland.[4] Since Lynch had always encouraged the SDLP's partnership approach and had been seen as unenthusiastic about Fianna Fáil's endorsement of a withdrawal policy, his statement came as a surprise, while Ó Fiaich's was a break with the generally non-political stance of his predecessor. Both statements reignited a debate that many party members believed had been defused with the adoption of *Facing reality*. Over the following few months, the re-emergence of the withdrawal debate created a degree of uncertainty and confusion as to how the party should respond. Initially, several leading members who had counselled against making British withdrawal the primary focus of policy, began advocating solutions that made it much more central. Reinforcing the withdrawal argument was the ECHR's finding that interrogation techniques used against those detained in August 1971, had amounted to 'inhuman and degrading treatment'.[5] The fact that fresh allegations of apparently similar techniques were then under investigation strengthened the view among many Nationalists that British justice meant 'no' justice, and that no British government would ever have the capacity to find a solution.

In making withdrawal a more central demand, the SDLP now felt compelled, as Hume's 1977 paper had suggested, to indicate the constitutional arrangements it believed would best suit the new Ireland envisaged. In a lively debate, some, like Paddy Duffy, favoured a two-state federal arrangement. Duffy argued that a federal Ireland would be a state

> under the control of the Irish people and free from British control. The constitution will have to clearly provide for a pluralist society and could not in any sense subject any religious group, however small, to the attitudes or doctrines of any other religious grouping, however, large.[6]

Hume himself seemed attracted to the idea, and caused a minor controversy when, in an attempt to appeal to Unionists, he argued that in a federal Ireland power-sharing might not be a pre-requisite for the northern state.[7] Many in the party disagreed, and Séamus Mallon publicly argued that power-sharing would be essential to guarantee equal treatment for the two communities. Denis Haughey seemed to favour the Hume approach, claiming that a federal Ireland should guarantee continuing UK citizenship to Unionists, and that the North should have a strong parliament, operating 'as near to normal as possible'.[8]

When an August editorial in the mass-circulation *Daily Mirror* expressed support for withdrawal, it seemed as if a significant section of British public opinion was also moving in that direction.[9] The *Mirror's* comment was sparked by the absence of political movement and the growing protest by PIRA and Irish National Liberation Army (INLA) prisoners who, denied their own clothes, refused to wear prison garb, wrapped themselves in blankets and refused to respect prison rules. It was no surprise, therefore, that at the SDLP's annual conference later in the year, withdrawal again featured in several motions submitted for debate. The motion selected for discussion was from Austin Currie's Coalisland branch. It stated that

> British disengagement from Ireland is inevitable and desirable; it ought to take place as part of an overall political solution which would provide

guarantees for both traditions in the North and minimize the possible dangers in the political, security, economic and financial fields and that the British government, immediately after the Westminster election, should call a quadripartite conference of the two governments in London and Dublin and representatives of the two traditions in the North with a view to finding a permanent solution to the Irish problem.[10]

While the motion reflected the desirability of a British 'disengagement', a word that lacked the dramatic impact of 'withdrawal', it was not a simple demand for immediate withdrawal.[11] Instead, its main focus, as Currie was at pains to point out, was the key recommendation that the British and Irish governments jointly convene a conference to which the major parties in Northern Ireland would be invited, with the aim of reaching agreement on a settlement. The debate on the motion resulted in it being carried almost unanimously, only two votes being cast against it and with one abstention.[12] With its endorsement, several harder-line withdrawal motions fell and, despite the considerable amount of comment on the matter earlier in the year, the conference referred a motion on federalism back for further study. An NIO observer at the conference accurately interpreted the debate as an expression of SDLP members' frustration

> that so little progress had been made in the search for an agreed form of devolved government . . . and a strong feeling that no progress would be made whilst the British government continued to offer Unionists the prop of the negative guarantee.[13]

STRESSING IRISH CONTEXT

The debate over withdrawal only confirmed the paralysis that had gripped Northern Ireland's politics; a paralysis in which the only movement seemed to be within each community, with none between them. Following the conference, a working party reported to a joint meeting of the party's executive and the constituency representatives group, and recommended a seven-point strategy based on the Coalisland motion and on motion 89 (which had proposed a federal solution).[14] The SDLP was now working on the premise that a solution to the Northern Irish problem could only be found in the wider Irish context. Creating this context, the report argued, would require British acceptance that this was the only realistic option and that 'withdrawal is central to it'. To muster the necessary pressure on the British government, the report recommended that the major parties in the South be persuaded to work more closely with the SDLP and that external support be sought in Europe and the USA and within the UK itself. The immediate objective would be a quadripartite conference, as called for in *Facing reality*. Regarding constitutional models for a new Ireland, the report argued that 'a federal system has some advantages which could make it more acceptable than either a unitary or an independent state in the North'. The report also commented, with a considerable degree of understatement, that for Unionists, 'a federal Ireland is simply a united Ireland in which they would be reduced to impotence'. It acknowledged that, like other models of unity, 'a federal solution leaves the fundamental problem of finding a consensus'. The implication was that, in present circumstances, any consensus would not be for a united Ireland, and that the only way to produce a consensus was through a quadripartite conference that would deal comprehensively with all of the issues at the heart of the conflict. Such an approach further implied that significant compromises would have to be made by Nationalists as well as Unionists.

While the focus on withdrawal could be characterized as the SDLP falling back into traditional Nationalist rhetoric, there was another objective behind this tactic. That objective was to stimulate discussion, particularly among parties in the South regarding their intentions for the North. The North's crisis had given rise to the frequent complaint that it was not sufficient to merely call on the British to withdraw, but that the implications of such a demand had to be honestly and carefully examined. Hume had already challenged his own colleagues over these implications in order to expose the shallowness of a simple withdrawal policy as well as underlining the need for more realistic answers. In the case of the parties in the South, this need was becoming acute and would eventually lead to the establishment of the New Ireland Forum (NIF) in 1983.[15]

PRISON CRISIS LOOMS

However, while the withdrawal debate was simmering within the party, the growing prison crisis was posing a considerable challenge to the SDLP in the wider community. Given the size of the Nationalist community, not surprisingly, many SDLP members had acquaintances and relations in the provisional movement, and were directly exposed to community pressures arising from the prison crisis. While opposed to paramilitary violence, the party was also opposed to internment without trial, to interrogation methods that violated the human rights of those arrested, to non-jury trials and to legislation such as the Prevention of Terrorism Act and the Emergency Provisions Act. Not only did the party believe that such measures and methods amounted to violations of human rights, but also that they had the effect of strengthening sympathy for the prisoners and their cause among Nationalists. Prisoners who demanded they be afforded 'special category', and, when refused, protested by refusing to wear prison garb, by daubing their cells with excrement, by refusing to wash and, eventually, by resorting to hunger strikes, gained a sympathetic response within the Nationalist community.

While the party was anxious to do whatever it could to defuse the crisis, it found itself caught in a no-win situation, best illustrated by events at a party meeting in the Ardoyne area of Belfast in September 1978. A crowd invaded the meeting, wielding placards that accused the party of inaction on the crisis, and assaulted several leading members, among them Austin Currie, Denis Haughey, Séamus Mallon and Bríd Rodgers.[16] In a statement released several days later, the SDLP accused those who had carried out the attacks of 'rampant fascism', and went on to outline efforts made by party members to bring the prison protests to an end. Sinn Féin and the PIRA, who had directed prisoners' relatives to make no contact with the SDLP, had spurned these efforts.[17] The statement added that when SDLP representatives visited the prisons, prisoners would not speak to them, and when the SDLP arranged meetings for relatives with NIO officials, the relatives were warned not to attend. Despite its best efforts, therefore, the very people on whose behalf it was acting prevented the party from trying to alleviate the situation. Nevertheless, motion 11 at the 1978 annual conference called on the party to support 'special status' being granted to 'political prisoners', while continuing pressure from individual members and branches reflected growing anger within the Nationalist community about the prison situation.

Special category status was ill-defined in practical terms, but essentially it meant that paramilitary prisoners should be treated differently from 'ordinary' prisoners. In the prisoners' eyes, special category amounted to recognition that the motivation for their crimes was political, and not personally or selfishly inspired. A paper on special category prepared for the party's executive recommended that the demands to wear their own clothes and to receive more visits should be granted to all prisoners and not just to those who regarded themselves as 'political'.[18] In support of its recommendation, the paper pointed to the practice in many countries where the wearing of special prison apparel was no longer prescribed. Adopting this position would mean that the party could support the prisoners, but not ally themselves either with paramilitary prisoners exclusively, or with the street protests being organized by groups and individuals overtly pro-PIRA. It would take some time, considerable controversy and communal upheaval before the authorities adopted the SDLP's recommendation.

NEW AND OLD CHALLENGES

The 1978 annual conference saw the election of Bríd Rodgers as chair in succession to Denis Haughey who, after five years, had not sought re-election. It was also a conference that saw the party prepare for two imminent election campaigns, a general election and the first direct elections to the European Parliament. A general election had been expected in the autumn, but when it was not called, it was certain to take place by October 1979 at the latest. Once again, the party decided centrally that all twelve seats would be contested, and by late 1978 many candidates had already been chosen. The constituencies awaiting candidates included the cockpit constituency of Fermanagh-South Tyrone, where the issue would again be the effect of a 'split' in the Nationalist vote, should the SDLP decide to oppose the sitting MP, Frank Maguire.

Few general elections have been called in circumstances quite as dramatic as those surrounding the end of Prime Minister James Callaghan's government in March 1979. Dependent as his government was on the votes of non-Labour MPs, it was obvious that when a vote of confidence was called for, these others would be crucial to the government's fate. When several Unionist MPs declared that they would vote against the government, notwithstanding the extra seats that Northern Ireland had been granted, all eyes were on Fitt and Frank Maguire. Maguire had seldom appeared in parliament since his election in 1974, but on this occasion he turned up only to 'abstain in person', as he said himself. Despite his long years of loyal support for Labour, Fitt also decided to abstain. In what many regarded as one of his finest parliamentary speeches, Fitt claimed that among the grounds for his abstention was Roy Mason's 'total and absolute disaster as Northern Secretary' by showing himself to be 'a complete and utter

Unionist'.[19] Secondly, he pointed to the findings of the report on interrogation techniques that officers of a force answerable to Mason had tortured prisoners.[20] By abstaining, Fitt and Maguire sealed the fate of the government, and the general election was called for 3 May.

Disregarding its decision that all twelve seats would be contested, the party executive decided that in the case of Fermanagh-South Tyrone, the decision should rest with the constituency organization itself.[21] At a convention called for that purpose, it was decided to contest the seat, but only if two Unionist candidates had been selected, otherwise the party would not. It was for such circumstances that Austin Currie was selected as the party's candidate, and when two Unionist candidates seemed likely, his nomination seemed assured.[22] At a special meeting some days later, however, the party executive set the convention's decision aside and, by a vote of 12–3, decided not to ratify Currie's nomination, whatever the circumstances. The reason given was that the margin at the convention in favour of contesting, 50–47, had been too narrow.[23] Currie himself believed that the real reasons may have had more to do with the perceived effect that a split Nationalist vote might have on support for the party in other constituencies, and in the forthcoming European parliamentary elections.[24] The decision precipitated the first major division within the SDLP. Within days, Austin Currie resigned as party whip, and announced that he would contest the election as 'independent SDLP'.

Currie was supported by many party members, both within and without the constituency, among them Gerry Fitt, but he was severely criticized by others. Séamus Mallon and Paddy Duffy, both candidates themselves, openly denounced Currie's decision. Paddy Duffy was standing in Mid-Ulster, where his main opponent for the Nationalist vote in this winnable seat was Pat Fahy of the recently formed Irish Independence Party (IIP),[25] while Mallon was the party's candidate in Armagh, a less winnable but nonetheless important constituency for the party. The fear was that by splitting Fermanagh-South Tyrone's Nationalist electorate, Currie's action would impact negatively on both Duffy's and Mallon's prospects.

In its election manifesto, the SDLP ignored the controversy, and concentrated on the frustration and anger of the party towards the British government's management of affairs in the North since the collapse of the 1974 executive.[26] The manifesto argued that since the convention, there had been no serious attempt to promote dialogue, that the focus had been on security solutions and that such initiatives as had been taken were biased in favour of

Unionists. The manifesto also pointed to the worsening economic situation as further evidence of Labour's mismanagement. The manifesto stressed, yet again, the SDLP's demand for a British re-assessment of its 'constitutional guarantee', stating that 'it is surely not unreasonable, at this stage, to insist that the British must abandon their present policy and commit themselves to seeking reconciliation between the peoples of this island'.[27] The party pledged that, following the elections, it would work for the convening of a 'quadripartite' conference to address all of the North's constitutional and political issues.

In the elections, the party's vote declined by 4 per cent and it won no extra seats. Once again Gerry Fitt was the only successful SDLP candidate.[28] In Fermanagh-South Tyrone, Frank Maguire retained his seat, while Currie came third. Despite his defiance of the party executive's decision, Currie remained a staunch member and returned to the constituency representatives group, but not as chief whip, a position now occupied by Eddie McGrady.

HUME'S TRIUMPH

Just over a month after the general elections, the electorate was again at the polls, this time to elect three members to the European Parliament (pl. 12). True to his belief that membership of the EC not only offered Northern Ireland new social and economic opportunities, but also wider horizons and examples of how age-old enemies were building common institutions to overcome the bitter legacy of their many wars, Hume's manifesto, *A new horizon*, focused exclusively on the challenges and prospects in the new parliament. He deliberately avoided local political issues over which the EC had no jurisdiction, and stressed the positive contribution that the EC's regional and agricultural policies and programmes offered. Uniquely among the main candidates, Hume also emphasized the global significance of the EC, particularly with respect to developing countries.[29] With a strong likelihood of victory, Hume's campaign did much to revive party morale, as he sought votes, presidential style, throughout the whole of the North. Hume polled 140,622 first preferences and was elected second after Paisley, who topped the poll, and far ahead of the UUP's successful candidate, John Taylor (pl. 13). His opponents for the Nationalist vote, Bernadette McAliskey, Paddy Devlin and the Republican Club's two candidates, managed just over 40,000 between them.

Hume's victory made him the undisputed democratic voice of northern

Nationalists.[30] He now had a stage in the European Parliament, where he could cultivate fresh influence to address the Northern Irish crisis, and he lost no time in doing so, primarily by having the parliament investigate specific issues such as economic development, rural development and the Irish language. In January 1980, he submitted a motion to the parliament calling on the EC to undertake a study of Northern Ireland's needs and recommending that the European Commission put forward proposals on how additional Community resources might be made available to help solve the North's economic ills. The study that followed, known as the *Martin Report*, would bring £63m to Belfast for inner-city redevelopment, and release a considerable sum for badly needed social housing.[31] Hume's initiatives on support for the Irish language contributed to the establishment of the Bureau for Lesser-Spoken Languages in 1982 with its location in Dublin.

THATCHER'S PLANS

Meantime, on the Northern Irish stage itself, the arrival of a Tory government led by Margaret Thatcher had not been greeted with any enthusiasm by the SDLP. Thatcher had been strongly influenced by her close friend and recently assassinated Northern Ireland spokesperson Airey Neave,[32] and was not thought to have any great interest in her troublesome province. Her initial instinct was to avoid any major initiatives. In Neave's place, the little-known Humphrey Atkins was appointed secretary of state, and his first moves to engage with the SDLP did not augur well for a positive relationship. A few weeks after his appointment, he called on the party to stop using Dublin and Washington to influence British policy in Northern Ireland, to nominate members to the Police Authority and to fully support the RUC,[33] advice the party ignored. Instead, the SDLP continued to refine its policy of seeking a solution in the wider British-Irish context and was happy to use whatever influence it could muster to impress that message on the two governments.

In a further development of those policies at a special weekend conference of the executive and constituency representatives held in early September, the party adopted a document which stated that

> the increasing electoral strength of Paisleyism and the lack of leadership and commitment to devolution of the Official Unionist Party (UUP),

the alienation of large sections of the population resulting from paramilitary influence ... and security strictures, convince us that it is now impossible to reach the agreement necessary to create an administration which would command the active support of sufficient numbers of people in both communities.[34]

The document further argued that

the search for a solution must shift from the Northern Ireland political parties to outside factors which have the power and the resources to create change and would allow political action to be taken without the constant threat of veto by any political grouping in Northern Ireland.[35]

In effect, the party proposed an approach that would, initially, by-pass the North's sectarian stalemate so that

a joint Anglo-Irish programme can be formulated which will seek a constitutional arrangement making provision for the special position of Northern Ireland within Ireland itself, within the UK and within the EC, while simultaneously promoting socio-economic development in areas where joint action would be obviously beneficial to the requirements of all parts of island.[36]

To give effect to its all-Ireland socio-economic proposals, the party suggested that a number of North-South commissions be established to take joint action in areas such as agriculture and fisheries, industry and commerce, health and social services, policing, education and European affairs. While there was no immediate action on foot of these recommendations, they were to become central, six years later, to the Anglo-Irish Agreement, and ultimately to the Good Friday Agreement in 1998.

There was, however, no appetite for such bold initiatives within the British government, as Thatcher's new government grappled with a worsening security situation. August 1979 proved to be a particularly bloody month. It opened with the killing of two British soldiers and closed with the assassination at Mullaghmore in Co. Sligo of Lord Louis Mountbatten, uncle of the Duke of Edinburgh, the Queen's husband, and three of his boating companions, and, on the same day, with the murder of eighteen members of the parachute regiment in a booby-trap bomb explosion near Warrenpoint, Co. Down. The PIRA was responsible for all three incidents, the nature and scale of which served to strengthen the case made by those who favoured a security solution first, only after which a political solution would be sought. Loyalist paramilitaries added weight to this argument, with an upsurge in the number of Catholics murdered over the following months.

The new leader of the UUP, James Molyneaux, compounded the negative prospects for political movement when he announced that his party was not contemplating any early move towards a devolved settlement. For Molyneaux, 'devolution would be impossible for at least five years and ... the most sensible course for the party was the improving of direct rule'.[37] Then, when Pope John Paul appealed for an end to violence during his visit to Ireland in late September, the PIRA responded that only violence would remove the British from Ireland and that, upon victory, 'the church would have no difficulty in recognizing us'.[38] The situation appeared more log-jammed than ever.

ATKINS' PLANS

It was, therefore, with some surprise that in early October, on the same day that the PIRA responded to the pope's appeal, Atkins was reported to be considering a political initiative to give the people of Northern Ireland 'greater responsibility for their own affairs'.[39] Based on Roy Mason's proposals for a gradualist approach to devolution Atkins had conducted some initial discussions with party leaders and, despite the huge gaps between parties' positions, seemed to believe that a new initiative should be attempted. In light of the worsening security situation, Gerry Fitt also expressed the view that 'some means had to be found to create a political forum to give power back to a broadly representative section of the Northern Ireland people'.[40] His view signalled a more modest approach than that endorsed at the party's think-in just a few weeks previously and, without consulting his colleagues, he indicated that the SDLP would be likely to cooperate with Atkins' initiative. According to the *Irish Times* political correspondent David McKittrick, Atkins would propose an elected assembly from which a number of representative committees would be established to advise and scrutinize the work of NIO ministers.[41] It was further envisaged, according to McKittrick, that power would be transferred incrementally, according to the level of agreement that the parties might reach, a proposal that

that did not rule out power-sharing, but one that did not envisage it happening for some considerable time, if ever. The UUP quickly dismissed the Atkins proposals, while the SDLP made clear that it remained committed to seeking a wider British-Irish initiative to deal comprehensively with the crisis and would not consider a purely internal approach.

Despite these rejections, Atkins persisted with his consultations, and issued an invitation to the main parties, SDLP, APNI, UUP and DUP, to attend an inter-party conference aimed at exploring possible ways of achieving devolution. Except for the absence of elections prior to the conference, the proposal was not dissimilar in purpose and scope to the ill-fated convention of 1975–6. In 1979, however, the prospects for success seemed even less positive, especially since the UUP quickly declared that it would not participate. When the DUP and the APNI announced that they would participate, attention focused on the SDLP's response. Fitt expressed a qualified welcome at the prospect of fresh talks,[42] but given the party's clear preference for a quadripartite conference, there was no enthusiasm for talks in any other context.

BRITISH-IRISH CONTEXT OR NOTHING

At the party's annual conference in early November, further emphasis was placed on the British-Irish context. The party adopted a new policy document, *Towards a new Ireland: a policy review*, which argued that 'the problems of Northern Ireland can only be solved by joint Anglo-Irish action taken as part of a clearly agreed programme between both governments'.[43] The document stressed the need for a partnership administration and stated that one should be set up, not as a first step, but as part of an overall agreement. Despite his willingness to go along with the secretary of state's proposals, in his conference address, Fitt reiterated the basic SDLP approach that the 'Irish government must be brought in because they cannot be isolated'.[44] However, this was not what Atkins was proposing.

When Atkins published *The government of Northern Ireland: a working paper for a conference*, setting out the parameters for inter-party talks, it was clear that there would be no discussion of any Irish dimension, and that the 1974 power-sharing arrangements would be an unlikely option for devolution. Again, Fitt expressed a guarded welcome, but it was immediately clear that other party leaders were highly critical of what was being proposed. Séamus Mallon stated that 'it would be wrong to assume that the SDLP saw merit in the document' and, at a meeting of the constituency representatives group, the document was rejected as 'absolutely inadequate as the basis for his [Atkins'] conference'.[45] This view was endorsed at a joint meeting of the executive and constituency representatives the following evening.[46] It was also decided that, in order to explore every possibility for dialogue, the leadership should continue talking to the secretary of state with the aim of agreeing a more inclusive agenda that would allow the Irish dimension to be discussed. But before that could happen, the party was faced, with the dramatic resignation of Gerry Fitt from both leadership and membership.

FITT DEPARTS

Although Fitt had been present at the meeting that had rejected Atkins' terms for the proposed inter-party conference, and had supported the rejection motion, he was clearly unhappy about it. Despite his conference remarks, the exclusion of the Irish dimension had not concerned him, since he had come to believe that it was of secondary importance to having a regional assembly and government with adequate safeguards for Nationalists. Obviously, he had not been keeping himself well informed as to the thinking and mood within the party. As one NIO official commented, 'if anyone is at fault (for the SDLP's rejection of Atkins' invitation), it is Mr Fitt for not keeping better in touch with feeling in his party'.[47] PIRA violence had also been sickening him and turning him against the Nationalist aim of Irish unity that he had so frequently and passionately articulated as a member of Republican Labour and, indeed, in his early years as SDLP leader. Another, more personal, factor may well have been John Hume's considerable influence within the party, an influence hugely strengthened by his recent election to the European Parliament with a Northern Ireland-wide mandate. While Hume and Fitt had never publicly clashed, Hume had provided the SDLP's intellectual muscle and Fitt its popular touch, but a touch that resonated more with working-class Belfast than with Northern Ireland as a whole, though it was also a touch that was becoming less sure as the years passed. Furthermore, he had little time for party organization and attended party meetings quite infrequently and, though he was proud of his socialist outlook, it was more instinctive than intellectually worked out. Attacks on his home had encouraged Fitt to spend more time in London, which inevitably reduced contact with his party colleagues. As Hume's influence increased and other figures like Séamus Mallon assumed significant roles, Fitt may well have seen himself more and more a figurehead leader, and so decided to step aside before being obliged to do so.

Fitt's own explanation for his resignation was that the party was becoming too 'green' and, echoing Paddy Devlin, claimed that it had lost its socialist soul. At the press conference to announce his resignation, he complained

> I thought I was going to form a party that would have links with the trade union movement and that would talk to Protestants to try to bring about a Northern Ireland situation where we would work at some internal arrangement. The others (co-founders) were Nationalists. While it was in my blood to be a labour man, it was in their blood to be Nationalists.[48]

These were the easy criticisms often levelled at the SDLP by its opponents, but were difficult to understand from the person who had led the party since its foundation, who had seen it link up with the European social democratic and labour movement, and who had said he fully supported its policies up until the day before he resigned. These policies included the significance that the party placed on the Irish dimension and on the need for a joint British-Irish initiative as the basis upon which to seek a solution. Indeed, at the end of the 'withdrawal' debate at the 1978 party conference, Fitt had boldly restated party policy on Irish unity saying that 'the SDLP wants to unite people of all religions and outlooks, not only in Northern Ireland, but the whole of Ireland, so that we can bring about the reunification of this country by consent, not coercion'.[49] It was difficult, therefore, to accept his argument about the 'greening' of the party.

Austin Currie, who had been extremely close to Fitt since entering Stormont in 1964, suspected that he 'had given to the British the impression that he could deliver the SDLP to the Atkins Conference, and was seriously embarrassed that he had failed to do so'.[50] This explanation was probably not the whole truth, more likely only the immediate cause of his resignation. Undoubtedly, Fitt had been unhappy with the growing emphasis the party had been placing on the need for a comprehensive approach, and the emphasis that some had previously placed on a British withdrawal. As he had confided to an Irish government official, the debate calling for a British withdrawal might well have led to his resignation two years previously. However, there is little evidence of him voicing his concerns at party meetings, though, as Chris Ryder's biography shows, he seems to have made a habit of voicing them to NIO officials. Nevertheless, Fitt's departure was a blow to the party, most of whose members had felt very affectionately towards him, even though some had become increasingly critical of what they had perceived to be a failure to effectively represent their sense of Irishness. An annual conference motion just two weeks before his resignation had demanded that he concern himself 'more with projecting the Irish dimension and leave others to project the British dimension'.[51] However, within the party, Fitt was widely respected, particularly for the single-handed campaign he had waged, after he had first been elected to Westminster, to make the British government aware of discrimination against Catholics, and for his role throughout the civil rights movement. He had resolutely opposed paramilitary violence and, as a result, had suffered several attacks on his own home. However, like Paddy Devlin's departure from the SDLP, Fitt's was not accompanied by any other significant resignations and, on 28 November, John Hume was the unanimous choice to be his successor, with Séamus Mallon the party's new deputy leader.

SDLP TO ATTEND CONFERENCE

Ironically, in view of Fitt's annoyance that the party seemed unwilling to engage in talks, Hume lost little time in negotiating terms with Atkins to enable the SDLP to participate in the proposed conference. After several meetings, it was agreed that all-Ireland relations would be discussed in a separate, but parallel series of meetings, in which parties might or might not participate. Not unexpectedly, the DUP announced that it would not be attending such meetings, nor would it discuss power-sharing of the 1974 kind.[52] But, having won the argument to have the agenda widened, the SDLP's executive decided that the party would attend the conference in the hope that the talks might prove the first step towards achieving the wider dialogue it believed necessary.[53] However, with only three parties scheduled to attend, and with the DUP intent on being present for only part of the agenda and, even then, unwilling to discuss power-sharing, no one rated the prospects for the conference very highly. Adding to the gloom as the year drew to a close were the deaths, just before Christmas, of six more members of the security forces at the hands of the PIRA. The year ended with a total of 125 deaths from violence, several of them in some of the bloodiest incidents of the Troubles.

Chapter 8

Conferences and hunger strikes

Violence marked the opening weeks of the new decade, just as it did the final days of the seventies. In the first week of 1980, three members of the UDR were killed by a booby-trap bomb and a policeman attending a football match was murdered. A week later, three passengers were killed when a bomb exploded on a train travelling from Belfast to Lisburn. For all seven deaths, the PIRA claimed responsibility. A few weeks later, a British soldier manning an army checkpoint in West Belfast shot dead a 16-year-old joy-rider in a car that was, allegedly, being driven in a suspicious manner. To many Nationalists, this killing was another example of callous British indifference towards members of their community. In the midst of such violence, the Atkins conference commenced its proceedings, but, with only three parties in attendance, there was little confidence that it would even help lower tensions, let alone reach an agreement that might help end the violence.

The SDLP submission to the conference was based on its well-rehearsed proposals for power-sharing and an institutionalized Irish dimension, but with no mention of a British withdrawal. As at the constitutional convention, the SDLP indicated that power-sharing need not be permanent, and again proposed that its operation be reviewed after eight to ten years, when a more 'normal' (voluntary) basis to the formation of an executive might be adopted.[1] But once again, these proposals were instantly dismissed by the DUP, whose own suggestions were almost exactly those set out by the UUUC at the convention five years previously. For the DUP, power-sharing was an alien concept on which to base the formation of a government and, as it stated at the time, the party 'emphatically rejects all suggestions which involve a participatory role in the executive for the minority'.[2] Ignoring the political reality in Northern Ireland, the DUP attempted to make a virtue out of accepting that whatever party or parties could command a majority in an assembly had the sole right to form a government. This argument was meant to indicate that the SDLP might be part of an executive if, on its own, or allied with some other party, it could achieve a majority in an assembly. However, since the existing political arithmetic gave Unionists a majority and the prospect of the SDLP being invited to help form a government was remote, the DUP's argument was seen as self-serving and not a constructive contribution to a solution.

These diametrically opposed positions only emphasized why a positive outcome to Atkins' conference was never likely. As for the parallel talks to allow the SDLP present its proposals on the Irish dimension, they too had an air of unreality surrounding them. Their main value from the SDLP's perspective was the opportunity to highlight the all-Ireland dimension to the crisis; to remind the British government that it had all but abandoned the Whitelaw position, and that the issue remained of fundamental significance. In further attempts to widen the agenda of the talks, the party also submitted papers on the economy, on poverty and on the economic and social benefits of closer cooperation between both parts of Ireland.[3] But, with no realistic opportunity to discuss them, submitting them was almost an academic exercise.

After three months of infrequent meetings, the conference adjourned, with the secretary of state promising to reflect on its proceedings before publishing his own proposals. The failure yet again to achieve any significant level of agreement between the local parties convinced the SDLP that it would never again pursue any route to a solution that was not explicitly based in the wider British-Irish context.

HOPING IN HAUGHEY

To develop that context, the party now focused its attention on the South, where Charles J. Haughey was the new Taoiseach.[4] Haughey was a politician whose strong, traditional, Fianna Fáil views made him something of an ogre in the eyes of Unionists and a man to be viewed with some suspicion by the British, not least because those views meant that he regarded Britain to be solely to blame for partition, and, by extension, also for the current crisis. Furthermore, his alleged involvement in the South's 1969 arms scandal rendered him doubly suspect.[5] On taking office, Haughey had made it clear that he would be guided by his party's 1975 policy on Northern Ireland that called for British withdrawal and for Irish unity, but, as with similar policies held by other parties, did not indicate how a sufficient number of Unionists might be persuaded to accept unification. While opposed to the PIRA's campaign, Haughey was less concerned than his predecessor to appear conciliatory, especially towards Unionists, an approach that at times was to cause serious difficulties for the SDLP.[6]

However, in practical terms, Haughey realized that for the northern crisis to be resolved it was essential that he work closely with the British government. He had little faith in the Atkins talks and, from the outset of his office, concentrated on developing relationships with Margaret Thatcher. In February 1980, he issued a statement in which he called on the British government to join him in seeking a solution and, in May 1980, he met with Thatcher in London in the hope that together they might undertake a new diplomatic initiative on the North. It was a meeting warmly welcomed by the SDLP, now more anxious than ever for a British-Irish initiative. John Hume met Thatcher just a few days before Haughey did, and put to her the case for withdrawing the guarantee to Unionists, and for convening a quadripartite conference under the auspices of the two governments.[7] Thatcher, whose government was reported to be thinking along more modest and pro-Unionist lines, was not persuaded, and on the eve of her meeting with Haughey, she reaffirmed that 'the future of the constitutional affairs of Northern Ireland is a matter for the people of Northern Ireland, this government and this parliament and no-one else'.[8] It was a statement like many others by British prime ministers, and was primarily intended to allay Unionist fears of a sell out on the constitutional position. On this occasion, however, it was also an expression of Thatcher's own belief in the union and a reminder to Hume and the Irish government that the British guarantee remained her basic position. Notwithstanding his views on the causes of partition or his party's demand for a British withdrawal, at his meeting with Thatcher, Haughey acknowledged that unity could only come about with the consent of a majority of the people in the North and signalled his intention to work closely with the British in seeking a way forward.[9]

END TO INTERNAL APPROACH

For the SDLP, the period following the Atkins talks was essentially one of marking time. In July, the secretary of state published a consultative document containing proposals for devolved government based on discussions at his conference with the hope that elections to a new assembly could be held by mid-1981.[10] Instead of a single, definitive proposal for government, Atkins presented several models ranging from the 1974 power-sharing model to government by committee, and invited parties' views. But since the SDLP remained convinced that only a genuine power-sharing model would win the support of its electorate, and since Unionists still rejected its demand for participation as of right in an administration, the situation remained deadlocked. As it had anticipated, the SDLP once again found an approach that began with the local parties to be a cul-de-sac, and was even more firmly convinced that only a British-Irish initiative had any chance of success.

LOCAL CONCERNS

However much the party now eschewed an internal approach to a solution, it remained conscious of the social and economic challenges that needed to be addressed in Northern Ireland. In September, as a follow-up to the submission on poverty made to the Atkins conference, the SDLP hosted a major one-day conference in Belfast on tackling poverty.[11] The conference was notable not just for the range of speakers from North and South who contributed, but also for the fact that it was a conference with no parallels by other political parties and was intended to highlight the SDLP's commitment to its social democratic principles, as well as answering the criticism that the party had lost its social conscience with the departure of Fitt and Devlin.

Another local issue that obliged the SDLP to adopt a strong line related, surprisingly, to teacher education. Education had always been an area that reflected the North's communal divide, and in June 1980 a review group, established to examine the provision of higher education, published a report on teacher education that recommended the amalgamation of the two Catholic training colleges in West Belfast, St Joseph's and St Mary's, together with their transfer to the site of Stranmillis College in South Belfast.[12] These recommendations were met with considerable opposition from the Catholic Church, as well as from political and other interests in West Belfast. Whatever about the case for its recommendations on economic and academic grounds, the committee had hit several raw nerves within the Catholic-Nationalist community. Not only were the only two higher education institutions in West Belfast to be amalgamated, they were then to be moved out of the area to a more Protestant part of the city at the site of an essentially Protestant institution. The church feared the loss of control and influence over the education of teachers for Catholic schools, while West Belfast feared the loss of jobs and the loss of institutions that contributed to local communities.

As the party representing a majority of Catholics and as a party consisting of many members of the teaching profession, the SDLP was expected to take a robust stand in opposition to the controversial recommendations. In its submission on the report, the party claimed that the proposals threatened a separate and distinct Catholic input to teacher education and, while agreeing the amalgamation of the two colleges, pleaded a civil rights case in defence of maintaining a clearly separate and distinct institution in West Belfast.[13] The civil rights perspective was the right to freedom of religion, and therefore to a distinctive institutional expression of that right, especially in education. This view prevailed, but only after a vigorous and very public campaign orchestrated mainly by the Catholic Church. The SDLP found itself closely allied with the church's position and, as a result, in opposition to the other Christian churches, which generally favoured the review group's recommendations. It was a campaign that inevitably traded on widespread suspicions and antagonisms towards the British government. It revealed once again the almost impossible position in which the British found themselves when trying to deal even with issues that appeared open to rational economic and educational solutions, but which ignored the equally, if not more important socio-political context. More fundamentally, the controversy also revealed the wide ramifications of the basic fault-lines in Northern Ireland society and the urgent need to address them.

PRISON PROTESTS ESCALATE

With the search for a political settlement in the doldrums, the most critical immediate issue was the continuing prison protests by PIRA and INLA prisoners in Long Kesh, now known as the Maze Prison. In October 1980, the protests escalated when seven prisoners began a hunger strike, making an already highly volatile situation even more inflamatory, as support groups outside began mobilizing public protests. Before then, the SDLP had continued its efforts to have the prison protests resolved. Earlier in the year, a party delegation together with a number of prisoners' relatives who had defied Sinn Féin's strictures about dealing with the party, met the secretary of state to urge a settlement and to warn about the possibility of a hunger strike and its likely effects.[14] Atkins' only response was to announce that special category status was to be ended for those few prisoners still in custody since before 1976 and who had retained that status, a decision guaranteed to make matters worse.[15] Soon after the hunger strikes commenced in October, the SDLP outlined its position and, in line with its previous stand, stated that 'the only punishment to which a prisoner should be subjected is the deprivation of liberty and ... government has a responsibility to safeguard the health and well-being of all prisoners, whether protestors or not'.[16] On the prisoners' refusal to wear prison-issue clothes, the party again reminded the government of the practice elsewhere of no prison garb, and claimed that there was no good reason why the same should not be allowed in Northern Ireland.

As the prison crisis intensified, historic dividing lines became ever more sharply drawn. Nationalists rallied against the government and for the prisoners, while Unionists rallied in support of the government and very much against the prisoners. Churches positioned themselves at almost polar opposites on the issue; trade unions, student movements, political parties, the Gaelic Athletic Association (GAA) and many other organizations found themselves increasingly under pressure as motions on the prison protest made their way onto their respective agendas.

Within the Nationalist community, sharp divisions also existed as to how a resolution to the crisis should be sought. The SDLP realized the huge emotional effect of a hunger strike by prisoners who had been, however misguidedly, motivated by the cause of Irish unity to enage in paramilitary activity, hence its anxiety to see the strike and the whole prison protest resolved as soon as possible. Nevertheless, as during the earlier phase of the protests and despite its efforts, public and private, on behalf of the prisoners, the party found itself accused of not doing enough. Demonstrators picketed John Hume's home in Derry and, during the annual conference in November, a large and very vocal protest demanded that the party do more. At the conference, an emergency motion called on the British government to work for a resolution and condemned its unwillingness to act. Speakers in the debate attacked the government for being inept and for allowing itself to become prisoners of the prisoners' demands. However, the party did not commit itself to seeking a return to 'political status', the core prisoner demand, nor did the conference call on the party to become formally linked to the protest movement, as the latter had demanded.

Following the conference, and as pressure on the British government intensified, Hume became closely involved in seeking a resolution. At a meeting with

Atkins in early December, he referred to the ruling in May by the ECHR that while 'political status' was not justified, the British government was obliged to have regard for the health and wellbeing of the prisoners.[17] On the basis of this obligation, the commission's judgment had criticized the British for not finding ways to defuse the dirty protest and so avoid the health risk faced by the prisoners. Hume held several more meetings with Atkins, at all of which he pressed the commission's judgment as a basis on which a resolution could be found. At first, the government seemed to respond positively and, when Atkins addressed the hunger strike issue in parliament in mid-December, he quoted liberally from the commission's judgment in order to set out the rights and privileges available to prisoners.[18] A compromise was then agreed that would allow prisoners to wear their own clothes during recreation periods and to have greater freedom of association. Three days later, on 18 December, the prisoners called off their strike.[19]

Although the hunger strikes ended, the dirty protests did not, since many of the prisoners believed that they had been deceived. Nevertheless, for a few days, people across Ireland, North and South, were able to relax and enjoy Christmas believing the whole protest would soon end. Tragically, however, there was to be but a short intermission before the prisoners' determination to win all of the concessions they had demanded led to the strike being renewed and to a drama that would propel the whole of Ireland and Britain into a period of unremitting tension and division.[20]

REINFORCING BRITISH-IRISH CONTEXT

Despite the pressures arising from the hunger strike, the SDLP maintained a focus on the political challenge. At the 1980 annual conference, a policy document, *Strategy for peace*, was adopted. It restated forcibly the case for a constitutional conference to be convened by the British and Irish governments in which 'the necessary negotiations for a New Ireland and for new forms of Anglo-Irish cooperation can take place'.[21] The document also made clear that partnership between Unionists and Nationalists still remained the only possible basis on which to achieve a consensus in the North. But, noting the continued refusal by Unionists to 'even consider a partnership administration', the document again questioned whether 'any agreement can ever be reached within the context of Northern Ireland as it is presently structured' and so again urged the case for a British-Irish framework as the way forward. The party was already developing its thinking as to the shape a formal British-Irish arrangement might take. A discussion paper, *Anglo-Irish relations*, had been prepared by the party's vice-chair, Seán Farren, in which a variety of possibilities were outlined, drawing on examples such as the Nordic and Benelux unions, and arguing that the historic links been the two states demanded something similar.[22]

The 1980 conference was also the first to be addressed by John Hume as party leader. In his main address, Hume elaborated on why the SDLP believed that it was now essential that the initiative be taken over the heads of Unionists. He claimed that it would be

> unrealistic to expect Unionists, habituated over generations to confident supremacy, to surrender their advantage spontaneously ... they will not, and probably cannot, make the leap of imagination alone (and surrender the constitutional guarantee given by Britain). They must be helped to do so by the British government, and only they can do it. In asking them to withdraw their guarantee to Unionists, the SDLP is not demanding any advantage ... We are asking that, for the first time, everyone stand on their own feet, which is surely the only basis on which there can be a true settlement.[23]

Answering critics who argued that withdrawal of the guarantee suggested that Unionists would be coerced into a united Ireland, Hume argued that, on the contrary, it would oblige Unionists

> to consider their real options ... and to work out what future relationships they want to have with the rest of Ireland, not on the basis of injustice and supremacy, but of viable political and economic considerations.[24]

TOTALITY OF RELATIONS

Surprisingly, given the general climate of the time, within a month of the conference, significant steps towards new British-Irish initiatives were taken when Margaret Thatcher and several of her ministers met Haughey and senior members of his cabinet in Dublin.[25] The communiqué from their meeting spoke about devoting their next meeting ... to special consideration of the totality of relationships within these islands. For this purpose, they had commissioned joint studies including institutional structures, citizenship rights, security matters, economic co-operation and measures to encourage mutual respect.[26]

This was the first time that the British and Irish governments had agreed to examine relationships between the two states in such depth, and the prospect of doing so marked a significant shift in the approach of each towards the other. The meeting was hailed in Irish circles as the beginning of a new era in British-Irish relationships. Haughey described the meeting as 'historic', and for the SDLP, John Hume praised the outcome as providing the framework within which a solution to the North's crisis could be found, adding that 'the Taoiseach had done a good day's work'.[27]

The British did not see things quite in such dramatic terms, however, and controversy over the scope of what was intended soon developed. For the British, the talks had been an opportunity to improve relationships between both governments, and they understood the studies to focus exclusively on questions of socio-economic and cultural cooperation. In contrast, Irish foreign affairs minister Brian Lenihan, interpreted the phrase 'totality of relations' to mean that 'everything was on the table ... (and) that as far as new institutional matters are concerned, we regard them as new political ways of resolving the problem that exists between North and South, within Northern Ireland and between the two parts of Ireland and Britain'.[28] In response, the British asserted that the North's constitutional position had not been discussed. Two months later, Lenihan compounded the controversy when he argued that the new inter-governmental approach would pave the way towards Irish unity within ten years.[29] As far as the British were concerned, Lenihan had overstepped the mark, but his claims served to whet Nationalist appetites, while doing nothing to allay the perennial fears of Unionists.

Unionist reaction was to express outrage, claiming that the worst was about to happen. Paisley launched himself into a series of protest rallies across the North, evocatively called the 'Carson Trail', in memory of Edward Carson the early twentieth-century Unionist leader. At these rallies, Paisley and other Unionist leaders denounced Britain's alleged betrayal of Ulster, warned against threats from the South and pledged to resist any attempts to hand the North over to its enemies.

While the SDLP had welcomed the outcome of the British-Irish meeting in Dublin, the party did not share Lenihan's exaggerated expectations. At a meeting between an SDLP delegation and the Irish government, Hume said that he believed the dispute over the proposed studies was largely irrelevant and claimed that 'when the proposals emerge at the end of the studies, people may not be as frightened as they sound today about constitutional proposals, particularly if there are adequate guarantees and safeguards for the interests of all sections of the community'.[30] However, Hume did expect that the studies would begin to address what he termed 'three frameworks of conflict: within the North, between North and South, and between Ireland and Britain'.[31] In other words, he wanted to see the three sets of relationships that the SDLP had identified as the basis to a solution in the North being addressed together. So, however minimalist or maximalist the interpretations of what the joint studies were intended to achieve, Hume and the SDLP saw in them an opportunity to advance the only agenda that they believed could ultimately lead to a solution, not something on which to build unrealistic expectations.

HUNGER STRIKES CRISIS

More immediate threats loomed as the respite from the hunger strikes evaporated and reports indicated that many of the prisoners regarded the ending of the strike as precipitate and felt they had been tricked into terminating their protest. On New Year's Day, the prison's Catholic chaplain, Fr Denis Faul, warned of the possibility of a renewed hunger strike and, at the beginning of February, protesting prisoners announced that a second strike would commence on 1 March, the fifth anniversary of the ending of special category status. Despite appeals from leading churchmen like Bishop Edward Daly,[32] who had been among those who had worked to find a resolution to the first hunger strike, PIRA prisoner Bobby Sands refused food, and he was followed over the next seven months by several others.[33] Their hunger strikes were to dominate the North's politics over this period, dividing its communities as they had never been divided before and eventually marking a watershed on the political landscape of a totally unforeseen kind.

The second hunger strikes faced the SDLP with a similar but more dangerous dilemma than the first. Initially, these strikes appeared as if they might rebound on the PIRA and on Sinn Féin, but the longer they continued, it was the SDLP that was to experience greater pressure. Hume again pressed the ECHR decision as the basis for a resolution, and argued that the commission be invited to undertake an investigation into conditions at the Maze.[34] His pleas went unheeded, as did those of many others, churchmen and politicians. Sands' hunger strike lasted sixty-six days and he died on 5 May.

ANOTHER FERMANAGH-SOUTH TYRONE DILEMMA

Before he died, Sands made a totally unexpected intervention into politics. Within a week of the hunger strikes recommencing, the Fermanagh-South Tyrone MP, Frank Maguire, died, and whether or not to contest the subsequent by-election became a critical question for the SDLP. Once more, it was a case of who else might be contending for the Nationalist vote, and the party immediately set about assessing opinion in the constituency. At first, the view seemed to be in favour of contesting, with the result that the party executive decided to hold a selection convention. Opposition to this decision quickly emerged, particularly within Fermanagh-South Tyrone and the neighbouring Mid-Ulster constituency. Nevertheless, after a highly charged discussion over the wisdom of contesting the election, the selection convention voted 59–42 in favour, with 27 abstentions, and then unanimously chose Austin Currie as the party's candidate.[35]

Meantime, it emerged that Noel Maguire, a brother of Frank's, would also be nominated. Nationalists would now be faced with a choice between two candidates, almost guaranteeing victory to the only declared Unionist candidate, Harry West. Despite considerable unease within its ranks, the party might well have stood by Currie's nomination had not Sinn Féin decided to nominate Bobby Sands as a candidate, dramatically facing the SDLP and Maguire with an unenviable decision.[36] Feelings in the constituency were divided, with a considerable number of members in favour of not contesting the seat. Indeed, one of Sands' assentors was Tommy Murray, a local SDLP councillor.[37] In the new circumstances, the party's executive voted not to ratify Currie's nomination, once again reversing the decision to contest. Explaining the reversal, Séamus Mallon commented that

> It was a very difficult decision. There were hours and hours of deliberation. As a political party, we have a right and indeed a duty, to take into

consideration the view of people who live in that area and are party supporters in that area. It was for that reason and for no other reason that the decision was taken.[38]

This time, Currie did not have himself nominated as an independent candidate, though he would have attempted to do so if Maguire's nomination had stood.[39] At the last moment, Maguire withdrew, leaving the election a straight contest between Sands and West. Sands won, but the SDLP was seen to have lost some of its credibility, despite the fact that, in the emotional context of the election, the party would almost certainly have received a low vote, as well as being accused of handing victory to West over a hunger strike prisoner in a 'British' jail, with the inherent threat to members that this could have meant. The advice that the party leadership gave to its supporters was not to support candidates who associated with organizations that used violence. Since Sands had been convicted in his capacity as a member of the PIRA, a vote for him meant ignoring that advice. That is precisely what a large number of SDLP supporters did, since without their votes it is clear that he would not have been elected.

Criticism of the decision was widespread, both from within the party itself and from without. Founder members Ivan Cooper and Paddy O'Hanlon were among the prominent party voices to denounce the decision. Cooper attacked the party's decision as 'scandalous', saying

> How anyone subscribing to the policy of the SDLP could justify a situation where the anti-Unionist population of Fermanagh and South Tyrone are left with a choice between two men who are anathema to everything we stand for is beyond me.[40]

O'Hanlon urged SDLP supporters to add Austin Currie's name to their ballot papers, but this advice was never likely to be followed. An editorial in the *Irish Times* offered perhaps what was the mildest criticism, saying of the party that 'they will be missed, and some will see their non-appearance as a defection'.[41]

Answering the charge that the SDLP had betrayed its own principles, Hume argued that

> The SDLP would have been accused of lifting the siege of pressure on the British. That would have reverberated through other elections ... Politics is not only about principles but about the ability to put principles into practice. The second is as important as the first.[42]

In effect, Hume was saying that it had been a choice between two evils and that the party had chosen the one it judged least likely to do it serious damage. Indeed, in the party's consideration about contesting the Fermanagh-South Tyrone by-election was the likely effect of its decision on the forthcoming district elections in May. The decision not to contest was seen as prudent, since blame for the loss of the seat would, almost inevitably, have had negative repercussions for the party, especially in Fermanagh and Tyrone. Nevertheless, a meeting of the party's central council in late April was an occasion of very heated exchanges on the issue, with a strong sense emerging from the meeting that, in future, all seats would be contested.[43]

Bobby Sands' death, two weeks before the district council elections and the massive turnout at his funeral, suggested that constitutional politics might well be swept aside in the emotional maelstrom that the hunger strikes had produced. Not surprisingly, the party did suffer a loss of some council seats, though its overall vote increased; a result that retrospectively seemed to vindicate the Fermanagh-South Tyrone decision.[44] Significantly, the party gained an overall majority on two councils – Derry, and Newry and Mourne, Nationalist areas where the by-election drama might have been expected to have caused some damage. Hume claimed that despite some losses, the result had been a considerable triumph for the SDLP, given the circumstances in which the elections had been held. Hume also stated that the party would continue to seek a solution to the prison crisis and pointed to the several prominent international figures, among them, Senator Edward Kennedy and Dr Robert Runcie, archbishop of Canterbury, 'who had taken up positions on the H-Block (the hunger strikes) issue similar to our own'.[45] Unfortunately, neither his voice, nor the voice of anyone else was being heeded by those who had the capacity to end the hungers strikes. Thatcher's attitude was essentially one of contempt for the hunger strikers. In her view, they had committed crimes, had been convicted, and had deliberately chosen to go on hunger strike. Therefore, they deserved no special consideration. It was an attitude that displayed little appreciation of the emotions stirred by the strikes, or of the possible consequences.

DIALOGUES OF THE DEAF

Following Sands' death, Hume had a very fraught meeting with Thatcher, at which he argued the folly of pursuing a prison policy that was only driving more and more Nationalists to support the provisional movement.[46] Hume's arguments made no impression and, as the British continued their 'no concessions' approach, his predictions were soon to be realized. Although delayed for some months, the by-election to fill the vacancy caused by Sands' death was called for late August. Once again, the party centrally committed itself to contesting the election, only to find that this time the selection convention voted 48–44 not to do so. Despite the narrowness of the vote and the views expressed at the recent central council meeting, the party's executive endorsed the decision.[47] So, for the third time in two years, the party removed itself to the sidelines of an election in the same constituency.

On this occasion, criticism was more acute and more strongly expressed, with many again accusing the SDLP of having abandoned its own principles. Ironically, the day before the selection convention met, Séamus Mallon spoke at a summer school in Carlow about the grave danger the North faced from paramilitaries like the PIRA, whom he accused 'of trying to assume political leadership of the Northern Ireland people and to destabilize politics in the South'.[48] Not surprisingly, the party's decision not to contest was seen as making it easier for the PIRA to do just that, and, this time, in its editorial two days later, the *Irish Times* severely criticized the party for ignoring the dangers its deputy leader had pointed out, arguing that 'the field is now abandoned to the PIRA'.[49]

The emotional tide among Nationalists was even stronger in August than it had been in May and had the selection convention agreed to contest, there would probably have been considerable difficulty persuading anyone to become the candidate.[50] Furthermore, with the British still as unyielding as ever, the SDLP, along with most of Nationalist Ireland, laid the blame for the crisis at the door of the government. As party chair, Seán Farren stated that

> Current fears about the possible growth of support for extremists are essentially the result of British failure to understand the implications of its stand on the hunger strikes. Its failure on this issue ranks with the British government's failure to support the power-sharing executive in 1974.[51]

Owen Carron, Sands' election agent, was chosen as the 'Anti-H-Block' candidate and, by election day on 20 August, ten prisoners on hunger strike had died. Carron's main opponent was the UUP candidate Ken Maginnis, whom many thought had a strong chance of winning the seat. In the event, Carron won with an even greater majority than Sands.[52] The presence of candidates from the APNI, and the Republican Clubs who had nominated when the SDLP declined, had no effect on the outcome. The impact of Carron's victory was not just immediate, it had longer term consequences. Shortly afterwards, Sinn Féin announced that, in future, the party would contest all elections, internal Northern Ireland as well as UK contests. The provisional movement had adopted what would later be described as the 'armalite in one hand and a ballot box in the other' tactic.[53]

From March until October, the hunger strikes and the two by-elections dominated politics and, despite the pleas and the efforts to mediate, the logjam persisted. The strikes held the whole of the North transfixed with their macabre series of deaths and mass funerals. For many Nationalists, anti-British resentment intensified at what was seen as a deliberate and callous decision to allow the strikers to die. For most Unionists, the strikes were incomprehensible, while their political leaders expressed nothing but contempt for what they regarded as a needless waste of life.

It was not until the families of some strikers, encouraged by Fr Denis Faul,[54] began to allow medical intervention when their striking relatives had lapsed into a coma, that significant steps towards ending the strikes were taken. The first such intervention was in July, but from early September the number increased, and by October, family interventions or threats of intervention succeeded in persuading the remaining hunger strikers to terminate their protests. Meantime, Jim Prior replaced Atkins as secretary of state for Northern Ireland. Prior adopted a more flexible approach, and soon after taking up office, he met some of the prisoners. Within weeks, he conceded their key demand, the right to wear their own clothes at all times, and the strike ended soon afterwards. Months of tension and drama were over, but not so the repercussions from the trauma that had so deeply affected the North's communities.

MARGINALIZING THE SDLP

Despite John Hume's attempts to influence the British government, the SDLP had been effectively sidelined, with little or no influence over the second phase of hunger strikes. The party condemned the strike and the leadership of Sinn Féin for not calling it off,[55] but none of the party's leading members was able to play any significant role in helping to end it.[56] The district council election results gave the SDLP a boost in an otherwise demoralizing period, but when the strikes ended, the party found itself seriously challenged by the arrival of Sinn Féin into the electoral arena. The challenge would become real within twelve months and would gradually change the balance of political influence within the Nationalist community.

In an effort to restore morale, the party executive and constituency representatives group met for a weekend in September, in Carrigart, Co. Donegal, to reflect on the situation.[57] Given the circumstances where the communities in the North were so polarized, the meeting re-emphasized its now well-established approach, that only a new British-Irish initiative could provide the context for political progress. The party acknowledged that the decisions regarding the hunger strike by-elections were damaging, particularly not to have contested the second by-election.[58] Other issues on the agenda included the need to improve party organization and to develop a more comprehensive range of social and economic policies. There was also considerable discussion around the future of the constituency representatives group, now expanded to include leaders of councillor groups. Concern had been often expressed about the original members' mandate and infrequent attendances at its meetings by some. No radical change was decided, however, and the group continued to function as it had for the previous six years.

Added to the criticism received over the Fermanagh-South Tyrone election decisions were attempts to discredit the party following revelations that a number of leading members, including John Hume and Séamus Mallon, had met representatives of Sinn Féin.[59] The meetings had been held at the request of the SDLP to discuss the hunger strikes and how the violence might be ended. Confirming that the meetings had been held, a spokesperson for the party said that 'the SDLP was willing to talk to anyone to try to solve the serious problems of Northern Ireland ... but talking to people does not confer approval of their attitudes or methods'.[60] For Unionist leaders, this was no excuse, and UUP leader James Molyneaux denounced the SDLP as fellow-travellers of Sinn Féin and the PIRA. Furthermore, he tried, unsuccessfully, to influence members of the European Socialist group against appointing Hume as one of the group's vice-presidents.[61] The SDLP's withdrawal from the two by-elections, together with its meetings with Sinn Féin, provided Unionists with convenient excuses for maintaining their policy of non-engagement.

NEW POSSIBILITIES

When the hunger strikes ended, there was a new opportunity to focus on more fundamental political issues. The SDLP initially found Prior and his team of ministers at the NIO open to its ideas on developing the British-Irish framework. In November, arising from their joint studies, the two governments established the Anglo-Irish Intergovernmental Council, a formal mechanism under which to conduct their discussions on British-Irish relationships generally and, in particular, the results of those studies.[62] The SDLP welcomed the new council, claiming it to be 'an SDLP concept', and seeing it as a means of assisting reconciliation between Ireland's two major traditions. Hume argued that 'our long-standing policy on the way to promote agreement in Ireland has at last been adopted by the British government'.[63] At this early stage, however, the council's agenda did not touch on the major political and constitutional issues that Hume wanted to see addressed. Nevertheless, the council did have this potential and the SDLP was anxious to see it develop.

VIOLENCE OVERSHADOWS

With the hunger strikes now in the past and the PIRA still active, Hume's address at the 1981 annual conference focused on what he described as the PIRA's determination to provoke civil war, and he pressed the need for urgent political action. To many, the hunger strikes had created a climate in which conflict on a greater scale looked increasingly possible. During the strikes, sixty-four people had been killed in violent incidents, many by the PIRA, and, on the second day of the conference, the PIRA murdered Unionist politician Revd Robert Bradford MP and the caretaker of his office, Kenneth Campbell, while the MP was holding a clinic for constituents. In September, Paisley had called for the establishment of a 'Third Force' to counter PIRA terrorism.[64] Following the killings, Paisley added to the PIRA's threat, claiming that he would make Northern Ireland ungovernable in order 'to exterminate the PIRA'. Members of Paisley's so-called 'Third Force' paraded at several locations across the North, while a 'day of action' consisting of work stoppages and rallies mobilized Unionist protests against what was claimed to be a worsening security situation.[65]

Despite the killings and the continuing political impasse, Hume's address also emphasized barely perceptible positive achievements in an otherwise bleak political landscape. In particular, he highlighted his early European achievements: the £16 million released for social housing in Belfast as a result of the *Martin Report*, and the small-farm plan, worth £80 million, for which he had lobbied.[66] More significantly in Hume's view was the establishment of the Anglo-Irish Intergovernmental Council and the intention to add a parliamentary tier to bring Irish and British parliamentarians into regular contact. In effect, Hume was contrasting what could be achieved by democratic politics with the devastation and despair that followed from the terrorism of the PIRA and loyalist paramilitaries. The achievements were, as yet, few in comparison with what was required in order to achieve a settlement.

As 1981 drew to a close, the total number killed in one of the most traumatic years of the Troubles was 117. The PIRA and other republican paramilitaries were responsible for 84 of those.[67] Several of these killings had been of Protestants in border areas where the PIRA was now being accused of conducting a campaign of 'ethnic cleansing'. It was no surprise that Unionist tempers had been at boiling point and, as loyalist paramilitaries mobilized, Hume's fears of more widespread violence rather than his hopes for a brighter future seemed as if they might be realized.

Chapter 9

Parallel assemblies

If the hunger strikes dominated politics in 1981, slightly more normal politics would dominate in 1982. After some initial discussions towards the end of 1981, including a day-long conference involving leading politicians that addressed Northern Ireland's economic difficulties,[1] Prior undertook a concerted drive to achieve devolved government in the New Year. Prior was encouraged because, despite rejections from the UUP, the SDLP and the DUP were making positive noises. The establishment of the Anglo-Irish Intergovernmental Council meant that one of the SDLP's basic requirements for political progress was now being put in place, and although not yet the kind of council of Ireland it envisaged, it was a step in that direction. Consequently, the party believed that it should explore what Prior had in mind for Northern Ireland itself. Secondly, when Prior hinted that among his considerations was an executive, appointed by him rather than by an assembly, the party began to see merit in what he was proposing. Prior seemed to be thinking of an executive in which some members could be drawn from outside the assembly – a US-type of executive,[2] possibly appointed after an unsuccessful attempt by assembly members to agree a cross-community administration. Such an approach seemed likely to meet the SDLP's power-sharing requirement and such an executive might also be better able to withstand the kind of pressures that had collapsed arrangements in 1974. It was because of these possibilities that Hume welcomed Prior's proposals, and, focusing on their evolutionary potential, he commented that 'the idea is that if the assembly developed sufficient political maturity to be able to accept the terms of shared responsibility, I think at that stage the secretary of state would cede his position'.[3]

ROLLING DEVOLUTION

Politically, the first few months of 1982 saw much speculation and debate around the details of what Prior would propose. The secretary of state held several meetings with party leaders, and for a while there was a sense that progress could be made. Contributing to that optimism were a number of high-profile Lenten addresses given by leading politicians, among them John Hume. The lectures were given to representative audiences at St Anne's Cathedral, Belfast, and at the Servite priory in Benburb, Co. Tyrone. Hume's address marked a determined effort to reach out to the whole community, almost as if he wanted to allay fears that had been created by the events of 1981, including the SDLP's own decisions not to contest the Fermanagh-South Tyrone by-elections. He acknowledged that all sides to the conflict were at fault and that

> we need a new and generous vision. We need to abandon the sterile exclusivity of "ourselves alone" and need the positive encouragement of the third party, the British government, not by creating structures which underline and advertise our abnormality, but by patient public policy which commits them and us to a new Ireland forged by mutual respect and agreement.[4]

Hume went on to say that he believed that 'there are those in the Protestant community who have that wider vision', and he called on them to present proposals that would challenge 'my own tradition to meet the responsibility we have not yet measured up to, to spell out in clear and tangible terms what we mean by unity, what we mean by partnership, what we mean by reconciliation'.[5] He concluded by saying that he was hopeful, rather than optimistic, about Prior's proposals.

Given past experiences, it was almost predictable that Hume's hopes would soon be dashed. As more details emerged, opposition to what Prior was suggesting increased. James Molyneaux remained opposed to partnership devolution in principle, and since his party's executive would only discuss devolution on the basis of the convention report, he rejected Prior's proposals. Within the SDLP, and even before Hume's Lenten address, Séamus Mallon was voicing concerns when Prior admitted to a party delegation that his executive proposals had to be dropped, and that the proposed assembly would have little more than consultative powers. Mallon accused Prior of 'basing his plan on what is essentially the loyalist and Northern Ireland convention report of 1975'.[6] The SDLP then effectively lost interest in the secretary of state's initiative.

Despite the opposition, Prior persisted with his discussions and, in early April, having gained cabinet approval, he published his final proposals for what was to be called 'rolling devolution'.[7] The APNI was the only party to welcome the proposals in full. The UUP launched a barrage of attacks but, curiously, the DUP did not.[8] In a lengthy statement issued after a joint meeting of the party's executive and constituency representatives group, the SDLP spelled out the reasons for its opposition, and its decision to try to dissuade the British government from proceeding to assembly elections as Prior had proposed. The SDLP argued that Prior's proposals contained no certainty of power-sharing.[9] The proposed requirement of a 70 per cent threshold in an assembly vote before devolution could be achieved effectively gave a veto to anti-power-sharing Unionists. The SDLP was also highly critical of a second requirement that 'there must be reasonable and appropriate arrangements to take account of the interests of the minority which are acceptable to the majority'.[10] As Denis Haughey pointed out, this meant that Nationalists could only enjoy such rights as Unionists were prepared to allow them, and this was an unacceptable proposition.[11] The party also condemned the proposals because of what it regarded as the absence of anything worthwhile on all-Ireland relationships. Finally, on the issue of identity, which Prior's paper stated was 'at the heart of the problems of Northern Ireland', the party pointed out that 'there is not a single concrete proposal in the white paper based on what it conceives to be the 'heart' of the problem'.[12]

Some years later, on his own admission, Prior agreed with much of what the SDLP said, when, in his autobiography, he blamed Thatcher for having removed a section that would have provided more concrete proposals on identity and all-Ireland relationships. Prior claimed that 'she insisted that the separate chapter on Anglo-Irish relations in my draft should be scrapped, and a less positive version incorporated at the end of the chapter on the "The Two Identities in Northern Ireland"'.[13] Removing that section meant that Northern Ireland was being treated exclusively within a UK context, and that the two governments alone would address wider Anglo-Irish relations. Obviously this was not the SDLP's approach, nor was it that of Taoiseach Charles Haughey, and both urged that no attempt be made to implement the proposals pending further discussion. Even before the white paper had been published, the Taoiseach and the SDLP had jointly expressed their reservations. Following a meeting with senior members of the SDLP on 22 March, Haughey said that

> both sides considered the proposals as they were emerging were unwork-
> able … they shared the conviction that … progress should be pursued

in the present circumstances through further development of the Anglo-Irish process initiated between the Taoiseach and the British prime minister at their meeting in December 1980.[14]

These objections were ignored, and legislation was prepared and passed at Westminster to give legal effect to Prior's proposals, and it was announced that elections to a new assembly would be held in the autumn. For the SDLP, the question now was whether or not the party should contest those elections. Interest was added to the question when Sinn Féin announced that while it preferred abstention, it too would contest should the SDLP decide to do so.

SENATOR MALLON

The commonalities that were developing between the SDLP's position and that of the Irish government were seen to take a step further when, in early May, Haughey unexpectedly appointed Séamus Mallon to Seanad Éireann, the Irish senate.[15] It was an appointment that caused some ripples of opposition within the party because it seemed like an attempt to create an alliance between the SDLP and Fianna Fáil.[16] Séamus Mallon had never hidden his belief that a Fianna Fáil government was better for northern Nationalists than any alternative, a belief that made him suspect, in the eyes of Irish Labour and Fine Gael.[17] When Mallon took his seat as an independent, however, fears were allayed and his presence offered an opportunity to have SDLP views heard for the first time in the Irish parliament. A more serious issue arising from his senate appointment was Mallon's eligibility to take a seat in any new assembly should he be a successful candidate in the forthcoming election. According to the existing legislation, he would be ineligible,[18] and when this was realized, efforts were made, unsuccessfully, to have amending legislation passed at Westminster.[19] Unionists would not be slow to exploit the opportunity to unseat Mallon when it arose.

OPTIONS FOR A NEW IRELAND

In June, as part of the outreach efforts that Hume had spoken about in his Lenten addresses, the SDLP organized a one-day public conference to commemorate the bicentenary of what was called Grattan's Parliament.[20] Entitled *Options for a new Ireland*, conference speakers came from a wide variety of political and church affiliations,[21] and the conference was attended by a cross-community audience of several hundred. While it was not invited to propose any recommendations, the conference did excite much comment, not least because of its inclusive nature, and the fact that it was taking place during a period of considerable debate on Prior's proposals. For the SDLP, it was an opportunity to highlight the importance of the British-Irish context for a resolution and to call for a new dialogue between Nationalists and Unionists. In his address, Hume made no reference to Prior's proposals, but appealed instead for a real debate about the forms and structures of government that would satisfy the aspirations of the different traditions in Ireland. The overall message was not only about reconciliation within the North, but also reconciliation between North and South. The immediate political message was also clear. The party was rapidly distancing itself from any involvement in the proposed assembly, but the question remained as to whether it would contest the elections, now scheduled for October. Only major changes to Prior's proposals were likely to influence the SDLP towards participation in the assembly, but with the legislation now in place, there seemed little chance of any changes being made. However, contesting the elections to protect its mandate was another matter.

The prospects for redressing the white paper's omission of meaningful proposals on the Irish dimension were not helped by the Dublin government's criticism of Britain's decision to retake the Falkland Islands by force, following Argentina's invasion of the islands in April 1982.[22] This 'unhelpful stance' as Thatcher saw it, led to an immediate cooling of relationships with Dublin and the cessation of progress on the intergovernmental council. Thatcher emphasized the coolness, saying that 'no commitment exists for Her Majesty's government to consult the Irish government on matters affecting Northern Ireland'.[23] For the SDLP, this was a significant set-back, since the party wanted a quickening of the pace on the British-Irish front, not a reversal which could endanger the whole process.

TO STAND OR NOT

The election issue gave rise to a serious divergence of opinion within the party. Established to provide positive leadership, for the SDLP not to contest elections was anathema to many members. Such a decision ran the risk of leaving a vacuum that others could fill. However, having made its opposition to Prior's proposals so absolute, the case for even contesting seemed to many very weak indeed. The party's dilemma was a choice between contesting the elections, but playing no part in the assembly, and not contesting at all and, in either position, hoping to influence the situation from the outside. A third alternative to emerge was to contest the elections, enter the assembly to test Unionists yet again on power-sharing and, in the likely event of rejection, to then withdraw. The third option was not given much consideration, since it would lay the party open to the accusation of not giving the assembly a chance and, furthermore that its assembly members would, following their withdrawal, then be paid for doing nothing.

A joint meeting of the party executive and constituency representatives group was held in late August to decide the issue and, after nearly six hours of intense debate, the decision was to contest the election, but not to participate at all in the assembly.[24] Although there was a clear majority in favour of contesting (25–14), many leading members voted against, expecting that Prior would then cancel, or at least postpone the elections. Those opposed to contesting also argued that if the elections proceeded, the SDLP's absence would deny the outcome any legitimacy, and would force Prior to reconsider his whole project. For those in favour of contesting, it was important to maintain the party's mandate, because without a mandate, the party would lack legitimacy. Austin Currie, who voted in favour of contesting, later contended that 'it would have been better to have boycotted, for we found ourselves involved in a campaign where the electorate, naturally enough, saw little difference between ourselves and Sinn Féin, and we suffered as a result'.[25]

COUNCIL FOR A NEW IRELAND

Having decided to contest the elections, the SDLP then had to determine what message it would present to the electorate, an electorate that for the first time during the Troubles would be faced with a significant Nationalist alternative in the form of Sinn Féin. Although in its own right it was an unknown electoral force, the Fermanagh-South Tyrone experiences had shown that Sinn Féin was likely to pose a threat in several constituencies, with its simple message of abstention from the assembly, coupled with its unrealistic demand for a British withdrawal. For the SDLP, such an approach would not be sufficient. The party had to demonstrate a workable alternative to abstention, and it found this in its council for a new Ireland proposal.

As it launched its campaign, the SDLP spelled out the reasons why it would not participate in the new assembly, and that it would seek a mandate to establish what it called the Council for a New Ireland. The proposed council would consist of representatives drawn from Oireachtas Éireann and Nationalist representatives from the North committed to constitutional politics elected at the forthcoming elections. According to the manifesto, 'the council should have a limited life and have the specific task of examining the obstacles to the creation of a new Ireland and producing for the first time on behalf of the elected democratic parties of this country who believe in a new Ireland, an agreed blueprint so that a debate on real alternatives can begin within the Anglo-Irish framework'.[26] The proposal was an extension of the party's emphasis on seeking a solution that took account of the wider all-Ireland dimension.

As to the origin of the proposal, there have many claims. Within the SDLP, frequent calls had been made for a deeper understanding among constitutional Nationalists, North and South, of the issues that needed to be resolved, the barriers to their resolution and the possible answers to those issues. Hume, Currie and Mallon, among others, had often alluded to the failure of southern parties to articulate a coherent policy that went beyond blaming the British for the evils that flowed from partition. At the 1976 conference, Séamus Mallon had called on the Irish government to establish an all-Ireland forum to discuss proposals for power-sharing and the Irish dimension. In 1978, Denis Haughey had suggested a conference of all constitutional Nationalist parties to address the crisis in Northern Ireland, while the conferences in 1979 and 1980 had endorsed motions calling on constitutional Nationalist parties to devise a common approach to the North.

In the South, while there had been much discussion of the North since the Troubles had broken out, and while Irish governments had followed a broadly similar line of opposition to terrorism together with support for the SDLP's approach, there was no shared analysis among the parties, nor was there any shared understanding as to what North-South relationships should entail. Southern understandings of northern society were often poorly informed and were frequently biased. So, while prominent politicians like Garret FitzGerald and Conor Cruise O'Brien were articulating new approaches to the North, the absence of agreement on the basic principles that should inform Nationalist thinking was glaring. The *Options for a new Ireland* conference had revealed significant differences between the approaches advocated by Martin Mansergh on behalf of Fianna Fáil and by Garret FitzGerald,[27] leader of Fine Gael. Hence the SDLP's proposal for a forum that would promote informed discussion out of which a consensus could be achieved. Persuading the parties and the government in Dublin of the value of the idea would not prove to be easy.

ASSEMBLY ELECTIONS

First, however, the election had to be fought and a sceptical electorate, for whom the proposed council for a new Ireland was a vague concept, had to be convinced to support the party. In its key message, the SDLP decided to focus on the weaknesses of Prior's proposals rather than on the virtues of a council about which there was, as yet, little support. Compared with previous manifestoes, this was an essentially negative message that stressed the possibility of a return to majority (Unionist) rule, an objective that the Unionist parties made no attempt to conceal.[28] Hume highlighted the 70 per cent threshold for achieving devolution, and the fact that 'Unionist leaders have already indicated their intention of using this plan to achieve a 70 per cent vote for the various Unionist parties and on that basis seek a return to majority rule'. It was not an unreasonable possibility and Hume strongly asserted that the SDLP was 'refusing to fall into such a trap'.[29]

The SDLP nominated twenty-eight candidates and contested seats in every constituency. Compared with the convention (seventeen seats) and the 1973–4 assembly (nineteen seats), the fourteen seats won on this occasion marked the first serious decline in the party's electoral fortunes. Overall, the SDLP's vote showed a significant drop from 159,773 in 1973 to 118,891 in October 1982 and while Sinn Féin's vote of 64,191 may have accounted for some of this decline, the party's absentionist policy probably persuaded many of its supporters not to vote.[30] These results were widely interpreted as a severe setback for the SDLP and a significant boost to Sinn Féin and, by implication, an indication of more support for the PIRA's campaign within sections of the Nationalist community than had previously been estimated.[31]

Although the absence of SDLP and Sinn Féin was a blow to Prior's hopes, it did not prevent the assembly from convening and proceeding with its immediate business of establishing committees to oversee the functioning of government. Conscious that the Nationalist community was divided on

abstention, Prior made several vain appeals to the SDLP to participate, belatedly suggesting that a North-South dimension could be developed.[32] However,
the only regret expressed within the party was that the decision deprived its
assembly members of financial allowances that could have assisted a very cash-
strapped organization.[33]

PERSUADING THE SOUTH

Persuading the main southern parties to adopt and activate the SDLP's
council for a new Ireland proposal took some time. The fall of the Haughey
government in November 1982, and the re-election of Garret FitzGerald as
Taoiseach, delayed responses until the New Year. In the course of the general
election, FitzGerald indicated that his preference would be a consultative
process involving Unionist as well as Nationalist parties, with the aim of
devising 'proposals to put before the people of Northern Ireland which will
reflect our vision of the kind of Ireland in which they (Unionists) would
have a secure place'.[34] Open-minded as the proposal was, there was little or
no chance that Unionists would engage in such a process. What the SDLP
envisaged was an exclusively Nationalist forum in which constitutional
Nationalists would develop common principles on which to base future
negotiations with Unionists and the British. More helpfully, from an SDLP
perspective, Labour Party leader Dick Spring called for an all-party consensus
on the North that would address 'the problem realistically and honestly'.[35]
Initially, Fianna Fáil said nothing about the proposal, preferring to wait and
judge its feasibility.

Adding urgency to the search for an initiative that would instil some energy
into the political process was a further intensification of terrorist violence. This
was the period of the INLA's 'Droppin' Well' bombing atrocity, in which seventeen people (five civilians and twelve British soldiers) were murdered.[36] It was
also the period during which the RUC and British army were accused of initi-
ating a 'shoot-to-kill' policy directed against the PIRA and the INLA in which
several of their members would be killed in highly suspicious circumstances.[37]
Once again, security forces' tactics were seen as being directed against the
Nationalist community without any regard for the norms of proper policing
practice, let alone the human rights conventions to which the British government was pledged. It was a policy that may have brought some satisfaction to

the security forces and the Unionist community, but served only to strengthen Sinn Féin, while at the same time weakening the SDLP.

MALLON UNSEATED

Following the assembly elections, the UUP lost little time in having Mallon unseated by taking legal action to deprive him of the assembly seat he had won in Armagh on the grounds of his continuing membership of Seanad Éireann.[38] Since the SDLP was not participating in the assembly, the loss of the seat meant little in practice. What the legal case did reveal, however, was that Unionists remained unwilling to indulge the party in any way. This was hardly an approach designed to encourage a rethink by the SDLP of its attitude towards the assembly. There was also an irony to Mallon's situation because within a month of the court case, his term as a senator was ended. When the Fine Gael-led coalition took office in November, Garret FitzGerald nominated Bríd Rodgers, then SDLP general-secretary, to the Seanad. Rodgers came from a staunch Fine Gael family in Co. Donegal and Mallon's Fianna Fáil sympathies ruled him out for re-appointment by a Fine Gael Taoiseach.

A BRUISED PARTY

The annual conference in January 1983 was one of bitter reflection for the party. For many, the assembly election had been a bruising experience and party members were seeking a boost to their morale. This was not helped when, to begin with, a small number of members used the conference to announce their resignation, while Paddy Duffy claimed that the party was 'doomed to disaster'.[39] For Séamus Mallon, the party was at 'a very stark cross-roads, where either constitutional nationalism could deliver on the question of progress to Irish unity or we open the door even further to the gun'.[40] Countering this fatalistic mood, party chair, Seán Farren, pointed to the opportunities that the council for a new Ireland could offer, and called on parties in the South to 'respond positively to the ... proposal'.[41] In his leader's address, Hume claimed that the council would 'open up the possibility of transforming the debate on Anglo-Irish relations and on our sad and destructive quarrel'.[42] The council proposal was the SDLP's main hope for political progress, but it remained a gamble since, as yet, there had been no guarantee that the main southern parties would respond positively.

The first party to signal a positive response was Labour, whose fraternal delegate at the conference, Ruairí Quinn, pledged his party's support for the proposal, though he did so without first consulting his party leader, Dick Spring.[43] While it took some more weeks of discussion, Fine Gael and Fianna Fáil eventually announced their support and, on 11 March, Garret FitzGerald indicated that the New Ireland Forum (NIF), as he chose to describe the council, would meet for the first time in Dublin Castle on 30 May (pl. 15). While FitzGerald accepted the case for a Nationalist consensus, his overriding motive was that 'I had come to the conclusion that I must give priority to heading off the growth of support for the IRA in Northern Ireland.'[44] He and his foreign minister, Peter Barry, who had developed close relationships with the SDLP, were extremely anxious to bolster the party's position, to take the initiative away from Sinn Féin, and to curb the damage they saw Haughey doing with his continuing emphasis on seeking a British declaration of intent to withdraw from Northern Ireland.[45] As Barry stated, 'The SDLP has been consistently supported by the Northern Ireland minority over the last ten years and deserve all the support and encouragement we can give them'.[46] Invitations to the forum were extended to all constitutional parties on the island to be represented,[47] but, as expected, the APNI, the UUP and the DUP ignored theirs, as did Sinn Féin-the Workers Party, and so the forum was to be the exclusively Nationalist gathering proposed by the SDLP.[48]

As the forum's main proponent, the SDLP approached it with a high degree of expectation. At another weekend meeting in Donegal, the executive and constituency representatives discussed its approach and prepared several position papers outlining its positions on key issues. The papers reiterated established SDLP positions such as the principle of consent for Irish unity,[49] its critique of the British guarantee and the need for a British-Irish framework within which to develop new institutions in the North, between North and South and between Ireland and Britain.[50] The papers also underlined the necessity to enshrine internationally agreed human rights norms in both parts of Ireland, to provide guarantees for minority rights, and to remove any suggestion that the Catholic Church could exercise undue influence over legislation in the South, or in a future united Ireland.[51] A critical task for the forum, according to a later SDLP paper, was to reach a clearer understanding of unionism and of the reasons why Nationalists had not succeeded 'to convince the Unionist population of the merits of the Nationalist aspiration'.[52]

Chaired by Professor Colm Ó hEocha, president of University College, Galway, the forum opened in a blaze of publicity on 30 May 1983. In his opening address, Hume stressed that the forum was

> not a Nationalist conspiracy, neither is it a Nationalist revival mission. It is nothing less than a major effort … to understand the encounter between our own ethos and the ethos of those who live with us on this island but refuse to share it with us.[53]

Hume spoke in trenchant terms about those 'whose message is hatred, their medium is murder, their achievement division and destruction', and said that the forum had to provide the alternative message, 'reconciliation yes, destruction no, democracy yes, your fascism never'.[54] While Garret FitzGerald and Dick Spring expressed similar sentiments, the gap between these three and Fianna Fáil's Charles Haughey was significant. Once again, Haughey laid all of the blame for the northern crisis at Britain's door, said nothing about the need to re-examine the public ethos of the southern state, and referred to the need for consent only in the context of agreeing the forms and structures of a united Ireland.[55] These differences would mark much of the forum's work and, in particular, the preparation of its final report.

During the summer months, the forum proceeded in private, commissioning reports and inviting submissions from individuals, groups and the public in general. With a Westminster election in June and five extra seats to be contested, the SDLP had a strong expectation that two or three could be won. In light of recent experience, the party was again pledged to nominate candidates in all constituencies, and overtures from Sinn Féin for an electoral pact, particularly in Fermanagh-South Tyrone and Mid-Ulster were dismissed out of hand. Eddie McGrady summed up the party's attitude, saying that 'there cannot be any compromise between those who seek a peaceful and united Ireland, as in the SDLP, and those who seek a violent and divided Ireland, as in Sinn Féin'.[56]

JOHN HUME MP

The new Foyle constituency, mainly Derry city and its environs, was regarded as a certainty for John Hume, and so it proved to be. In West Belfast, however, where Gerry Fitt decided to defend the seat as an independent, Joe Hendron's chances against Gerry Adams were considerably reduced, and he failed to win, by over 6,000 votes. Hendron came second, but Fitt, having received just over 10,000 votes, had clearly deprived him of an excellent chance of winning the seat. Elsewhere, the SDLP's best chances were seen to be in South Down and in the new seat of Newry-Armagh. Eddie McGrady once again opposed Enoch Powell in South Down, but failed to take the seat by just 650 votes, while Séamus Mallon was 1,500 behind Jim Nicholson of the UUP in Newry-Armagh. Both of these seats were to become key targets for the party in future elections. In Fermanagh-South Tyrone, the party's candidate, Rosemary Flanagan, split the Nationalist vote, with the result that Owen Carron lost the seat, which was won by the UUP candidate, Ken Maginnis. Worrying for the party was the overall gap between it and Sinn Féin, which had shrunk to 4.5 per cent (17.9 against 13.4 per cent of the vote). Nevertheless, the party now had John Hume in both Westminster and in the European Parliament, and had the forum in which to influence the main parties in the South.

Hume's election was a significant boost to the party, and when he made his maiden speech at Westminster, he demonstrated the full force of the SDLP's analysis of the crisis in the North. Outlining the horrors of violence together with the social and economic ills suffered by people in his own and other constituencies, he invited the House of Commons to

> imagine 2,000 people being killed on the streets in Yorkshire, 20,000 maimed and injured, and £430 million spent on compensation for bomb damage; two new prisons built and a third under construction; the rule of law drastically distorted, with the introduction of imprisonment without trial; senior politicians and policemen murdered, and innocent civilians murdered by the security forces.[57]

He then posed the question whether such events would have been major issues in the general election, and challenged parliament to face the crisis with the urgency required if they had been happening in Yorkshire. Hume accepted that all involved – Irish, British, Unionist and Nationalist – had to re-examine traditional positions, otherwise progress towards a resolution would be impossible. It was a powerful speech and was widely acknowledged as such on all sides. Although a lone voice, Hume would now ensure that the SDLP's approach did not go unnoticed at Westminster.

FORUM DELIBERATIONS

When the forum reconvened in September, its agenda demonstrated that it intended to make a valuable contribution to the general understanding of the complexities of the northern crisis and to the search for a political way forward. Reports on the economic effects of partition, on the effects of the violence, on agriculture North and South, and on an all-island approach to energy and to transport, were pioneering studies and gave participants considerable material for discussion.[58] Central to the forum's agenda were the many public sessions at which various groups and individuals from a wide variety of backgrounds and interests made presentations of their views about the North, about North-South and British-Irish relationships as well as about economic and social matters relevant to those relationships.[59] These public sessions and the special studies on social and economic matters commissioned by the forum gave its deliberations considerable significance, and helped dissipate much of the scepticism that had surrounded its establishment.

For SDLP members, the forum brought them into an entirely new political context where they had to contend with the rivalries of southern politics, and where some of their own dispositions towards those same parties were exposed, and at times exploited. In the course of the public sessions, the SDLP's members demonstrated their unique first-hand insights into and perceptions of the issues being addressed. Among the more significant occasions on which they did so was the long-awaited and eagerly anticipated presentation by leading clergy of the Catholic Church.[60] On behalf of the SDLP, Séamus Mallon's questioning of the delegation was notable for two of the themes that he explored. The first was the delegation's view of the morality of PIRA violence, to which Bishop Edward Daly replied in unequivocal terms: 'I declare in the name of the whole episcopal conference that it is totally unjustified, immoral ... that it is totally defeating the very aims it proposes to set itself to accomplish'.[61] The response provided clear moral support for the position of all of the constitutional parties, and, in particular, for the SDLP. The second issue was the church's stand on the vexed question of divorce that was legally available in the North, but constitutionally denied in the South. Séamus Mallon asked if the delegation could 'envisage a situation where Unionists, or northern Catholics ... were asked to live in a new Ireland which diminished the availability of civil divorce as it at present applies in the North of Ireland'.[62] He received a reply that surprised those who had expected the traditional Catholic demand that divorce be prohibited by state law. Several members of the delegation insisted that there would have to be complete separation of church and state and, in the words of Bishop O'Mahony, that 'in no way would Northern Ireland Protestants lose in any way any one of their civil or religious liberties'.[63] Mallon's very direct probing of the delegation on such a sensitive issue won him considerable praise, and showed the SDLP leadership willing to openly address fears that underlay Unionist antipathy to a united Ireland.

FORUM DIVIDES

The most challenging part of the forum's work was to agree its final report. In this task, the division that had been noted at the opening session re-emerged, and focused on whether the forum should recommend particular constitutional models for a united Ireland. Fianna Fáil recommended that only one model, a unitary state, should be mentioned, but since other models, a federal/confederal arrangement and joint authority or condominium had also been discussed, the other parties argued that these be included. Hume's view was that since the forum had been more concerned with identifying the principles that should underlie any future settlement, constitutional models were unnecessary and would only prove an unhelpful distraction. Séamus Mallon also opposed setting out a variety of models, which he disparagingly termed a collection of 'dolly mixtures'.[64]

As the forum's report was being finalized, the status to be afforded the unitary state option created a deadlock that threatened the whole project. Haughey continued to insist that the unitary model be the only option, while FitzGerald, Spring and Hume insisted that the other options had to be included, if any option was mentioned. It was only the intervention of Séamus Mallon, the SDLP member seen as most likely to have influence over Haughey,[65] which helped achieve the necessary compromise. Mallon produced the formula which stated that while the parties to the forum regarded a unitary state as their preference for a united Ireland, the federal/confederal and condominium models were also options. A fourth option was also agreed, which was an invitation to propose models that had not been considered at the forum.[66] This was included at the SDLP's insistence as a signal that, in negotiations, agreement might have to be found on a model that had not as yet been developed.

In the context of the whole report, the SDLP regarded chapter 5, *Framework for a new Ireland: present realities and future requirements*, as of much greater significance than the discussion of constitutional options. This chapter spelled out the reassurances the party believed would be required if new arrangements were to be agreed between Unionists and Nationalists. Critically, they included several key principles. These were: a rejection of any form of coercion, in other words new arrangements would have to be freely negotiated and agreed by the people of the North and by the people of the South, the principle of consent; an acceptance of the validity of the Nationalist and Unionist identities, both having secure and durable, political, administrative and symbolic expression and protection; a commitment to equal rights and opportunities for all; a provision for effective guarantees protecting individual, communal and cultural rights of both Nationalists and Unionists; and acceptable security arrangements that all could identify with and support.[67] These commitments were intended to be the common basis for the main Nationalist parties in whatever negotiations would lie ahead, and indeed were to provide, fourteen years later, the main building blocks for the Good Friday Agreement.[68] Meantime, now that the forum had concluded its deliberations, the focus was on whether the British government would pay any attention to its report and, if so, how would they act upon it.

SENATOR BRÍD RODGERS

If the forum provided a platform for most of the SDLP leadership, Seanad Éireann provided Bríd Rodgers with opportunities to bring the party's messages to the attention of all of Ireland's legislators. In the Seanad, Rodgers spoke out on many issues, but one of the most important was the allegation that a 'shoot-to-kill' policy was being followed by sections of the security forces. While several police officers had been prosecuted following a number of such incidents, none was convicted and it was strongly believed that colleagues had engaged in cover-ups. One case provoked considerable outrage when, despite evidence of false statements and other forms of collusion, an RUC officer was acquitted of the unlawful killing of an unarmed civilian alleged to have been involved in paramilitary activity.[69] Not only was the police officer released, but he was also complimented by the judge for his work. Rodgers tabled a motion asking that the Seanad 'express grave concern at the implications for peace and stability in this country of the decision handed down … in the case of the shooting dead of an unarmed civilian in County Armagh'.[70] Her speech on the motion provided an opportunity to reflect the deep anger and sense of outrage felt throughout the North's Nationalist community at the manner in which the security forces were attempting to deal with the paramilitary threat.

Her remarks won cross-party sympathy and support and echoed the party's message to the forum that an exclusively military response was not the answer to what was inherently a political problem, and was only exacerbating an already dangerous situation. Instead, she called on the British government to act decisively, and for the people of Ireland, North and South, to 'stop posturing, and party politicking', to engage in dialogue, and to make the necessary compromises in order to achieve a resolution.

Chapter 10

Forum to Hillsborough

Despite the significance given to the forum's report by each of the four party leaders, the immediate outcome was not positive. The very day the report was published, two sharply contrasting emphases emerged – that expressed by Charles Haughey on behalf of Fianna Fáil, and that expressed by the leaders of the other three parties. For Haughey, the significance of the report lay in its endorsement of the unitary option as the forum's preference, and his call for a conference of the two governments to decide 'the form and constitutional structures' of a united Ireland. Haughey did not share the more flexible approach emphasized by the other three and, in particular, the emphasis John Hume placed both on the forum being willing to consider other proposals, and on the recognition afforded to the Unionist tradition in chapter 5. The goal of a Nationalist consensus had not been fully achieved. Had the parties been able to agree, it might have been better had no model been mentioned, since none of the three models was ever likely to have an immediate appeal to Unionists and, therefore, would not be acceptable to the British. Indeed, at his press conference, Hume downplayed the significance of the models, and appealed to both the British government and Unionists to enter into a new round of discussions, saying that the immediate problem was 'constructing a (negotiating) table, not defining precisely what would be on it'.[1] However, it was on these models rather than on Hume's more open-ended approach that responses to the report focused.

Despite these diffent emphases, a significant degree of agreement had been achieved. At the heart of the report was the 'principle of consent' (that any change in the status of Northern Ireland could only be achieved with the consent of a majority in the North). So, notwithstanding differences as to the models for governing a united Ireland, all parties had now accepted this principle, thus enabling FitzGerald's government to use it and the *Realities* chapter as the basis for a renewed engagement with London on how to achieve progress in the North. The next fifteen months were to prove just how effective FitzGerald would be, though in the immediate aftermath of the forum the prospects were by no means positive.

Critical to the SDLP's objectives for the forum had been the need to demonstrate that constitutional nationalism could achieve more progress towards a settlement than the PIRA's campaign of violence. In his remarks at the forum's closing session, John Hume had again attacked those who promoted violence, especially the PIRA, and those Unionists and Nationalists who refused to respect the rights and identities of others. He contrasted the courage, imagination and generosity of the report with the 'malignant big lie of those who destroy life while pretending to serve freedom, and the pusillanimous half-truths of those who cannot bring themselves to face the full dimensions of our problems'.[2] So, with most to lose, and also most to gain from the forum, the SDLP hoped that momentum would now develop towards a new initiative, this time to be jointly sponsored by the two governments.

REACTION TO FORUM

Unionist reaction to the report was, not surprisingly, uniformly hostile and dismissive. The DUP pasted 'Ulster is British' posters on prominent locations across the North and in Dublin, and, focusing on the models for a united Ireland, denounced what they predicted would be an international campaign to 'to try to force Irish unity down the throats of Ulster Unionists'.[3] The DUP immediately published a counter document, obviously prepared in advance, *The Unionist case: the Forum Report answered*.[4] Less flamboyant in tone, the UUP also dismissed the report and declared as 'bogus' the forum's remarks about the principle of consent.[5] Sinn Féin joined Unionists in dismissing the report, saying that it had 'fudged' the issue of British withdrawal.[6] British government reaction was more cautious. Secretary of State Prior said that his government would study the report and would afford time for a parliamentary debate on it, a response that the SDLP welcomed.

The report also produced considerable international interest, something that particularly pleased the SDLP. In the US, a number of leading politicians led by Senator Edward Kennedy moved a resolution in the US Senate urging 'all political parties in Northern Ireland, the British government and the Irish government, to review the findings of the forum report in the spirit in which it is offered'.[7] The vote was carried unanimously, while a similar motion in the House of Representatives was also carried unanimously.[8] An opinion poll conducted North and South showed a surprisingly high level of public knowledge about the forum in both parts of the country, as well as support for a conference on the report's proposals.[9] Welcome as these signs of support were, the British government's response would be the most crucial and, as yet, that response was not forthcoming.

HUME'S LEADERSHIP CONFIRMED

The second European parliamentary elections in June witnessed a direct confrontation between the SDLP and Sinn Féin. John Hume was again the SDLP's candidate, while Sinn Féin nominated their press officer, Danny Morrison, an indication that Gerry Adams would not be risked against Hume. Hume's manifesto again focused on European matters and avoided even mentioning the forum. In it, Hume stressed his record over the previous five years and set out his plans for the future. It was an impressive record, ranging from the *Martin Report*, to his support for lesser-used languages, to the more recent report on Northern Ireland from Danish MEP, Neils Haagerup.[10] Haagerup's report was the result of a motion which had called on the parliament to examine the situation in the North with a view to recommending how the EC might be of assistance. The report was quite political, recommending the establishment of an Anglo-Irish parliamentary body, as well as increased European assistance for social and economic development.[11] Much to the annoyance of the British government and Unionist MEPs, who viewed the report as unwarranted interference, the parliament adopted it and, in doing so, implicitly endorsed SDLP strategy.

Hume's confidence that he would defeat Sinn Féin was not misplaced. He was again elected second after Paisley with 151,399 first-preference votes, an increase of over 11,000 compared with 1979. Morrison, who had claimed that he would defeat Hume on the first count only received 91,476. The result was a significant endorsement for Hume personally, and for the SDLP in general, as well as a vindication of its work in the NIF. For Sinn Féin, the result was a serious setback, and several party members questioned the wisdom of taking part in electoral politics, saying, naively, that force was the only effective means whereby change could be achieved.

WESTMINSTER DEBATES REPORT

The Westminster debate on the NIF report took place in July and provided Hume with an important opportunity to impress his British audience with the case for comprehensive negotiations between all interests in the North. In his speech, Hume stressed the need for all sides to re-assess their attitudes, just as constitutional nationalism had done in the forum. He acknowledged that Irish nationalism had been 'sectional and exclusive and Gaelic', but was now anxious to engage with Unionists and the British government in a new search for a solution. He praised a recent UUP document, *The way forward*,[12] for its tone, saying that it was new and completely different from anything he had read from the UUP before, adding that 'if that party's leaders believe what they say when they claim that they want to accommodate the different loyalties in Ireland, I am ready to talk with them'.[13] Hume invited members of the commons to read the 'realities' chapter (of the forum's report) and, if they disagreed to spell out what *they* believed were the realities in Northern Ireland. However, if they agreed, he argued, they must accept that 'the only major proposal in the forum report is to get the governments together to create a framework and atmosphere in which the realities can be discussed to bring an end to the Irish nightmare'.[14] The Labour Party supported his call for new talks on an open agenda[15] and, speaking for the government, Prior hoped that over the next few months progress could be made, a hint that the kind of talks urged by the SDLP might soon take place.

Prior acknowledged that there were positive aspects to the report and he instanced the emphasis on respecting the Unionist identity and its openness to other views, but he was critical of its dismissal of British efforts to achieve progress and, more emphatically, he dismissed the three models saying 'it is a dangerous fallacy that the Unionist majority in Northern Ireland will agree'.[16] However, he accepted that any return to devolved government was only possible with the assent of both communities; that the 'minority' had a sense of grievance and frustration which history had created, and that the government was prepared to recognize the sense of Irish identity that many people in Northern Ireland held. He also reiterated British commitment to the majority of the people in Northern Ireland on their right to self-determination, and suggested that an Anglo-Irish parliamentary body 'could be of value' in expressing the close relationship between the UK and the Republic. Such sentiments paralleled aspects of the forum report and indicated a willingness to explore new ways forward. In a further significant statement, Prior confirmed that the Irish government had the right to speak on behalf of northern Nationalists.[17] The Irish government welcomed Prior's approach[18] and, notwithstanding Unionist dismissal of the forum report, the scene seemed set for a fresh round of negotiations with an Irish-British summit likely later in the autumn. In a move seen as a signal from Thatcher that she might not move quite so quickly, Prior was replaced by Douglas Hurd in early September. Hurd had no record of any particular interest in Northern Ireland and was viewed as likely to be quite sympathetic to the Unionist parties.

PRESSURE FOR INITIATIVE

Throughout the summer of 1984, Hume used every opportunity afforded him to stress the need for a comprehensive agenda and for the British government to 'open their minds and to rethink and see that everybody's views are taken into account in an approach to a settlement, but nobody's views shall be over-riding'.[19] At the same time, pressure also mounted on the SDLP to take its seats in the assembly and to acknowledge that considerable reform had already been achieved in addressing grievances regarding employment, identity and policing. A meeting of the party's central council in September was addressed by a former civil rights activist and renowned human rights academic, Kevin Boyle, who pointed to such reforms and advised the SDLP to reconcile itself to an 'internal solution',[20] while an opinion poll indicated that a majority of Catholics believed the party should enter the assembly.[21] However, both the Irish government and the SDLP were convinced that a wider basis for a settlement was essential, and that the assembly was an irrelevance. The Irish government was also convinced that the British and, in particular, Mrs Thatcher, were now approaching the Northern Ireland problem with a new seriousness, and that the forthcoming summit would have a positive outcome.[22] Indeed, with contacts between the two governments intensifying since the early summer, the Taoiseach and his colleagues had every reason to expect a positive outcome. It would turn out to be a false expectation.

BRIGHTON BOMBING

In October, the PIRA exploded a bomb at the hotel in Brighton where the British Conservative Party was holding its annual conference, killing five people and seriously injuring many more. Margaret Thatcher narrowly missed being caught in the blast. At once, the mood in Britain became decidedly hostile to any major political initiative and, instead, the focus shifted back to security. Thatcher dismissed the prospect of an initiative, saying that 'if there were any sudden quick initiatives that would be equally acceptable to both parts of the community, they would already have been taken'.[23] Nor did Hurd's conference address suggest any imminent development. Instead, he made yet another appeal to the SDLP to enter the assembly, and, while he described the forum report as 'a sincere attempt by constitutional Nationalists in both parts of Ireland to address the problem', he too gave no indication that a fresh initiative was being prepared.[24] His most positive points, from an SDLP perspective, were to repeat Prior's acknowledgment that many in Northern Ireland had a strong affinity with the South and, secondly, that he would continue to work within the Anglo-Irish Intergovernmental Council to strengthen relationships with the South.

'OUT, OUT, OUT'

With no shortage of ideas and advice as to what might be done, there was considerable media speculation throughout the early autumn of 1984 on the possibility that the Thatcher-FitzGerald summit meeting in mid-November would herald a new initiative, despite what Hurd and Thatcher herself had been saying in the wake of the Brighton bombing. Within the SDLP, Hume expected 'either the beginning of a new process or a considerable development of the Anglo-Irish process initiated by Charles Haughey'.[25] He was not expecting an immediate move towards all-party talks, but rather, at government level, 'agreement on a common set of realities about the situation in the North which would form the agenda for an all-party conference'.[26] The talks with London had begun on the basis of the forum's three models which, not surprisingly, London had rejected.[27] Nonetheless, the British did seem to be moving towards accepting that the Irish government should have a special role in the affairs of Northern Ireland,[28] but then drew back from this proposal after the Brighton bombing, and emphasized security focused cooperation. Not surprisingly, the Irish government would not commit to increased security cooperation without a significant political *quid pro quo*,[29] and continued to press for 'shared decision-making' on the North. Thatcher rejected this suggestion, offering instead a joint security commission, in turn rejected by FitzGerald. With no compromise in sight, the November summit was a disaster for the Irish government, a huge disappointment for the SDLP, and a severe setback for all who had expected significant progress following the forum.

The summit was characterized by one word used three times by Margaret Thatcher at her press conference. When questioned about the forum's models for governing a united Ireland, she said that each one was 'out', giving rise to the headline 'out, out, out'.[30] While the prime minister did not dismiss the whole forum report, her blunt rejection of the three models was interpreted as if she had and, indeed, an indication that she was not considering any significant initiative. At his press conference in Belfast a day after the summit, Hurd added to the Irish government's disappointment and frustration by rejecting any decision-making role for the Irish government in Northern Ireland's affairs, saying that 'joint authority is really not workable in practice nor acceptable in principle here'.[31] FitzGerald's own account of the summit and its aftermath reveals the extent of his frustration and annoyance that so many months of negotiation had been brought to nought by Thatcher and Hurd's negative approaches.[32]

Within the SDLP, the disappointment was made more acute by the triumphant consolation that Unionists took from the prime minister's words. Party members were outraged and Pascal O'Hare, a Belfast councillor and a forum delegate, said that FitzGerald had been humiliated by Britain, and called on the Irish government to 'stop spending £100 million of taxpayers' money on their security forces along the Border, propping up Britain, and playing into England's hands'.[33] In an uneasy television discussion with Ian Paisley, Séamus Mallon listened as Paisley triumphantly dismissed the forum realities as 'Nationalist realities' unacceptable to Unionists and then, mockingly, invited the SDLP to enter the assembly.[34] Hume referred to Thatcher's comments at her press conference as 'simply vindictive and deeply offensive',[35] adding later that 'not for the first time, the intransigence and extremism of Mrs Thatcher has fuelled the anger and bitterness upon which violence in Ireland is fed.'[36]

REBUILDING RELATIONSHIPS

For the SDLP, it seemed that its efforts at the forum to establish a new basis for negotiations with the British and Unionists had been in vain. Despite the anger and disappointment, however, Hume realized that a way forward required building positive relationships with both, otherwise the situation would deteriorate to the advantage of those who claimed that democratic politics could solve nothing. Over the next few months that challenge would be spear-headed by the Irish government, which lost no time in emphasizing that it sought 'the transformation of the political, security and judicial systems in Northern Ireland', and that its objective was to achieve agreement on this agenda.[37] That determination led to one of the most intense diplomatic initiatives of the period, during which every effort possible was made to persuade leading figures in the British establishment of the urgent need for the government to revise its position.[38] With the assistance of his department officials, FitzGerald sought to engage the interest of influential government backbenchers in a new initiative, central to which would be the principle of consent, and recognition by the Irish government of the legitimacy of the Unionist tradition and the benefits that would flow from a new British-Irish relationship in addressing the North's crisis.

UNIONIST APPROACHES

Meantime, the SDLP was being urged to enter talks with the other parties. To appeals from the secretary of state were added invitations to join in talks from the UUP leader James Molyneaux, then Paisley, and then APNI leader John Cushnahan. Knowing that it would have to eventually engage with these parties, the SDLP did not formally reject their invitations, but was reluctant to engage in talks with parties that had so contemptuously dismissed the forum report, and had declared themselves opposed to any involvement by the Irish government in the affairs of Northern Ireland. A joint meeting of the party's executive and constituency representatives in early December ruled out inter-party talks that would not include the forum report on the agenda.[39] Instead, the party drew up proposals for a 'permanent all-Ireland commission on North-South affairs',[40] to be composed of public representatives from both North and South to advise on all-island matters. The proposals never became a matter for serious discussion at the time and were essentially a signal of where the SDLP's focus lay, and a reaction to the Unionist refusal to consider any North-South dimension. However, the proposals did anticipate ideas that would be developed in negotiating North-South arrangements following the Good Friday Agreement.

With all parties expressing their anxiety for talks but none actually talking, the gaps between them remained as wide as ever. Tragically, the killing and bombing reinforced those gaps. By the year's end, seventy-two people had been killed by violence, forty-five of them by the PIRA. The necessity to ensure that constitutional politics could prevail was as urgent as ever. Realizing this, the two governments resumed their negotiations in the New Year; John Hume met with Margaret Thatcher; and the SDLP held its fourteenth annual conference, having eventually stated that it was prepared to meet the DUP.[41] At his meeting with Thatcher, Hume argued that inter-party talks on their own would not solve the problems of Northern Ireland, and underlined once again the need for a joint British-Irish approach. According to Paul Routledge, Hume was assured that Thatcher 'was committed to doing something about the Northern Ireland problem within the parameters of the Chequers' communiqué', which had been issued following the November summit.[42] Then, on the eve of the SDLP's annual conference, Hurd hinted that the South might be given a formal consultative role in the North's affairs, saying that 'some greater recognition of the interest of the Irish government in the affairs of the province' could be granted.[43] The SDLP began to hope again that its key objective since the forum might be realized.

INTERNAL SETTLEMENT RULED OUT

Anticipatitng the approaches of the other parties in any talks, party chair Seán Farren made it clear at the annual conference in January that the SDLP had ruled out an internal settlement, saying that the SDLP party sought instead

> to build upon the New Ireland Forum by strengthening the role which democratic nationalism must play in reaching an agreed accommodation with our Unionist neighbours and in developing a framework for friendly and co-operative Anglo-Irish relationships.[44]

Commenting on an invitation from the UUP to enter into discussion with the SDLP,[45] Hume expressed the SDLP's willingness to enter into talks with other parties, but added that 'we are obliged to ask whether the talks now offered are based on a change of heart or are merely for short-term advantage'. Citing recent developments – Unionists' post-Chequers triumphalism, and attempts to have Derry city council divided in two – one council for the predominantly Protestant east bank of the Foyle, the other for the predominantly Catholic west bank – Hume asked whether Unionists were prepared to recognize and respect the Nationalist tradition and, if not, questioned the sincerity of requests for inter-party talks.[46] Briefed as he had been on the renewed contacts between Dublin and London, Hume was not anxious that the SDLP should rush into talks that might have the effect of distracting from what the two governments were hoping to achieve, especially since Unionists were reacting negatively to what Hurd had said about the possibility of a new role for the Irish government. The fear was that Unionists were more concerned to prevent that role developing than they were to negotiate a new power-sharing arrangement. The SDLP focus remained, therefore, firmly on a British-Irish initiative. Calling for talks Hume again challenged the 'Irish and British governments to get together without preconditions on either side and create the framework that we need'.[47]

SHOOT-TO-KILL

At the conference, delegates addressed a number of specific issues that were on the agenda of both governments, one being the administration of justice, which had again given rise to considerable concern within the Nationalist community.[48] The use of supergrass evidence in trials of suspected paramilitaries, the strip-searching of prisoners, especially of females at Armagh prison, and continuing allegations of the so-called 'shoot-to-kill' policy, were among the abuses highlighted and condemned. Another key security demand was the disbandment of the UDR, which Séamus Mallon, as justice spokesperson, had long called for, pointing to the many terrorist-linked offences in which serving or former UDR personnel had been involved.[49]

Considering the likely aftermath of local government elections the following May, the conference also discussed how the party's councillors should behave towards any future Sinn Féin colleagues, a debate that again revealed just how deep was the Unionist-Nationalist divide. A motion from the executive recommending that no voting pacts be entered into, was hotly debated, with some delegates arguing that not having working arrangements with Sinn Féin could hand a number of councils over to the control of Unionists. Fergus McQuillan from Fermanagh represented the views of many councillors when he argued that while condemning Sinn Féin for supporting the PIRA, he would 'prefer any one of them as chairman to the "moderate" Raymond Ferguson, whose every vote is Unionist down the line'.[50] The executive motion was carried, but it was understood that, short of formal pacts with Sinn Féin, councillors were free to develop working arrangements with other parties according to local circumstances.

TALKS, BUT WITH WHOM?

With pressure continuing on the SDLP to engage with the Unionist parties, a few days after the annual conference, Hume took an initiative that had the effect of instantly reducing that pressure. In a radio discussion with Gerry Adams, he declared that rather than meeting with Sinn Féin, as Adams was urging him to do, he would prefer discussions with Sinn Féin's masters, the leadership of the PIRA. It was a move that took most people completely by surprise, and risked relationships with the Irish government. Unionists immediately threatened not to engage with the SDLP if the talks went ahead. Garret FitzGerald diplomatically stated that while he 'recognized John Hume's passionate dedication to end violence ... I do not believe he will persuade them to drop their plan to take over this island, but I recognize his courage and conviction in attempting to do so'.[51] Dick Spring argued that such talks should not take place while violence continued, while Hurd claimed that the proposed talks would only give credibility to the PIRA. However, there was strong support for the initiative from within the SDLP and the wider Nationalist community. Séamus Mallon described the proposed talks as 'courageous', and Bishop Edward Daly said that 'it was imperative that someone of his (Hume's) standing told the PIRA that there were other ways to achieve aims than a campaign of violence'.[52] The PIRA, quick to respond to Hume's request, welcomed the opportunity to put its case, saying that there was 'plenty to discuss'.[53] But, when the encounter between Hume and PIRA representatives took place at the end of February, it was a non-event. Hume was driven on a journey of several hours to an unknown location where the PIRA representatives insisted on video-recording the meeting. Hume refused, on the grounds that the recording could be edited, and at that point the encounter ended.

Meantime, the momentum for meetings with Unionist parties had dissipated, and attention returned to discussions at inter-governmental level, and the forthcoming local government elections.

Following the aborted PIRA meeting, Unionist leaders heaped scorn on the SDLP, accusing the party of 'taking a hard green line' and that it had 'now made it quite clear that they're not going to participate in any structure within Northern Ireland'.[54] Unionists suggested, therefore, that the requirement for cross-community assent be dropped from any devolution plans. This was an unwise and dangerous suggestion, since it only reinforced the SDLP's case that inter-party talks outside the framework of a British-Irish initiative would be a waste of time. Gerry Adams joined the criticism, accusing Hume of engaging in 'an empty propagandist effort to avoid meaningful dialogue with the Sinn Féin leadership'.[55] The PIRA gave its own answer with a devastating bomb-attack on the RUC station at Newry in early March, killing nine officers. In a situation crying out for meaningful dialogue, few were talking, and those who were – the two governments – were still a long way from an agreed initiative.

SINN FÉIN'S ELECTORAL CHALLENGE

The SDLP now prepared for the district council elections scheduled for May. January's annual conference had already anticipated one of the most significant aspects of these elections – how Sinn Féin would perform and, in particular, how they would perform against the SDLP. The SDLP, with 104 seats on the outgoing councils, nominated 169 candidates, only 15 per cent of whom were women. With unemployment at a record high of more than 120,000, the party concentrated its message on social and economic issues, as well as on its policy of power-sharing. It avoided the wider constitutional matters over which councils had no control, though that did not prevent such issues from influencing the elections.[56]

The results gave the SDLP 101 seats, compared to 59 for Sinn Féin, an indication that the latter's participation had not seriously damaged the SDLP; rather Sinn Féin won support from many voters who had never given their vote to the SDLP. Sinn Féin had inhibited further SDLP growth, however, and had even pushed the party back a little, an outcome that many saw as signalling a growing threat to the SDLP. As the new councils met to elect their officers, attention focused on how the SDLP would relate to Sinn Féin's councillors. In the event, the party operated the pragmatic approach advised at the annual conference. In some councils, such as Fermanagh, the SDLP supported Sinn Féin nominees, in others it accepted Sinn Féin support to have its own councillors elected to the various offices and that cross-community power-sharing be safeguarded. Unionists regarded every vote for a Sinn Féin councillor as further evidence of the SDLP's unwillingness to engage with them, notwithstanding that Unionist councillors seldom supported SDLP councillors for any senior office, and, in principle, still opposed the rotation of senior offices among the major parties. Defending the party against this criticism, Hume argued that 'we have applied the principle of proportionality consistently. This means that in those councils where we have a major say we have supported nominations from all parties and from none ... (because) once people are elected ... they should receive the same treatment as any other elected representative'.[57]

GOVERNMENTS ENGAGE

On the wider political front, British-Irish talks continued to focus on a more significant role for the Irish government in the affairs of the North, but for a while they were overshadowed by serious divisions between government and opposition in Dublin. At the Fianna Fáil Ard Fheis in April, Charles Haughey maintained his hard-line anti-British rhetoric, declaring that 'the political expedient (partition) imposed on this country sixty years ago has failed and is the basic cause of all the violence and bloodshed. Any attempt to prop up that expedient now by ad hoc palliatives will only prolong the tragedy'.[58] His remarks were intended to denigrate FitzGerald's efforts as he negotiated with Thatcher on a 'decision-making role' for the Irish government in the affairs of Northern Ireland. To Haughey, this amounted to formally recognizing partition, and he repeated his demand for fundamental constitutional change in the North, leading to the ending of partition, a demand far removed from the immediate goal of the government and the SDLP.

In view of Haughey's position, and to reduce the risk of him influencing leading members of the SDLP, FitzGerald took first Mallon[59] and later Currie[60] into his confidence; Hume had been involved from a very early stage. The key objective of the talks was to formalize how the Irish government could be involved more directly in the affairs of Northern Ireland. While the establishment of the intergovernmental council in 1981 had initiated an era of much closer relationships between both governments, it had not included a guaranteed day-to-day role in decision-making. This was what FitzGerald and his government were now determined to achieve.

Among other issues being addressed by the two governments were the establishment of an assembly and a power-sharing executive, the future of the UDR, the possibility of joint North-South courts to deal with terrorist offences,[61] the restructuring of the RUC, a bill of rights and all-island economic cooperation. In other words, this agenda was an attempt to achieve all that Sunningdale had gained, but doing so much more comprehensively and explicitly. If granted the formal role it sought, the Irish government would effectively become a stronger guarantor of the Nationalist community's rights and, together with the British government, also a guarantor of Unionist rights. The hope was that, in such a context, parties in the North would feel secure and more willing to establish a power-sharing administration. Furthermore, it was hoped that the reforms and changes sought would reduce and eventually seriously undermine support for the PIRA.

As the talks advanced, the SDLP published its own proposals for reform of the justice system.[62] *Justice in Northern Ireland* highlighted imbalances in the composition of the judiciary, predominantly Protestant and Unionist, the use of single judge courts to try terrorist-type offences, the so-called Diplock system,[63] the pronounced Britishness of court symbolism, and the high rate of acquittal of RUC members and British soldiers. The document criticized the police authority for not being robust in exercising its powers, and called for a ban on the use of plastic bullets by the security forces. The reforms proposed included: the presence on the bench of southern judges in terrorist cases; an overhaul of the police and judicial services; and the abolition of the UDR.

Negotiations between both governments continued into the early autumn and, as speculation mounted that an agreement was imminent, Hume began stressing that whatever agreement would emerge it would not be a final solution. He argued that a successful outcome would be the establishment of a new framework within which further progress could be made in talks with Unionists. But, rather than prepare for talks with the SDLP, Unionists who feared the worst began threatening strong opposition to any agreement, including withdrawing from district councils, disrupting business in parliament, and organizing work stoppages leading to the possibility of an all-out strike, as in 1974.[64] Fianna Fáil's opposition also intensified, with Haughey warning that his party would not countenance 'any departure from the sound principles set down in the New Ireland Forum ... (and that) Fianna Fáil will not accept any agreement not in accordance with the basic principles of Irish unity enshrined in the constitution'.[65]

Haughey's continuing criticism of what he understood was being negotiated might have been expected to pose difficulties for the SDLP, some of whose members were still more inclined to believe that Fianna Fáil was 'sounder' on the North and more robust in dealing with British governments, than the Fine Gael-Labour coalition. Indeed, some of Haughey's remarks were interpreted as an attempt to influence the SDLP against supporting an agreement.[66] To guard against any internal divisions, particularly at leadership level, special meetings of the SDLP's executive and constituency representatives were held in September and October to keep members informed about the negotiations, and to assure them that party policy was influencing those negotiations, especially with regard to economic, social, judicial and security force reform. Hume also publicly reminded Haughey that the negotiations were a product of the process that he and Thatcher had initiated when they had established the intergovern-mental council, and further suggested that whatever might be agreed could be developed by future Irish governments of whatever hue, including obviously a Fianna Fáil government.[67] Hume also took care to keep his key political contacts in the US informed and, together with the Irish government to ensure that an agreement would be followed by significant investment support from the US government.[68]

The party's fifteenth annual conference took place at the end of October, shortly before the two governments concluded their negotiations. Consequently, it was a more muted conference than might otherwise have been the case. The main motions rehearsed what the SDLP wanted to see as part of the imminent agreement – a greater role for the Irish government in the affairs of Northern Ireland, together with the judicial and security reforms it was demanding. Hume underlined his support for the talks, indicating that for the SDLP, the 'yardstick for measuring their outcome will be simple. Will the proposals which emerge from an agreement ... help us to make progress with the healing process ...'?[69] Séamus Mallon addressed the contention that the agreement would impede the achievement of unity, and declared that no agree-ment would deter the SDLP from expressing the aspiration for unity:

> we cannot, we will not and we must not put this aspiration on the back
> boiler. We cannot make liars of ourselves, we cannot leave it in

suspended animation for any length of time, or, like in Co. Armagh, the boys in balaclavas will come along and say 'We are the only people pursuing this course'.[70]

Mallon's words were a reminder that a goal existed ulterior to what might emerge from current negotiations. In effect, he was signalling that Haughey's fears had been noted, but also that the Taoiseach had to be conscious of Nationalist sensitivities.

ANGLO-IRISH AGREEMENT

The long-awaited Anglo-Irish Agreement was signed on 15 November at Hillsborough Castle, the residence of the secretary of state for Northern Ireland, by delegations led by Margaret Thatcher and Garret FitzGerald. It was an agreement many thought impossible, given Thatcher's blunt dismissal of the forum report a year earlier. More significantly, it was the first substantive agreement between any British and Irish governments to address the internal affairs of Northern Ireland and, once signed, it was to prove a watershed that would gradually transform relationships, not just between Britain and Ireland but, as intended, between Unionists and Nationalists in Northern Ireland.

PART III

Hopes dashed, hopes renewed (1986–1994)

Chapter 11

Slow process

Greeted with considerable satisfaction by the SDLP, the Anglo-Irish Agreement precipitated a lengthy period of protest within the Unionist community characterized by demonstrations against government ministers, mass rallies, confrontation with the security forces, resignations from parliament, and the disruption of local council business. Notwithstanding its guarantee of no constitutional change without the consent of a majority, for most Unionists, the agreement represented a betrayal that had, in the words of Peter Robinson, placed them 'on the window-ledge of the union'.[1] In what must rank as one of the most poignant Unionist statements ever in the British parliament, Harold McCusker, MP for Upper Bann, said

> I never knew what desolation felt like until I read this agreement ... Does the Prime Minister realize that, when she carries the agreement through the house, she will have ensured that I will carry to my grave with ignominy the sense of injustice that I have done to my constituents – when ... I exhorted them to put their trust in this British House of Commons.[2]

Paisley described it as 'a document of treachery and deceit',[3] his outrage heightened by the fact that Thatcher's dismissal of the NIF's proposals had been so widely welcomed as an end to Nationalist 'pipe' dreams. For her to have signed an agreement, just twelve months later, granting the Irish government a formal role in the affairs of Northern Ireland was seen as a huge betrayal. Added to this sense of betrayal was continuing PIRA violence. Members of the RUC and the UDR remained deliberate targets and, since such victims were almost invariably from the Unionist community, the sense of betrayal was intensified.[4] With no sense of irony, Sinn Féin also described the agreement as 'a disaster', saying the 'claims of progress made by the Dublin government, and which will undoubtedly be heralded by the leadership of the SDLP, are hollow claims'.[5] Charles Haughey's denunciation of the agreement was accompanied by a threat to repudiate it whenever Fianna Fáil would be returned to office.[6] To confirm its disapproval, Fianna Fáil then voted against the agreement when it was debated in the Dáil on 21 November, where it was endorsed 88–75.[7]

FIRMER FRAMEWORK

For the SDLP, the agreement meant that one of the steps essential to making a longer term settlement possible had been taken. In an international agreement, the British and Irish governments had established a firm framework within which they would now jointly manage the affairs of Northern Ireland, albeit that the British still retained sovereignty and ultimate responsibility. The agreement gave nothing to the SDLP in any direct sense, but as an intergovernmental initiative it was one Unionists could not veto. By affording the Irish government a formal consultative role on key issues affecting Northern Ireland, it formalized and strengthened its role as guarantor of the rights of the Nationalist community, and vindicated the party's claim that the two governments had to share responsibility for dealing with the North's crisis. Specifically, the Irish government now had a voice on '(i) political matters; (ii) security; (iii) legal affairs, including the administration of justice; and (iv) the promotion of cross-border co-operation'.[8] The Irish government would also become an important conduit through which the SDLP could make representations on behalf of the Nationalist community and expect expeditious and effective responses. The party organized itself to do so by establishing direct contacts between its constituency representatives, ministers and key officials in the Dublin administration who had responsibilities for northern matters.[9] The party was no longer on its own in dealing with the British government and its administration. The Irish government was a more influential ally than ever before, and, having long advocated this kind of agreement, the SDLP was anxious to reap considerable benefits for the Nationalist community. Unionists were not slow to present an excellent opportunity for the SDLP to do so.

SÉAMUS MALLON MP

Among the first acts of Unionist protest was the resignation in early December of all fifteen of their MPs to allow their electorate express opposition to the agreement in the by-elections that would follow. The SDLP regarded the by-elections as a Unionist stunt and decided that it would not contest, except where it perceived a tactical advantage. In the constituencies of Mid-Ulster, Newry-Armagh, Fermanagh-South Tyrone, and South Down, there was a considerable party vote, and in two of them, South Down and Newry-Armagh, there was a strong chance of winning the seats. The party decided that it would contest these seats. Once again, suggestions from Sinn Féin that the SDLP enter an electoral pact to nominate unity candidates in the two western constituencies were rejected. Séamus Mallon was selected to contest Newry-Armagh, Eddie McGrady South Down, Austin Currie Fermanagh-South Tyrone and Adrian Colton Mid-Ulster.[10] This concentration enabled the party to mobilize considerable effort and resources into a vigorous campaign. In Newry-Armagh, future party leader, Mark Durkan, was appointed as Séamus Mallon's campaign manager and helped to organize a campaign described by one commentator as the 'most intensive ever mounted by the party' (pl. 17).[11]

The SDLP's message to the electorate was that the British government must not concede to Unionist threats, but that it must uphold the agreement so that talks could eventually take place in a framework that guaranteed both communities' basic positions.[12] The party's hope that the results would endorse its stand in favour of the agreement was well realized. While fourteen of the fifteen Unionist MPs were returned, in Newry-Armagh the SDLP gained a significant victory, with Mallon winning the seat from Jim Nicholson of the UUP (pl. 18). Mallon's election and the strong performance of the party's other three candidates together with a decline in support for Sinn Féin were seen as strong endorsements for the party's position on the agreement and the first visible signs of the benefits from it.[13]

The results proved to be a considerable boost to party morale. A second presence at Westminster and one whose attention was not divided between responsibilities to another parliament, as John Hume's was, added considerably to the party's influence there. Mallon impressed from the outset. His maiden speech was widely praised for its eloquence, its generous tribute to his predecessor, and for the conciliatory note struck when he argued that two choices faced the people of Northern Ireland: 'we can live together in generosity and compassion or we can continue to die in bitter disharmony'. He concluded by inviting Unionist leaders to engage with the SDLP and to 'come and build with us'.[14]

Unionist anger at this early post-agreement stage was still such that virtually all energy was directed into rallies against the agreement, demonstrations against British ministers, and attempts to disrupt meetings of the new Anglo-Irish Conference – which had replaced the intergovernmental council – all represented by the large 'Belfast Says No' banner mounted across the dome of the city hall at the insistence of Unionist councillors. So, rather than the agreement providing an opportunity for fresh inter-party talks, as the SDLP had hoped, Unionists spent the following eighteen months in a sullen, withdrawn state of protest against Thatcher and her government. MPs absented themselves from parliament while councillors in Unionist-dominated councils disrupted business for long periods. More ominously, loyalist paramilitaries increased their attacks on the Nationalist community.[15]

While waiting for Unionist anger to abate, the SDLP also had to cope with the very clear break in the South's bipartisan approach to the North, signalled by Fianna Fáil's denunciation of the agreement. Haughey based his criticism on his claim that the agreement was in conflict with the Irish constitution, in particular with Article 2, which laid claim to the territory of Northern Ireland, and was, therefore, in conflict with the aspiration to unity.[16] His strong condemnation of the agreement was not far removed from the attitude adopted by Sinn Féin, whose leaders had attacked the agreement for 'stabilizing' partition. Haughey was particularly anxious that his position on the agreement be fully understood in the US, and he despatched one of his closest colleagues, Brian Lenihan, to impress on Tip O'Neill and other leading Irish-American politicians the case for rejecting the agreement. O'Neill indicated that on this matter he took his advice from John Hume and the Irish government and would, therefore, support the agreement (pl. 16).[17]

Much as the SDLP regretted Fianna Fáil's opposition to the agreement, not least because it undermined the consensus that the forum had attempted to create, it had no significant effect within the party. Councillor Pascal O'Hare, whose sympathies were close to those of Fianna Fáil, did resign, but his was the only resignation. According to O'Hare, the agreement had 'copper-fastened the guarantee to Unionists' and that the Irish government 'had welched on the sterling work which was put into the New Ireland Forum'.[18] It was a strange position to take, given the u-turn that Thatcher had taken from her 'out, out, out' comments to conceding the role for the Irish government in the affairs of the North which the agreement provided.

As a result of Haughey's stand, relationships between the SDLP and Fianna Fáil cooled for a considerable period. This was illustrated by a notable incident at the European Parliament, when a leading member of the party referred to Hume in derogatory terms as 'Lord Hume' and accused him of allowing Unionist politicians decide when Ireland would be united.[19] Ironically, on the same occasion, Fianna Fáil MEPs joined the UUP's John Taylor in opposing a motion that welcomed the agreement, but were heavily outvoted in a parliament that would soon also vote to increase financial assistance to Northern Ireland. Hume's influence was obvious in both outcomes, and the same was true when the US Senate voted to endorse the agreement.[20] There too, financial assistance would be voted to support economic and social development in the North.[21]

The SDLP's answer to Fianna Fáil as well as to the provisional movement was to point to Article 1 of the agreement, which committed the British and Irish governments:

> if in the future a majority of the people (in Northern Ireland) wish for and formally consent to the establishment of a united Ireland, they will introduce and support in their respective parliaments legislation to give effect to that wish.

Hume argued that this commitment amounted to a statement by the British government that it no longer had any interest, strategic or otherwise, in remaining in Ireland and that it was now a matter for those who believed unity to be in the country's best interests to convince those who did not. In other words, unity had to be based on the consent of a majority of the people in Northern Ireland, and, therefore, was essentially a matter for the people of Ireland to decide, and not one a British government could ever impose. Directing his argument to Sinn Féin and the PIRA, Hume further asserted that 'the text of the agreement removed any justification for the use of violence in pursuit of Irish unity'.[22] This argument provided the SDLP with the basis for a dialogue that was to develop with the leadership of Sinn Féin over the following two years and that would eventually help to pave the way for what would become known as the 'peace process'.

ADDRESSING UNIONIST OPPOSITION

Answering Unionist objections to the agreement, the SDLP pointed out that one of Unionists' longstanding demands was also explicitly addressed in Article

1; that the Irish government accept that any change in Northern Ireland's status could only be effected with the consent of a majority of the people of Northern Ireland.[23] Unionists' demands for devolved government were also provided for. In article 4, the agreement offered the opportunity for local parties to assume responsibility for some of the matters on which the Irish government had been granted consultative rights, thereby reducing the latter's role in Northern Ireland. Given these guarantees, the SDLP believed that Unionist opposition had to be firmly withstood, since only then would its leaders agree to dialogue. In a speech in the US shortly after the agreement had been signed, John Hume recognized that Unionist

> opposition may be considered understandable, even inevitable, but it is not justifiable or justified ... Unionists will have to be brought to see that, this time, they cannot defy the will of the British parliament to which they profess loyalty, as they did successfully in 1912, and in 1974. They must be brought to realize that they cannot have matters all their own way.[24]

An international agreement between two sovereign governments had to be upheld. It was a message directed primarily to the British government, whose record of standing up to Unionist threats was not a positive one, from a Nationalist perspective. But the two governments did stand firm, even though Thatcher and Secretary of State Tom King[25] were prone to the occasional gaffe that raised Nationalist suspicions. Thatcher did so when she claimed, contrary to Article 2(b) of the agreement, that her government was not obliged to consult the Irish on anything.[26] King did so with his comment that the agreement meant that the South had accepted 'partition in perpetuity'.[27]

The first sign that Unionists might be willing to engage in fresh talks came with the condition that the agreement be abolished, a demand that neither government nor the SDLP could accept, not least because it was accompanied by threats from the DUP to plunge the North into 'the most major political crisis that this province has seen in my [Peter Robinson's] lifetime'.[28] Unionists claimed that their by-election mandates were sufficient to justify the abolition of the agreement, whereas for both governments it was a treaty that each was entitled to make as being in the best interests of their relationships, and of their responsibilities for Northern Ireland. Faced, therefore, with no prospect of the agreement being abolished, Unionists intensified their protests, calling a day of action across the North in early March 1986 and, in Unionist-dominated councils, refusing to strike a district rate. The day of action shut down commerce and industry in predominantly Unionist areas, with rioting in Belfast, where loyalist gunmen attacked the RUC. Later in the month, the banning of an Apprentice Boys' parade sparked off further loyalist-led rioting, attacks on the RUC and on Nationalist homes. The assembly, which had become exclusively Unionist after the APNI withdrew in December, was dissolved in June and the summer months witnessed more street protests, riots and further attacks on the RUC, on Catholic workers (especially at Shorts aircraft factory in East Belfast), and on Nationalist homes, including Séamus Mallon's.

The PIRA added their violence to what was becoming an increasingly tense and volatile situation, murdering several more RUC and UDR personnel, as well as business people, Catholic and Protestant, whom they 'executed' because of work they were carrying out for the security forces.[29] The total number of people killed in the first seven months of 1986 was almost twice the figure for the same period the previous year; thirty-eight were killed, half of whom were security force members, the others civilians and paramilitaries. Whatever else it had brought, the agreement had not helped reduce the level of violence.

For the SDLP, these months were a period of logjam as far as the prospect for talks with Unionists were concerned. Party leaders frequently expressed their willingness to talk, but given continued Unionist insistence that the agreement be suspended while any talks took place, and the governments' rejection of that condition, a political stalemate persisted. In an address to the social studies summer school in August, Bríd Rodgers called for 'positive leadership from the ranks of unionism … a leadership that … will negotiate with Nationalists as partners in a new beginning'.[30] But a statement from UUP leader James Molyneaux the same day made it clear that talks were unlikely for a long time. In Molyneaux's view, 'even if the Anglo-Irish Agreement disappeared within the next six months, fruitful talks would not be possible because political tensions between the two communities were so high'.[31]

SDLP relationships with Unionists were not helped by the outcome to the South's June referendum seeking the removal of the constitutional prohibition on divorce.[32] The SDLP, in line with its NIF approach, had called for a 'yes' vote, only to see the government's proposal rejected when 60 per cent voted against. The result reinforced Unionist views that civil rights in a united Ireland would be restricted when they did not comply with Catholic Church teaching, and so provided another excuse for having as little as possible to do with the South. Expressing considerable disappointment with the outcome, Austin Currie commented that 'the result underscores the nature of the two states that we have in Ireland: two confessional states, one in the North and one in the South and the only way to bring about a pluralist society is to bring the two together'.[33] But that possibility appeared more remote than ever.

REFORM AGENDA

In the absence of talks, the SDLP stressed the need for both governments to vigorously pursue the reform agenda promised by the agreement. But reforms were slow to materialize. Several required legislation at Westminster; others, like those affecting the RUC and UDR, were, according to the British, dependent on the security situation. Furthermore, with the British increasingly reluctant to further antagonize Unionists, delay became inevitable. Meetings of the inter-governmental conference repeatedly addressed such issues as repeal of the Flags and Emblems Act,[34] strengthening anti-discriminatory and public order legislation, increasing the number of judges in the Diplock courts from one to three,[35] enhancing the status of the Irish language, and ensuring more Nationalists were appointed to public bodies. Bríd Rodgers complained that many of these issues were basic civil rights matters, long in need of attention, and that 'those who expressed impatience at the slow, indeed the lack of progress in removing discriminatory legislation and practice are entitled to demand that those changes ... should be brought about without further delay'.[36]

If promised reforms were slow to materialize, the SDLP began making full use of the Irish presence in the Anglo-Irish secretariat based near Belfast.[37] As they monitored the situation, the officials there became important contacts for party representatives, recording complaints about security force behaviour, the routing and conduct of contentious parades, and receiving recommendations on a wide variety of social and economic matters.[38]

Although both governments hoped that calm would soon descend on the political scene, the months passed without any sign that Unionist protests would soon end. SDLP spokespersons kept repeating the party's willingness to talk, but not if the condition remained a suspension of the agreement. Unionists, however, maintained the position that without a suspension of the agreement 'no self-respecting Unionist can or will demean himself by accepting such terms'.[39] Fianna Fáil spokespersons also continued their attacks on the agreement, with Ray McSharry TD arguing that only British withdrawal from the North, followed by a united Ireland, would bring peace and stability.[40] These remarks sparked open controversy with the SDLP, when Séamus Mallon commented angrily that Unionists were now pinning their hopes on Fianna Fáil being returned to government at the next general election in the South, because of the latter's pledge to renegotiate the agreement.[41] Later, Mallon warned that any attempt by Fianna Fáil to renegotiate or repudiate the agreement 'could result in the British government sliding out of their commitments and responsibilities'.[42] For the SDLP, the agreement was a precious building block upon which further progress could be made, and it should not be put at risk.

CONFIDENCE RENEWED

Despite the inter-party logjam and the slow progress on promised reforms, the party met in a buoyant mood for its sixteenth conference in November. The theme for the conference, 'Agreement: the Only Way', summed up the confidence of members, and the sense that the previous twelve months had been good for the party. The central motion endorsed the agreement and called

> on all parties to accept the opportunities offered by the Anglo-Irish framework and, in a spirit of mutual respect, to tackle the serious problems that still face our community (and) towards that end the SDLP renews its willingness to enter into discussions with other parties without preconditions.[43]

The conference also debated several policy documents on fair employment, the economy, the Irish language, education, violence against women, judicial reform and the treatment of prisoners – all signs of considerable vigour and a firm commitment to the party's social democratic values.

That vigour and renewed confidence were reflected in Hume's address. He touched not just on local issues but on conditions in developing countries, the evils of apartheid in South Africa and developments in the EC, as well as the urgent need for an end to violence, and for dialogue and engagement between the parties in Northern Ireland. He bitterly condemned the viciousness of the

PIRA campaign and their recent murders of business people and workers. Extolling the Anglo-Irish Agreement, he directly addressed the provisional movement's leadership on the British government's commitment to legislate for Irish unity if that was the wish of a majority, saying that 'we are being challenged by this agreement, and rightly so, to cut out the rhetoric, to stop talking about Irish unity and start working for it and to set out our strategy for achieving it'.[44] In making this point, Hume was publicly laying out the basis upon which the party would later engage in talks with Sinn Féin. Hume's message to Unionists was that the SDLP was willing 'to join with our fellow citizens in every institution of this society in order to combine our talents in building prosperity, stability and peace'.[45]

SOME UNIONISTS WILL – MAJORITY WON'T

Among Unionists, however, a mood of protest still dominated, although some, like those in the recently formed Charter Group,[46] were beginning to urge that the party negotiate a settlement with the Nationalist community, and that the agreement only be suspended for a period to allow talks take place. A British conservative MEP, Fred Catherwood, originally from Northern Ireland, made a similar proposal. In a widely publicized address in October, he argued that 'we in Northern Ireland have in these next two months an opportunity in which we can negotiate a fair and lasting settlement that will enable both the majority and minority communities to live together in peace'.[47] But most Unionists clung to a hard line. According to Peter Robinson, independence would serve Unionists better if full union with the UK was not on offer.[48] This message was reinforced when, to mark the agreement's first anniversary, Ian Paisley and leading members of the DUP presided at a rally in Belfast's Ulster Hall at which a new group, 'Ulster Resistance', was paraded as a force that was 'prepared to take direct action as and when required to defeat the Anglo-Irish Agreement'.[49] A few days later, 200,000 people attended another protest at Belfast City Hall addressed by Unionist leaders who proclaimed that they would 'never, never, never' accept the agreement. Unionist anger intensified when, two weeks later, the secretary of state announced that the British government would repeal the Flags and Emblems Act, and would reform public order and incitement to hatred legislation.[50] Such decisions were seen by Unionists as concessions to the SDLP and the Irish government, and not justifiable in themselves. Early in

1987, an anti-agreement petition to Queen Elizabeth was launched and, with over 400,000 signatures, it was eventually presented at Buckingham Palace. Molyneaux's prediction about the impossibility of inter-party talks for some time was proving only too accurate.

The first significant sign of a fracture in Unionist ranks emerged in late January 1987, when the New Ulster Political Research Group, which had close UDA associations, published a discussion document entitled *Common Sense*, containing proposals for a constitutional conference, a written constitution for Northern Ireland, and a power-sharing administration.[51] While welcomed by the SDLP as a sign of fresh thinking within unionism, mainstream Unionist politicians rejected the proposals, repeating that there could be no talks while the agreement remained in operation. A suggestion from Austin Currie that political parties meet to discuss the grave economic situation, which had over 130,000 unemployed,[52] was likewise rejected, with Paisley describing it as an invitation to engage 'in back-door, undercover deals' and that there would be no compromise on seeking the agreement's suspension.[53] Nevertheless, what *Common Sense* demonstrated was that some Unionists now realized that it was no longer sufficient to protest, and that fresh thinking was essential. This was reinforced when Thatcher herself showed no sign of compromise, saying that such agreements 'are signed between countries, not parties. The Anglo-Irish Agreement will, therefore, continue'.[54] While some Unionists reacted by making the absurd threat to establish a parallel administration for the North 'to take over the running of government affairs ... in which Ulster people can put their trust and to which they look for leadership',[55] others accepted that protests had run their course. Eventually, the two main Unionist parties announced the establishment of a taskforce to examine ways of resolving the impasse.[56] It was a start, but there was still a long road to travel before inter-party talks would be convened.

HEALING SOUTHERN DIVISION

SDLP attention during this period was focused on the South, where a general election was taking place, raising fears that if Fianna Fáil returned to office, it would repudiate, or at least try to renegotiate the agreement. These fears were allayed when, having won the election, Fianna Fáil quickly made clear that it would uphold the agreement and, rather than renegotiate, would seek to have it fully implemented. The most public early demonstration of this commitment was in the US at the St Patrick's Day reception in the White House, where, in the presence of President Reagan, John Hume, Garret FitzGerald and leading Irish-American politicians, Haughey, with no sense of irony, declared that his government would uphold the agreement and expressed appreciation for the financial support which the US was about to donate to the International Fund for Ireland.[57] A further step in implementing the agreement was the decision by British and Irish parliamentarians that an inter-parliamentary tier to the Anglo-Irish Conference would be established, as provided for under Article 12 of the agreement.[58]

Notwithstanding Haughey's acceptance of the agreement, a legacy of the poor relations between Fianna Fáil and the SDLP was his decision not to nominate any party member to the Seanad in succession to Bríd Rodgers.[59] However, now that Haughey was upholding the agreement, the party was anxious to restore relationships with Fianna Fáil, so that it could continue influencing the manner in which the agreement would be implemented. The party welcomed Foreign Minister Brian Lenihan's early indication that his government would pursue a programme within the intergovernmental conference aimed at 'accelerating the rate of progress on social reforms, economic cooperation, legal reform and the reform of the police service'.[60] High among these priorities was reform of fair employment legislation, which the Irish government, along with the SDLP, regarded as in need of significant strengthening. With these assurances, the fraught relationships of recent years were soon left in the past, and positive working relationships with the Irish government were restored.

EDDIE McGRADY MP

In May, Thatcher called a general election and the SDLP prepared for what it hoped and expected would be a contest marked by further electoral gains. The target constituencies on this occasion were South Down, where Eddie McGrady was again the candidate, and West Belfast, where Joe Hendron was also re-nominated. The expectation was that John Hume and Séamus Mallon would hold Foyle and Newry-Armagh respectively. Although the party nominated candidates for nine other constituencies, considerable effort was mobilized for the two where gains were expected. Over and above these particular contests, the election was another contest for the leadership of northern nationalism.

With the Anglo-Irish Agreement beginning at last to show results, the SDLP expected that its overall vote would increase and that the gap between it and Sinn Féin would widen.

In a lengthy manifesto, the SDLP again stressed its commitment to a comprehensive solution to Northern Ireland's crisis, and expressed satisfaction that the agreement had provided a framework for achieving that solution. The manifesto urged dialogue between all parties 'to agree on institutions that will allow this whole community to work together',[61] and indicated the SDLP's readiness to enter into such dialogue after the election.

In the elections, the party achieved three out of four of its objectives; the overall vote increased to 21 per cent, a 10 per cent lead over Sinn Féin; the Foyle and Newry-Armagh seats were held, and Eddie McGrady won South Down from Enoch Powell (pl. 19).[62] The disappointment was not winning West Belfast, where Gerry Adams held his seat, albeit with a reduced majority. SDLP accused Sinn Féin of having resorted to a massive campaign of fraudulent electoral practices to achieve its victory, practices vividly described by former PIRA activist, Brendan Hughes, in Ed Moloney's book *Voices from the grave*.[63] However, the overall result was a significant boost for the party, and was seen as further vindication of the Anglo-Irish Agreement. Unionist opposition was, however, as strong and as solid as at any time since November 1985, with over 390,000 votes cast for candidates opposed to the agreement. The challenge of finding a solution remained as great as ever, if not greater.

Chapter 12

Exploratory dialogues

The weeks preceding the 1987 general election offered some tantalizing hints that new dialogues might be possible. The Unionist task-force was preparing its report and one of its leading members, Frank Millar, spoke of the 'need to ascertain from minority representatives whether their hearts' desire is a role in the government of Northern Ireland or if they wish to defer to Dublin and to have it represent their interests and act as their custodians'.[1] Those desires could only be ascertained if some form of dialogue was to take place. Then, in May, at the instigation of a German lawyer active in the Lutheran Church and with an interest in reconciliation, Eberhard Spiecker, a weekend of discussion took place in Essen to explore ways of getting parties to the conference table.[2] Among those present were Austin Currie and Seán Farren of the SDLP, and the Revd Martin Smyth and David Trimble of the UUP. Neither Millar's suggestion nor the discussions at Essen yielded anything of substance at the time, but at least a dialogue of sorts was underway. Sinn Féin also contributed to the sense that dialogue might happen when, in its election manifesto, *Scenario for peace*, the party hinted that a way out of the violent impasse might be found, though as yet there was no suggestion that the PIRA was ready to declare a ceasefire, or even suspend its campaign, nor was there any suggestion that loyalist groups would do so. The continuing brutality of PIRA activities was evident in the targets they chose at this time. There was a fatal attack on RUC officers and a civilian at Magee College in Derry, and the assassination of a senior member of the judiciary, Lord Justice Gibson, and his wife as they drove home from Dublin. Not to be outdone, loyalist gangs planted firebombs in Dublin and Donegal and continued to kill Catholics randomly. But the PIRA also suffered its own greatest loss of life in a single action when SAS soldiers ambushed a unit about to attack Loughgall RUC station, killing all eight of its members. It was believed at the time that intelligence about the raid had come from within the PIRA itself, a possible indication that some activists, tiring of the violence, were seeking a way out.

UNIONISTS' PROPOSALS

In July, the Unionist task-force published its report, *An end to drift*, and recommended that their leaders open discussions with the British, aimed at achieving devolved government. The report did not call for an end to protests against the Anglo-Irish Agreement, which it described as 'tantamount to joint authority',[3] but, significantly, it did not recommend a suspension of the agreement before talks would commence. The SDLP's Denis Haughey claimed that the report was 'a step forward, in that Unionists must move away from their entrenched positions as we have done on our side'.[4] However, since a large question-mark hung over the extent to which the two Unionist parties accepted the task-force report, no immediate progress was possible. Neither Molyneaux nor Paisley ever formally endorsed the report, and public references to it from other leading Unionists were noticeable by their absence.[5] On several occasions during the summer of 1987, Paisley and Molyneaux did engage in 'talks about talks' with government officials but, since their condition for meetings at ministerial level remained a suspension of the agreement, the situation continued to be log-jammed.[6] Neither the government nor the SDLP was yet prepared to agree to any suspension and, eventually, Unionists were obliged to recognize this reality. In September, Molyneaux and Paisley agreed to meet the secretary of state to discuss the possibility of wider talks. This second round of 'talks about talks' continued over the next few months with no sign of any willingness to engage with the SDLP until early in the New Year, when both leaders unveiled a scheme for administrative devolution.[7] Instead of embracing the more open-ended approach recommended by the task-force, however, they chose to re-present previously unacceptable proposals. Their scheme, which recommended an assembly working through a number of committees, was almost identical to the schemes proposed at the convention and by Secretaries of State Mason, Atkins and Prior. Given their history of failure, these latest proposals attracted no interest, either from the current secretary of state, or from the SDLP.

FAIR EMPLOYMENT CONTROVERSIES

With Unionists ignoring their proposals for comprehensive talks to include the Irish government, SDLP attention increasingly focused on the social and economic issues that the Anglo-Irish Agreement had promised to address.

Among the issues on which the party was most anxious to see reform was fair employment legislation. Ensuring fairness and equity in the workplace had been a key civil rights demand and, from its inception, the SDLP had campaigned for strong anti-discriminatory legislation. The 1976 Fair Employment Act was the first significant attempt to address the issue when it imposed a statutory obligation on employers to be fair in their hiring practices. However, that act was essentially exhortatory in its approach, and did not contain any clear requirements for affirmative action by employers in order to achieve fairness in the workplace. So, when reports from the Fair Employment Agency (FEA) showed persistent disparities between the employment profiles of Catholics and Protestants, to the former's disadvantage, stronger legislation became essential. The issue figured at several of the SDLP's annual conferences and at the 1986 conference a policy document, *Equal and just opportunities for employment*, detailing proposals for changes to the 1976 Act, was adopted.[8] Following the Anglo-Irish Agreement, the party joined with the Irish government in pressurizing the British for new legislation. Critically, for this phase of the campaign and because of significant US investment in the North and the general desire to increase that investment, the issue became a major focus for Irish-American groups, a development that became a particular source of controversy for the SDLP.

That controversy arose when the SDLP clashed over tactics with the Irish-American lobbying organization, the Irish National Caucus (INC). The INC had been highlighting job discrimination against Catholics for some time, focusing on US companies with investments in Northern Ireland. The INC's aim was to pressurize those companies into adopting a set of anti-discriminatory principles called the MacBride Principles and, in doing so, the INC lobbied for the support of state and federal politicians.[9] While the SDLP accepted that most of the McBride Principles were laudable, the party did not regard them as strong enough, and declined to fully endorse them, saying that its own proposals were more far-reaching and comprehensive.[10] Furthermore, because of his active involvement in trying to attract US investment to the North, Hume feared that some of the tactics employed by the campaign could have disinvestment effects, leading to a loss of jobs in an economy suffering over 20 per cent unemployment. To the SDLP, adding to the register of unemployed seemed to be no way of resolving issues of job discrimination.

In May 1987, just before the general election, Seán MacBride, then an international human rights advocate and the person after whom the McBride

Principles were named, made a particularly strong attack on Hume. In a letter to the *Belfast Telegraph*, he alleged that Hume was content to support the *status quo* as far as employment legislation was concerned and was not serious about further reform. Hume issued a trenchant response, arguing that the SDLP had no objection to the MacBride Principles as such but, essential as fair employment legislation was, tactics that would lead to disinvestment would

> not solve the legacy of serious unemployment in areas of high unemployment of Northern Ireland ... Anything which hinders, obstructs or prevents the influx of new investment or new jobs deflects from this twin-track strategy and the victims are the unemployed.[11]

Hume believed that a two-fold approach was required: effective employment legislation and an effective investment strategy.

For not fully endorsing the MacBride Principles, the SDLP, and John Hume in particular, came under strong criticism from some Irish-American groups such as the Ancient Order of Hibernians (AOH), who were close to NORAID, and who accused him of not upholding civil rights. Notwithstanding the party's reservations about aspects of the MacBride campaign's tactics, the SDLP did not actively campaign against the principles being promoted and, gradually, the principles were endorsed by several state legislatures, mainly states with large Irish-American communities. Given the significance of US investment, actual and potential, the publicity surrounding the MacBride campaign only added to the pressure for reform mounted by the SDLP and the Irish government.

Beginning in September 1986 when the British government published a consultative paper on possible reforms, a lengthy public debate commenced that eventually culminated in new legislation being enacted in 1989.[12] The debate was lengthy and controversial, both because of vehement Unionist opposition and a British reluctance to be seen as acting precipitately in the face of that opposition. Unionists refused to accept that discrimination existed at the levels indicated by the Fair Employment Agency (FEA) and, in councils where they were in the majority, their members refused to endorse the agency's pledge to uphold fair employment practices. Nevertheless, with the case for reform overwhelming and the pressure relentless from the SDLP, the Irish government, the British Labour Party,[13] the MacBride campaign and the trade union movement, the new act came to be more far-reaching than many had originally expected. The outcome was that, over the following years, it would prove a potent instrument in addressing workplace discrimination and in eliminating the worst features of the structural imbalances that, for decades, had so adversely affected employment opportunities for Catholics.

POLICING AND JUSTICE

The other areas where the party strongly advocated reform were policing and the administration of justice, but here progress was much slower. With no sign of an end to the terrorist campaigns these were two areas the British government was very reluctant to reform. Yet, in policing, considerable disquiet focused on continuing allegations of an RUC 'shoot-to-kill' policy, while single-judge courts and the use of informer evidence in terrorist trials had raised serious questions about judicial standards. Such questions reinforced concerns raised by allegations of the miscarriage of justice, not just in Northern Ireland, but also in high-profile cases in Britain, such as those of the Birmingham Six the Guildford Four and the Maguire Seven.[14] Several of these issues and cases came to prominence in late 1986–7 and created what was to be a very testing period for the Anglo-Irish Agreement and, as a consequence, for the SDLP.

The 'shoot-to-kill' allegations had first been raised by the SDLP, among others, when six unarmed PIRA and INLA activists were killed in suspicious circum-stances at various police checkpoints in 1982.[15] Following sustained complaints by the party and the Dublin government, the allegations were subjected to a special investigation conducted first by John Stalker of the Manchester police service and, when he was replaced in controversial circumstances, by Colin Sampson of the West Yorkshire service.[16] The findings of their unpublished report revealed that sufficient evidence to prosecute police officers did exist, but no prosecutions ever took place. Despite strong representations, within and without parliament, from the SDLP, the British Labour Party and the Irish government, no action was taken against the officers suspected of acting outside the law. The issue was raised at several meetings of British and Irish ministers, but to no avail. For the British, the war against terrorism implied a degree of toler-ance for some questionable security force measures, human rights considerations and the effects on the Nationalist community notwithstanding. For the Irish government and the SDLP, however, this was a major set-back. The agreement that seemed to have promised Nationalists a strong advocate in the form of the Irish government, now appeared impotent, and the Anglo-Irish Conference seemed to be nothing more than a talking shop. Adding to the pressure on Anglo-Irish relations in early 1988 were more very questionable security force killings, namely of a young man by a British soldier at Aughnacloy, Co. Tyrone, and of three PIRA members in Gibraltar, all four unarmed.[17] The combined effect of such killings and the refusal to prosecute suspect police officers challenged the SDLP's claims that the Anglo-Irish Agreement had brought more control and accountability over security force operations. The most positive answer that the party could offer was Hume's comment that

> our protests led to the appointment of Mr Stalker. Mr Barry (Irish minister for foreign affairs) put the matter on the agenda of the Anglo-Irish Conference and Mr Lenihan (Barry's successor) kept it there. If that had not happened all this would not have come out.[18]

But, for many Nationalists, simply putting matters on the agenda and holding inquiries that led nowhere was not sufficient evidence of change.

The supergrass trials entailed prosecuting suspects charged with terrorist offences exclusively on the evidence of informers. The scale of the trials, some with as many as twenty suspects tried together, had attracted considerable criticism from their introduction in 1981. Since most of the informers were themselves former terrorists who had been granted immunity in return for their evidence, many regarded the trials as travesties of justice that brought the whole system into disrepute. SDLP annual conferences featured many motions condemning the practice and accused the RUC of using illegal means of persuading informers to give evidence. As justice spokesperson, Séamus Mallon frequently denounced such trials and demanded that the practice cease. His criticism added to other voices of concern in the Irish government, the British Labour party, lawyers and civil rights organizations, causing severe embarrassment to the British government, which appeared to be condoning a form of 'show' trials. Following the Anglo-Irish Agreement and the successful appeals by several of those convicted, supergrass trials ceased in 1986.

VIOLENCE ESCALATES

Neither aggressive security, nor extraordinary legal measures were having much effect on the terrorist campaigns, which by the closing months of 1987 were intensifying. On 1 November, the French authorities arrested the *Eksund*, a vessel containing a large consignment of weapons intended for the PIRA. The seizure revealed that earlier consignments had not been detected and that the PIRA was now equipped with a large armoury of sophisticated weapons. The indications were that the PIRA was planning a new and more vicious phase to its campaign, soon to be demonstrated in a most tragic and devastating manner. On Sunday 8 November, the PIRA perpetrated one of its most notorious attacks when it detonated a bomb close to where the Remembrance Day cere- mony at Enniskillen was to be held. The bomb killed eleven people and caused horrific injuries to sixty-three others. The attack caused a huge sense of outrage across the whole community and beyond, but particularly within the Unionist community, for whom honouring the dead of two world wars was a sacred duty. Once again, demands were made for tougher security measures, even though experience had consistently shown their ineffectiveness. It was time for bold political initiatives, but the question remained as to who would take them.

The Enniskillen bombing occurred on the same weekend as the SDLP's annual conference, at which the attack was roundly condemned. John Hume strongly denounced the PIRA, saying that it had been responsible for the intro- duction of emergency legislation, for the provision of extra prison places, for the end to jury trials and for the continuing presence of armed police and soldiers on the streets. He accused it of violating people's human rights, of inhibiting economic development and of perpetuating conditions in which discrimination and abuses occurred.[19] A few days later, Hume called on the PIRA to cease its violence, saying that if that were to happen, he believed Sinn Féin would be entitled to participate in talks. He also reiterated his call on Unionists to enter talks, saying that the sign of the parties talking would itself be an act of strength that would 'give confidence to people and reduce the despair that recent events have tended to create'.[20] Hume's suggestion that Sinn Féin should be talked to was, to say the least, not well received, especially since it was made in the wake of the Enniskillen attack, and the arrest of the *Eksund*. However, talk to Sinn Féin was precisely what the SDLP leader was about to do.

TALKING TO SINN FÉIN

If 1987 ended in the shadow of the Enniskillen tragedy, 1988 opened with attempts to breathe new life into the political process. Tentatively, Unionists began talking about the desirability of better Anglo-Irish relations. Molyneaux spoke about an agreement that would 'supersede the present one',[21] and John Taylor claimed that 'what we have to do is to get to a situation where Belfast and Dublin can begin to negotiate'.[22] When the SDLP suggested talks with Unionists, however, the party received a very frosty reply. It seemed that Unionists, taking a leaf from the SDLP's own book, now wished to by-pass the party and to engage directly with London and Dublin. Paisley dismissed the SDLP's repeated suggestion that the parties might begin by discussing social and economic issues, asserting that 'Unionists are not going to be dragged or deceived into negotiations with the SDLP or any other party by back-door methods'.[23] Whatever their tactics, Unionists did not abandon their demand that the 'dreaded' Anglo-Irish Agreement, or 'diktat' as it was frequently termed, be suspended as a condition for substantial talks. Nonetheless, the secretary of state believed that the basis existed for some progress and, in February, he invited the SDLP to talks; an invitation the party accepted. Before these talks took place, however, a more significant development occurred, as the SDLP and Sinn Féin embarked on a series of meetings that were to continue over several months.

Ever since his aborted attempt to engage with the PIRA in February 1985, Hume had become increasingly conscious that the violence had to be ended if conditions for a genuine dialogue leading to the kind of overall agreement he believed essential, were to exist. By the close of 1987, the total death-toll had reached 2,899, with many thousands more injured and millions of pounds worth of property and businesses destroyed.[24] The overall economic damage could be gauged in the North's high level of unemployment, over 120,000, and, against a backdrop of ongoing violence, new investment was almost impossible to attract. The PIRA remained the terrorist group most responsible for that violence and destruction. After more than a decade and a half, however, its campaign had reached a stalemate and, despite acquiring a huge addition to its arsenal, there was no prospect that the key objective set by the PIRA leadership, a British declaration that it would withdraw from Northern Ireland, could be achieved, either in the short or long term. Furthermore, riddled with informers, an increasing number of attacks were being intercepted by the security forces with activists killed, injured and arrested. Within the provisional movement, some individuals were reported to be acknowledging both the stalemate, and the reality that the PIRA could not win.[25] But if the PIRA had no prospect of achieving its goals, neither had the security forces any prospect of doing other than containing and, at best, reducing violence. Within the British military establishment, the view was being expressed that 'the PIRA cannot be defeated'.[26] The clear implication of both positions was that politics had to take the initiative.

If the PIRA could not achieve its goal, the reality was that its close associate, Sinn Féin, had established itself on the political scene with a core vote of approximately 10 to 12 per cent of the electorate. While the party's links with the PIRA still precluded it from direct involvement in the wider political domain, it was becoming clear that its voice could not be completely ignored. Significantly, Sinn Féin's analysis was now changing from one of total support for the PIRA's armed struggle to one that claimed violence to be only one means of achieving British withdrawal, and if a viable peaceful alternative was on offer that it should be pursued. This suggestion had been first hinted in *Scenario for peace*, a document that was otherwise very hard-line in its expression of Sinn Féin demands.[27] In November, Adams was more explicit about the violence option, saying that a military solution was no longer possible and that 'there were numerous short-term political objectives that could be achieved before the final solution of a British withdrawal allowing self-determination'.[28] Realizing the change, Hume believed that an opportunity existed whereby the violence might be brought to an end. He first indicated his willingness to meet the Sinn Féin leadership to Belfast solicitor Paddy McGrory, who passed the message on to Sinn Féin.[29] Subsequently, an intermediary for Adams, Fr Alec Reid,[30] contacted Hume to ask if some engagement between the two parties might be possible. Hume readily agreed, claiming that it was the responsibility of democratic politicians to engage in dialogue if they believed that dialogue might help to end the violence. Following several meetings with Reid, the first meeting between Hume and Adams took place early in the New Year, and was followed by a series of meetings lasting until September 1988, some of which included other members of both parties.[31] These meetings took place in the Redemptorist house on the Antrim Road in Belfast and took the form of a series of discussions based initially on papers prepared by both parties.[32]

From the beginning, this dialogue concentrated on two critical issues, the legitimate means by which Irish unity should be pursued, and whether or not Britain would facilitate or oppose unity. From the SDLP's perspective, violence in pursuit of Irish unity or, as Sinn Féin put it, British withdrawal, had no legitimacy. The SDLP argued that Nationalists had the right to determine the means by which unity would be brought about and, whatever their other differences, election results showed the overwhelming majority of Nationalists in Ireland did not support violence in pursuit of that aim.[33] Furthermore, violence was counter-productive, given that members of the community that needed to be persuaded of the merits of Irish unity were victims of many PIRA attacks, and thereby very unlikely to be persuaded. In effect, whatever the provisional movement might argue about targeting the British presence, PIRA violence had become a war on Irishmen and women of the Unionist tradition that had provoked further violence from loyalist paramilitaries, mostly against innocent Catholics. As far as British attitudes towards Irish unity were concerned, the SDLP argued its belief that the British commitment in the Anglo-Irish Agreement to facilitate unity, should that be the wish of a majority of the people of Northern Ireland, meant that they were now neutral on the issue. On that basis, the party argued that no case existed for the PIRA's campaign. Instead, it was for those who believed in Irish unity to democratically persuade those who did not, since the latter would hardly be persuaded by any other means. This was the classic SDLP message, but it was the first time the message was delivered in such a concerted manner to members of the Sinn Féin leadership.

Sinn Féin's counter-argument rested on its interpretation of Ireland's right to self-determination, and the denial of that right by the country's partition. Partition, Sinn Féin claimed, was imposed to create a Unionist dominated state that would serve British economic and military interests, and history showed that the British would not be moved except by violence. In effect, Britain was the root cause of Ireland's ills. While the SDLP accepted that Northern Ireland had been Unionist dominated, and that Nationalists and Catholics had experienced discrimination, the party rejected the argument that partition was the root cause of division. Deep-seated divisions between Unionists and Nationalists had long pre-dated partition, and it was those divisions that had caused partition and had, subsequently, sustained it.

The one point of significant agreement between Sinn Féin's analysis and that of the SDLP was in the former's statement that 'only the domiciled people of Ireland, those who live in this island can decide the future of Ireland and the government of the island'.[34] While accepting this statement, the SDLP delegates made the obvious point that the 'domiciled people of Ireland' remained profoundly divided on the island's constitutional future, and that violence could not force them into an agreed position. Furthermore, by virtue of their numbers and concentration in the North, Unionists had been, and still were in a position to frustrate Irish unity. In effect, as long as Unionists were in a majority in the North and wished to retain the British link, they held a practical veto over Irish unity, and there was nothing the British government could do to deny them that veto. For the SDLP, the problem that Sinn Féin and all Nationalists had to face was 'the presence of the Unionist people, domiciled on the island of Ireland, their numbers and their geography that requires of necessity their agreement on how we share this island'.[35] Hence the critical need was not to force, or necessarily to persuade the British to withdraw, but to achieve agreement with Unionists.

MIXED RESPONSE

Not unexpectedly, these meetings evoked considerable reaction. Before the talks, Hume had confided in only a small number of party colleagues, but when he reported on his first encounter with Adams to a meeting of the constituency representatives, reaction was extremely supportive.[36] There was some criticism of the talks when the larger teams took part.[37] Eddie McGrady was one of the more prominent members who expressed concern from the outset and, when the talks continued, he argued that they should terminate as soon as it became clear that no progress was being made towards ending PIRA violence.[38]

Hume was denounced by all of the other parties. Unionists claimed that the SDLP was attempting to create an alliance with Sinn Féin. According to Paisley, Hume saw the joint approach by Unionist leaders as 'a menace to his united Ireland, therefore he turns to seek new allies with the political wing of the PIRA murderers'.[39] Others, like the APNI's chief whip Tom Campbell, argued that

> for one who is seriously suggesting he wishes to engage in dialogue between all sections of the community, this is an astonishing move. The fact that Mr Hume has chosen to meet with Sinn Féin in the aftermath of the Enniskillen murders is a sad commentary on this so-called desire for dialogue.[40]

The British government made its displeasure known when Thatcher declared in the House of Commons that 'members of this government have had no contact whatever with Sinn Féin and will have no contact with them. I would have thought that most people in this house hold the same view'.[41] Later, one of the SDLP's most severe critics, Conor Cruise O'Brien, claimed that SDLP strength rested 'on the back of the PIRA's 'armed struggle', and that the party was joining with Sinn Féin to pressurize Unionists into a united Ireland.[42] O'Brien forecast that 'further and greater violence' would result. Indeed, PIRA killings throughout the period of the talks brought considerable pressure on the SDLP to cut off all contact with Sinn Féin, forcing Hume to emphasize several times that since the talks were aimed at bringing violence to an end, the SDLP would persist for as long as that possibility existed.[43] But, as the talks continued, that prospect appeared to be no closer, and by the end of the summer the two leaders decided that no further meetings would take place.

NO COOPERATION

Realizing that there would be no meeting of minds on fundamentals, Sinn Féin proposed that the parties cooperate on two more immediate issues. The first was on fair employment, where they suggested a joint approach to achieve reform of existing legislation.[44] Secondly, Sinn Féin proposed that the two parties 'jointly issue a call to the Dublin and London governments for them to consult together to seek agreement on the policy objective of Irish reunification'.[45] To neither proposal would the SDLP agree, arguing that for as long as Sinn Féin supported the PIRA's campaign of violence there could be no cooperation between the two parties and, in any case, talking to the British about Irish unity over the heads of Unionists would not, in the SDLP's view, be a very productive exercise. The SDLP further underlined that Sinn Féin could expect no participation in any substantial talks or negotiations for as long as it maintained its support for the PIRA.

For the SDLP, the immediate objective in the talks had been, in the words of one of the party's delegates, to try to 'establish a basis for the permanent cessation of all military and violent activity'.[46] Clearly, this objective had not been achieved, but the talks had at least initiated a dialogue, which, in time, would result in Sinn Féin gradually moving into the political mainstream, creating conditions for a PIRA ceasefire and leading to the comprehensive negotiations that the SDLP believed to be essential. In the words of one prominent commentator, Barry White of the *Belfast Telegraph*

> If the SDLP has forced some republicans to look at what they are doing, and see the truth in John Hume's taunt that the 'methods have become more sacred than the cause' something will have been achieved.[47]

Viewed positively, therefore, the seeds of a political process had been sown, but it would be some years before they would bear the hoped for results. The problem for the SDLP was that, in 1988, those results could not have been foreseen and, at the end of the talks, the SDLP leadership had only demonstrated that it was prepared to take risks in pursuit of peace, and to suffer strong criticism for doing so. While many in the political sphere had denounced the talks, the party had gained considerable public support from its initiative. An opinion poll in the *Irish Independent* in April indicated that 68 per cent of those polled approved of the talks,[48] and, where opinion really counted, in the ballot box, the party would soon reap electoral benefits from taking those risks.

UNIONISTS SHIFT GROUND

While Unionists remained resistant to immediate talks with the SDLP, signs of a change of mind at leadership level continued to emerge, particularly within the UUP. James Molyneaux repeatedly emphasized the need for a new British-Irish framework to replace the Anglo-Irish Agreement, but now, borrowing SDLP language, he talked about assisting 'the British and Irish governments in a determined effort to end the ancient quarrel between the two nations', by addressing the 'totality of relationships' between the two sovereign governments.[49] From a Unionist leader, there was a freshness and openness in these sentiments that seemed to suggest possibilities. Hume welcomed the remarks and, in the hope that talks could take place, had already established a working group within the party to prepare for negotiations.[50] Taoiseach Charles Haughey, anxious to circumvent the Anglo-Irish Agreement and forge his own concord with Unionists, also responded and offered to talk to Unionists. For a while it seemed as if some in the UUP would accept Haughey's offer, but when Paisley made it clear that there should be no talks with Dublin until after a devolved government was in office in the North, the possibility quickly dimmed.[51] Throughout the summer and early autumn, therefore, the SDLP-Sinn Féin talks remained the only manifestation of political dialogue.

Attempts by the secretary of state to inject momentum into the political process had also come to nought. Tom King held several meetings with the parties, including the SDLP, with a view to convening inter-party talks on devolution. Unionist resistance to any talks while the Anglo-Irish Agreement continued to operate meant that King's initiative made no progress. A clear impasse had been reached and there was an urgent need to find a way around it. In the search for a means of breaking the impasse, attention began to focus on the review of the operation of the agreement scheduled to take place three years after its ratification, by December 1988. For Unionists whose protest campaign against the agreement had virtually collapsed, the review was seized upon as an opportunity to have the whole agreement replaced, but with neither government willing to consider such a move, the only way was for Unionists to enter talks which might aim at replacing the agreement, but which would not start with its suspension.

Nevertheless, in the spirit of the task-force report, some Unionists were again prepared to explore possibilities, and an occasion to do so presented itself at another informal inter-party discussion convened by Eberhard Spiecker in October. On this occasion, the talks took place in Duisburg and the SDLP was represented by Austin Currie.[52] According to Currie's account, those present agreed to put a proposal that he had drafted to their respective parties. The proposal read 'that meetings of the (intergovernmental) conference will not be held for a period (specified) to facilitate dialogue involving the major constitutional parties in Northern Ireland'.[53] It was a simple formula and one that was eventually to be adopted by both governments and the parties, but at the time did not elicit support. This was due primarily to exaggerated claims about what had transpired at Duisburg and to the fact that the talks were but one part of a number of inter-party contacts then underway, aimed at breaking the political impasse.[54] The SDLP was also still concerned that once any interval was allowed, Unionists would use it to delay reconvening the intergovernmental conference. Later, Hume was in contact with Unionist representatives from whom he received a document outlining possible scenarios in which talks might take place, including the Duisburg proposal for an interval between conference meetings.[55] Hume's response was not to dismiss the 'interval' proposal, but rather to suggest an SDLP alternative, that talks take place 'completely outside the framework of the Anglo-Irish Agreement', with the objective of achieving an agreement that would 'transcend in importance any previous agreement ever made and that the agenda of the talks will address all the relationships that can contribute to the realization of peace and stability'.[56] The proposal was a reminder that for the SDLP, important though the Anglo-Irish Agreement was, it could be superseded by a more comprehensive agreement involving all parties, as well as the two governments. Indeed, the latter was what the party was ultimately aiming to achieve. Hume's proposal was not acceptable to

Unionists, despite the fact that it referred to 'transcending previous agreements', precisely the language that Molyneaux had been using in recent months. For the SDLP, talks aimed at an agreement that would transcend the Anglo-Irish Agreement were much more acceptable than talks that would require the suspension of an agreement on which the party placed so much value.

SDLP REVIEW AGREEMENT

With the prospect of talks in the balance, John Hume requested Eddie McGrady to review the party's negotiating position and to prepare a submission to the review of the operation of the Anglo-Irish Agreement.[57] The ensuing discussion paper on negotiations was essentially an update of existing party positions. It restated the key objective to be the establishment of a 'framework for cooperation and reconciliation both within Northern Ireland and between North and South'.[58] The paper argued that such a framework would be 'the political embryo out of which unity could grow, since it must be obvious that Irish unity ... will only persist in agreement between the Nationalist and Unionist traditions'. It went on to argue that the SDLP should seek the maximum possible degree of devolved powers for a regional assembly and exec-utive, a North-South council and new institutional arrangements for relationships between the North and Britain. The paper also strongly recom-mended that any agreement be simultaneously placed 'before the people of Ireland, North and South, for their endorsement'.[59]

In its submission to the review of the Anglo-Irish agreement, the SDLP emphasized the agreement's achievements, noting that for first time, the prob-lems of Northern Ireland were being dealt with 'in their proper British-Irish framework, rather than the narrow ground of Northern Ireland alone'.[60] The achievements included the repeal of the Flags and Emblems Act, the removal of voting restrictions that had affected those born outside of Northern Ireland,[61] and the stand taken by the Irish government in defence of the status of the Irish language in the school curriculum.[62] The submission went on to recommend a more concerted approach to social and economic issues, to redressing discrim-ination, and to dealing with the policing of contentious parades. Despite the delays and frustrations, after only three years the agreement's achievements were at last beginning to mount up and the party felt strongly justified in not conceding its suspension very readily.

As 1988 ended and a New Year began, the prospect of political progress on any front still remained distant, despite the occasional green shoots of hope. Sinn Féin and the PIRA still seemed impervious to any appeal to end the latter's violence, while Unionists were still struggling to find a way of talking with other parties that did not require acceptance of the agreement. Nevertheless, for the SDLP, developments over the previous two years were now viewed very positively. At the party's annual conference, the engagement with Sinn Féin was singled out for special praise. But it was the Anglo-Irish Agreement that was the source of most satisfaction and hope. Despite Unionist protests and Sinn Féin's denial of its significance, the agreement had endured and had created a permanent framework for consultation between both governments, within which tensions could be defused, misunderstandings addressed and, more significantly, joint action planned for the future. Furthermore, it provided a forum in which matters of concern to the SDLP's electorate could be addressed on a wider stage than Northern Ireland itself. More significantly, as Hume reminded the party, the agreement 'has removed the unjust Unionist veto on British policy, it has removed their exclusive hold on power and, this time, the British government, unlike many of its predecessors, has not succumbed to blackmail'[63] – a development that Hume had long believed to be essential if serious negotiations were to take place. Despite their deep sense of betrayal the agreement was not all negative for Unionists, even if they were not willing to admit it. While the Unionist veto over British policy regarding Northern Ireland had been decisively challenged, the principle of consent to constitutional change had been firmly enshrined in Article 1 of an international agreement to which the Irish government was a prime party. That principle would be the bedrock on which any future agreement would have to be built.

Chapter 13

Talks on-off-on

The early months of 1989 saw the prospects for inter-party engagement continue to see-saw between possible and unlikely. The Duisburg initiative had not produced any immediate movement, nor had the exchange of papers between Unionist leaders and John Hume. Nonetheless, occasional hints emerged suggesting a more positive prospect. Brian Mawhinney, minister for education and Tory MP for Peterborough, who was originally from Northern Ireland, was charged by the secretary of state with developing relationships with the parties to assess the prospects for talks. As a result, dialogue of a sort did take place, if only indirectly. A sign of improving relationships between the parties was a delegation of party leaders which met Tom King in February to discuss the future of the Harland and Wolff shipyard, then about to be privatized.[1]

STANDING BY AGREEMENT

Preconditions for talks remained the major barrier, and the height of that barrier was starkly revealed in two in-depth interviews conducted by Frank Millar, the former chief executive of the UUP and then a journalist based in London. The interviews appeared in the *Irish Times*, the first with John Hume and the second with James Molyneaux.[2] Both interviews provided detailed insights into how the two party leaders viewed the prospects for serious negotiations and the general political situation.

For the SDLP, the Anglo-Irish Agreement remained the key to progress. It had, in Hume's analysis, transformed the political situation by creating a level playing pitch between Unionists and Nationalists as well as producing a considerable number of important changes and reforms, not least in fair employment and in policing. On the latter, Hume cited significant improvements in the manner in which controversial Orange Order parades were being managed since the passing of the 1987 Public Order Act. On the question of inter-party negotiations, he once again appealed to Unionists to accept an open-ended approach involving representatives from both parts of Ireland and aimed at 'reaching agreement on how they share this island'.[3] Answering the point that such negotiations would not result in Unionists having to vote themselves into a unitary Irish state, he emphasized that if agreement was the objective, the SDLP would accept whatever could be agreed. The implication was that while Nationalists would argue the case for a united Ireland, faced with determined Unionist opposition, there would have to be compromise. The *quid pro quo* was that Unionists would have to recognize Nationalist aspirations as legitimate and accept institutional means whereby those aspirations and the general Nationalist identity could be afforded legitimate expression. These means would have to include a presence in government together with institutions of an all-Ireland kind. Given Unionist concerns about Sinn Féin's links with the PIRA, Hume emphasized that 'you can't expect anyone to sit around a table with someone who reserves the right to pull a gun if he doesn't get his way',[4] a clear indication that the PIRA would have to end its campaign before Sinn Féin could be admitted to any negotiations.

In his interview, the ever-cautious and still very integrationist Molyneaux ruled out a major conference of the Northern Ireland parties and two governments, as proposed by the SDLP, and described power-sharing as a form of government that 'would not work in any civilized, democratic state'.[5] As for relationships between Northern Ireland and the South, he declared them to be a responsibility of the British and Irish governments. Referring to the Duisburg talks, he dismissed them, and, indirectly, those of his own party who had participated, as of no significance, describing the people who organized such events as 'very innocent … very worthy people who organize themselves into groupings, who are obsessed with the notion that they have a mission in life to bring the warring factions of political parties together'.[6] As far as Molyneaux was concerned, discussions could take place between himself, Paisley and Hume on practical matters such as the future of the Belfast shipyard, but ultimately it was for the British government to propose what form of government Northern Ireland might have, though in saying that, he ignored Unionist rejection of what had been proposed in 1974, as well as the Anglo-Irish Agreement. Molyneaux seemed content for Northern Ireland to remain in the UK so long as Unionists could continue to reject British proposals and not suffer any penalty. As the Duisburg initiative indicated, Molyneaux's views did not represent the only thinking within the UUP at the time, but he was party leader and he was firmly ruling out the kind of process the SDLP believed essential.

SOUTHERN FRUSTRATIONS

The SDLP's insistence on not suspending the operation of the Anglo-Irish Agreement and on a comprehensive approach involving the two governments as well as the North's political parties, came under intense criticism from influential sections of public opinion in the South at this time. Such criticisms had emerged during the talks between the SDLP and Sinn Féin, when the party's old foe Conor Cruise O'Brien attacked it for adopting positions that he believed to be inherently helpful to the PIRA, providing them with a layer of respectable cover. Then, in April 1989, at the annual conference of the Workers' Party in Dublin, party president Proinsias de Rossa referred to what he described as a growing disenchantment with the SDLP because of the absence of political progress. Blaming the SDLP, de Rossa directly attacked John Hume, saying that 'we can assist the South in its slow and shocked reappraisal of John Hume, who once had the status of a saint in the South but is now exposed as another tribal leader whose main asset is that he says tribal things very slowly and very quietly'.[8] Another high-profile public commentator, Senator John A. Murphy, a professor of history at University College, Cork, added his criticisms of the SDLP, arguing in very questionable terms that there was no case for the party's all-Ireland approach. For Murphy, there was 'no community of interests, no real temperamental or cultural affinity between northern Nationalists and 26-county citizens. The southern perception of fellow-Catholics north of the border is different only in degree from the southern perception of the Unionists'.[9] Most of the criticism could be attributed to frustration with the continuation of violence and the failure to make progress with Unionists towards an acceptable resolution. The North still commanded a lot of news coverage and the government was devoting much of its energy to seeking a solution, but none was forthcoming. Not surprisingly, the result was that some sections of public opinion wanted to turn their backs on the North. For the SDLP, the concerted nature of the criticism was worrying, given the party's dependence on southern sympathy and understanding for its approach, but however frustrating for southerners, the situation was much more frustrating as well as dangerous for people in the North.

ELECTORAL SUCCESSES

Elections in the late spring and early summer distracted from any general discussion of talks as the party prepared to contest both district council and European parliament seats. The district council elections in May saw the party contesting an electorally more experienced Sinn Féin than four years previously. However, with the achievement of the agreement, together with the party's involvement in talks with Sinn Féin, improvements in the policing of controversial parades, and progress towards more powerful fair employment legislation to its credit, the expectation was that the outcome would be very positive.

The party's manifesto for the local elections, *Make a difference*,[10] reiterated the case for power-sharing in councils, noting that the policy had eventually led to informal arrangements between SDLP and UUP councillors on some councils to ensure this would happen. The manifesto condemned the many Unionist-dominated councils where SDLP and other Nationalist representatives were still deliberately excluded from senior positions and also denied opportunities to represent their councils on external bodies such as the Housing Council.[11] The manifesto also re-emphasized

> that the Anglo-Irish Agreement is the proper framework through which the central problem of relationships on this island can be resolved ... We therefore once again reiterate our desire for a genuine and sustained political dialogue to commence as soon as possible without any preconditions.

The manifesto went on to denounce Thatcherite policies that were attempting to privatize council services and, in a section on international development, uniquely among the North's parties, the SDLP drew attention to the need to 'think globally and to act locally' and commended the Derry-Addis Ababa link as a model to be emulated in other councils.[12]

The election results saw the SDLP increase its number of councillors from 101 to 121, while Sinn Féin's decreased from 59 to 43. Furthermore, from having more councillors than the SDLP in four councils after the 1985 elections, Sinn Féin was now ahead in none.[13] This was a very satisfactory outcome and was seen as further vindication of the party's approach to the Anglo-Irish Agreement, and of its belief that the agreement was having positive practical effects. Overall, the election results, which also saw the DUP suffer reverses to the advantage of the UUP, indicated that the majority of voters now supported parties most likely to engage in talks. The SDLP and the UUP responded to this message when several councils met to elect their senior officers and adopted cross-party rotational arrangements for the allocation of these positions. The policy of power-sharing was winning more converts, although as yet only in councils where Unionists did not have an overall majority.[14]

REVIEW OF THE AGREEMENT'S OPERATION

A week after the local government elections, the two governments published their long awaited review of the Anglo-Irish Agreement's operation. The *Review of the working of the conference*[15] was deliberately quite limited, since neither government wanted to signal that any significant changes to the agreement were required. In essence, the review expressed satisfaction with the manner in which the agreement had been implemented, emphasized the continued commitment of both governments to encouraging the parties towards devolution and noted the legislative and other measures taken to deal with parades, fair employment, recognition for the Irish language and a more balanced range of appointments to public bodies. On the controversial issue of the non-jury Diplock courts, however, the review acknowledged that the British government had not been persuaded of the merit of three-judge courts and so would not be introducing any change. Other issues of concern to the SDLP addressed in the report included the social and economic disadvantages experienced in many Nationalist areas and, secondly, cross-border economic cooperation. For the former, a programme of action for the most disadvantaged areas of Belfast and other deprived areas was announced[16] and both governments committed to intensifying joint activity on cross-border cooperation, pledging that 'future conference meetings will include a systematic programme of assessment of all of the main sectors to determine where the process of cooperation can most fruitfully be expanded'.[17] Critically, on a matter that was also exercising the SDLP, the report recognized the need to prepare for 'the completion of the internal market in the EC in 1992' claiming that it would 'generate common opportunities for both parts of Ireland as well as common difficulties arising from peripheral island status'.[18]

The SDLP viewed the achievements of the agreement with considerable satisfaction, convinced that they had given Nationalists a new sense that their rights and identity were being recognized and upheld more effectively than ever before, and that action was being taken to address socio-economic issues that impacted on their daily lives. With respect to political matters, however, the major disappointment was that, despite the agreement's guarantees on funda-mental constitutional issues, Unionists remained unwilling to engage in talks unless the agreement was suspended. Nevertheless, confident that neither government would renege on the agreement, the SDLP could now afford to wait until Unionists found their way to the negotiating table.

CURRIE DEPARTS

Shortly after the local elections, the SDLP suffered the unexpected loss of Austin Currie, who accepted an invitation from the leadership of Fine Gael to contest a seat in the Dublin West constituency in the South's forthcoming general election. With the prospects of resuming a full-time political career in the North still very uncertain, Currie had decided that a seat in the Dáil would offer an opportunity to bring a much needed northern perspective to many of its deliberations. So, while his departure from the party was regretted by his colleagues, he left with their good will and gratitude for the 'the services he has given both to it and to the people of Northern Ireland'.[19] Those services had been immense. Since his first election to the old Stormont in 1964, Currie had played a pivotal role in the civil rights campaign, had advocated the establish-ment of a modern left-of-centre party and had contributed significantly to the growth and development of the SDLP. He and his family had paid a heavy price for his political involvement. Not only had he lacked regular employment since the fall of the power-sharing executive in 1974, but he had also seen his home attacked and his family abused on several occasions. His subsequent career as a member of the Dáil and as minister of state for children enabled Currie to realize his potential for public office, as well as providing him with an impor-tant platform from which to speak on northern matters.

FOCUS ON EUROPE

As attention in the North turned to the European elections, Hume again deter-mined that only EC-related issues would feature in his campaign. He declared his major priority to be more effective use of European resources for job creation, to help solve the unemployment crisis of more than 100,000 men and women. He strongly criticized the British government's approach to Europe for not accessing all of the resources that were available to assist Northern Ireland.[20] He proposed that European investment could be used to support 'programmes aimed at industrial development, integrated rural development, new infrastructure and a social guarantee for young people, providing jobs, training and education'.[21] The prospect of the European single market was another key issue in the SDLP's manifesto. Already the party had published two pamphlets outlining the advantages that would flow from the market,[22] and, alone among the local parties, the SDLP emphasized the market's potential for Northern Irish exports.[23]

While the SDLP's electoral messages were all explicitly focused on Europe, it was impossible to conceal the fact that the Anglo-Irish Agreement was a key factor, particularly for the Unionist parties, who regarded the election as another opportunity to express their opposition. In the event, however, a low turnout of 48.3 per cent and 150,000 fewer voters than in 1984, suggested a degree of boredom and frustration at the failure of many politicians to move beyond protest. Ian Paisley saw his vote drop by more than 80,000, while Sinn Féin's Danny Morrison had to admit disappointment at a more than 4 per cent drop in his support. John Hume was the only candidate to record a significant increase, his vote increased by 3.4 per cent to a record 25.5 per cent. Following the local government results, this achievement was a further expression of support for SDLP policies. Hume used the victory to renew his call to Unionist leaders to join the SDLP in urgent talks about the political future of the North.[24]

UNIONISTS SAY 'NO BUT'

As yet, there was no tangible sign of progress towards such talks. For UUP leader James Molyneaux, the 1985 agreement was still 'a bad dream' for Unionists and he saw cooperation with the SDLP on such matters as the Belfast shipyard as the only basis upon which to build new relationships with Nationalists. Even then, the proviso was that the agreement must be set aside.[25] In July, Unionists, who had deeply resented Tom King's pro-agreement stance, greeted his replacement by Peter Brooke MP, a close confidant of Margaret

Thatcher, as a new opportunity to have the agreement replaced. King had grad-ually earned respect from the SDLP for the manner in which he had insisted on upholding the Anglo-Irish Agreement in the face of Unionist opposition, and the party was slightly apprehensive lest the new secretary of state might prove less committed. In the event, there was little to be concerned about. Following a somewhat uncertain beginning, when he revealed a poor grasp of what the agreement stated,[26] Brooke was to display a dogged determination to address the political impasse within its framework.

In August, John Hume used the occasion of the twentieth anniversary of British troops on the streets of Northern Ireland to reiterate the SDLP's reas-surance to Unionists that the party had no interest in their 'conquest or domination', but rather wanted to 'discuss how we resolve our human relation-ships to our mutual satisfaction'.[27] He again called for a conference between the parties and invited Unionists to put any proposal they might wish on the agenda suggesting that whatever would be agreed be put to the people of Ireland, North and South, in joint referenda requiring a majority in both. The message was reinforced by Seán Farren, who claimed that Unionists should accept the reassurance provided in the agreement's commitment that 'any change in the status of Northern Ireland would only come about with the consent of a majority of the people of Northern Ireland' as a guarantee that their fundamental position was respected and, therefore, they should not be unwilling to enter talks.[28]

REFORMING THE UDR

Unionists remained unwilling to accept the SDLP's invitation, and the absence of political dialogue allowed security to become the dominant issue. Since the Anglo-Irish Agreement had been signed, the SDLP and the Dublin government had been pressing for considerable reform of the RUC and the UDR. Some progress had been achieved with respect to the former, a new police authority had been appointed and changes made to the managing of controversial parades, but, despite the many allegations of collusion with loyalist paramili-taries, the UDR had remained unaffected. These allegations reached a climax in September 1989, after it was revealed that security documents were in the possession of some of these paramilitaries. The SDLP called for the UDR to be disbanded,[29] and the deputy chief constable of Cambridgeshire, John Stevens, was appointed to investigate the theft and the leaking of intelligence documents from UDR sources.

Invoking the commitment in the Anglo-Irish Agreement to undertake 'a programme of measures ... to improve relationships between the security forces and the community with the object in particular of making the security forces more readily accepted by the Nationalist community',[30] the Irish government made collusion and reform of the UDR a central matter for discussion at the October meeting of the intergovernmental conference. The result was the introduction of several measures affecting recruitment to the regiment, the handling of intelligence, and ensuring a police presence as part of UDR patrols,[31] all welcomed by the SDLP, even if far short of what the party ultimately sought – the disbandment of the regiment.

ACKNOWLEDGING THE ROLE OF THE SOUTH

In the autumn, the DUP's Peter Robinson, followed by some members of the UUP, re-opened the debate over devolution. In the course of a BBC discussion with Hume, Robinson acknowledged that the South had a role to play in finding a solution for the North. Echoing the SDLP's emphasis on the three dimensions to the problem – relationships between the two communities in the North, between the two parts of Ireland, and between Ireland and Britain – Robinson insisted that Unionists had 'to sort out their relationships with the government in Dublin', as well as those with their Nationalist neighbours in the North.[32] Critically, Robinson also made it clear that Unionists were no longer insisting that the Anglo-Irish Agreement be withdrawn before negotiations could begin. Instead, a suspension of the working of the agreement would suffice. Fearing that suspension, once achieved, could be prolonged indefinitely, Hume again suggested that a declaration be made that negotiations take place 'without prejudice to the different parties' views on the Anglo-Irish Agreement', with the object of seeking 'an agreement that would transcend in importance any previous agreement ever made'.[33] While Robinson did not agree, Hume's suggestion was not completely rejected and the implication was that both politicians were beginning to move towards an understanding that would allow talks to commence.

A few weeks later, at the UUP's annual conference, a motion calling for the strengthening of the North's position at Westminster was amended with a demand that devolution be restored. The amended motion was passed, though in the debate strong opposition to devolution continued to be expressed by pro-integrationists, among whom was a future prominent politician, Jeffrey Donaldson, who denounced devolution if it meant having 'John Hume, Séamus Mallon and Eddie McGrady governing this country'.[34]

FRESH EVIDENCE

Peter Brooke added to the sense that fresh possibilities were being explored when in November he acknowledged that while it was difficult to envisage the PIRA being militarily defeated, it was possible to envisage talks with Sinn Féin, should the PIRA end its campaign of violence. Calling for an ever more aggressive security policy, Unionists condemned such a suggestion, but the SDLP and the Dublin government welcomed it. Séamus Mallon described the secretary of state's remarks as 'a quantum leap' in that they recognized the 'self-evident fact' that when violence stopped in the North, all political parties would have to become involved in the exercise of self-determination.[35] At the SDLP's annual conference some days after Brooke's remarks, Hume added to the pressure on the PIRA to declare a ceasefire by pointing to the number of people they had killed, 1,565 from a total of just over 3,000, many with no security force or British government connection. He accused the PIRA of regarding the campaign to be 'more sacred than their cause' and of not having the courage to end its violence. To emphasize its callousness, Hume also accused the PIRA of allowing the Birmingham Six, the Guildford Four and the Maguire family, all falsely convicted of bomb attacks in Britain, to remain in prison while their own members responsible for those attacks were at liberty.[36] The message was that whatever the PIRA's objectives when the campaign had started, it was now characterized by purposeless death, destruction and tragedy, to the point that violence had become an end in itself. But, as before, his words went unheeded, and while the year ended with a slight decline in the violent death toll, eighty-one compared with ninety-four the previous year, there was no sign that any of the terrorist groups intended to call an early an end to its campaign.

Despite Robinson's remarks and the re-emergence of a more determined pro-devolution wing within the UUP, politically the year also ended with renewed uncertainty as to where the Unionist parties stood with respect to talks. While the possibility of some kind of gap between meetings of the intergovernmental conference was gradually being established, Molyneaux began insisting that the two governments would also have to indicate what changes they would be prepared to make to the agreement before he would consent to talks.[37] Then, in January, Paisley openly contradicted his deputy when he demanded the suspension both of the intergovernmental conference, and of the functioning of its secretariat as preconditions to any talks.[38] For the SDLP, this confusion of messages rendered it difficult to establish where Unionists stood, and the party stuck firmly by its insistence on no prior suspension of the agreement and, secondly, that while any new agreement would have to *transcend* the Anglo-Irish Agreement, it should first be put to the electorate North and South in joint referenda. So, while not completely opposed to talks during gaps between meetings of the intergovernmental conference, the party maintained a very cautious approach, not least because it still feared that gaps might be prolonged, but also because it believed that the Irish government's participation had to be beyond question, another issue on which Unionists were sending ambivalent messages. Indeed, the almost exclusive emphasis placed by pro-devolution Unionists on talks being primarily about restoring a regional, non-power-sharing, government only added to the party's caution.

BROOKE FORCES PACE

Notwithstanding this uncertainty, whether out of frustration or because he genuinely believed that a new opportunity existed, Brooke began an intensive period of consultation with the parties in January, aimed at agreeing a basis for talks. Launching the process, Brooke claimed that 'it was just possible that the will might exist to achieve some political progress in the near future'.[39] It was a process that would only very slowly gain momentum, but one that would, despite serious setbacks, eventually lead to talks, though not until a year later. Not only were there suspicions between Unionists on one hand, and the SDLP and the Irish government on the other, suspicions also surfaced between the Unionist parties, revealing wide gaps between the more pro-devolution DUP, and the divided, but still more pro-integration UUP. At intergovernmental level, a variety of issues also complicated discussions, the most controversial of which was extradition. New legislation in 1987 had been intended to remove previous barriers to the extradition of suspected terrorists from the South to the North.[40] However, when the Irish Supreme Court ruled, in March, against extraditing two Maze prison escapees,[41] controversy on the issue was revived, leading Thatcher to remark that the Republic seemed to be a 'safe haven for terrorists'. Nevertheless, both governments persisted with their efforts to break the political deadlock and, in April, announced that while they could not yet say for definite that they would succeed, they felt they were making progress.[42] But if the governments were making progress on conditions for negotiations, it was not at all clear that the parties would soon be willing to accept those conditions.

For the SDLP, safeguarding the advances gained from the Anglo-Irish Agreement was critical, and the party maintained its opposition to any suspension of its operation and even more to any suggestion that it be abandoned. While there was no likelihood of the agreement being totally abandoned, suspension of the agreement's operation without firm commitments to its full restoration should a more comprehensive agreement not be reached, met with the party's strong opposition. The party's suggestion that a new agreement would transcend the Anglo-Irish Agreement was, therefore, to be understood as an agreement that would subsume and go beyond the former. In effect, as far as the SDLP was concerned, a new agreement should have to be even more comprehensive than the existing one.

While Unionists insisted that a precondition to talks had to be the prospect of a new agreement, they were not envisaging a more comprehensive agreement than that of 1985. Unionists had now accepted the need for new relationships with Dublin, and gave some indications of what a new agreement should contain. These were far from what the SDLP was ever likely to accept. To improve relationships with the South, Unionists suggested the establishment of a Republic of Ireland consular-type office in Belfast, 'in common with accepted international practice. Such an office would provide a point of contact no less adequate to those who desire it, than that available through Maryfield (where the intergovernmental conference office was located)'.[43] The very language stressed the traditional Unionist view that the South was a 'foreign' state and the role envisaged for the 'minority' was essentially the same as that offered at the 1975 convention, chairs of assembly committees on which Unionists would retain a majority. Unionists also insisted that as a precondition for talks the Anglo-Irish Agreement should not operate while negotiations towards its replacement took place.

The SDLP continued to argue that suspension was not justified, claiming that Unionists should negotiate without prejudice to their opposition to the agreement, knowing that a new agreement might well be reached to replace it. Complicating the preconditions for talks was a Unionist demand that the Irish government not be permitted to participate in discussions on the internal government of Northern Ireland. The SDLP insisted that, since the discussions would be aimed at replacing the Anglo-Irish Agreement, the Irish government had to be involved from the outset, even if not directly in negotiating the details of a government for Northern Ireland. In support of its argument, the SDLP pointed to article 4(c) of the agreement, which stated that the Irish government could 'put forward views and proposals on the modalities of bringing about devolution in Northern Ireland'. So, when Brooke seemed to endorse Unionist opposition to any Irish government involvement in such discussions, the party accused the secretary of state of being in breach of the agreement.

Nonetheless, the two governments painstakingly manoeuvred their way through these demands and preconditions and their surrounding suspicions, and by mid-June 1990 the basis for talks proceeding in the autumn appeared to have been agreed. All sides had eventually accepted that there would be a gap of at least eight weeks between meetings of the intergovernmental conference to allow for talks. It was also accepted that the talks would comprise three strands, each dealing with one of the three sets of relationships so frequently outlined by the SDLP. But a problem arose over when the second strand, addressing all-Ireland relationships, would commence. Since this would be the stage at which Unionists would come face-to-face with the Irish government, the former insisted that it should not commence 'until substantial progress' had been made on Strand 1 issues, the internal government of Northern Ireland.[44] Both the SDLP and the Irish government claimed that this precondition would enable Unionists to determine what 'substantial progress' would mean and therefore would amount to a delaying veto over when the Irish government could become involved. The party also feared that Unionists might strive for agreement in Strand 1, but then find excuses for not progressing to Strand 2.

Consequently, a firmer commitment on the Irish government's participation was sought, but when Brooke accepted the Unionist position in his draft parliamentary statement, the process stalled.[45] In addition to the 'substantial progress' precondition, Unionists had also demanded that their talks delegates be regarded as members of the wider UK delegation, a condition intended to indicate that they would be talking to a 'foreign' government and not doing so exclusively on their own behalf.[46] Unionists seemed to fear that with the SDLP and the Dublin government working in very close collaboration, they would be

isolated and so needed the counter-balance which membership of the UK delegation would provide. These preconditions were unacceptable to the SDLP and
the Irish government, which was also unimpressed by the decidedly Unionist
tone to the whole document.[47] Despite frantic efforts to bridge the gaps that
were appearing between all sides,[48] when Brooke made his statement on the
possibility of talks at Westminster on 5 July, it was to announce that he was still
unable to say when they might commence.

Two weeks later, SDLP leader John Hume attempted to break the impasse
when he met with Unionist leaders to present them with the draft of a statement that he proposed the secretary of state make.[49] Explicitly including many
of the same points as Brooke's own draft, Hume's draft differed on some key
Unionist demands. His draft omitted the reference to membership of the
British delegation, substituted 'substantial progress' with a commitment to
'launch all sets of discussions within weeks of each other', and expressed the
SDLP's desire to have any agreement submitted to referenda North and South.
Not unexpectedly, it was the turn of Unionist leaders to say 'no'. This they did
and, while the gaps that had inhibited Brooke's initiative at this stage seemed
not insurmountable, the prospect of autumn talks faded over the summer
months.

A POSITIVE INITIATIVE

While efforts to initiate negotiations on a new agreement were faltering,
contacts were developing between the SDLP and the two Unionist parties that
would demonstrate that the three parties could agree on a practical initiative. In
January 1990, following an invitation from several academics at the University
of Ulster's Centre for the Study of Conflict, the parties were invited to participate in a workshop on 'Northern Ireland in Europe' at George Mason
University in Virginia in the US.[50] The focus on Europe had been prompted by
the imminence of the single market and the belief that Northern Ireland should
position itself more effectively to take advantage of the economic opportunities
it would present, a case that the SDLP had been making for some time. Each
party nominated two participants and the outcome of their deliberations was a
feasibility study into the possibility of establishing a Northern Ireland centre in
Europe.[51] Discussions continued throughout the first part of the year, culminating with a second workshop at the University of Grenoble in France,

following which it was decided that the Northern Ireland Centre in Europe (NICE) would be established. The launch took place the following January with the support of all three parties as well as significant voices from civil society, particularly from the business and the community sectors.[52] While a modest achievement, the NICE showed that, despite widely differing attitudes towards Europe and their continuing absence of engagement on more fundamental talks, the parties were prepared to work together and were able to win support from civil society in the North. As well as extending the range of contacts between the parties, the workshops in the US and France had also provided an opportunity to exchange views on the wider political situation, and so kept alive the prospect for negotiations.

TALKS AGENDA

After the summer, Brooke renewed his efforts to initiate a viable talks process and, at the intergovernmental conference meeting in September, a sub-committee was established to work on the issue of the Irish government's involvement. Parties were invited to submit their proposals for an agenda, and the secretary of state met with the SDLP to discuss its submission at the end of September. Borrowing from the approach adopted at the NIF, the submission proposed that, at the outset of the talks, each party outline what it understood to be 'the nature of the problem to be solved'.[53] The SDLP's proposed agenda also suggested, again borrowing from the NIF, that the objective of the talks should be

> to accommodate two sets of legitimate rights: the right of Nationalists to effective political, symbolic and administrative expression of their identity; and the right of Unionists to effective political, symbolic and administrative expression of their identity, their ethos and their way of life.[54]

From a discussion of these objectives, the SDLP hoped that 'agreed realities' would be identified 'as the starting point for genuine dialogue, leading to reconciliation and agreement'.[55] The basic realities that the SDLP had in mind were that two 'political and cultural traditions' existed in the North, 'each equally valid and legitimate, but with loyalties and aspirations which transcend the borders of Northern Ireland'.[56] In practical terms, the party claimed that 'these realities are dimensions of three interlocking and interdependent sets of relationships and must be accommodated within such a framework'.[57]

While the agenda for the talks that eventually took place would reflect very closely the SDLP's proposals, the autumn months saw little progress towards breaking the preconditions impasse. Indeed, the lack of progress brought leading SDLP members to call for the whole approach to be recast, fearing that the focus would be too narrowly on devolution. At a fringe meeting during the British Labour Party's annual conference, Séamus Mallon emphasized the Irish government's role, saying that the SDLP would not accept that as a co-signatory to the Anglo-Irish Agreement its participation could be subject to the determination of Unionists.[58] Several days later, John Hume suggested that Brooke's approach should be abandoned because of Unionist insistence that talks start with devolution and only move on when agreement had been reached, the very approach that had led to the failure of previous talks. He called instead for a greater emphasis on the wider context and on what an agreement that would transcend the Anglo-Irish Agreement might look like.[59]

STRESSING FAR-REACHING CHANGE

At the party's annual conference, the leadership again stressed the need for significant constitutional reform embracing the whole island, and dismissed an exclusive focus on devolution.[60] Hume emphasized that the SDLP preferred negotiations without any preconditions and reminded Unionists that the Anglo-Irish Agreement was not set in stone and could be built upon and transcended.[61] Answering Unionist criticism that the SDLP was not interested in restoring regional government to the North,[62] Séamus Mallon stressed that any future government would have to be radically different from previous administrations. In addition to what would be the normal competencies of a devolved administration, Mallon insisted that it should have wide fiscal powers, as well as the authority to negotiate separately with the EC on the North's behalf.[63] Stressing the SDLP's commitment to an all-island economic policy as well as political cooperation, the conference also endorsed a comprehensive document detailing proposals for cross-border economic cooperation with particular reference to disadvantaged border areas.[64]

BROOKE 'TALKS' TO PROVISIONAL MOVEMENT

Notwithstanding the political impasse, Brooke continued to press the case for talks, stating that he might have 'to set the pace and show the way'.[65] In other words, he would impose his own framework and dare the parties not to attend, a risky threat given the experiences of his predecessors, Humphrey Atkins and James Prior. Wisely, Brooke did not pursue his threat. Instead, with no sign of progress, he risked more Unionist wrath by engaging in further open dialogue with the PIRA.[66] In a speech delivered in his London constituency, he argued, in a comment that John Hume had been urging him to make for some time, that 'the British government has no selfish strategic or economic interest in Northern Ireland; our role is to help, enable and encourage'.[67] He underlined the fact that the provisional movement had to persuade Unionists of the benefits of a united Ireland, not wage a campaign of terror against them. He also repeated that Sinn Féin would be entitled to a place at any negotiating table should the PIRA end its campaign. This was very far from Thatcher's assertions that 'Northern Ireland was as British as Finchley' and that there could be no talking to terrorists.

Following the 1988 talks with Sinn Féin, Hume had also maintained a kind of public dialogue with Adams, as well as occasional face-to-face meetings. The dialogue had been conducted in Hume's various public pronouncements with the intention of impressing on the Sinn Féin and PIRA leadership the futility of the latter's campaign, that it had no prospect of achieving any of its declared objectives and that the only viable way forward was through democratic dialogue. An essential pre-requisite for Sinn Féin's participation in dialogue was, therefore, a ceasefire. In his statements, Brooke was now making the same offer and setting the same precondition. As was subsequently revealed,[68] the British government had also permitted the re-opening of a secret channel to the PIRA, along which similar messages were being more directly conveyed.[69]

Sinn Féin answered Brooke, saying the party was ready to engage with the British government, but rejected the secretary of state's claim of British disinterest, and made no mention of a ceasefire. In its response, Sinn Féin described Unionists as a minority of the Irish nation whose rights would be upheld, but 'only in an independent Ireland'.[70] In a very traditional and militant interpretation of the 'real problem', Adams denied the charge that Unionists were being forced into anything. Rather, he argued, it was a case of 'forcing Britain to get out, and to grant democratic self-determination to all of the Irish people without reference to their religion'.[71] Apparently, nothing had changed in Sinn Féin's position since the dialogue with the SDLP. The only hint of a possible end to the PIRA's campaign lay in Adams' reiteration that, for the PIRA, 'armed struggle was not dogma' and was only resorted to in the absence of a viable alternative.[72] This of course ignored the fact that Sinn Féin, like all other parties, could organize openly, could publicize its policies and could nominate candidates in all elections. Ironically, in view of his role as the PIRA's contact with the British, Martin McGuinness put the case for continuing the campaign more bluntly when he posed and answered the rhetorical question: 'is there a group of people within the republican movement or within Sinn Féin who believe that the freedom of Ireland can be won only through political involvement or in elections? ... it's a total and absolute nonsense.'[73] The provisional movement still had a curious understanding of people's democratic rights.

TALKS MOVE CLOSER

Brooke's efforts at breaking the political deadlock continued and, from the end of November 1990, the possibility of talks moved ever so slowly closer.[74] Paisley and Molyneaux presented the secretary of state with what became known as the 'Christmas Eve' document, in which they replaced the 'substantial progress' requirement with the phrase 'in the light of progress made' as the criterion for moving to talks with Dublin.[75] It was a positive move, but it was not sufficient for the SDLP or Dublin, who still feared that Unionists would stall until they had achieved 'substantial' progress on a devolved government.[76] From mid-January, the SDLP leader began working on a new draft statement.[77] According to Hume's draft, there would be no mention of 'significant progress' as the criterion for North-South talks, thus depriving the Unionists of their veto. As recommended by the Irish government the previous June, Brooke would be the arbiter of when precisely the talks would move to address Strands 2 and 3, and so involve the Irish government. Following several weeks of intense consultation, during which the prospects for talks continued to see-saw, a final version incorporating much of Hume's draft was agreed and Peter Brooke announced the terms for talks at the end of March.[78] For the SDLP, the thematic structure of the talks would be as the party had recommended, that 'the talks must focus on three relationships: those within Northern Ireland; ... among the people of the island of Ireland; and between the two governments'.[79] As further reassurance for the SDLP, and for the Irish government, Brooke announced that all had 'agreed that the three sets of discussions will be under way within weeks of each other'.[80] The Unionist demand that they be part of the British delegation was not conceded. On the vexed question of the operation of the intergovernmental conference, it was agreed by both governments that there would be no meetings between two pre-specified dates and that its secretariat would not be required to 'discharge its normal role of servicing conference meetings provided for in Article 3 of the agreement'.[81] The SDLP could, therefore, claim that neither was being suspended.

The statement drew to a close the long saga of quite tortuous negotiations on when and what would be discussed, but it was to be only a pause before the parties would return to more procedural wrangling when the talks finally commenced in June. Meantime, paramilitary violence continued, with the PIRA adopting a new, more sinister and cynical tactic, the use of 'human bombs'. The first was exploded when a Catholic worker, Patsy Gillespie, who supplied sandwiches to army bases among other outlets, and whose family was taken hostage, was forced to drive a car loaded with bombs into an army checkpoint outside Derry, killing himself and five soldiers.[82] Incendiary bombs in several towns destroyed many Protestant-owned businesses, while loyalist paramilitaries intensified their murder of Catholics in a vicious phase of 'tit-for-tat' killings. The weary acceptance of persistent violence seemed destined to continue.

1 John Hume addresses demonstrators at a civil rights
protest in Derry, 1969 (SDLP archive).
2 An early SDLP press conference. Left to right: John Hume, Gerry Fitt,
Austin Currie and, behind, Paddy Duffy and Michael Canavan (SDLP archive).

3 A sit-down anti-internment protest in Derry, August 1971 (Willie Carson archive).
4 Michael Canavan, facing camera, at an anti-internment demonstration in Derry, August 1971 (Willie Carson archive).

5

6

5 Hugh Logue, John Hume and Ivan Cooper under army escort after an anti-internment rally (Willie Carson archive).
6 John Hume calming demonstrators, accompanied by Hugh Logue at an anti-internment protest (Willie Carson archive).

7 John Hume being frisked by a British soldier in Derry (Willie Carson archive).

8

9

8 SDLP assembly members with Irish-American civil rights lawyer Paul O'Dwyer (seated centre, between Fitt and Hume) at Stormont in 1973 (SDLP archive).

9 SDLP chairman Denis Haughey addressing the media at the launch of the party's manifesto for the February 1974 general election (SDLP archive).

10

11

10 Gerry Fitt making the leader's address at the SDLP's annual conference in 1975 (SDLP archive).
11 Paddy Devlin and Denis Haughey at a conference of European social democratic and labour parties (SDLP archive).

12

13

12 John Hume accompanied by his wife, Pat, and Gerry Fitt and party colleagues after he was officially nominated as candidate for the first European parliamentary elections in June 1979 (SDLP archive).

13 The three newly elected MEPs, John Hume (SDLP), John Taylor (UUP) and Ian Paisley (DUP), June 1979 (SDLP archive).

14

15

14 John Hume and his election agent Berna McIvor and party worker Ann McCartney view the damage caused by a PIRA fire-bomb attack on the party's Derry offices during the 1983 general election campaign (SDLP archive).

15 John Hume, Séamus Mallon, Eddie McGrady, Joe Hendron and Austin Currie at a session of the New Ireland Forum in Dublin Castle, 1983–4 (SDLP archive).

16

17

16 John Hume accompanies Speaker of the US House of Representatives, Tip O'Neill, on a walk-about in Derry in 1982 (SDLP archive).
17 Séamus Mallon accompanied by Councillors Frank Feeley and John McArdle canvassing in Newry during the parliamentary by-election of 1986 (Pacemaker).

18 Séamus Mallon carried in triumph after his victory in the 1986
by-election (SDLP archive).
19 Eddie McGrady, with his wife Patricia, hearing the declaration of his victory in
the South-Down constituency at the 1987 general election (SDLP archive).

20 Joe Hendron carried in triumph after his victory in the 1992 general election, on his right is SDLP councillor Alasdair McDonnell (SDLP archive).

21 Eddie McGrady, Joe Hendron, John Hume and Séamus Mallon, the SDLP's four MPs (1992–7) (SDLP archive).

22 Gerry Adams, Albert Reynolds and John Hume shake hands on the steps
of government buildings, Dublin, October 1994 (photograph by Matt Kavanagh/
Irish Times).
23 SDLP negotiators Mark Durkan, Denis Haughey, Bríd Rodgers and Seán Farren
with South African President Nelson Mandela at the inter-party seminar in June 1997
(SDLP archive).

24

25

24 Bríd Rodgers under police escort at a Drumcree march protest (SDLP archive).
25 John Hume accompanied by party colleagues greets the Good Friday Agreement
(photograph by the *Irish Times*).

26

27

26 U2 lead singer Bono introduces David Trimble and John Hume to the audience
at the pro-agreement concert in Belfast, May 1998 (SDLP archive).
27 SDLP assembly members at Stormont 1998 (SDLP archive).

28

29

28 Deputy First Minister Séamus Mallon addresses the Northern Ireland Assembly, watched by ministers Mark Durkan and Seán Farren (SDLP archive).

29 John Hume, accompanied by party colleagues and friends, displays his Nobel Peace Prize medal following the ceremony of presentation in Oslo, 10 December 1998 (SDLP archive).

30

31

30 John Hume introduces Mark Durkan and other party colleagues to President Bill Clinton during the latter's visit to Northern Ireland in 1998 (SDLP archive).
31 First meeting of the power-sharing executive led by First and Deputy First Ministers, David Trimble and Séamus Mallon at Stormont, December 1999 (SDLP archive).

Chapter 14

Dress rehearsal: Brooke-Mayhew talks

As the four parties, the APNI, the DUP, the UUP and the SDLP, assembled to participate in what became known as the 'Brooke-Mayhew talks',[1] hopes were high that they would be successful. An *Irish Times* editorial described success as likely to amount 'to a more far-reaching set of arrangements than any that has been attempted – much less put in place – since the settlement of 1921–2'.[2] However, it was not long before the scale of the challenge was emphasized in several weeks of procedural wrangles about the location, the agenda and the chairing of the second, North-South, strand of the talks, all of which would ultimately bring the talks to a premature close. Although the procedural issues were often dismissed as trivial, they in fact were manifestations of the more difficult political and constitutional issues that had to be addressed.

PROCEDURAL WRANGLES

The Unionist leaders, who continued to act jointly at this early stage of the talks, and who frequently raised objections to procedures proposed by others, did so because they were determined to negotiate the Anglo-Irish Agreement out of existence, and to have Articles 2 and 3 removed from the Irish constitution. But the nature of their objections had a touch of unreality that questioned their commitment to genuine engagement. They objected strenuously to Dublin as a location for the Strand 2 talks, arguing that, since it was from there that the claim on the North emanated, Unionists could not go to Dublin lest they be seen as acknowledging that claim. Curiously, Unionists also objected to the Irish government negotiating in Belfast, since that would mean the 'foreign' power claiming the North being officially in the North! Furthermore, the Unionist parties then objected to an outside chair for the Strand 2 talks, insisting that the secretary of state fill the role, and that the talks be in London. When the recommendation of an independent chair was eventually accepted, they objected to several names, among them Lord Carrington, former UK secretary of state at the Foreign Office, on the grounds that he had supported the Anglo-Irish Agreement.

Throughout the several weeks of such procedural disputes, the SDLP was effectively on the sidelines as Brooke devoted his time to addressing Unionist concerns. The one procedural principle that the SDLP insisted on was that Strand 1 could not commence as long as doubt existed regarding the operation of Strand 2. The SDLP had assumed that once it had agreed the formula outlined in Brooke's statement of 26 March, subsequently endorsed by the Irish government at the Anglo-Irish conference of 6 April, the secretary of state would determine when Strand 2 would commence, and that there would be no further obstacles to negotiations commencing. So, when the Unionist leaders entered their various objections, the SDLP regarded them as unreasonable, and as signs of bad faith. Séamus Mallon accused Unionists of displaying weakness and an inability 'to stand on their own two feet', and dismissed their suggestion that Strand 2 talks take place somewhere in Europe, saying 'wouldn't we all look very silly getting on to airplanes to go off for five weeks to Strasbourg, Paris, Brussels or wherever it might be to discuss our future'.[3] Hume argued that the SDLP had assumed the talks would alternate between North and South,[4] and the party suggested Armagh, Ireland's ecclesiastical capital and, ironically, Ian Paisley's birthplace, as a compromise location, but it was rejected. The party then proposed that Strand 2 should open in London, continue in Belfast and close in Dublin. After a four-week delay the logjam was eventually broken when the parties agreed that an independent chair would preside over Strand 2 and accepted the SDLP proposals for the venues. All four party leaders, Hume, Molyneaux and John Alderdice of the APNI, then agreed that the talks proper would commence on Monday 17 June.[5] However, given the loss of negotiating time, only three weeks of the gap between meetings of the intergovernmental conference remained, there was little likelihood that the talks could achieve very much.

SINN FÉIN WANTS IN

As the talks began, Sinn Féin protested its exclusion, ignoring the condition that their participation required an end to PIRA violence, or their disavowal of that violence.[6] As if to underline the reason for their exclusion, the PIRA embarked on a series of blatantly sectarian attacks on predominantly Protestant housing estates across the North.[7] The contradiction between the terrorist activity of its military wing and the overtures of Sinn Féin could hardly have been more strongly emphasized. By continuing to highlight the futility of the former and the possibilities that could be available to the latter, Hume still hoped to convince the Sinn Féin leadership and through it the provisional movement as a whole, that the peaceful road was the only one that offered any hope of progress towards the goal of Irish unity. It would be some time before the dialogue would have that effect.

TALKS COMMENCE

The talks opened on 17 June[8] and in his address to the opening plenary session, Hume outlined what he hoped would be the steps that parties would follow, saying

> when each party has tabled its analysis of the problem, we should seek through debate and discussion, to identify whatever common ground and common perceptions exist between us. Having done that, we believe that we should seek to identify those requirements which will be necessary to the survival of any new arrangements we may wish to make.[9]

The essence of the SDLP's position was contained in the paper *The SDLP analysis of the nature of the problem*.[10] It was a vintage SDLP statement, emphasizing the historic British-Irish context to the problem, the need to recognize the identities and allegiances of Unionists and Nationalists, and to accommodate their interlocking relationships. The SDLP also highlighted its conviction that support for policing arrangements would require fundamental reforms in policing and in human rights legislation. Finally, the party addressed economic and social disadvantage and called for a concerted investment programme in deprived communities. As regards the Anglo-Irish Agreement, the party described it as 'an irreversible breakthrough in understanding and tackling the underlying causes of the Anglo-Irish conflict' and defended the right of the Irish government 'to involvement in the affairs of Northern Ireland'.[11] On Irish unity, the SDLP reiterated that 'the consent of a majority of the people of Northern Ireland' would be essential, and, to achieve it, 'the task of Irish nationalism must be to seek to persuade the Unionist tradition in Northern Ireland that their

interest lies in reaching an encompassing and mutually enriching accommodation with political nationalism on the island'.[12] The document also condemned
without reservation those who had recourse to violence, which, the party
claimed, was only producing a 'more deeply divided people'.[13]

When the Unionist parties' analyses were examined, the gaps between them
and the SDLP were, not surprisingly, wide, but there were some surprising
parallels and convergences, especially in the DUP's submission. In it, the DUP
accepted the three relationships, within the North, between North and South
and between Ireland and Britain, to be essential to an agreement.[14] Given its
strongly devolutionist approach, the DUP also stressed the need for a workable
form of government in which the Unionist majority would be respected, but
which would also provide a role for the minority. Not surprisingly, the DUP
denounced the Anglo-Irish Agreement as having 'proved entirely incapable of
delivering on its declared objectives ... (and it) remains as unacceptable to the
vast majority of the people of Northern Ireland today as it was on 15 November
1985'.[15] Also denounced were Articles 2 and 3 of the South's constitution,
although the DUP did acknowledge that in the Anglo-Irish Agreement the Irish
government had accepted the principle of consent to constitutional change. By
comparison, the UUP's document was heavily integrationist, made scarcely any
reference to the Nationalist community, indeed attempted to diminish the scale
of Nationalist disaffection from the northern state by suggesting that many
Catholics were Unionist, and while as equally opposed to the Anglo-Irish
Agreement as the DUP, proposed an essentially minimalist, internal approach
to any new structures and made no reference to relationships with the South.[16]
These differences between the two Unionist parties suggested that despite the
agreements that had been reached between them in *An end to drift*, negotiations
with the SDLP would not be conducted on the basis of an agreed Unionist
position.

The short period of time until the next meeting of the intergovernmental
conference meant that the talks were unable to achieve anything more than a
cross-examination of each party's opening statements, and an initial discussion
of a second set of papers focusing on what was termed 'requirements for new
structures'. The requirements discussion was intended to move the talks
towards agreeing key practical features of new institutions, though in effect they
amounted to not much more than a set of general commitments. For the SDLP,
the key requirements for new structures included that they: 'be capable of
providing peace and stability'; 'be based on democratic process and founded on

consensus'; uphold 'parity of esteem between the two traditions'; be based on 'equity of treatment for both traditions'; recognize 'the totality of Anglo-Irish relationships'; include a 'European dimension'; are 'innovative' (looking beyond traditional types of structures); be 'confidence-building' between the two traditions; and that as well as being 'durable', they be 'capable of evolving'.[17] Again, there were close parallels between the requirements put forward by all parties, but timetable constraints did not allow for any detailed discussion.

TALKS ADJOURN

Faced with the two governments' determination to adhere to the agreed timetable, and despite Unionist pressure for more time, the talks ended abruptly on 3 July. Notwithstanding their brevity, the SDLP acknowledged the value of the exchanges that had taken place, but stressed 'our consistent view that such talks should take place without preconditions, and we hope this can happen in the near future'.[18] For the SDLP, the talks had the added satisfaction of having been based on its long-advocated three-stranded formula, with the proviso that issues related to all three would have to be resolved before an agreement could be reached. The party had also tabled its proposal for joint referenda as the most effective means of democratically endorsing whatever might ultimately be agreed. While it would not be until the following April that talks would recommence, the parties had re-engaged after many years of false starts and acrimony and, for the first time together had commenced a fundamental examination of the issues to be resolved.

Despite engagement and the hope that talks could recommence in the autumn, relationships between the parties were to sour over the ensuing months as uncertainty grew about Unionist willingness to revive the talks. A combination of pre-election tensions – a British general election was anticipated from late 1991 – caused by Unionist hopes that a minority Conservative government would be returned, and that their Westminster influence would, consequently, be enhanced;[19] together with new Unionist preconditions for reconvening talks;[20] and their refusal to even commit to talks should a Labour government be returned, were responsible for no early resumption.[21] An intensification of PIRA and loyalist paramilitary activity added to those tensions and inhibitions.[22]

In the immediate aftermath of the talks being adjourned, Unionists accused the SDLP of conspiring with the Irish government to prevent an extension to the gap between meetings of the intergovernmental conference so that the talks could have continued. Some Unionists claimed that the party was more concerned to protect the Anglo-Irish Agreement than to have it replaced by a comprehensive agreement.[23] However, given the Unionist parties' responsibility for the protracted procedural delays that had dominated the first month of the talks, their unwillingness to accept that talks would continue following the scheduled meeting of the conference, the SDLP found it difficult to accept that Unionists were entirely committed to the process. Furthermore, since it was Hume who had helped broker the breakthrough that moved the talks into substantive mode, the party believed its own commitment to be beyond question. True, the SDLP refused to table substantive proposals for the government of Northern Ireland, as other parties had, but, given the increasing likelihood of closure, the party felt justified in not doing so.[24] At a meeting with the Irish government and opposition parties the day after the talks ended, the SDLP reiterated its wish that 'a formula would be found to enable them to recommence', and hoped that this would happen as soon as possible.[25] In September, Brooke held a series of meetings with the parties in an attempt to restore the talks, but given Unionist vacillations on the conditions under which they would agree to re-entering talks, no progress was made.[26]

COMING OF AGE

In the autumn, the SDLP prepared to celebrate its 'coming of age' conference marking twenty-one years of its existence. While the party had much to celebrate in terms of leadership, the stresses and strains of the period had put huge pressures on the party organizationally. Although structured along the lines of many other political parties, with local branches, constituency councils and a central executive, there were always too few activists to effectively shoulder all of the essential tasks. By the late 1980s, active membership had declined compared with the years of early enthusiasm, and the need for renewal and fresh faces was becoming evident at many levels. Some new faces had already begun to emerge at leadership level, in the likes of Mark Durkan, John Hume's parliamentary assistant since the latter's election to Westminster in 1983 and a future party leader in 2001. Durkan had become party chair in 1990 and was a member of the party's delegation to the Brooke talks. Other new faces included Alex Attwood, like Durkan a former student leader and now a Belfast city councillor,

John Fee who worked with Séamus Mallon, and Margaret Ritchie, Eddie McGrady's parliamentary assistant who also chaired the association of SDLP councillors and who would become party leader in 2010. All four would rise to considerable prominence in the party in later years. However, more new faces were needed if the party was to sustain its leadership of the Nationalist community, but successive failures to break the impasse had made politics less and less attractive over recent years. Crucially, the party also needed a more secure financial basis, as the precarious nature of its situation became clear when the party's finances were reported to the twenty-first conference.[27]

Financially, the party had been dependent on the usual forms of fund-raising adopted by all voluntary organizations, together with occasional donations from generous benefactors, particularly at election times. But, as the executive's report to conference revealed, such efforts were yielding lower than expected returns.[28] External sources, particularly the Dublin support group, provided significant funding and at each annual conference the group presented the party with the proceeds of its efforts over the previous twelve months. But all of this was insufficient for a party endeavouring to maintain a headquarters with several staff serving the growing needs of a small, but modern political party. From the late eighties, additional significant assistance had been provided for several years through the generosity of a London-based Irish businessman, Eddie Lawlor. Lawlor had been so impressed by John Hume that he offered financial and other support to the SDLP. This resulted in large new premises being acquired and extra staff being employed.[29] However, it was support that could not be sustained and, in 1991, the party was faced with a crisis. As party chair Mark Durkan bluntly commented, 'we allowed ourselves such a drift in our financial position, deluding ourselves that any problems were for the treasurer or staff rather than the party'.[30] Staff cut-backs and the disposal of the new premises became necessary, and although the former was strongly resisted by some delegates, the measures enabled the party to overcome its immediate funding problems. The lack of finance continued to haunt the party, however, leaving its central organization the perennial victim of inadequate resources.

The twenty-first conference was marked by another controversy that highlighted inter-generational differences within the party. The issue was whether the party should support the establishment of a branch of the Brook pregnancy advisory clinic in Belfast. The clinic's reputation was that it not only provided advice on sexual behaviour, particularly to young people, but that it also referred pregnant teenagers to abortion clinics in Britain. In line with the other parties in Northern Ireland, the SDLP was strongly pro-life. Consequently, when the Brook clinic announced that it would open a centre in the North, strong opposition was expressed from many quarters. Two opposing motions appeared on the SDLP's conference agenda, one from the Queen's University branch, which, while not mentioning the Brook clinic by name, called for 'the extension of relationship and sex education in schools, and welcomes the establishment of accessible advice services under medical supervision'.[31] The opposing motion from the East Belfast branch deplored 'any moves to establish a Brook clinic in Northern Ireland'.[32] A lively debate divided delegates between traditionalists on matters of sexual morality, who opposed the clinics because of their alleged referral service, and the more liberal, especially younger members, who viewed the issue as one of freedom of information. The matter was referred back to the executive, which meant that no decision was ever taken.

More significantly, the conference agenda also reflected the party's continuing concern about social and economic disadvantage, particularly in areas like West Belfast and, while condemning the 'insane campaign of violence by the PIRA' as a disincentive to potential investors, called for 'massive inward investment' as the only realistic way of reducing the dole queues'.[33] Other related issues highlighted on the agenda included calls on the government to adopt fully the European social charter in order to provide proper protection for workers, and for the publication of affirmative action measures required of employers to ensure fair and balanced workforces. These and other motions showed that, whatever its financial difficulties, the SDLP, after twenty-one years, still maintained its original commitments to civil rights and social justice.

Notwithstanding its financial and organizational weaknesses, the SDLP remained confident that its approach to the North's political and intercommunal crisis was the correct one. In a number of district council by-elections[34] during 1991, the party had generally maintained its electoral position and was looking forward with considerable expectation to improving its support in the forthcoming general election. In his leader's address to conference, Hume laid considerable stress on the success of the EC as a model of conflict resolution and suggested that its institutional framework offered an example that the North could well emulate.[35] He spoke of the people of Europe coming ever closer together as the single market approached, and he pointed to the huge advantage he saw it bringing to the whole of Ireland. Hume called for talks to resume so that the parties could 'agree institutions, North and South, which not only respect our differences and our diversity but allow us to carry out the increasingly necessary task of working our considerable common ground together'.[36] To PIRA and Sinn Féin, Hume directed the simple question 'could they tell us how a group of people could unite about anything without agreement', and he called on them to lay down their arms and to join with the SDLP 'in the challenging process of finally breaking down the barriers between the people of Ireland'.[37] It was the same question and the same invitation that the SDLP had put directly to Sinn Féin in the 1988 talks, and while efforts to engage Sinn Féin in the political process had been intensifying from several quarters, there was as yet no sign that the PIRA was preparing to call the necessary ceasefire.

TALKS RECONVENE

As the New Year opened, Brooke renewed contact with the parties in a final pre-election bid to have talks re-launched. Unionist leaders reiterated their position on not committing to talks in the event of a Labour government taking office,[38] a condition that Hume described as '... amazing. The problems that we are discussing and trying to resolve don't change simply because governments change'.[39] Attempts by Unionists, with some support from Brooke and the APNI, to have the talks recommence only with respect to Strand 1, and that, in the event of Labour coming to power, the situation would then be assessed to see if talks could be continued, found no support from the SDLP.[40] The SDLP firmly opposed a partial resumption, insisting that only the comprehensive three-stranded agenda previously agreed would suffice.

Just when it appeared that no further progress could be made, PIRA violence claimed the lives of eight Protestant workmen returning home from work at the British army barracks in Omagh, and the UVF's retaliation attack on a book-maker's shop in Belfast two weeks later killed five Catholics. These events had a sobering effect. British Prime Minister John Major insisted that the talks had to be resumed and, with the support of the new Taoiseach, Albert Reynolds, meetings took place with the party leaders, at which they agreed 'to discuss obstacles in the way of further political dialogue in the hope that political dialogue might be able to recommence at an early date'.[41] At a further meeting and after assurances that a change of government in Britain would not alter the terms of the talks, the four leaders stated that they saw 'no obstacle to the resumption of talks as soon as possible'.[42]

Consequently, the talks reconvened on 9 March, but given the imminence of the British general election, it was acknowledged that the meeting could only be symbolic and that substantive talks would not take place until after the election. Discussion on 9 March focused on the Irish constitution, with Unionists emphasizing their demand that Articles 2 and 3 be dropped, and the SDLP responding by insisting that the 1920 Government of Ireland Act be on the agenda.[43] That was as far as the discussions went. Following the announcement, two days later, that the general election would be held on 9 April, no further meeting took place until a new government had taken office.

JOE HENDRON MP

With attention now focused on that election, the SDLP prepared a manifesto that claimed the party's strategy for political dialogue had been vindicated by recent developments, and, on that basis, sought a renewed mandate for that strategy. The manifesto indicated that the SDLP would 'follow the European example by proposing institutions of government to give expression to all our relationships which respect our differences but which also allow us to work our common ground together', a further hint that the party's detailed structural proposals would borrow significantly from the EC's institutional model.[44] The manifesto also contained proposals related to social justice, economic development, human rights, environment, world development and international policy, making the manifesto the most comprehensive issued by any party in the election. The party nominated thirteen candidates, having decided not to contest the Unionist-dominated constituencies of East Antrim, East Belfast, North Down and Lagan Valley.

Once again, there was considerable interest in how the SDLP would perform compared to Sinn Féin. Expectations were high that the party's overall vote would increase, and that in West Belfast, Joe Hendron, again the party's candidate against Gerry Adams, would be successful. In fact, the results marked a resounding victory for the SDLP. Not only did the party's overall vote increase to a new high of almost 24 per cent (over 184,000 votes), from 21 per cent in 1987, but Joe Hendron defeated Adams to join the party's three sitting MPs, Hume, Mallon and McGrady, all of whom increased their majorities. The results also saw the Sinn Féin vote decline from just over 11 to 10 per cent (slightly more than 78,000 votes). As a result, the SDLP became the larger of the two parties in such Nationalist strongholds as Mid-Ulster and Fermanagh-

South Tyrone. Extremely pleased with the outcome, the party regarded it as a clear endorsement of its brand of non-violent, constitutional nationalism, and of its commitment to a comprehensive political solution that would respect all traditions.

Joe Hendron's victory (pl. 20) gave particular satisfaction and was seen as a strong signal that people desired an end to violence and a new political arrangement that would recognize and respect all traditions. Ever since Gerry Fitt lost his seat to Adams in 1983, West Belfast had been regarded as an almost impregnable Sinn Féin stronghold, and not a constituency that the SDLP could easily regain. But Hendron, who had long represented part of the constituency on Belfast City Council, and whose medical practice served some of its most deprived areas, was highly respected as a strong advocate for the SDLP, a fearless opponent of the PIRA and a representative with a deep concern for his constituents' welfare. Ironically, for a party that claimed it was pledged to uniting 'Protestant, Catholic and Dissenter', Sinn Féin bitterly attributed Hendron's victory to tactical voting by Unionists in the constituency, suggesting that their support should not be welcomed by any Nationalist party.[45] On the contrary, the message the SDLP took from its success in West Belfast and elsewhere was that it should continue its engagement with Unionists in reconvened talks, as well as pursuing its contacts with Sinn Féin leaders to bring an end to the PIRA's campaign.

ENCOURAGING WIDER DIALOGUE

John Hume, who was then in regular contact with Gerry Adams, had recently called for a wider community dialogue with paramilitaries and those politically associated with them, in order to increase pressure for an end to violence. In February, in the course of a radio interview, he had criticized church leaders for giving politicians 'advice from the sidelines', and for not, themselves, engaging with paramilitary organizations. He appealed to churchmen 'to talk with the paramilitary organizations, the sinners in your camp. Talk to them. Because you are the people who should be talking to them ... and get them to stop'.[46] While Sinn Féin had been engaged in contacts with some senior clergy of the Catholic Church, Hume wanted a more sustained form of engagement, not just to influence PIRA, but also other paramilitary groups in both communities. Immediate reaction to Hume's remarks was quite critical but, interestingly, Prime Minister

John Major, whose own intelligence service was also in contact with Sinn Féin and the PIRA, stated that 'it is to the advantage of everyone in Northern Ireland for the politicians of Northern Ireland, of all shades of opinion, to come together to talk and express their mutual wish for peace', and that would, of course, have to include Sinn Féin.[47]

Among the first churchmen to respond positively was Bishop Edward Daly in Derry, who met Sinn Féin leaders in the city. More significantly, because of its cross-community dimension, two highly respected Presbyterians, the Revd Godfrey Brown, and the Revd Jack Weir, met with Gerry Adams soon after the general election, and began a series of meetings that would continue over the following months. They described their first meeting as 'an attempt to open fresh channels of communication'.[48] While there was no immediate outcome, these meetings brought new voices into the process of persuading Sinn Féin that to fully take its place in the political process violence had to end. It also meant that a wider, parallel process to the inter-party talks was developed and the prospect, however dim, was emerging that all parties might eventually negotiate with each other. Adding to the urgency of developing this wider dialogue was continuing PIRA activity, marked by two massive bombs that exploded at the Baltic Exchange in London on the day after the general election. The explosion killed three people, one a 15-year-old girl, and caused damage of more than £700 million, a sum greater than all of the compensation hitherto paid out in Northern Ireland over the previous fifteen years.

STRAND 1 TALKS

For the immediate future, most political attention was now directed at the reconvened Strand 1 of the inter-party talks. Following the announcement of a new gap between meetings of the intergovernmental conference,[49] the talks recommenced on 29 April, this time convened by Brooke's successor, former Attorney-General Sir Patrick Mayhew. The talks would last until November and, while they would not end in success, they provided the most intense set of inter-party discussions to date, covering most of the key issues related to the political crisis. For the SDLP, the talks were the opportunity to further explore the analysis it had presented at the aborted process the previous year, and to also present its proposals for a new set of institutional arrangements reflecting the three-stranded relationships that were now the generally accepted basis for any agreement.

At the first plenary session, the SDLP stressed, in language echoing the NIF's report, that the problems the parties were required to consider long pre-dated the 1920 partition of Ireland and 'were therefore more fundamental than the mere existence of Northern Ireland or the form its institutions took'. Two different, but equally legitimate, traditions existed. 'There should be an acceptance that the rights of Nationalists *and* Unionists to effective political, symbolic and administrative expression of their identity, their ethos and their way of life had to be addressed in the talks process'.[50] The party then tabled its proposals for new political structures. These marked a radical departure from the structures that the party had agreed to in 1973, and which had been its assumed position any time it had referred to power-sharing. But, as SDLP leaders had been suggesting in recent months, the proposals were radical and drew heavily on the EC's institutional framework.

SDLP'S EUROPEAN MODEL

In introducing its proposals, the SDLP argued that new structures 'should be sought in areas which have endeavoured to overcome problems of conflict and division', and went on to point to the European model as the 'most conspicuously successful and original' model in modern times.[51] The party proposed that an assembly with very limited scrutiny and budgetary powers be directly elected, and that a powerful, but separately constituted executive take responsibility for the government of Northern Ireland. Echoing proposals made in its first policy document, *Towards a new Ireland*, the party now proposed that this executive consist of six commissioners, three of whom would be directly elected, and the other three appointed, one each by the British and Irish governments, with the third appointed by the EC.[52] To obviate any criticism that the talks might be simply focused on an internal solution, the SDLP's submission also signalled that it would be proposing a North-South council of ministers in Strand 2 talks, and a parallel institution dealing with British-Irish relations in Strand 3.[53]

Anticipating strong criticism of its proposals, not least from the Unionist parties, the SDLP argued in an accompanying memorandum that 'we have reiterated our acceptance of the fact, articulated in Article 1 of the (Anglo-Irish)

Agreement, that no change in the status of Northern Ireland can come about without the consent of the majority there'.[54] The memorandum went on to state that

> the purpose of our proposal is not to dilute the British identity of the Unionist community. It is rather to put in place positive conditions which will allow the minority community to identify with, support and defend the institutions of government in NI. In our view, the presence of the Irish Government nominee in the NI Executive will provide the symbolic and practical reassurance required to achieve this objective.[55]

The SDLP further suggested that the three externally appointed commissioners could be from Northern Ireland, and that

> they would not be present to dictate to the people of Northern Ireland. As with commissioners appointed to serve in the European Commission, each commissioner would be required to take an oath committing himself/herself to working alongside the directly elected commissioners on behalf of the people of Northern Ireland.[56]

The proposals were certainly very novel and completely unexpected.

Arguing in support of its proposals, the SDLP stated that it wanted to break the dependence of the executive on the assembly, which it saw as a fundamental weakness of the 1974 arrangements. The party claimed that dependence 'had been shown to lie at the centre of failed attempts to establish cross-community administrations'.[57] In other words, the SDLP argued that an institutional separation of executive from scrutiny functions, would avoid a repetition of those failures. Since the party also proposed that the commissioners should be required to act in unanimity, the pressure for agreement would, hopefully, overcome traditional divisions. How critical divisions between assembly members would not also be strongly reflected among the commissioners, three of whom would be directly elected, was difficult to imagine. The obvious hope was that the commissioners would develop an independence from local political influences which together with a strong working relationship would enable them to overcome any tensions that would arise.

Not surprisingly, these proposals faced a barrage of criticism from within and without the talks, and, for the first time, the party found itself accused of not being serious. An *Irish Times* editorial suggested that the proposals could not be the party's bottom line because, if they were, 'then the party would surely have a case to answer for leading the talks into a cul-de-sac'.[58] Unionists dismissed the proposal for an Irish government-appointed commissioner as amounting to even greater Dublin interference in the affairs of the North, an interference they were determined to diminish, not increase. John Taylor, a UUP delegate, bluntly stated that 'I absolutely and totally reject these proposals'.[59] The DUP accused the SDLP of 'making a submission which substantially widens the gulf and introduces new conditions'.[60] The APNI dismissed the executive proposal as

> unrealistic and impractical ... if implemented it could not ensure effective decision-making, and the powerlessness of the proposed assembly would serve to encourage a destructive and disruptive attitude amongst its members.[61]

There was also scepticism as to the EC's willingness to become involved in the manner proposed. Indeed, Jacques Delors, president of the European Commission, would make it clear that he did not believe the proposal could be supported since it would mean the commission interfering 'in the internal problem of a country, of a province'.[62] Within the SDLP itself, there was not unanimous support for the commissioner-type proposal, with several delegates believing that it had no chance of being agreed, not least because of its complexity and questions about its practicality.[63]

Despite the strong criticism, there were those who regarded the proposals as having merit, if only because of their novelty and because they challenged the received wisdom regarding the nature of a future government for Northern Ireland. An *Irish News* editorial commended the European influence on the SDLP's proposals, adding that 'there would be very clear and obvious attractions to Britain in wanting the rest of the EC to share the burden with London and Dublin of resolving the conflict in Northern Ireland'.[64] The Irish government also saw merit in the proposals, indicating that 'we would have no objection to appointing a commissioner in Northern Ireland; we want more than a consultative role'.[65] However, it was soon clear that if a stalemate was to be avoided and if the talks were to progress to Strand 2, compromise would have to be considered.

UNIONISTS RESURRECT CONVENTION PROPOSALS

The Unionist parties and the APNI rejected the SDLP's commission-type administration, not only on political and practical grounds, but also because the proposed assembly would have no more than consultative powers and would be unable to overturn commissioners' decisions. In contrast, Unionists proposed a legislative assembly which would also exercise an executive role through departmental committees composed of assembly members whose chairs would be appointed in proportion to party strengths. These proposals were almost exactly the same proposals Unionists had been making since the 1975 convention, proposals that had never found favour with the SDLP. The slight advance on the convention proposals was that departmental committee chairs would be heads of departments, a ministerial like position, and, might meet together to coordinate business and perform quasi-executive functions. These proposals were intended to circumvent the direct power-sharing type executive agreed to in 1973 and to which Unionists remained resolutely opposed ever since. However, from the SDLP's perspective, their essential weakness was that the committee system would mean a Unionist majority on most, if not all committees and, consequently, would result in a scarcely concealed return to 'majority' rule, rather than a genuine form of power-sharing. At the first substantive hurdle, the talks were faced with two mutually exclusive sets of proposals, and some compromise had to be sought if progress was to be made.

POSSIBLE COMPROMISE

No formal compromise was reached on the various proposals, though a framework paper prepared by NIO officials as a result of exploratory discussions between the parties at sub-committee level, suggested, among other possibilities, that a directly elected 'panel' of three instead of six commissioners, might be acceptable to the SDLP.[66] This panel would have consultative, monitoring, referral and representative functions. In other words, it might have powers to oversee an assembly's business, a much reduced role from that envisaged in the SDLP's proposal. These suggestions provided a form of compromise, but one that fell far short of what the SDLP had sought. The party agreed that it would merely note the report.[67] As far as agreement, even in principle, on Strand 1 was concerned, all that the parties could state was that there could be an assembly.

As to an assembly's powers, and where executive authority might lie, no agreement of any kind was reached.

STRAND 2 TALKS

Unionist hopes that considerable progress would be made on Strand 1 matters before the talks moved into Strands 2 and 3 were not realized. So, when pressure mounted to move the talks into those strands, Unionists resisted and for a while another breakdown seemed likely. The SDLP countered Unionist resistance, saying that further progress on Strand 1 issues, in particular the role of the Irish government, was 'dependent on matters which other parties claim are pertinent to Strands 2 and 3 discussions, when the Irish government will be a participant in the talks',[68] and, therefore, it made sense to move without delay into those strands. Following discussions with the parties and the Irish government, and private assurances to the Unionist parties that the British government had no enthusiasm for the SDLP's proposals,[69] this is exactly what transpired. On 1 July, Brooke announced that 'no more work can be usefully done in Strand 1 at present ... and the most constructive route forward is to build on the work done ... and to move forward now into those strands (2 and 3) of discussion'.[70] Effectively, this was an acknowledgment of the SDLP's case that all three strands were so inter-related that a resolution in one was dependent on a resolution in the others, and that all three needed to progress in parallel.

For the SDLP, moving into Strand 2 was not only essential, it was something of a relief from its sense of unease and isolation arising from the strong criticism it had experienced during the Strand 1 talks. Strand 2 was where the party believed serious negotiations could really start. In the SDLP's analysis, it was Unionist mistrust of the rest of the people of the island that had led to partition, and it was only by bringing all of the parties and the two governments together that relationships could be fully addressed and resolved. For Unionists, Strand 2 was the opportunity to confront the Irish government about Articles 2 and 3 of its constitution, and to demand that it commit to removing these articles as an essential component in any agreement. Following such a commitment, Unionists said that they would discuss North-South institutions, but not of the kind envisaged by the SDLP.

The opening of Strand 2 talks marked an historic moment in British-Irish relationships. It was the first time ever that representatives of both governments and all of the main constitutional parties in Northern Ireland met to negotiate their future relationships. The first sessions were held over three days at Lancaster House, London, and beginning on 6 July, were presided over by independent chair, Sir Ninian Stephen. In the SDLP's opening remarks, Hume presented essentially the same analysis as the party had presented in Strand 1. Ominously for the SDLP, in his opening remarks, Sir Patrick Mayhew indicated that the talks were taking place 'on the premise that any new political institutions in Northern Ireland would be based on the structures outlined in the Strand 1 sub-committee report',[71] the report on which the British government's framework paper had been based. This suggested that when the talks returned to Strand 1 issues, the SDLP would be required to accept the compromise or risk causing a breakdown. In the event, it was not a challenge that ever materialized.

The following two weeks of discussions witnessed an intense engagement between Unionist and Irish government delegates on a wide variety of issues, including the constitution, security, the role of the Catholic Church, and the fate of the Protestant minority in the South. As expected, Unionists strongly pressed the case for a unilateral commitment from the Irish government that its constitution would be amended before they would be willing to discuss any new North-South structures. While rejecting this demand, the Irish government delegates did, however, suggest that amendments might be possible in the context of an overall agreement,[72] a position that the SDLP broadly endorsed. The talks adjourned on 24 July with agreement to reconvene in September, but with no agreement, even in principle, on any of the substantial matters discussed.

'COULD' OR 'WOULD'

When the talks resumed there were just over two months until the next scheduled meeting of the intergovernmental conference during which the negotiations would have to be completed. From the outset, the SDLP and the Irish government once again found themselves subject to intense Unionist arguments on the constitution, but the Irish government would only repeat that amendments *could* be put to a referendum as part of an agreed package, not that they *would* be put. As Minister Dessie O'Malley argued, the

> the package would be a signal at the end of these talks towards ... new
> relationships, and the Irish people would be able to decide to accept this
> package, but the articles wouldn't be removed simply by someone asking
> for them to be removed unilaterally.[73]

In somewhat more graphic language, Séamus Mallon stated that 'Nationalists
in Ireland, particularly in Northern Ireland, are not going to lie down like pups
and wave their feet in the air and welcome a unilateral change in Articles 2 and
3'.[74] While the Irish government formally indicated that it 'does not rule out
constitutional change resulting from the present negotiations', it made clear
that there would be no unqualified commitment to do so, and that it would be
'particularly sensitive to the impact any proposed amendment might have on
the position of the Nationalist minority in Northern Ireland who, unquestionably, have been the victims of the Government of Ireland Act'.[75]

PRACTICAL PROPOSALS

For its part, the SDLP continued to argue that Articles 2 and 3 were not the root
cause of the relationship problem between Unionists and Nationalists, but like
the Irish government, it accepted that constitutional amendments could be part
of any final package. When it came to the party's own submission on new
North-South structures, the SDLP ignored the constitutional issue and instead
focused on the kind of institutions it believed should be agreed. The party
recommended that a North-South council of ministers be established with
responsibilities in such areas as economic development, agriculture, tourism
and transport, security and legal affairs, environment, health and social welfare,
and cultural and educational matters.[76] The party also proposed that such a
council should have special responsibility for EC programmes affecting the
whole island. Finally, the SDLP proposed the setting up of a parliamentary
body with members drawn from a new northern assembly and the Oireachtas
with the right to 'discuss policy, review progress, make proposals to the secretariat, question ministers etc.'[77] The submission reflected much that had been
agreed at Sunningdale in 1973. Unlike the fate of its proposals in Strand 1, the
SDLP found its submission for North-South institutions positively acknowledged by the British government in its summary document for discussion by
the Strand 2 committee.[78]

When the talks moved to Dublin, the focus returned to the constitutional issue, but with no progress beyond the stated positions of both the Dublin government and the Unionists. Pressure on the Irish government to make a firmer commitment to holding a referendum to amend Articles 2 and 3 came not just from Unionists and the British, but also from several sections of public opinion in the South, among them the main opposition party, Fine Gael. The party leader, John Bruton, urged that the government formally commit to a referendum if a satisfactory package was agreed, arguing that 'this is the big difference between 'could' and 'would' … if the government would say they would do it, I believe it would unblock the talks'.[79] However, the government was not prepared to go beyond what it had already indicated, and the logjam remained.

Notwithstanding this impasse, some useful discussion took place on possible North-South structures, on possibilities for cooperation, including security and terrorism, identity and allegiance, with the result that a further British government summary document in early October indicated areas of potential agreement.[80] These again included much that the SDLP had been proposing. However, wide gaps remained to be negotiated since the UUP, which had acknowledged the need for new institutions to deal with North-South matters, had proposed they be functions of a wider 'council of the British Isles', an idea that was unacceptable to the SDLP.[81] By this stage, the talks had entered their final month and, while Strand 2 discussions continued throughout October, the prospect of an agreement in this or any other strand quickly faded, and an orderly closure was agreed. In the last weeks of the talks, Sir Ninian Stephen conducted one-to-one talks with all of the parties, the result of which was a document entitled *Elements of an agreement*, which set out the areas where agreement in principle seemed to have been reached.[82] Although, at the time, the parties did not accept Stephen's document, it did address key issues related to all three strands and, in many respects, anticipated what the Good Friday Agreement would contain some five-and-a-half years later.

TALKS END BUT NOT OVER

When the talks ended on 10 November, the SDLP acknowledged that 'deeper levels of understanding have been established as to participants' positions and as to the difficulties which must be overcome in reaching a comprehensive settlement'.[83] The party also hoped that talks could be renewed in the near future.

After the long months of logjam and stalemate, there was a sense of public disillusionment with the politicians and the process. The SDLP was severely criticized by the other parties for not making any compromise on its Strand 1 proposals, with suggestions that the party had not been fully committed to the process. However, most criticism was reserved for the Irish government's unwillingness to make a firm commitment that it would recommend amendments to Articles 2 and 3 in the event of an agreed package on all other issues.[84]

As the talks ended, the reality of political violence continued to be felt. In the closing months of the year, the PIRA again bombed London, Belfast and predominantly Protestant towns like Bangor, Coleraine and Lisburn, and murdered several members of the security forces while loyalists continued to murder Catholics. The year ended with ninety-one deaths from violence, and no sign of an end in sight. The only hope lay in the contacts which Hume and others were now developing with the provisional movement.

PART IV

Hopes realized (1995–2000)

Chapter 15

Self-determination

The SDLP's 1992 annual conference was a celebration.[1] The party had recorded its highest ever vote at the general election that year; it now had four MPs and, despite the imminent collapse of the Brooke-Mayhew talks, it had the satisfaction of having much of its analysis and basic framework for an agreement accepted for whenever one would be negotiated. The party felt a degree of confidence not experienced since the early seventies, and looked forward to successfully contesting the electoral challenges ahead, especially the local government elections in May 1993. John Hume reflected this confidence as he criticized Unionists for what he claimed was their 'lack of self-confidence', manifest in persistent demands that the British government reiterate the constitutional guarantee of no change without majority consent.[2] Hume called on Unionists to recognize that when the SDLP spoke of an 'agreed Ireland', the party was speaking about agreed constitutional and political arrangements in Ireland that would require the assent of Unionists as well as of Nationalists, not an Ireland in which one identity would have achieved victory over the other. Conscious of his dialogue with Sinn Féin leader Gerry Adams, Hume also stressed that the one organization that could make the greatest contribution to a climate conducive to an agreement was the PIRA, which he called on to declare a ceasefire.

POLICE REFORM FUNDAMENTAL

Reflecting on a key issue given scarcely any attention during the Brooke-Mayhew talks, Séamus Mallon highlighted the need to address reform of policing and security. Conscious of the 1973 failure to satisfactorily address the issue, the party was anxious that the same would not happen again. While some reform had taken place since the Anglo-Irish Agreement, the SDLP believed it was not sufficient and that more fundamental change was essential if Nationalists were to support and participate in the police service. The SDLP had raised policing and judicial reform at the Brooke-Mayhew talks and had listed both in a paper to Sir Ninian Stephen setting out areas of disagreement,[3] but Unionists and the APNI, and indeed the British government, had not shared SDLP's concerns. As in 1973, the assumption was that the RUC did not require fundamental reform to make it acceptable to Nationalists. That was clearly not the SDLP's position, and Mallon argued that

> unless we solve this problem – the administration of justice – we don't solve any of the political problems. That is not because we don't want to – but because it is the harsh reality, for us within our constituencies and within our party.[4]

The party could not afford to repeat the Sunningdale experience of not having the issue adequately addressed in future negotiations.

PARTY PROBLEMS

Despite the party's success in recent elections, the executive's report to conference lamented the continuing fall in registered members and took no consolation from the fact that electoral support seemed to be moving in the opposite direction. The report commented that 'whatever sense of irony or relief which this might stimulate, we should consider how much better we could do with improved membership and organization'.[5] Further success did not arrest this decline, a decline that would eventually lead to a weakening of party structures and, by the end of the decade, contribute to a considerable loss of electoral support. For the present, however, notwithstanding membership decline, the party continued to demonstrate an enthusiastic capacity for policy development. A compendium of policies circulated just before the conference listed a total of 123 significant policy initiatives over the previous twenty years, covering the full range of political, social and economic areas, to which the twenty-second annual conference added several more.[6] It was a considerable record for a party neither in government nor, officially, in opposition.

As the SDLP prepared for the 1993 local government elections, there was considerable discussion about reconvening inter-party talks. There was a widely shared sense that, despite the absence of agreement, enough progress had been made during the Brooke-Mayhew talks to encourage the parties to re-engage.

At a meeting with the secretary of state on 23 April, Hume acknowledged that public opinion wanted politicians to resume talks, and he declared that the SDLP was ready and willing to do so.[7] Eddie McGrady argued that 'the only thing that would truly defeat the ingrained paramilitarism of this country is the untried will of the entire community'.[8] However, it was also clear that momentum had been lost and that not all the parties were willing to re-engage. The political focus now moved to the developing dialogue between John Hume and Gerry Adams that was coming to public attention.

WHO SELF-DETERMINES

Following Peter Brooke's statement in November 1990 indicating that Britain no longer had any selfish, strategic or economic interest in remaining in Ireland, discussions on how to bring about a PIRA ceasefire moved to a new level. Hume began drafting a declaration setting out the terms and conditions for talks that would include Sinn Féin, which he believed could be made by the British and Irish governments. He worked on the draft, first on his own, then in consultation with Taoiseach Charles Haughey and Irish officials, notably Haughey's adviser, Martin Mansergh and with Gerry Adams.[9] Initially private, his meetings with Adams were brought to public attention in April 1993, when the latter was spotted entering Hume's house in Derry.[10]

Following the revelation that they were meeting, Hume and Adams issued a statement in which they addressed the thorny issue of self-determination, and for the first time a shift in the traditional Sinn Féin analysis was becoming more publicly evident.[11] Until then, Sinn Féin's position had remained as it had been outlined to the SDLP during the 1988 talks between both parties. In other words, the people of Ireland as a whole had the right to determine the country's future, a positon that effectively dismissed any special concern for Unionists' views. Hume believed that a basis for progress towards a comprehensive agreement would be laid if the leadership of Sinn Féin and the PIRA could be persuaded to accept the SDLP's interpretation of self-determination: that while the people of Ireland had the right to self-determination, the right could not be exercised without consulting Unionists who, at least by virtue of their numbers and geography, held a practical veto over how the right to self-determination would be implemented. The April statement marked a slight move in this direction when the two leaders stated that the Irish people as a whole have the right to self-determination. This is a view shared by a majority of the people of this island though not by all its people. The right of self-determination is a matter for agreement between the people of Ireland. It is the search for that agreement and the means of achieving it on which we will be concentrating.[12]

For the leader of Sinn Féin to accept that not all of the people of Ireland (an oblique reference to Unionists) shared the same view as to how self-determination should be exercised, and, more importantly, that agreement had to be sought on the exercise of that right, was a significant break with his party's previous approach. Seeking agreement clearly implied working for it peacefully and democratically, and that required an end to violence. Adams' move, though slight and still tentative, offered the possibility of further movement.

Unionists, however, were not easily convinced and did not interpret the statement in those terms. Instead, they dismissed the joint statement as evidence of a conspiracy to coerce them into a 'united' Ireland, and indicated that they would not re-enter talks with the SDLP while the Hume-Adams dialogue continued. Chris McGimpsey of the UUP wrote that 'John Hume's pursuit of an "agreed Ireland" did not focus on obtaining the autonomous agreement of Unionist consent, but on the independent inducement of Unionist consent'.[13] Nonetheless, from Hume's perspective, the statement marked an important step towards comprehensive negotiations, and in any case the primary audience at this stage was the British government. The British had to be persuaded to accept a formulation on self-determination with which Sinn Féin and PIRA could live, and *vice versa*. If such a formulation could be found, then it would be a matter of engaging with Unionists. From this point onwards, it was a matter of building on the gradual changes in the provisional movement's thinking and, in particular, of convincing Unionists that seeking their agreement was sincerely meant.

Building on those changes would not be easy. At a meeting of the constituency representatives on 27 April 1993, just three days after the second of two encounters with Adams that month, Hume tabled papers from Sinn Féin and the PIRA's Army Council which showed the distance yet to be travelled.[14] The papers contained the provisional movement's own proposals for a joint declaration from both governments. In it, both would commit to achieving Irish unity within a specified period of time, and in a manner to be determined according to the principle of self-determination. While the papers also emphasized the willingness of the movement to end violence, the demand on unity was so extreme as to render it unacceptable. Neither the Irish nor the British governments were ever likely to commit to a process aimed at achieving unity within a specified period, however long. The proposition clearly overrode the principle of consent, but since, as the Hume-Adams statement had indicated, the provisional movement was beginning to accept that Unionists could not be taken for granted and their rights would have to be respected in a united Ireland, the prospect of achieving progress could not be ruled out. Dialogue had opened a door, slightly, and further dialogue held out the prospect of it opening wider.

SDLP CONCERNS

Weighing the hope that the Hume-Adams dialogue would lead to a PIRA cease-fire against the ongoing violence, it was no surprise that within the SDLP's leadership there was a degree of scepticism as to the provisional movement's seriousness about wanting peace, and a concern, therefore, about the value of pursuing the talks. However, most were supportive of the dialogue with Adams.[15] Hume was trusted to do what he judged best. In the proposed declaration by the two governments, Hume also hoped that the Irish government would constitutionally acknowledge the principle of consent by amending Articles 2 and 3 to make clear that unity 'cannot be achieved without the agreement of the people of Northern Ireland', and together with the British government would commit to working for institutions of government, North and South, that would respect the diversity of the people of Ireland.[16] In other words, Hume was seeking a balanced declaration from both governments that would also be acceptable to the provisional movement and, crucially, also to Unionists. His initial draft would undergo considerable amendment during several phases of discussions before appearing as a formal declaration by both governments in December 1993.

WIDESPREAD SCEPTICISM

The revelation that Hume was once again engaged in dialogue with Adams brought howls of protest from Unionists, as well as degrees of scepticism and sharp criticism from shades of political opinion in the South. The DUP accused Hume of having made common cause with the PIRA and, according to that party's press officer, there was 'no doubt that John Hume is now working hard to rehabilitate the blood-stained spokesmen of the PIRA. He wants them involved in any talks to add weight to the pan-Nationalist front he is putting together to cover his own back'.[17] APNI leader, John Alderdice, claimed that 'many people who have previously admired Mr Hume's abilities and judgment will be dismayed that he now feels it easier for him to make common cause with Sinn Féin than with Alliance'.[18] More significant was the intense criticism from commentators in the South. Michael McDowell of the Progressive Democrats believed the talks 'would set back the inter-community peace process and ... were doomed to failure'.[19] Contributors to the *Sunday Independent*, Conor Cruise O'Brien and Eamon Dunphy, launched trenchant attacks on Hume and the whole SDLP. Dunphy described Hume as 'a political bomber flying over Unionist heads trying to kill them'.[20] O'Brien, whose views of the party were as critical as ever, commented that under Hume's leadership the SDLP had become 'a coldly sectarian party, which is not above doing a deal with terrorists in order to gain collective community and sectarian advantage'.[21] Adding to the anger of those who condemned Hume's initiative was an intensification of PIRA bombing attacks in the North and in Britain. In Britain, a bomb exploded in the centre of Warrington, killing two young boys, 3-year-old Jonathan Ball and 12-year-old Timothy Parry,[22] while another massive bomb-attack in London killed one person and caused damage of over £1,000 million.[23] It was difficult to appreciate the value of dialogue with representatives of a movement that callously continued to put civilian lives in danger. But Hume persisted in the conviction that his message would have to be heeded.

SDLP HOMES ATTACKED

The Hume-Adams dialogue and PIRA's ongoing campaign combined to raise communal tension and became the excuse for loyalist paramilitaries who launched a series of attacks on the homes of SDLP public representatives. Between April and September, the homes of fifteen councillors, as well as that of MP Joe Hendron, were attacked, luckily without any serious personal injuries being caused. The UDA made it no secret that the attacks had been motivated by Hume's contacts with Gerry Adams. Although none of the representatives involved called for the talks to be abandoned, Joe Hendron did state his belief that the talks were undermining his position as MP for West Belfast.[24] But in a follow up statement with his three MP colleagues, Hendron made clear his support for the talks and denied any suggestion of a party rift.[25]

POSITIVE SUPPORT

The Hume-Adams talks also elicited positive comments. Garret FitzGerald wrote that

> those who criticize such initiatives must surely ask themselves: if they were in a similar position to John Hume, and if they had been given by other people of good will and rational judgment reason to believe that such a contact might, even by remote chance, advance peace in Northern Ireland, could they justify to their own consciences taking the easy way out by refusing these risks?[26]

Bishop Cahal Daly of Down and Connor also welcomed the dialogue, saying that it was 'very good news to hear that there are still people there who don't want talk of war but who want talk of peace'.[27] Because it was also engaged in its own discussions with Sinn Féin at the time,[28] the Irish government maintained a neutral position, merely indicating that Hume 'was an experienced politician and it was a matter for him to decide whether something useful could come out of the talks'.[29] Hume answered his critics, saying 'if I fail to achieve the objective of bringing violence to an end the only damage will be that I have failed, but not a single person extra will be supporting violence as a result. But if the talks succeed, then the entire atmosphere will be transformed'.[30] Some weeks later, in June, the Hume-Adams dialogue received indirect endorsement when the informal Opsahl commission, *Initiative '92*,[31] published its report. Among the commission's significant findings was that 'there was almost across-the-divide agreement among presenters at the oral hearings that a settlement that excluded Sinn Féin would be neither lasting nor stable, and that some way had to be found to bring Sinn Féin into the process'.[32] This was precisely the objective that had motivated Hume in the first place.

CONVINCING GOVERNMENTS

In June, Hume prepared an amended draft which sought to move the debate on self-determination forward by acknowledging that while 'the people of Ireland have the right collectively to self-determination ... they have been divided on how to exercise that right' and the aim should be 'to reach agreement on the exercise of self-determination'.[33] By stressing agreement, Hume was again indicating that Unionists would have to agree to the manner in which self-determination would be expressed and, of course, their expression would, in all probability, not be in accordance with the wishes of the provisional movement.

Meantime, electoral politics resulted in the SDLP increasing its number of seats at the district council elections in May. Emphasizing the continuing need for cross-community partnership at council level, the party's manifesto, *Progress through partnership*, acknowledged that 'a few councils with large Unionist majorities have felt secure enough to display a measure of generosity to councillors from other parties'.[34] The party hoped that this example would be followed more widely, because not doing so had contributed significantly to the SDLP's suspicions of Unionist intent during the Brooke-Mayhew talks. The situations that prevailed on the two largest councils, Derry and Belfast, were contrasted. On the former, senior offices rotated between all parties while Belfast council had, in the words of the manifesto, 'become a by-word for sectarian, obstructionist politics of a kind that most of us, of whatever political persuasion, hoped we had seen the last of twenty years ago'.[35] In effect, the party was challenging Unionists to become more committed to partnership as a basic requirement of political life at all levels, and to demonstrate that commitment in practical terms at local government level, the only level where representatives of both communities could do so.

ELECTORAL ENDORSEMENT

In the elections, the SDLP won 127 seats, up from 121 in 1989, while Sinn Féin also increased its number of seats from 43 in 1989 to 51. The combined vote for both parties reflected a rise in the Nationalist proportion of the electorate and a corresponding decline in the Unionist share, a trend that would continue over the following years, and which would add to the imperative on Unionists to make an agreement. The results also strongly suggested that the SDLP was continuing to gain from its approach during the Brooke-Mayhew talks, as well as from Hume's engagement with Gerry Adams. Despite ongoing PIRA atrocities, however, Sinn Féin was also gaining and now represented over 30 per cent of the Nationalist vote. These figures underlined the growing conviction, reflected in the Opsahl report, that it could not be ignored, and if Sinn Féin were to accept the same terms as other parties (a disavowal of violence), it would not be excluded from future negotiations.

With no early revival of inter-party talks in prospect, the political focus for the rest of 1993 remained on the Hume-Adams dialogue. In that context, John Hume and the SDLP in general were subjected to unrelenting criticism. Unionists maintained that the SDLP had abandoned any interest in devolution and, given Major's declining majority in the commons, had begun to press for concessions at Westminster, in particular for a select committee that would allow greater opportunities for scrutinizing and amending legislation proposed for Northern Ireland.[36] Conor Cruise O'Brien and similarly minded southern commentators maintained their attacks on the SDLP, with O'Brien claiming that neither it nor Sinn Féin had any 'serious intention of seeking Unionist agreement. What they want from Unionists is capitulation'.[37] However, as Hume was later to comment, he did not care 'two balls of roasted snow' about the continuing criticism of his engagement with Adams.[38] He had set himself the goal of ending violence, and dialogue was his only means. While the SDLP continued to protest the *bona fides* of Hume's strategy, continuing paramilitary violence from loyalists and the PIRA still left the party with no evidence of a positive response. The summer months witnessed an intensification of loyalist attacks on Catholics, while the PIRA exploded large bombs in towns like Newtownards, Bournemouth and Armagh, causing huge damage. Whatever Hume and Adams had been discussing, it remained very difficult to believe that violence might be nearing an end.

US INTEREST INTENSIFIES

In September, a new factor entered the political scene with the arrival of a delegation from the US, led by former Congressman Bruce Morrison and consisting mainly of business people, most with an Irish-American connection. While delegations from the US were not new to Northern Ireland, this one

came at a time of heightened speculation that recently elected President Bill
Clinton would soon appoint a special 'peace envoy' and Morrison had been
among those instrumental in gaining the president's interest in the proposal.
During his visit, Morrison and his colleagues met with several political parties,
including the SDLP, to discuss the contribution that such an envoy might
make. With long experience of the value of US interest in Northern Ireland, the
SDLP was anxious to encourage the proposal and indicated this view to
Morrison and his colleagues. In his meetings with all of the parties, including
with Sinn Féin, Morrison's message reflected that of the SDLP – violence had
to stop if the US was to become involved in helping to achieve political agreement and, beyond that, in encouraging greater US investment in the North.
The visit was an early signal of the role that the US government was to play in
the quest for peace and for an agreement.

MAJOR SAYS 'NO'

With no sign of a British response to his proposals for a declaration, Hume met
John Major in mid-September to urge him to make a declaration along the lines
that he had developed with Adams, but with no positive effect. Hume and Adams
then issued another joint statement that was to cause considerable confusion
and annoyance both in Dublin and in London. In it, the two leaders indicated
that, having made considerable progress, they would be forwarding a report to
the Dublin government for consideration by the two governments, but released
no details. Furthermore, they announced that they had 'suspended detailed
discussions' pending a response.[39] Hume departed for several mainly business-
related meetings in the US, leaving behind a sense of expectation that neither
government had wanted, but which fuelled huge media speculation.[40] The two
governments had hoped to keep details of contacts with Sinn Féin confidential
until such time as they had jointly agreed a response. As a result, they were very
unhappy with the pressure created by the Hume-Adams statement. The Irish
government was particularly annoyed, given that the version of the declaration
being discussed was far from a finished product and, in its view, the Hume-
Adams draft still contained unacceptable wording on self-determination.

While Hume had briefed the party's leadership about his talks with Adams,
he did not always share full details of what was being discussed. Consequently,
when he departed for the US, some of his closest colleagues were confused as to

what the 'report' to Dublin contained. At a fringe meeting of the British Labour Party's conference two days after the joint statement, Séamus Mallon spoke about the need for patience if peace was to be achieved. But he also pointedly warned that patience

> cannot survive continued killings and bombing of towns and villages. Whatever the logistics of their (PIRA) own internal deliberations, and whatever timescale their tactics demand, if they are serious about developing a strategy for peace ... they can let the silence of their guns, the silence of their bombs be the absolute tangible, humane declaration of their intent to work for peace.[41]

Mallon was expressing not only his own annoyance, but also the frustration of colleagues about the length of time it was taking the PIRA to decide whether or not it would declare a ceasefire. Joe Hendron expressed his frustration when he again publicly declared that the Hume-Adams talks were undermining his position in West Belfast, but added that his electoral survival was secondary to the search for peace and that he fully supported Hume's efforts.[42]

Following the joint statement, Hume adopted a more studied approach in public, saying that while much had been achieved with Adams, 'the process is not finished. It has reached a certain stage and there is obviously more work to be done. It must involve all the parties and its purpose is to bring about a cessation of all violence'.[43] Since details of the discussions were unknown to the public, reaction focused on the fact that they were still taking place. Unionists continued to allege that Hume and Adams were intent on coercing them into a united Ireland, and that any short-term proposals would be merely 'staging posts' in that direction.[44] Leader of Fine Gael, John Bruton, said that the only solution that would work would be one 'supported by moderate Unionists and moderate Nationalists. Secondly, a solution that rewarded violence was not likely to work because it would encourage the renewal of violence at a later stage to get a little more'.[45] Government spokespersons avoided direct criticism of Hume but, by denying that any report had been received, they raised questions about his credibility. Despite the government parties' reluctance to openly criticize Hume, many commentators highlighted the fact that Reynolds and Spring were very unhappy with the joint statement. The British government said that it would consider any document passed to it by Dublin, but Mayhew made it clear that 'the status of Northern Ireland is that it is part of the UK ... It could only be changed if people change their minds about it'.[46] In other words, there would be no single *collective* expression of self-determination as demanded by Sinn Féin, and the British would not become persuaders for Irish unity, a matter they believed had to be left to the people of Ireland.

GOVERNMENTS TAKE CONTROL

When Hume returned from the US, he briefed the Irish government on the details of his discussions with Adams. The proposals they had agreed consisted of three broad principles.[47] The first stated that the people of Ireland as a whole had a right collectively to self-determination. The second accepted that Unionist consent would be required for any solution in Northern Ireland. The third called on the two governments, particularly the British government, to become persuaders for unity. The first was a truism, but only acceptable to both governments if it was not to be understood as requiring a single act of self-determination. The third was never likely to be accepted because it required the British to support only one possible outcome to negotiations. The second principle was the most significant, representing as it did the shift in the provisional movement's position. But, surrounded by the ambiguous first principle and the refusal of the British to become persuaders for Irish unity, the package as a whole was doomed. In the event, when the Irish government eventually did forward a copy of the draft declaration to London, the British government rejected it out of hand.[48]

The controversy and speculation caused by the Hume-Adams statement raised questions about the SDLP's credibility and, most particularly, about John Hume's tactics. More widely, the effect was that the two governments took sole charge of creating a framework for discussions, though they would be careful to build on the advances achieved in the Hume-Adams dialogue. So, while Hume had not achieved a ceasefire by the autumn of 1993 as he had hoped, his engagement with Adams had resulted in significant, if yet only partial changes in the provisional movement's thinking on self-determination. If sustained, these changes could lead to a ceasefire as their next logical step. Making it happen would take a little longer, not least because there were those in the PIRA still intent on viciously pursuing their campaign of violence.

SHANKILL AND GREYSTEEL MASSACRES

Paramilitary violence in October underlined the scale of the challenge to be faced in ending that violence. On 22 October in the House of Commons, Hume spoke of his dialogue with Adams as 'the most hopeful dialogue and the most hopeful chance of peace that I have seen in twenty years'.[49] The very next day, his words were cynically and brutally contradicted. On a busy Saturday afternoon, the PIRA exploded a bomb in a fish shop on Belfast's Shankill Road, killing ten people and injuring fifty-seven. The PIRA claimed that their bomb was intended to kill members of the UFF who, they mistakenly believed, were meeting in an office above the shop. Tensions, already high because of recent paramilitary attacks, rose sharply as retaliatory murders by loyalist paramilitaries followed quickly, the worst coming a week later, when two UFF gunmen murdered seven customers celebrating Halloween at the Rising Sun bar in Greysteel, Co. Derry. October ended with twenty-seven dead from violence, the highest monthly figure since 1976.

The violence seriously called into question the sincerity of the PIRA's support for the Hume-Adams dialogue, and posed a huge threat to its continuation. Hume expressed himself shattered at the news of the Shankill bombing, and broke down in tears when, at the funeral of those murdered at Greysteel, he spoke to their relatives. A daughter of one of those killed encouraged him to continue his work for peace, saying that 'when we said the rosary around my daddy's coffin, we prayed for you and for what you are trying to do to bring peace'.[50] He reiterated his call for an early and positive response to the proposals that he and Adams had made, and pledged to continue their dialogue. He was again widely criticized, but also received considerable support from such unlikely quarters as the London *Independent*, which said that he 'should pursue his dialogue with Gerry Adams ... Such discussions may seem inappropriate ... But abandoning talks now would be a mistake'.[51]

NEW INITIATIVE UNDERWAY

The Irish government responded almost immediately, when, during a debate on the North, Foreign Minister Dick Spring outlined six democratic principles that would 'underpin a peace process, and which can be combined through negotiation and dialogue to secure sustainable peace'.[52] Critical to those principles was the right of a majority in the North to determine its constitutional status (principle 3), and the right of Unionists to give or withhold their consent to such change (principle 4). The sixth principle reaffirmed that a place would be available to those who had previously supported terrorism, but only following 'a total cessation of violence'.[53] These principles said nothing new, but they did emphasize that the Irish government would not accept a commitment to self-determination that ignored the wishes of a majority in the North, or that overrode the wishes of Unionists.

A few days later, the two governments agreed to use these principles as the basis for developing the framework for negotiations on which they were working, while also indicating that, in the event of a renunciation of violence, 'new doors could open and both governments would wish to respond imaginatively to the new situation which would arise'.[54] In their statement, both premiers praised John Hume for 'his courageous and imaginative efforts' in engaging in his dialogue with Gerry Adams, but stressed that any initiative 'can be taken only by the two governments and that there could be no question of their adopting or endorsing the report of the dialogue that was recently given to the Taoiseach'.[55] In the House of Commons three days later, when questioned by Hume as to why his proposals had been rejected, Major replied that 'I reached the conclusion, after having been informed of them by the Taoiseach ... that it was not the right way to proceed',[56] adding that this was also the view of the Irish government. Hume recognized that the proposals could not in themselves 'be the basis for action', but he did expect that both governments would build on them.[57] So, while some commentators viewed the statement as a total rejection of Hume-Adams, the fact that both governments were now taking the initiative in a concerted and determined manner, was precisely what Hume had been working towards. The principles upon which they were working were essentially the same as the SDLP had traditionally followed in its approach to a resolution. The difference now was that the leadership of Sinn Féin was slowly coming to accept these same principles, and the question was how long would it take before the PIRA would call a ceasefire and allow comprehensive talks to commence.

HUME HOSPITALIZED

Within the SDLP itself, the Shankill bombing and the apparent rejection of the Hume-Adams proposals caused considerable unease, and took a grave toll on

John Hume's health, with the result that he was hospitalized for a time. In hospital, he received hundreds of messages of support, expressing ordinary people's appreciation of his efforts to achieve peace and anger that those efforts did not appear to be receiving a response. Reinforcing those messages were the results of several opinion polls; one for the *Sunday Independent*[58] showed that 72 per cent of those questioned supported the Hume-Adams dialogue, while a *Guardian* poll indicated that 59 per cent of people in Britain thought that Major should talk to Adams.[59] A statement by a group of professionals from the Nationalist community expressed their wholehearted support for John Hume, claiming that since signals had been given indicating a cessation of violence to be achievable, 'if we ignore those signals now we are in danger of condemning the next generation to another quarter-century of bloody violence'.[60] Hume's talks with Adams had generated such a degree of sympathy within Irish and British public opinion that both governments had no option but to be seen to build on them.

DOWNING STREET DECLARATION

John Major significantly boosted the momentum towards a new initiative in a speech at the Lord Mayor of London's annual dinner in mid-November. He began by echoing Hume's own words that 'there may now be a better opportunity for peace in Northern Ireland than for many years', and then stated that his government was 'actively seeking a framework to deliver peace, stability and reconciliation'.[61] A week later, at the SDLP's annual conference, Hume called on the British government to ensure that such a framework would lead to a solution 'capable of earning the allegiance and agreement of all traditions and respect their diversity', and that it would also be a framework 'in which such an agreement can take place'.[62] In other words, Hume was emphasizing the need for a framework that would enable PIRA violence to end.

A secret, parallel British-PIRA dialogue was also gradually moving in the same direction. In the correspondence related to that dialogue released in late November, it was clear that the terms under which PIRA violence could end and negotiations could commence were being painstakingly developed.[63] Not surprisingly, the same differences on the critical issue of self-determination were reflected in this dialogue as in the Hume-Adams discussions. The PIRA had claimed that 'the route to peace is to be found in the restoration to the Irish people of our right to national self-determination – in the free exercise of this right without impediment of any kind', and it confidently stated that 'the wish of the majority of the Irish people is for Irish unity'.[64] The British insisted that its guarantee of no change in the North's constitutional status without the consent of a majority would not be withdrawn.[65] There was, as yet, no hint of the more subtle position reflected in some of the Hume-Adams' statements. The furthest that the British were prepared to go was, as stated in the Anglo-Irish Agreement, to accept 'that the eventual outcome of such a process (negotiations) could be a united Ireland, but only on the basis of the consent of the people of Northern Ireland'.[66] Notwithstanding these differences, the dialogue was continuing, paralleled by the Irish government's own contacts with the provisional movement.

The revelation of the scale and extent of these parallel dialogues raises questions as to the value of the Hume-Adams initiative. As far as the Hume-Adams and Irish government contacts were concerned, Sinn Féin had hoped to create a broad political axis of the kind it had proposed to the SDLP during the 1988 talks. In this, it had succeeded up to a point.[67] The point beyond which it did not succeed was the basis upon which constitutional change could take place. Whatever they might say about Irish unity being a possible outcome to negotiations, neither government nor the SDLP was prepared to accept that self-determination could be exercised in a single 'collective' manner. It was also clear that public opinion in the South did not favour Sinn Féin's interpretation. An *Irish Times* opinion poll in early December showed that the majority of Irish people did not support Irish unity as their immediately preferred choice for Northern Ireland; most respondents favoured a power-sharing government within existing constitutional arrangements.[68] For the SDLP, as for the two governments, dialogue with the provisional movement was justified because it was critically important that the movement fully understood the basis upon which it could participate in talks, and upon which principles any talks would have to be based.

The new document that both governments were preparing was intended to elaborate these principles. The document, eventually revealed in mid-December has, ever since, been referred to as the *Downing Street Declaration*. In its essentials, the declaration stated nothing new, but was more explicit in spelling out those essentials. It repeated commitments that had been well-rehearsed over the years, and particularly in the Anglo-Irish Agreement: respect for the democratic wish of a majority in Northern Ireland on whether they preferred to support the Union or a sovereign united Ireland; that the role of the British government was to encourage and facilitate agreement between the parties, and that it had no selfish, strategic or economic interest in the North; that agreement between the parties could take the form of agreed structures for the island as a whole, including a united Ireland achieved by peaceful means; that the people of Ireland by agreement between both parts respectively could exercise their right of self-determination on the basis of consent, freely given, North and South, to bring about a united Ireland if that was their wish; that the democratic right of self-determination by the people of Ireland as a whole must be achieved and exercised with and subject to the agreement of a majority of the people of Northern Ireland.[69]

What was new about the declaration was that it went further than the Anglo-Irish Agreement in spelling out the existing constitutional framework, as well as the constitutional possibilities that could inform any negotiations that might follow. While not committing the British to become *persuaders* for Irish unity, their guarantee of no constitutional change was now qualified by a commitment to encourage agreement between the parties, and if unity was the wish of majorities North and South, to facilitate it with the appropriate legislation. The two governments also stated that in the event of a permanent end to the use of violence

> democratically mandated parties with a commitment to exclusively peaceful methods and which have shown that they abide by the democratic process, are free to participate fully in democratic politics and to join in dialogue in due course between the governments and the political parties on the way ahead.[70]

The two governments would also assist in creating 'institutions and structures which, while respecting the diversity of the people of Ireland, would enable them to work together in all areas of common interest'.[71] For its part, the Irish government undertook to establish an all-party Forum for Peace and Reconciliation, to 'make recommendations on ways in which agreement and trust between both traditions in Ireland can be promoted and established'.[72] Sinn Féin had pressed for a permanent convention of Irish parties, with a wide remit to consider all-island issues, not just reconciliation between 'both traditions'. In other words, they had been pressing for an embryonic all-Ireland parliament. The forum would go some towards those objectives, but by no means as far as Sinn Féin had proposed.

The SDLP warmly welcomed the declaration. In parliament, on the day of the declaration, Hume said that he regarded it as the most important statement ever made on British-Irish relations, and acknowledged that the declaration was based on the SDLP's understanding of the conflict. In Hume's words

> the declaration identifies the problem as the deeply divided people of Ireland ... it recognizes that that division can be healed only by agreement, and by an agreement that earns the allegiance and agreement of all our traditions and respects their diversity. I welcome also the fact that the government have committed themselves to promoting such agreement and to encouraging such agreement, and whatever form that agreement takes, the government will endorse.[73]

Joe Hendron stated that there was now no excuse for the PIRA to continue its violence and he called on it to implement a total cessation.[74] Hume announced that he would be renewing his contacts with Adams, since the challenge was to all parties 'to come to the table in a totally peaceful atmosphere and to begin what is the very difficult process of reaching agreement'.[75] His objective was to reinforce the message that whatever justification had previously existed, in the PIRA's own terms, the case for violence no longer existed.

Sinn Féin's immediate response was not encouraging. Ignoring the SDLP's response, it claimed that there was 'disappointment amongst Nationalists about the joint declaration' because it did not appear to contain anything new. In particular, it attributed this disappointment to the manner in which the declaration dealt with self-determination 'by agreement with the two parts of Ireland rather than with the island as a whole',[76] something neither government had suggested was ever likely. Having raised expectations as to what it could achieve through the various dialogues in which it had been engaged, Sinn Féin and the PIRA were now faced with the most formal expression of the terms and conditions on which negotiations would take place. Both would have to accept those terms and conditions or consign themselves back to the margins of politics. Significantly, neither denounced the declaration and, instead, announced that clarification would be sought of what precisely the declaration meant with respect to such specific points as self-determination, the Unionist veto and the question of prisoners.[77] Seeking clarification signalled a willingness to engage in talks about talks, a normal preliminary to real negotiations.

The SDLP, having strained itself to make those terms and conditions as facilitating as possible for the provisional movement, was, like everyone else, forced to wait several months while Sinn Féin deliberated and decided its ultimate response. A public opinion poll indicated overwhelming support for the declaration, with only 4 per cent of Sinn Féin supporters in the North disapproving, and an overall 56 per cent of all political opinion in its favour.[78] Another significant step towards both comprehensive negotiations and the cessation of violence had now been taken, but finally achieving both would entail a period during which many would have reason to doubt if a positive response was ever likely.

Chapter 16

Peace at last

Over the 1993 Christmas holiday period, internal discussion within Sinn Féin-PIRA about the Downing Street Declaration was, according to reports,[1] intense, but generally negative. This negativity was conveyed in devastating terms at the beginning of 1994, when the PIRA fire-bombed shops and other business premises in and around Belfast, including the famous Linenhall Library, where over 1,000 books were destroyed. The message was blunt. The PIRA was still in business, no matter what the two governments had stated in their recent declaration. According to its spokespersons, Sinn Féin was still studying the declaration and had given no indication that it was likely to be accepted as the basis for entering negotiations. However, both governments asserted that the declaration was their definitive pronouncement on the principles and conditions that would underlie negotiations. The prospect for such negotiations was gloomy, and it seemed only a matter of time before Sinn Féin would formally reject the declaration.

According to the provisional movement, the main barriers to accepting the declaration included a significant difference between the declaration and the Hume-Adams document on how Irish self-determination was to be applied, as well as issues related to an eventual British withdrawal and the fate of paramilitary prisoners. On self-determination, despite its various hints of change, Sinn Féin officially clung to its traditional interpretation. In its view, by re-stating the majority consent principle, the declaration underwrote the Unionist veto on constitutional change.[2] The problem for Sinn Féin-PIRA was that John Hume fully endorsed the declaration and was urging all parties to accept it. Hume rested his acceptance of the declaration on the British government's assertion that it had no 'selfish economic or strategic interest in Northern Ireland', and that

> it was for the people of the island of Ireland alone, by agreement between the two parts respectively to exercise their right to self-determination on the basis of consent, freely and concurrently given, north and south, to bring about a united Ireland if that is their wish.[3]

Hume also pointed out that, in the declaration, the British government had pledged to legislate for a united Ireland, if that was what both parts agreed. He restated his conviction that whatever reasons might have justified the provisional movement's armed struggle in the past, they no longer existed. He called on the leadership of Sinn Féin-PIRA to accept the challenge of peace and to grasp the historic opportunity presented by the declaration. His words received no immediate positive response. Instead, Hume and his colleagues were once more heavily criticized.

SEEKING CLARIFICATIONS

The SDLP, like everybody else in the North, were now witnesses to a very public dialogue between Sinn Féin and the two governments on clarifying the declaration. To many, it seemed a very cynical exercise given the continuation of the PIRA's campaign. Despite the fact that both governments had devoted long hours negotiating the declaration following the lengthy Hume-Adams dialogue and their own separate contacts with the Sinn Féin-PIRA leadership, the latter was still not satisfied and, through its requests for clarifications, seemed to be demanding more, though what was being demanded was unclear. It was not surprising that a sense of irritation was expressed about what were seen as deliberate delaying tactics. Séamus Mallon forcefully expressed this irritation for the SDLP when he claimed that there was not 'a whisker between the two documents, Hume-Adams and the Downing Street Declaration, on the issue of self-determination'.[4] He called on the Sinn Féin leadership to 'be courageous and to clarify three basic realities to the IRA and their supporters: that violence could never achieve Irish unity; that the right to self-determination was not based upon coercion; and that all Nationalists who wanted Irish unity must become persuaders'.[5] Sinn Féin ignored the call and persisted with its claims that the differences between the two documents remained significant, arguing that the joint declaration was 'substantially different in key areas to the Irish position (Hume-Adams)',[6] a claim that implied not just a British unwillingness to compromise, but also the Irish government's failure to achieve what the Hume-Adams document had proposed. In an article that was clearly intended to refute this suggestion, Hume pointed out that the British position was not one of supporting the *status quo*, but rather that it wanted 'to see peace, stability and reconciliation established by agreement among all of the people who inhabit the island'.[7] He again positively acknowledged the British position on self-determination to be one for the Irish people alone to exercise 'on the basis of consent, freely and concurrently given'.[8] There was, therefore, no ambiguity as to where Hume stood on the declaration, whatever Sinn Féin might claim. Yet, in the belief that clarifications posed no threat to the process, Hume favoured some clarification as demanded by Sinn Féin. He also stressed that Sinn Féin should use the occasion of its ard fheis at the end of February to announce its definitive decision. His request went unheeded and, while some speeches at the conference indicated a slightly more positive approach to the declaration, the conference as a whole did not endorse it, focusing instead on what it continued to describe as British support for the 'Unionist veto'.[9]

SDLP FRUSTRATIONS

As the early months of 1994 passed without a clear response from the provisional movement, the political process seemed once again frozen in stalemate. The stalemate tested relationships within the SDLP, as members witnessed Sinn Féin being wooed, particularly in the US, where Gerry Adams was received almost as an international statesman during a highly publicized visit to address the National Committee on American Foreign Policy.[10] In contrast to Adams' messages about peace, PIRA fire-bombs in the North and mortar-bomb attacks on London's Heathrow airport[11] made it difficult to believe those messages. A meeting of constituency representatives in Toomebridge in early March gave voice to SDLP members' understandable unease, and several questioned where attempts to persuade the provisional movement to adopt exclusively peaceful means were really heading.[12] To many of those present, there was a cynical contradiction between ongoing PIRA violence and Adams' claims to be a peacemaker, and they queried why a definitive decision on the declaration was taking so long. In response, Hume argued that a satisfactory outcome was still likely, that patience was required and that a genuine discussion was underway within the provisional movement. SDLP members were further unsettled as party representatives' homes and the party's head office came under more attacks from loyalist and the PIRA.[13] In late March, in an extremely brutal attack by a PIRA gang outside his home in Crossmaglen, Councillor John Fee suffered multiple injuries and had to be hospitalized.[14] The murder of so-called 'informers' also caused huge anger and led Eddie McGrady to accuse the PIRA of denying its victims the justice it so often demanded for itself.[15] As a result, Hume came under even more criticism for his continued confidence that his engagement with Adams would meet with success. To critical voices at home were added the doubts of Irish-Americans who had supported Adams' visit to the US, and who were particularly upset at the attacks on Heathrow, which received wide media coverage internationally, and at warnings that more could happen.[16] Feeling the pressure, Hume's answer remained simple and straight-forward: 'no stone should be left unturned to bring about peace'.[17]

EUROPEAN LINKS

Of more immediate concern to the SDLP were the forthcoming elections to the European Parliament. Expectations within the party were high that Hume, given his peacemaking role, would perform exceedingly well. In its approach to the election, the party adopted the by now well-established practice of focusing exclusively on Europe-related issues. On this occasion, the campaign high-lighted the party's membership of the PES, one of the larger groups in the parliament, whose commitment to tackling unemployment, to investment in economic renewal, and to the defence of democratic and human rights resonated strongly with SDLP policies.[18] The EU programmes that were bene-fiting Northern Ireland, such as the common agricultural programme, and the funding of infrastructural development, were also highlighted, as well as those, like Interreg, that promoted North-South cooperation. All were cited as evidence of the positive outcomes from EU membership. The SDLP empha-sized the new trading opportunities offered by the single market and, over the previous two years, had organized several public meetings and seminars aimed at encouraging the business sector to avail of the greater freedom of movement for goods and services that the single market would facilitate.[19] Hume's positive approach to such programmes and his reputation as a frontbench member of the PES had increased the party's opportunities to become involved in a truly supra-national movement, and to engage in politics beyond the confines of local concerns.[20]

With the results almost entirely predictable, the 1994 European election campaign was very low-key. For the SDLP, the goal was to increase the percentage of first-preference votes so that Hume could be elected on the first count. Sinn Féin seemed resigned to the fact that the party would not win the seat and, instead of one strong candidate, nominated three relatively unknowns.[21] Consequently, the results for the SDLP were much better than expected. Hume received 161,992 first preferences (compared with 136,335 in 1989), a figure that represented almost 29 per cent of the total vote, the highest ever recorded for the SDLP at any election. In contrast, the Sinn Féin vote amounted to 55,215, a very poor result given the high profile that the party had achieved since the Downing Street Declaration. The results demonstrated the very high regard in which Hume was held across the community and were a brake on criticisms of his peace strategy, especially from within the party. Above all, the results provided a very strong endorsement of that strategy, and added further pressure on Sinn Féin to make a definitive and positive response to the declaration.

CEASEFIRES

Signs that Sinn Féin would soon announce its response to the Downing Street declaration came when it arranged a special meeting of its members to be held in Letterkenny, Co. Donegal, at the end of July. But when it took place, the decision was again neither to accept, nor to reject the declaration.[22] Somewhat disingenuously, Sinn Féin discussed the declaration almost as if it were exclusively a British government document, ignoring its joint authorship and its endorsement by all other parties of the Irish Nationalist tradition. Sinn Féin claimed that the declaration was replete with reassurances for Unionists, and that the right of the Irish people to self-determination was once again undermined by the statement that it must be exercised 'by agreement between the two parts (of Ireland) respectively … on the basis of consent freely and concurrently given', and by the reaffirmation in paragraph 2 of 'Northern Ireland's statutory guarantee'.[23] As in its initial reaction, however, Sinn Féin claimed that despite the declaration's alleged weaknesses, 'the potential to build a real peace still exists'. The implication was that slowly but surely the provisional movement was accepting, but not admitting, that the declaration was not going to be changed, and that negotiations would take place within the constitutional parameters it set.

To many, the unwillingness to explicitly accept the declaration after nine months of clarification and debate, even if it had not been rejected outright, was a huge disappointment. In Hume's absence in the US, Séamus Mallon gave the

SDLP's first reaction, pointing out that every other Nationalist political party had accepted and supported the joint declaration, 'yet Sinn Féin say it has not dealt adequately with the core issues'.[24] The tenor of Mallon's remarks reflected the dismay and annoyance widely felt in Nationalist Ireland. Foreign Affairs Minister Dick Spring expressed grave disappointed and felt that not much hope could be taken from the Sinn Féin position.[25] However, with so much invested in the process, neither government was yet prepared to turn its back on the process. Taoiseach Albert Reynolds saw some positive signals in the outcome,[26] while the British government did not comment directly, preferring instead to emphasize that it continued to work with the Irish government on a new framework document that would go beyond the declaration and contain the broad headings for an agreement to be submitted to renewed inter-party talks.[27] The message was that such talks would soon go ahead and, without an end to PIRA violence, Sinn Féin could not expect to participate.

Notwithstanding the negative perceptions and ongoing PIRA violence,[28] expectations began to grow that a ceasefire was imminent. A special meeting of SDLP executive and constituency representatives in the middle of August assessed the situation, but those present were divided as to how much longer the party should share that expectation. In a lengthy and highly critical analysis of the provisional movement's continued prevarication, Séamus Mallon challenged the movement to either cease its violence immediately or be 'removed from any further involvement in the process of creating peace and a new political dispensation on the island of Ireland'.[29] Mallon caustically challenged the Provisionals' claim to be 'the champions of the rights of the Irish people', saying that they were actually denying the right of self-determination by pursuing a relentless campaign of violence to force Irish unity. While Mallon's statement summed up the frustrations of several members at the meeting, the majority accepted Hume's view that a positive outcome was still likely, and that some more time should be allowed before making definitive judgments.[30] In this assessment, Hume was to be vindicated before the end of the month.

As speculation about a ceasefire mounted, the political focus was never off Sinn Féin, particularly when Bruce Morrison led another group of Irish-Americans to meet Sinn Féin, the Irish government and the SDLP. Given its connections to the White House, the group was believed to be conveying the US government's strong desire for an end to PIRA violence as well as offering a form of guarantee that Sinn Féin's democratic rights would be upheld.[31] Following the meeting with Sinn Féin, Morrison expressed a strong belief that progress was being achieved towards an early end to PIRA violence.[32] His colleague Bill Flynn praised Hume as the 'principal architect' of the peace process, and claimed that if he had been fooled by Adams 'it would not be the first time I have been fooled', but he believed his optimism to be justified. A day later Hume and Adams met and issued a statement strongly hinting that significant developments were about to be announced. They referred to an 'effective peace process' being the result of their joint efforts, and of 'the essential ingredients … being available' to develop 'an overall political strategy to establish justice and peace in Ireland'.[33] The statement ruled out an 'internal solution', and asserted that a lasting solution had to be based on 'the right of the Irish people as a whole to national self-determination'. This assertion was immediately followed by recognition of the reality that 'the exercise of this right is, of course, a matter for agreement between all of the people of Ireland and we reiterate that such a new agreement is only viable if it enjoys the allegiance of the different traditions on this island'. What the statement indicated, apart from the likelihood of a PIRA ceasefire, was that Sinn Féin had now effectively accepted that self-determination could only be expressed in the manner set out in the Downing Street Declaration and long advocated by the SDLP.[34] Two days later, on 31 August, the PIRA declared 'a complete cessation of military operations', and placed its hopes for a solution on 'inclusive negotiations'.[35] After twenty-five years of bombing and killing aimed at forcing a British withdrawal from the North, the provisional movement was settling for the kind of process in which its political wing could have been involved at any time since the early 1970s, had it not supported the campaign of violence.

The SDLP joined in the general welcome that most people expressed towards the PIRA announcement, and looked forward to a renewal of the wider political process, hopefully this time a process that would be comprehensive in terms of participants and its agenda. But it would take a further eighteen months of 'talks about talks' before that process would get underway. The first cause of the delay was the criticism that PIRA's statement did not describe the cessation as 'permanent', but instead had used the word 'complete'. Hume regarded the cessation as permanent, and party vice-chair Jonathan Stephenson pointed out that '*The Collins national dictionary* defines the word "complete" as, "entire, finished, perfect with no part lacking"'.[36] Those who rejected equivalence were described as unhelpfully 'nit-picking'. It took until the middle of October for the British government to make what John Major described as 'a working assumption' that the cessation was permanent, and, consequently, that preliminary talks might commence between government officials and Sinn Féin before Christmas.[37] Since these talks would not involve other parties, the focus of SDLP attention was on developments in Dublin and, in particular, the establishment of the Forum for Peace and Reconciliation.

HISTORIC HANDSHAKES

One of the most dramatic events to mark the cessation occurred a week after the PIRA announcement when Taoiseach Albert Reynolds invited Hume and Adams to a meeting after which a now famous three-way handshake was photographed on the steps of government buildings in Dublin (pl. 22). The three leaders, representing three strands of Irish nationalism, committed themselves to jointly working for agreement in the North by democratic and peaceful means, and on the basis of the principle of consent. The Forum for Peace and Reconciliation would help confirm this commitment by bringing Sinn Féin, for the first time, into a political process involving all of the other parties that shared the same goals. Modelled on the NIF, the new body held its opening session on 28 October. By then, a complete cessation of loyalist campaigns had also been declared and Ireland was enjoying a peace not known for almost a whole generation.[38]

SUPPORT IN WASHINGTON AND BRUSSELS

Hume now took the opportunity to publicize recent developments in visits to the US and to Brussels. In the US, he briefed President Clinton and Vice-President Gore on the cessation,[39] and witnessed the House of Representatives pass a motion calling for the creation of a $60 million equity fund to encourage investment in Northern Ireland. Appearing before the Senate's foreign relations committee, Hume outlined such opportunities for US businesses in the North, and urged easier access to US markets for Northern Irish products.[40] An early signal that Europe would also commit more resources to economic development came when, in another example of Hume's influence, president of the European Commission, Jacques Delors, stated that he was 'ready to propose to the commission an increase in our aid to Northern Ireland ... in order to reinforce peace'.[41] In the European Parliament, Hume was afforded a standing ovation from members and was nominated by his socialist colleagues for the Nobel peace prize.[42] This was the first of many awards for which Hume would be nominated in recognition of his efforts to bring about an end to PIRA violence.[43] A further notable event recognizing his work for peace came when he was invited to address the British Labour Party conference at the beginning of October. Hume used the occasion to stress familiar SDLP themes: the need to accommodate diversity; the need for both Unionists and Nationalists to abandon traditional mind-sets; the rights of people over territory and the need to underpin political agreement with referenda in both parts of Ireland.[44] He was at the pinnacle of his political achievements and influence, and the SDLP basked in his glory.

Hume's emphasis on the need for fresh economic investment resulted in a number of initiatives in the months following the PIRA and loyalist ceasefires. Among them was the establishment of a working group to prepare proposals in response to Delors' promise of additional European Union (EU) assistance. Hume nominated the working party in conjunction with the North's other two MEPs, Ian Paisley and Jim Nicholson.[45] The SDLP's own submission to that working group outlined several key areas,[46] which, the party argued, would benefit from new EU investment. A number of these proposals were incorporated into the final proposals for an expenditure of £240 million over three years when the package was approved by the Council of Ministers in December.[47] Among the SDLP proposals were schemes for urban and rural development, social inclusion and reconciliation projects, as well as cross-border development. Eventually to be known as the European peace fund, it would contribute several hundred million to projects, North and South, over the next two decades.

FORUM FOR PEACE AND RECONCILIATION

Politically, the most important post-ceasefire initiative in which the party was involved was the Forum for Peace and Reconciliation. Like its predecessor, this new forum convened in Dublin Castle. The SDLP was allocated five seats,[48] and, although the Unionist parties had declined to attend, the range of individuals and parties present were testimony to the significant changes now underway. All parties represented in the Dáil agreed to participate and from the North, the APNI and the Workers' Party as well as SDLP and Sinn Féin accepted invitations. Present also was independent Senator Gordon Wilson from Enniskillen, whose daughter, Marie, had been among those killed by the PIRA on Remembrance Day 1987.

In his opening address, Hume suggested that the forum should 'work on a planned basis to break down the barriers of distrust and prejudice, which were the real barriers. The border is in the hearts and minds of our people, and the real task of the forum is how we break down that border'.[49] Following a procedure recommended by the SDLP at the Brook-Mayhew talks, the forum's initial focus was on how the different parties understood the causes of the northern troubles. Eddie McGrady outlined the SDLP's contribution to this debate, drawing on the party's well-known analysis of the three relationships embracing the people of Ireland, North and South: relationships between communities within the North, between North and South and between Ireland and Britain.[50] McGrady argued that an accommodation between all three was required, and that consent lay at the heart of such an approach.

'WE KEPT OUR HEAD, OUR HEART, OUR NERVE'

The SDLP's annual conference in November was an occasion for the party to offer its own gratitude and congratulations to Hume and to the rest of the leadership for their contributions to ending the violence. A deep sense of pride and vindication ran through many of the motions, exemplified in that from the Ballycastle branch that read: 'in acknowledging our party leader's contribution, conference also wishes to pay tribute to the entire party leadership and membership for their relentless commitment to peaceful and democratic politics over the past twenty-five years'.[51] As party chair, Mark Durkan stated 'We kept our heads. We kept our heart. We kept our nerve and we kept our promises. We can draw confidence and patience for our future work by reflecting on how well our party and our leadership have served as pathfinders for progress'.[52] Pointing to the negotiations that now seemed inevitable, Durkan emphasized the centrality of police reform to achieving agreement, and deplored the views of those like the chief constable who had suggested that significant reform was not required because sufficient reform had already taken place.

In his leader's address, John Hume acknowledged the significant contributions to the peace process made by the two prime ministers, but reserved special tribute to his party colleagues, especially those whose homes had been attacked.[53] He called for a special focus on economic development, seeing in it new opportunities for both communities to work together, and to join in working with others from the South. The party was expectant with the hope that it would soon be engaged in negotiations that would gradually switch the focus of politics to those 'bread and butter' issues.

The conference also debated the contentious issue of electoral pacts raised in a motion that recommended that, at the next election, the party only contest the four Westminster seats it then held. Elsewhere, it was suggested, the party should stand aside for others, or enter electoral pacts. For some members, since Sinn Féin was no longer supporting a paramilitary campaign, electoral pacts to the advantage of the Nationalist community could no longer be judged improper. The motion was defeated following strong opposing interventions, notably one by Séamus Mallon, who described it as 'dangerous, farcical and incompetent' and said that it was really endorsing 'not pan-nationalism' but 'pan-Catholicism'.[54]

If Mallon's comments suggested that the traditional community mould of northern politics could be easily broken, the peaceful context now taking shape would demonstrate just how enduring that mould was, and that it would be within it that progress would have to be made. The strength of the mould would also be manifest in the length of time it would take to move from the ceasefires to meaningful inter-party dialogue.

Shaping the negotiating table

Following the ceasefires, the SDLP shared the general Nationalist expectation that little time would be lost before meaningful inter-party negotiations would commence. The establishment of the Forum for Peace and Reconciliation within two months of the PIRA declaration stressed the need to replace violence with dialogue as quickly as possible. But the forum was mainly a Nationalist institution, notwithstanding the presence of the APNI and Senator Gordon Wilson, and its brief was to investigate barriers to reconciliation, not to negotiate a settlement. For that purpose, a wider forum had to be created, one that would obviously have to involve the main Unionist parties and the British government, all of which had adopted a cautious approach to the ceasefires, in particular to that declared by the PIRA. Unionists did not share the British assumption that the PIRA ceasefire was permanent and demanded more time and evidence before they would be convinced. The Unionist approach was supported by public opinion in a poll that indicated that only 30 per cent of those questioned believed the ceasefire to be permanent.[1] The sceptics seemed justified when, in early November, the PIRA accepted responsibility for the murder of Newry postal worker, Frank Kerr, during a robbery at a local sorting office,[2] and by the continuation of so-called 'punishment' beatings for alleged anti-social behaviour in communities where the provisional movement's influence was strong.

DECOMMISSIONING PROBLEM EMERGES

Politically, the ceasefires were followed by a period of apparent inaction on the part of the British government. Anxious about a lengthy delay in convening talks, Hume and Adams issued a joint statement in late November, calling for 'inclusive talks aimed at securing agreement and an overall settlement' and, echoing the words of the Downing Street Declaration, they urged that the British demonstrate that they were 'persuaders for agreement between the Irish people'.[3] The British response was to insist that talks with Sinn Féin would initially be to clarify the latter's *bona fides*, and to determine how and when arms would be decommissioned (an issue that now began to emerge as a serious impediment to talks). Speaking at an investment conference in Belfast in early December, Major declared that 'huge progress' would have to be made on the decommissioning of PIRA weapons before Sinn Féin could be admitted to formal negotiations.[4] When John Hume claimed that progress could only be made by allowing talks to go ahead first, he was roundly criti-cized by the secretary of state, who repeated the prime minister's insistence that the arms issue had to be resolved first.[5] The PIRA had no intention of making any significant move to decommission before talks commenced, however, claiming that there had been no demand for decommissioning prior to the ceasefires, and both the SDLP and the Irish government accepted that this was the case.[6] While both agreed that weapons disposal would have to be addressed, both also believed that only talks would create the context likely to lead to their disposal. The British government would eventually accept this position, but not until after a long delay and protracted 'talks about talks' with Sinn Féin.

The talks with Sinn Féin commenced in the closing weeks of 1994, at first with British officials at the NIO, but not for several months more with the secretary of state and his ministers. Throughout these early engagements, the British maintained that decommissioning remained a precondition and, without it, full inter-party talks could not take place. So protracted were these talks that many Nationalists questioned the government's sincerity in wanting to see Sinn Féin involved at all. Speaking at a seminar in the University of Ulster, Bríd Rodgers described the British position as totally 'inadequate', and the demand for early decommissioning as 'a delaying tactic'. While welcoming some aspects of the British response such as the removal of the ban on Sinn Féin representatives being interviewed on radio and television, Rodgers claimed that these did not amount to the 'creative' response that had been promised.[7]

FRAMEWORKS

Progress towards all-party talks had been unexpectedly interrupted when the Fianna Fáil-Labour coalition in the South fell in mid-November and was replaced by another coalition involving Labour and Democratic Left, and led by Fine Gael, whose leader John Bruton became Taoiseach. While Bruton was openly hostile to the provisional movement, he continued building on the opportunities offered by the ceasefires. In particular, he continued work on a new document intended by both governments to set out the parameters for reviving inter-party talks.[8] The basis for this document was the proposals advanced during the Brooke-Mayhew negotiations. Entitled *The frameworks for the future*, it was released with considerable publicity on 22 February 1995. In the House of Commons, Hume praised Major for his government's input, and the leaders of the other British parties for their positive responses which, he claimed, meant that the Northern Irish issue was 'above party politics, which is where it belongs'.[9] Mindful of the need to encourage Unionists to take part in whatever negotiations lay ahead, he addressed their MPs, saying

> I understand their fears and tensions given the twenty-five years we have been through ... this problem cannot be resolved without the participation and agreement of the Unionist people ... If they do not agree with this (document) they should come to the table and join all the parties and both governments as soon as possible to begin the difficult process of reaching agreement.[10]

Séamus Mallon stressed the challenges facing both the SDLP and the Unionist parties, saying that 'we ... have an awesome responsibility to pursue the noble objective of peace and to make the concessions which are going to be required, not just from unionism but from nationalism as well'.[11]

The document contained two parts: the first outlined proposals for 'accountable government in Northern Ireland; the second outlined the British and Irish governments' shared understanding 'as to how relations in the island of Ireland, and between these islands, might be based on cooperation and agreement to the mutual advantage of all'.[12] In summary, the two governments' main proposals included an assembly of approximately ninety members, elected by proportional representation, with committees overseeing the work of Northern Ireland's departments. As suggested at the Brooke-Mayhew talks, the two governments could propose a directly elected three-person panel to oversee the work of the assembly as a whole. On North-South relationships, the document emphasized the centrality of the principle of consent to constitutional change, and that the main functions of any new all-island institutions would be to promote agreement between the people of the island of Ireland;

to carry out on a democratically accountable basis delegated executive, harmonizing and consultative functions over a range of designated matters to be agreed;

and to serve to acknowledge and reconcile the rights, identities and aspirations of the two major traditions.[13]

Significantly, the Irish government committed to introducing proposals for changes to the Irish constitution that would reflect the principle of consent, and to rejecting any suggestion of a territorial claim over Northern Ireland. The long-standing SDLP proposal that joint referenda should be held North and South as the means of endorsing any agreement was also included. Building on the principles enunciated in the Downing Street Declaration, *Frameworks for the future* presented the most detailed set of proposals ever drawn up by both governments to deal with the North and, in its broad outline, it paralleled much of what the SDLP had been proposing over the previous two decades. With the parameters now set for talks, it remained to be seen if the parties would engage.

Given the comprehensive nature of the proposals, the SDLP's willingness to engage in substantive talks was never in question. But despite the strong echoes of what had emerged from the Brooke-Mayhew talks, and despite strong assurances on the constitutional position of Northern Ireland, Unionists were dismissive of the proposals and, in early March, the UUP formally rejected them in their entirety.[14] The UUP had believed that they had a good working relationship with Major; one that allowed them to support the Conservatives against any risk of the government being prematurely brought down,[15] but they were outraged at the comprehensive nature of the document. In particular, they objected to the scope of its North-South proposals, and refused to be convinced by the guarantees for their position within the UK. In the words of UUP MP William Ross, the document was 'a manifesto leading to the creation of a united Ireland'.[16] On talks in which Sinn Féin would also participate, both the UUP and DUP remained adamant that the PIRA would have to decommission first. However, while broadly welcoming the *Frameworks* proposals as a basis for discussion, Sinn Féin reiterated that, by virtue of its electoral mandate, it was fully entitled to participate in talks, and that no precondition on PIRA decommissioning should prevent it from doing so. Since the British government and Unionists insisted on the opposite, the stalemate looked likely to persist unless someone offered a concession. In early March, in Washington, Secretary of

State Mayhew moved slightly to break the stalemate, when he said that there 'must be a willingness in principle to disarm progressively', and that a start must be made as a tangible confidence-building measure.[17] But even this softening of the decommissioning requirement met with no positive response from the PIRA, and was roundly denounced by Unionists as an unwarranted concession.

RE-ENGAGING WITH UNIONISTS

Notwithstanding the stalemate on establishing comprehensive talks, the SDLP met both main Unionist parties informally to discuss pressing social and economic issues as well as addressing the general political situation. Several meetings took place, especially with the UUP, including a joint meeting involving the SDLP, the UUP and John Major.[18] While the meeting with Major focused on social and economic matters, and did not touch in any detail on the prospects for political progress, the fact that meetings were taking place at all suggested the parties were at least becoming meaningfully engaged again, and that political progress might be made. Reinforcing this view were the first meetings between Sinn Féin and British ministers. Minister of State Michael Ancram met a delegation in March, and Mayhew met Adams at the Washington investment conference in late May but, as was frequently the case, hopes of a breakthrough were not realized. Resolving the decommissioning issue remained a British precondition to comprehensive talks. Consequently, the suspicion grew that the British would be prefer if the SDLP and the Unionist parties would fully re-engage, and Sinn Féin participate when the decommissioning requirement had been met. Having devoted so much to achieving the PIRA ceasefire, the SDLP was, however, not willing to put it at risk by side-stepping Sinn Féin and entering full inter-party talks with Unionists without them.

NORTH-SOUTH AND EAST-WEST ARRANGEMENTS

Talks of a kind continued at the Forum for Peace and Reconciliation in Dublin where, in addition to evidence from prominent individuals and organizations, the parties debated new institutions within the North, between North and South and between Ireland and Britain, as well as opportunities for all-island economic development, human rights and, critically, the principle of consent. On institutions for the North, the SDLP did not revisit its commission-type proposal, stressing more the need for a partnership approach along the lines that it had traditionally proposed. On all-Ireland arrangements, the SDLP recommended that their remit should go beyond mere cooperation to a fully coordinated and integrated level of planning on key infrastructural needs such as roads, transport, energy, water supply, and environmental protection, in order to break down the back-to-back provision of such services that had grown up since partition. On east-west (British-Irish) structures, which were less frequently discussed than the others, the party argued that these had the potential for developing ever closer mutually beneficial links between the two islands on a wide range of social and economic matters. Addressing the forum on these structures, Mark Durkan underlined the reassurance such structures would give Unionists 'who are fearful of being trapped as the ultimate minority and of being abandoned as the ultimate minority'.[19] The proposal was evidence of the SDLP's willingness to recognize the need to provide expression for Unionists' sense of identity, as well the practical benefits that such cooperation could provide.

CONSENT AND DECOMMISSIONING

While most of the debates at the forum produced a high level of consensus, those on self-determination witnessed a sharp division between Sinn Féin and most of the other participants. Despite its gradual move towards accepting the principle of consent, Sinn Féin was not yet willing to do so formally. So, when the forum published the report *Paths to a settlement in Ireland: realities, principles and requirements*, Sinn Féin dissented from the section which asserted that the consent of a majority in the North would be required for any new agreement.[20] The party still clung to its traditional view that this requirement denied Irish self-determination and amounted to a 'Unionist veto'. Significantly, in a forum that included all of the major Nationalist parties in Ireland, Sinn Féin could find no support for its view, revealing how out of touch it was with mainstream democratic Nationalist thinking.

The impasse over decommissioning persisted throughout the summer and autumn of 1995, with no apparent resolution. Anxious to nudge the process towards all-party talks, the SDLP pressed the case for the appointment of an independent international arbitrator, but the British were slow to accept the proposal. At Westminster, Eddie McGrady received a very non-committal reply when he urged Major to respond to what was becoming a compelling case.[21] Instead, the British government almost seemed as if it wanted to cause tension within the Nationalist community and to delay progress. In early July, a British soldier, Lee Clegg, who had been convicted of murdering a teenage Catholic girl, Karen Reilly, and who only served two years in custody, was released. His subsequent readmission to the army caused outrage in the Nationalist community, and rioting ensued in many areas. The contrast was drawn with paramilitary prisoners on whose behalf the Irish government had been unsuccessfully lobbying for release after much longer periods in custody. Joe Hendron accused the British government of releasing Clegg in order to boost its waning public support.[22] Tension over the release was soon followed by disturbances at several Orange Order parades, confrontation at Drumcree near Portadown being among the most serious.[23] Such disturbances, long common in many areas during the 'marching' season, were soon to escalate and become a major issue over the following years.

STALEMATE AGAIN

With tensions growing, the prospect for political progress receded.[24] To complicate matters, the UUP added to the stalemate when, to the decommissioning precondition, the party's new leader, David Trimble, added a demand for elections to a new assembly. Trimble claimed that, in an assembly, Unionists would talk to all those who had a mandate, including Sinn Féin.[25] Recalling the 1975 convention and the stalemate it produced, and the UUP's more recent dismissal of the *Frameworks* document, the SDLP rejected the proposal, fearing that an election campaign would harden party positions and create less, not more negotiating flexibility. Nevertheless, the demand would continue to be made over the coming months, and would eventually be conceded.

In an attempt to break the decommissioning stalemate, the SDLP proposed that preparatory inter-party talks commence not later than 30 November, and that a three-person international body 'advise both governments on the commitment of all parties to peaceful and democratic means ... and consequently of their commitment to the removal of all weapons from Irish politics. The international body will also be asked to ascertain and advise on how the question of arms ... can be finally and satisfactorily settled'.[26] The party hoped for a parallel approach in which the political parties could commence talks, while at the same time, an independent body would address decommissioning on the understanding that its recommendations would be accepted by those concerned, the paramilitaries. The proposals were immediately rejected by the UUP and the DUP, both of which restated that there would be no talks of any kind without prior decommissioning.

CLINTON'S VISIT

The imminence of President Clinton's visit to Britain and Ireland scheduled for December 1995 gave urgency to breaking the stalemate. By now, Clinton's government was deeply involved in counselling almost all of the party leaders whose visits to Washington had become nearly as frequent as their visits to London and Dublin, and there was growing US impatience at the lack of progress. Then, virtually on the eve of Clinton's visit, the two governments announced that agreement had been reached on a way forward.[27] The agreement closely paralleled what the SDLP had proposed: on decommissioning, an international body would report by mid-January on 'a suitable and acceptable method for full and verifiable decommissioning'; preparatory talks with the political parties would commence immediately to determine the nature of the talks proper (who would attend, the structure and format to be adopted, and general procedures to be followed); and all-party talks would then begin by the end of February.[28] In recognition of the role played by the US, George Mitchell, former majority leader in the US Senate, was invited to chair the international body on which he would be joined by former Finnish prime minister, Harri Holkeri, and General John de Chastelain, former chief of staff of the Canadian army. On 30 November, Bill Clinton became the first serving US president to visit Northern Ireland, and he did so at a moment when it seemed that both governments and all the political parties might finally engage.

Clinton's visit was a triumph. Enthusiastic crowds greeted him everywhere he went in Belfast and Derry. In Derry, SDLP Mayor John Kerr and party leader John Hume welcomed him as he urged political leaders to engage in the search for agreement and to work with the international body on decommissioning. No sooner had he departed than the euphoria of his visit dissipated. First David Trimble and then the PIRA dampened expectations that progress towards that engagement would be smooth. Trimble demanded that the Irish government first revoke the Anglo-Irish Agreement, and that it remove Articles 2 and 3 from its constitution. Furthermore, he stated that he would not negotiate the internal affairs of Northern Ireland with a foreign government.[29] Then the PIRA announced that 'there is no question of the IRA meeting the ludicrous demand for a surrender of IRA weapons'.[30] Intransigence rather than steps towards a resolution seemed, once again, the preferred option.

A slightly more optimistic message was conveyed when, at the same time, the SDLP held its first meeting with the UUP under David Trimble's leadership. As with earlier meetings, the parties focused on a wide agenda that included socio-economic matters as well as the immediate political situation, and again agreed that they should jointly meet with the prime minister.[31] The SDLP continued to express its reservations about Trimble's proposal for an assembly, but by now the Irish government had joined the British in supporting the call for assembly elections, and the party was becoming somewhat isolated in its rejection of the idea.[32]

SOBER ANNUAL CONFERENCE

The SDLP's twenty-fifth annual conference in November was essentially a very sober occasion, with the party reflecting on the impasse that was continuing at the time. Mark Durkan severely criticized the British government for allowing the stalemate to persist for so long, accusing it of 'retailing preconditions for the Unionists'.[33] Hume reminded members that the SDLP's message remained as relevant as ever – the need to cherish diversity and to respect human rights. He stressed that 'all politics in a normal society is about the right to existence – the right to life, but also to a decent standard of living – to jobs and housing',[34] objectives that had been at the heart of SDLP policy since its foundation, and would remain there when politics in Northern Ireland had become 'normal'. He spoke too of the sacrifices that many members had made, and the challenges that still lay ahead in establishing partnership institutions in the North and between North and South.

The most heated debate at the conference was another motion calling on the party to consider electoral pacts with others, wherever tactically appropriate. The argument in favour was the same as the previous year – now that the violence had ceased, Sinn Féin could no longer be accused of supporting physical force politics, and it might be advantageous to negotiate electoral pacts. However, given bitter memories of Fermanagh-South Tyrone, and the possible negative effects of any pact on the prospect for talks, conference decided not to vote on the issue, but to consign it to the party executive for further consideration, traditionally the polite way of rejecting it. Of more immediate significance was the outright rejection of the UUP proposal for an elected assembly, which Séamus Mallon described as a Unionist attempt to achieve an internal settlement that would ignore the wider Irish context.[35]

One of the most important debates was on the party's recently published policy document, *Policing in Northern Ireland*, which recommended not only radical structural changes in the police service, but also changes in its symbolism and ethos to make it possible for all sections of the community to support policing, and, more importantly, to serve as police officers. Speakers recognized the challenge posed, particularly to those on whom the SDLP would be calling to join a reformed service, and it was for that reason, among others, that the party was anxious to see a service that could accommodate officers from both traditions. Mindful of the effects of the PIRA's campaign against the RUC, Alex Attwood said the pain and hurt inflicted on its members and their families, would have to be acknowledged, and that while the provisional movement said that 'the RUC was unacceptable, there were many good and decent members of that police force who would be members of a future police service'.[36] Getting the balance right on policing was never going to be easy, but the SDLP's proposals would go a long way towards eventually achieving it.

ELECTION CONTROVERSY

While the first full year of the ceasefires ended with a huge drop in the number of violent deaths, terrorism had not gone away. The ceasefires meant fewer troops on the streets, less frequent roadblocks and a more relaxed atmosphere generally. Nine individuals lost their lives through violence, compared with sixty-two the previous year. But nine deaths were still nine too many and, worryingly, paramilitaries continued to mete out, with no sense of irony, 'punishment' beatings to those whom they judged to have engaged in 'anti-social' behaviour. Peace was still a very fragile plant.

In January, having consulted widely, the international body reported its assessment of the decommissioning issue and proposed a number of compromises.[37] On the central issue of disarming paramilitaries, it accepted that 'while there is a clear commitment on the part of those in possession of ... arms to work constructively to achieve full and verifiable decommissioning ... that commitment does not include decommissioning prior to ... negotiations'.[38] The body recommended that the parties *consider* some decommissioning taking place during negotiations, in effect a recommendation that did not require any decommissioning at this stage. As reassurance to those who were insisting on prior decommissioning, it also recommended that participants in negotiations should commit 'to exclusively peaceful and democratic means' in a formulation that became known as the 'Mitchell principles'.[39] Rather tentatively, the report touched on the issue of elections prior to negotiations, and suggested that 'if it were broadly acceptable ... an elective process could contribute to the building of confidence'.[40]

Two days later, John Major presented the report at Westminster, and provoked the anger of the SDLP when he seemed to exaggerate the significance given to elections in building confidence for negotiations. Major favoured the recommendation because, in the absence of prior decommissioning, he argued that 'an elective process offers a viable alternative direct route to the confidence necessary to bring about all-party negotiations. In that context, it is possible to imagine decommissioning and such negotiations being taken forward in parallel'.[41] To Hume, the prime minister was obviously supporting the UUP proposal, and angrily suggested that the option was being endorsed to retain Unionist support for the government.[42] Instead of elections, Hume urged that a date be fixed for all-party talks. Major rejected both suggestions. So, despite an earlier commitment to convening talks by the end of February, the governments were now faced with the reality that, in the absence of some prior decommissioning or elections to some form of assembly, no Unionist party would attend. On the other hand, the SDLP might not attend if assembly elections were to be held. Also, the overriding fear existed that paramilitaries, especially the PIRA, would claim that the opportunity for peaceful negotiations had been squandered, and would return to violence. Unfortunately, that fear would soon be justified.

For several weeks, it seemed as if stalemate would again grip the process. Unionists, who still clung to their prior decommissioning requirement, now had a second precondition to talks, and taunted the SDLP for its apparent refusal to seek a democratic mandate.[43] To avoid stalemate, the party advanced a more qualified approach to elections. Mark Durkan indicated that it was not a question of whether to have elections or not, but rather when, and of what kind. He pointed to the South African experience, where elections had only been held as part of the negotiating process after parties had defined that process, and he argued that 'there is not sufficient common understanding about the "process", never mind proposals, for an election to yield constructive or convergent mandates'.[44] However, the SDLP maintained its opposition to an assembly being elected *prior* to negotiations and, despite Bruton's apparent earlier sympathy for elections, it had convinced the Irish government of its case. Dick Spring expressed grave reservations, and was extremely annoyed that the British had committed themselves to the election proposal without any prior consultation.[45] In early February, the party was forced to reconsider its position when the PIRA broke its ceasefire with a massive bomb at Canary Wharf in London, killing two men, injuring over a hundred others and causing millions of pounds worth of damage.

Renewed PIRA violence immediately ruled out any prospect of Sinn Féin being admitted to negotiations, at least not until a new ceasefire had been firmly established, and that was unlikely to be soon. If talks were to take place as both governments planned, they were now only likely to involve the SDLP, the Unionist parties and APNI, all of which, except the SDLP, were in favour of an assembly. Anxious to avoid appearing negative, Hume gave the first clear indication that the SDLP might be changing its position. Writing in the *Independent* some days after the ceasefire broke down, he first set out the party's objections to elections – their divisive effects and, in particular, their focus on the 'constitutional' options rather than on what might be 'feasible'.[46] However, in the changed circumstances, he did not rule out some test of public opinion. He acknowledged a 'rational kernel in the Unionist case, as Mr Trimble and his colleagues believe they require some form of popular mandate in order to take part in all-party talks'. To meet that requirement, Hume advocated that a referendum 'for peace' be held to seek popular endorsement for inclusive talks, and for 'a total cessation of violence'.

The SDLP had now accepted the need for some form of popular mandate before talks could begin, and although the party rejected the suggestion of an assembly,[47] the likelihood was that elections would be favoured with the possibility of a referendum at a later stage. This is precisely what the two governments announced when they met at the end of February, and agreed the steps towards all-party talks set to commence on 10 June. Those steps included: an elective process; cross-party pre-talks meetings to agree the structure, format and agenda for negotiations; consideration of the advantage of a referendum 'to mandate support for a process to create lasting stability, based on repudiation of violence for any political purpose'.[48] Despite its reservations about an assembly-type election, the SDLP welcomed the proposals, and Séamus Mallon viewed the declaration as

> a statement of intent by the political process that our problems will be solved in one way, and one way only: through peaceful, democratic means. This is a moment of truth for all paramilitary, terrorist groupings in Northern Ireland, who will have to make a choice whether they will join in creating that peace or will isolate themselves in standing against the express wishes of the Irish people who want that peace so desperately.[49]

Anxious to ensure that, if at all possible, the talks did not proceed without Sinn Féin, Hume and Adams met the PIRA leadership to argue the case for restoring the ceasefire.[50] Because he understood that prior decommissioning had not been a requirement in pre-August 1994 communications with the PIRA, Hume believed that some dramatic intervention was required to rescue the peace process. In his subsequent statement, he called for a ministerial meeting not just with Sinn Féin, but with the PIRA itself in order to clarify matters.[51] Should such a meeting have been considered, the defiant stand of the PIRA ruled out the chance of one taking place. The paramilitaries re-stated that they would accept no preconditions to talks, either for themselves or for Sinn Féin, and declared that the armed struggle was pursued, 'because of conditions in the six counties and the British claim to sovereignty in Ireland'.[52] The SDLP leader now faced the prospect of the process in which he had committed so much of his credibility coming to nought. Furthermore, his party faced a decision about participation in elections leading to negotiations from which Sinn Féin would be excluded. As Séamus Mallon had stated, the choice for the paramilitaries and their political associates was clear – participation in the talks depended on the existence of a genuine ceasefire.[53]

SDLP TO CONTEST

Over the following weeks, the party faced a crucial decision as the two govern-ments published a consultation paper setting out the 'basis, participation, format and agenda of all-party talks',[54] and stating that participation in talks was to be confined to 'all those political parties ... which achieve representation through an elective process and which ... establish a commitment to exclusively peaceful methods and which have shown that they abide by the democratic process'.[55] At a central council meeting called to assess members' views at the end of March, the general opinion was in favour of contesting the elections, but not of participating in the Forum for Political Dialogue, as the new assembly would be called.[56] The party feared that the forum, with its inevitable Unionist majority, would become a constraint on negotiations. According to Jonathan Stephenson, 'our fear is that David Trimble will take decisions made in the forum to all-party talks for ratification, and that he will try to constantly link the two bodies'.[57] In the event, the forum would turn out to be a much less significant body, operating purely as a debating chamber that the SDLP would not grace for very long.

In March, the British government announced the format for the elections to the forum and to the negotiations.[58] A modified regional list system was chosen on the grounds that delegates nominated by their parties would conduct the negotiations and, therefore, party strengths needed to be clearly determined. From each constituency, parties would nominate up to five delegates in proportion to its vote; with a further twenty nominated by the parties in proportion to their overall strength across the North. The two governments also agreed that the elections be confined to no more than fifteen parties, a safe number to ensure no significant point of view would be absent. The SDLP continued to express serious reservations about the forum's purpose, seeing it as an unnecessary and unhelpful distraction to the negotiations. To a certain extent, these fears were allayed, but not removed, when the governments made clear that the negotiations would have 'precedence over the forum'.[59]

SDLP-UUP PRE-TALKS

While the two governments were determining the terms and condition for negotiations, the SDLP engaged in a further series of unpublicized meetings with the UUP in order to explore issues to be determined in the negotiations ahead. Four such meetings took place, focusing on two issues; the UUP's assembly proposals; and the nature of a North-South body. According to the UUP, one of the main reasons they had pressed for the forum was to ensure the

DUP's participation, since without a fresh mandate, the latter would certainly boycott any talks, while the UUP itself would not talk with Sinn Féin since the latter had not convinced Unionists of their full commitment to the democratic process. The UUP believed that it would have to deal with whoever else would be in the forum. According to SDLP's notes of the meeting, 'the UUP was impressed by what our North-South paper says, (it) does not scare them and (it) provides a basis for negotiation; a lot of time was spent teasing out some illustrations as to how the body might operate'.[60] The UUP also showed considerable interest in the SDLP's ideas on relations between Ireland and Britain, an issue in which they had not expected the party to have much interest and one that the UUP was anxious to highlight during the negotiations. While the talks were informal and not intended to reach any agreement, they did serve to familiarize the parties with each other's proposals on key issues.

UNUSUAL ELECTION

With elections set for 30 May, the SDLP drew up its lists of potential constituency and 'top up' delegates. A combined total of eighty-four names was entered for both lists, although the realistic expectation was that the party would emerge with approximately twenty-five delegates. Given the sharp divisions within unionism, the likelihood also existed that the SDLP could be the largest party. Unionism was now split between the UUP, the DUP, Robert McCartney's newly formed UK Unionist Party (UKUP),[61] and two loyalist parties, the Progressive Unionist Party (PUP), linked to the UVF, and the Ulster Democratic Party (UDP), linked to the UDA. Of these, the DUP and the UKUP were vehemently opposed to talks that would include Sinn Féin, unless preceded by full and verifiable decommissioning, while the UUP was divided between those who, like Trimble, had a more flexible approach, and those who took a line similar to that of the DUP and the UKUP.

On the question of participation in the forum, the SDLP declared at the launch of its campaign that it would work 'with the other main parties on matters of common concern, particularly on serious social and economic problems', and so would participate.[62] The election campaign was short and intense. The SDLP stressed its role in the peace process, in particular the role played by John Hume, and its framework for new partnership institutions in the North, between North and South, and between Ireland and Britain. Indicating trouble ahead for the process, Trimble ruled out any role at the talks for George Mitchell, now tipped as chair, but nonetheless insisted that the Mitchell principles would have to be fully respected. Paisley spoke in cataclysmic terms about the election being 'a life-and-death struggle' in which the very existence of the North as part of the UK was at stake. As the SDLP had frequently stated, the elections would not reveal anything new about party positions, and they did not.

The results gave the SDLP 160,786 votes, a significant drop of 23,659 when compared with 1992. Sinn Féin recorded an increase of 39,050 over the same period, despite the fact that the PIRA had resumed its campaign and had set off more bombs in London. In the key West Belfast constituency, the results did not augur well for the next Westminster election; there, Sinn Féin took four of the five seats, outpolling the SDLP by over 11,000 votes. In Belfast as a whole, the party's vote dropped to 28,835, against Sinn Féin's 34,353, a gap of 5,518. For the SDLP, the result was disappointing, given the party's very high vote in 1992, and the role Hume had played in the peace process. Ironically, rather than punish Sinn Féin for the breakdown of the PIRA's ceasefire, many Nationalists seem to have sympathized with Sinn Féin because of the British government's failure to advance talks more expeditiously. Overall, the results made the UUP the largest party (30 seats), the DUP second (24), the SDLP third (21) and Sinn Féin fourth (17), followed by the APNI (7), UKUP (3) and others (6).

The negotiating table had now been shaped and the mandates given, but the talks originally intended to include Sinn Féin, would now commence without its participation, and there was no sign that the PIRA would soon cease its campaign. As if to underline that point, almost on the eve of the talks' opening session, on 7 June, a PIRA unit murdered Garda Jerry McCabe during an attempted robbery of a post office in Co. Limerick. The prospects for Sinn Féin's participation soon, or at any stage, rapidly receded. This murder caused considerable anxiety within the SDLP, with several leading members questioning whether the peace process could bear early results.[63] For the present, however, all eyes were on the talks and the possibilities they might contain.

Chapter 18

Negotiating agreement

The talks opened in a tense and ominous atmosphere on 10 June 1996. Sinn Féin, excluded from the talks because of the PIRA's breach of its ceasefire, appeared in strength to demonstrate outside the talks' venue, a large fortress-like office-block on the Stormont estate, close to Parliament Buildings. Inside, there were further demonstrations as the Unionist parties declared their opposition to George Mitchell acting as overall chair, together with his colleagues from the decommissioning consultations, Harri Holkeri and General John de Chastelain, as co-chairs. Prime Minister John Major and Taoiseach John Bruton formally opened the proceedings, stressing the historic opportunity the talks offered, an assertion immediately contradicted by Unionist objections about how negotiations should proceed. It took another long day of intense behind-the-scenes discussions before Mitchell was confirmed in the chair during a very stormy session in the early hours of 12 June. The DUP and UKUP noisily withdrew, accusing the UUP, whose delegates remained, of treachery for accepting the governments' chairing arrangements. The parties present then committed themselves to upholding the Mitchell principles, a required condition for participation, and the talks commenced.[1]

PROCEDURAL WRANGLES, BOMBS AND PARADES

The resolution of Mitchell's role did not mean an end to disputes and delays during the opening weeks. Having been thwarted over the chairing arrangements, the DUP determined to accept neither the rules of procedure, nor the agenda tabled by the two governments, despite these having been arrived at during pre-talks discussions with the parties. For the following seven weeks, the sessions were entangled in disagreements over both. Finally, with some slight modifications, agreement was reached at the end of July on rules of procedure, but not yet on the agenda, and the talks adjourned until September.

If the situation at Stormont was fraught, it only mirrored what was happening on the streets. On 15 June, the PIRA exploded a massive bomb in Manchester, causing three hundred million pounds worth of damage, and launched mortar bombs at a British army base in Germany. In Northern Ireland, a menacing situation developed on the streets as the height of the loyal orders marching season was being reached. Renewed Nationalist opposition to the routes for a number of parades resulted in confrontation between marchers, local residents and the police. At issue again was the right to march versus the claim that such a right should not be exercised without the consent of residents living along a parade route. As the summer of 1996 progressed, the number of incidents surrounding such parades increased, with politicians on both sides of the community increasingly drawn into the controversies.

Recognizing a parade as an example of the freedom of expression, the SDLP argued that exercising this right had to have regard to the views of local communities through whose areas parades were intended to pass. This meant that dialogue between parade organizers and those communities was essential. Since the loyal orders regarded their right to parade as non-negotiable, and since several community groups leading the protests were perceived as being under Sinn Féin influence, representatives of the loyal orders refused to engage in dialogue. With the police left to manage the situation, confrontation was almost inevitable.

Once again, the most serious confrontation took place at Drumcree, where the local Orange lodge and thousands of supporters gathered to defy a police order prohibiting the lodge from marching along the mainly Nationalist Garvaghy Road.[2] A five-day stand off with the police ensued, with the result that across the North, protests, roadblocks and riots occurred in several predominantly Unionist areas. At Drumcree, calls for direct dialogue between the residents and the local Orange lodge went unheeded, and attempts at mediation did not produce a solution. After five days, and citing their fear of more widespread trouble, the police allowed the parade proceed as originally intended and forcibly removed Nationalist protesters who attempted to block the route. This decision was seen in Nationalist eyes as the police conceding to pressure from Unionist politicians and the Orange Order. Nationalist anger was profound and Bríd Rodgers (pl. 24), recently elected to the forum for Upper Bann, pointedly posed the question, as she stood watching protesters being dragged off the road, 'is this how Northern Ireland is to be governed, by mob rule and threat?'[3]

RESIGNATIONS FROM FORUM

Nationalist outrage at what they perceived was a return to the days when the police were the tools of Unionist politicians, led to more rioting, this time in Nationalist areas. At a special meeting of the SDLP's forum and executive members, the party claimed that the events at Drumcree had 'seriously damaged the trust and confidence essential to the political process', and decided that its members would resign their forum seats forthwith.[4] The events at Drumcree had exposed such raw, inter-communal tensions that the party felt that a strong stand had to be taken. Resignation from the forum, about which the party still harboured profound reservations, seemed the most effective step to take. Indeed, at its first session, Mark Durkan had declared that 'if the forum can be of any assistance in promoting a better atmosphere for dealing with the political problems, we will be there. Equally we will do everything to ensure that the negotiating process is protected'.[5] Following the incidents at Drumcree and elsewhere, the SDLP judged that the forum could not contribute that 'better atmosphere', and that concentrating on making the talks a success should be its sole focus.

Major street confrontations persisted until the end of the marching season in September, though one of the most nakedly sectarian protests, the picketing by loyalists of Catholic churches in North Antrim, continued for the next eighteen months.[6] Such confrontations together with continuing PIRA activity made the prospects for talks anything but positive when they resumed in September.[7] Concerned that a combination of these incidents and procedural wrangling could undermine the negotiations, the SDLP met with the UUP to assess the situation just before the talks reconvened.[8] While no conclusion was reached, the two parties decided to liaise regularly in order to more effectively and expeditiously progress the talks, and to defuse tensions.

IMPOSING ENTRY CONDITIONS

Agreement on the agenda was reached by mid-October,[9] but then the talks stalled over how to deal with decommissioning, further delaying discussion of a substantive kind. At issue were the conditions under which Sinn Féin could enter the talks. Unionists argued that Sinn Féin should only be admitted following a credible PIRA ceasefire and a verifiable start to decommissioning.

The SDLP insisted that compliance with the Mitchell principles should determine participation in the talks, not the preferences of particular parties, and following a new ceasefire there should be no delay in admitting Sinn Féin. In other words, the SDLP argued that there should be no prior decommissioning, nor a lengthy period to test the 'credibility' of a ceasefire, and that the talks should proceed by conducting all three strands in parallel, as well as issues related to decommissioning.[10] Accused by Unionists of not being serious about decommissioning, the SDLP responded that

> the only way political violence will finally be eradicated from our society is through the achievement of a lasting, just and balanced political settlement, which respects the rights of all our people and reflects equally the aspirations and identities of both traditions.[11]

The party pointed to the folly of trying to force decommissioning in the absence of progress towards such a settlement, and challenged the Unionist parties to accept that 'all conceivable interpretations of the Mitchell Report involve a process of negotiations on this issue'. The SDLP also posed the question as to whether Unionists were 'willing to engage in good faith on this, in parallel with the political negotiations'.[12] A series of meetings involving the SDLP, the UUP and APNI in early December produced some meeting of minds, but did not reach full agreement over decommissioning before the talks adjourned for the Christmas break.[13] In the New Year, the talks followed a similar pattern, but, despite several bilateral and multi-lateral meetings between the parties, no resolution was reached.[14] With local and general elections due in May, the talks adjourned on 5 March to allow the parties to conduct their respective campaigns. The only positive achievement since the talks began was the passing of decommissioning legislation at Westminster and in the Oireachtas to provide a legal framework for the process, should it ever happen.

Throughout the autumn of 1996, John Hume maintained contact with Gerry Adams in further attempts to have the PIRA ceasefire restored, but to no avail. Once again, Hume feared that an opportunity for peace and dialogue would be lost if Sinn Féin's entry to the talks was to be constrained by stringent preconditions and, worse, that the PIRA would return to all-out violence. Faced with the prospect of the Unionist parties withdrawing from the talks should the terms of entry be relaxed, the British government maintained that a new ceasefire would have to be seen as credible.[15] A lengthy period would be unacceptable to the provisional movement and was regarded by the SDLP as risking the whole process. This view was shared by the Irish and US governments. Dublin and Washington wished to see the rapid entry of Sinn Féin to the talks once a new ceasefire had been declared.[16] The impasse reinforced the perception that Major's government was so dependent on Unionist votes to stay in power that he could not be more flexible. In these circumstances, the SDLP became impatient for the general election, due sometime in the first half of 1997, and for the change of government it was predicted to bring.[17]

At the SDLP's twenty-sixth annual conference in early November, the frustration of members at the non-progress of the talks found full expression. Referring to the lengthy delay between the paramilitary ceasefires in 1994 and the opening of the talks in June 1996, party chair, Jonathan Stephenson, said that 'it was one of the great tragedies of the past twenty-seven years that Sinn Féin's commitment to democracy was not put to the test', and he accused the British government of not having the courage to call all-party talks while the PIRA ceasefire had lasted.[18] Hume blamed the British for delaying the talks, saying that it was his conviction that 'had they started soon after the ceasefire, we would have lasting peace by now', and he appealed to the PIRA 'to renew their ceasefire and create the circumstances where all the energies of all our people are devoted to building a new Ireland based on respect for both our traditions'.[19] His appeal received no positive response. Instead, the PIRA maintained its campaign of bomb-attacks and shootings.

CALLS FOR PACTS

Against strong opposition, some delegates once again proposed election pacts with Sinn Féin for the forthcoming Westminster elections, in order to deny Unionists seats that they would otherwise retain because of split Nationalist votes; the principal one being Fermanagh.[20] Prominent among those opposed to a pact was Séamus Mallon, for whom the differences between the SDLP and Sinn Féin were profound. He described Sinn Féin as part of a 'defenderist culture',[21] of being 'introverted, narrow and corrosive' in contrast to the SDLP, which, he said, was 'visionary in Northern Ireland political life'.[22] Later, after Sinn Féin had written to the party requesting discussions of a pact, Hume indicated that a pact could only be considered on two conditions: the first, if the PIRA had declared a new ceasefire; and the second, if Sinn Féin had abandoned its policy of non-attendance at Westminster so that effective representation would be provided for the Nationalist community.[23] Since neither condition was acceptable, Hume accused Sinn Féin of really being more intent on embarrassing the SDLP, than on working in the best interests of the Nationalist people. The issue led to one of the SDLP leader's most trenchant attacks on Sinn Féin and the PIRA. In an *Irish News* article,[24] Hume elaborated on the reasons why there could be no electoral pact with Sinn Féin, a party he accused of engaging in malpractices at elections, of intimidating SDLP election workers, and, above all, of supporting the use of violence for political ends. For the SDLP, 'to make an electoral pact with Sinn Féin without an IRA ceasefire would be the equivalent of asking our voters to support the killing of innocent human beings by the IRA'. He asked Nationalist voters to consider the consequences of voting for people

> who pretend to be democrats while stealing people's votes, and who pretend to stand for the rights of the Irish people while defying and denying the will of the Irish people for peace expressed in election after election these last twenty-five years.

It was an attack that ended any further talk of an electoral pact. However, the attack went deeper than the issue of a pact; it expressed Hume's growing frustration that, after all his efforts to bring the provisional movement into the democratic process, the North was again caught in a spiral of violence, and a talks process carefully designed to accommodate Sinn Féin was being spurned.

MANAGING PARADES

The other key issue addressed at the annual conference was the management of controversial parades. Introducing the party's submission to the British government's special commission examining how parades should be managed, the North Commission,[25] Bríd Rodgers talked of her 'tears of anger and despair and frustration' when the police forced the parade down the Garvaghy Road, and bitterly regretted the absence of direct dialogue between the Orange Order and local residents.[26] Others highlighted the work of the party in helping to defuse tension around the Apprentice Boys' parades in Derry as an example of how local dialogue could be effective.[27] In its submission, the party argued that decisions over whether or not particular parades would be permitted should no longer be a matter for the police, who were not seen as impartial, and who had to implement their own decisions. Instead, the SDLP recommended the creation of a special commission to assess applications to hold parades, to determine if they should be allowed to proceed, and, if so, under what conditions. The party also recommended that the commission should promote inter-community dialogue in order to obviate the kind of confrontation that had surrounded disputed parades. When the North Commission reported the following January, the party noted with satisfaction that many of its recommendations featured in what was proposed.[28]

TESTING ELECTION

The 1997 general election campaign was one of the most testing in the SDLP's experience. Outlining the challenge, Séamus Mallon said that the election would effectively be a choice as to who would lead the Nationalist community into the next century, 'constitutional politics' or 'violence'.[29] Graphically underlining this choice, the party's main election poster featured three pint glasses, representing 'violence', 'intransigence' and 'sectarianism' together with the slogan 'we don't want another round'. The message was intended to distance the SDLP from Sinn Féin, and to emphasize its distinctive peaceful and constitutional approach. Determined to maximize its vote, the SDLP nominated candidates to contest all eighteen constituencies, confident that it would retain its existing four seats, and possibly add Mid-Ulster and West Tyrone. The manifesto, *Real leadership; real peace*, stressed the consistent SDLP messages of 'partnership and inclusion' and its opposition to violence and sectarianism, and pointed to its three relationships analysis as having been adopted as the agenda for the ongoing negotiations.[30] As in previous manifestoes, the party outlined proposals for socio-economic reform, which was now a slightly more realistic possibility, given those negotiations.

The election results were both a triumph and a disappointment for the SDLP. With over 190,000 votes, the highest ever achieved in a parliamentary general election, the party emerged as the second largest in the North. However, while retaining its seats in Foyle, Newry-Armagh and South Down, the achievement was marred when Adams retook the West Belfast seat. Sinn Féin also won Mid-Ulster, while the SDLP failed to make its anticipated gain in West Tyrone.

So, while the party won back most of the votes it had lost in the forum elections a year earlier, in several constituencies where previously the SDLP had been ahead by a substantial margin, the gap between it and Sinn Féin narrowed considerably. Worryingly for the party's future performance, in West Belfast the margin was now over 8,000 votes in Sinn Féin's favour, a very disappointing result given Joe Hendron's strong representation during the five years he held the seat. Once again there were widespread allegations against Sinn Féin of fraudulent electoral practices, especially in these key constituencies. Overall, the election again revealed the growth in the Nationalist electorate, now at just over 40 per cent, and, as predicted by Séamus Mallon, the contest for its leadership was becoming intense.

As the electoral gap between the two parties narrowed, one of the most notable characteristics of Sinn Féin rhetoric was the extent to which it had now borrowed SDLP concepts and language. As the political commentator David McKittrick wrote, Sinn Féin 'have certainly been stealing the SDLP's clothes'.[31] Concepts like partnership between Nationalists and Unionists, calls for the Irish and British governments to work closely together, as opposed to Sinn Féin's traditional message of 'Brits out', and recognition that Unionist consent to new arrangements would be essential, were increasingly becoming part of the party's discourse, signalling the compromises that negotiations would inevitably require. The move away from an exclusively militant discourse towards that of constitutional nationalism was now taking firmer roots within Sinn Féin, and the party's participation in the talks would mark another significant move in that direction.

In Britain, the election was a triumph for Labour, now under Tony Blair's leadership. Blair had already familiarized himself with the situation in Northern Ireland, and he appointed Mo Mowlam as secretary of state, with instructions to get the process moving again and, in particular, to ensure that it would be inclusive. Before a new phase could begin, the parties had to mount their campaigns for the district council elections a few weeks later. The SDLP nominated 167 candidates and, hoping to repeat its recent overall result, expected to add to its 127 seats gained in 1993. But the results did not match expectations. In a turnout of 53 per cent, well below the 67 per cent recorded at the general election, the party won only 120 seats, and saw its overall percentage drop to just over 20, while Sinn Féin's climbed to almost 17, halving the gap between the two parties.

BRINGING SINN FÉIN IN

Elections over, the talks reconvened on 3 June. Blair had already permitted officials to renew meetings with Sinn Féin and, on a visit to Belfast, he had made it clear that his response to a new ceasefire 'would not be slow'.[32] He also warned that the 'settlement train' would soon be leaving the station, with or without Sinn Féin on board. In remarks aimed at reassuring Unionists, Blair declared that his agenda was 'not a united Ireland … None of us in this hall today, even the youngest, is likely to see Northern Ireland as anything but a part of the UK. This is the reality, because the consent principle is now almost universally accepted'.[33] The new prime minister conveyed an air of balanced urgency that suggested he was determined negotiations should not only proceed, but also be focused and productive.

More direct evidence that a new and more hopeful phase in the talks was likely came with the participation of all major parties, including Sinn Féin, in a four-day workshop in South Africa, in early June.[34] The workshop provided insights into the peace process there, and enabled participants to engage with some of the country's leading figures, including President Nelson Mandela (pl. 23), Cyril Ramaphosa of the ANC and Rolf Meyer of the National Party. Although both the UUP and the DUP decided not to formally engage with Sinn Féin at the workshop, a decision that astounded their South African hosts, and insisted on parallel and exclusive sessions for themselves, their attendance at the event indicated a new seriousness about the negotiations, and the likelihood that Sinn Féin would participate, sooner rather than later.

PARTNERSHIP IN BELFAST

Just before the talks reconvened, local government politics in Belfast signalled the kind of changes that the SDLP and many others were hoping for, when the party's long-serving council member, Alban Maginness, became the first Nationalist Lord Mayor of the city, with a Unionist, Jim Rodgers, as his deputy.[35] It was an auspicious sign, and one that the SDLP warmly welcomed. Accepting his office, Maginness stressed the SDLP's policy of partnership, saying

> Tonight the political mould has been broken. Its fracture does not mark
> a defeat of one political tradition by another, nor mark a defeat of one

political tradition by another, nor is it a victory. Rather it signifies a bold step towards the creation of a partnership amongst the political traditions of this divided city.[36]

Coincidentally, another SDLP councillor, Martin Bradley, was elected Mayor of Derry, also with a Unionist deputy, the first time ever representatives from the Nationalist tradition simultaneously held the office of first citizen of the North's two main cities. Partnership in local government, if not yet fully accepted by all parties, was now becoming the norm in most councils.

Political change in the South had also taken place when, following the general election on 6 June, a Fianna Fáil-Progressive Democrats government was formed with Bertie Ahern, a former finance minister, as Taoiseach. Ahern was very supportive of the talks in Belfast and would quickly develop a close working relationship with Tony Blair that would strongly influence their progress. Soon after the talks reconvened, the two governments moved swiftly to resolve the impasse on conditions for Sinn Féin's entry, and on 25 June they spelled out their agreed position.[37] At Westminster, Blair stated that once a new PIRA ceasefire had been declared, six weeks later an assessment of its credibility would be made, and, if the governments were satisfied, Sinn Féin would be permitted to join the talks.[38] Within the talks, the governments proposed that two sub-committees would be established, one to deal with confidence-building measures, the other to consider decommissioning, which the prime minister stated would have to proceed in parallel with the talks. The proposed international commission on decommissioning would also be established to deal with the practicalities of decommissioning in accordance with the recent legislation. With substantive talks scheduled to start in September and to conclude not later than the following May, there was a now a sense that the opportunity had to be grasped. In welcoming this development, Hume echoed the prime minister's warning that talks would proceed with or without Sinn Féin, saying 'let the rest of us get together and work quickly and strongly with both governments to reach ... agreement, to put it to the people, and to provide lasting peace and stability'.[39]

PARADES THREATEN TALKS

While the parties debated the governments' proposals, events on the outside were not conducive to progress. The marching season was again approaching its climax, and when attempts at mediating a settlement at Drumcree met with no success, fears mounted that a repetition of the previous year's incidents would occur. And so they did. As previously, police removed protesters from the Garvaghy Road to allow the Orange parade through, and, predictably, rioting broke out in many Nationalist areas. When an SDLP delegation met with Mo Mowlam, she was quite depressed at what had happened, and readily acknowledged the breakdown in relationships with the Nationalist community.[40] A delegation led by John Hume conveyed the deep sense of outrage to the Irish and British prime ministers, and, in an attempt to defuse the situation, put forward proposals for the re-routing of contentious parades.[41] Much to many people's surprise, a few days later, the Orange Order announced that some parades would be re-routed, and others cancelled.[42] It was an important gesture that helped reduce tension at a time when events could have seriously derailed the talks at Stormont.

PIRA'S SECOND CEASEFIRE

In mid-July, rumours began circulating that a new PIRA ceasefire might be declared. On 17 July, Hume and Adams met and issued a joint statement referring to 'considerable progress' towards restoring the peace process, a statement widely understood as the prelude to a ceasefire announcement. The announcement came two days later. The expectation now was that Sinn Féin would be invited to join the talks in September. While widely welcomed, within the talks the announcement added to Unionist concerns that decommissioning would not be addressed to their satisfaction. Trimble had insisted that if Sinn Féin entered the talks, it would be coming in 'with the expectation that it immediately starts disarming and that all the mechanisms will be in place to facilitate that'.[43] It was clear, however, that Sinn Féin would only consider decommissioning during the course of the talks, just as the international body had suggested, and that there was no obligation to commence the process. Also, much as the two governments might have liked to see some decommissioning at this stage, it was clear that they were not going to support Trimble's demand.[44] The days that followed the renewed ceasefire saw the prospects for the talks proceeding hang very much in the balance.

The main Unionist parties tabled amendments to the governments' proposals, all intended in one way or another to oblige a start to PIRA decommissioning. But, as the SDLP reminded delegates, 'there were two choices facing everyone – the weapons could be either taken out or talked out. The former option had had little success over the past 27 years and, as yet, the process of talking them out hadn't been tried'.[45] When put to the vote, all of the amendments failed to meet the requirement of a 'sufficient consensus'.[46] The question then remained as to whether the Unionist parties, in particular the UUP, would be at the talks when Sinn Féin entered in September. Signalling their refusal to accept the governments' paper, the DUP and the UKUP withdrew, and vowed not to return. Trimble adopted a more flexible approach, and decided that the UUP would consult with a wide section of opinion within and without the Unionist community, before coming to a decision about its future participation.[47] Meantime, Trimble made it clear that his party would have no direct dealings with Sinn Féin until after decommissioning had commenced.

HUME FOR PRESIDENT!

Faced with what would be the most important British-Irish negotiations since 1920–1, the SDLP devoted considerable time during August to preparing its input. August also saw a very public campaign to persuade John Hume to become a candidate in the South's presidential election, due at the end of October. Hume was at the height of his popularity throughout Ireland, and it was generally believed that were he to declare his candidacy, he would be elected unopposed, the main parties in the South having indicated that they would not nominate candidates to oppose him. For a time, it appeared that he might seek the nomination.[48] Within the SDLP, however, many felt that his departure would leave an enormous gap at what was a crucial time in the negotiations he had done so much to bring about. Although it was left to Hume's own personal decision, there was a general sense of relief among party colleagues when, in early September, he announced that he would not be a candidate. In making that announcement, Hume emphasized the crucial stage being reached in the talks and his belief that he should stay with his colleagues 'to devote all our energies towards achieving a new and agreed Ireland'.[49]

PARTIES IN AND OUT

Sinn Féin entered the talks on their resumption in September, but for the following two weeks there was uncertainty as to the UUP's position.[50] When the UUP decided, despite the opposition of many within the party, including several of its MPs, to remain at the table, it said that its purpose would be to challenge Sinn Féin's right to be present. The UUP challenge was an indictment alleging Sinn Féin to be in breach of the Mitchell principles, and therefore that they were not entitled to participate in the talks.[51] The indictment failed, but crucially the UUP did not withdraw. Following an SDLP-brokered motion that stressed the resolution of the decommissioning issue to be 'an indispensable part of the process of negotiation', the parties agreed to move to substantive negotiations.[52]

In early October, almost sixteen months after the talks had commenced, delegates began discussing the substantive agenda on new institutional arrangements and on a wide range of confidence-building measures, including decommissioning. Speaking at the launch of discussions on Strands 1 and 2, John Hume and Séamus Mallon, respectively, recalled the NIF's approach to an agreement – the need to recognize the right of Nationalists and Unionists to effective, symbolic and administrative expression of their identity – saying that this was the basis to the SDLP's submissions.[53] The SDLP then submitted a comprehensive set of proposals covering the institutional requirements for each of the three strands; the protection of human, civil and cultural rights; economic and social development; and policing and judicial reform, as well as decommissioning and the manner in which an agreement should be validated.[54] These proposals reflected long-established SDLP policies and, as the *Frameworks* document had indicated, they were broadly shared by the two governments.

Progress towards agreement remained slow throughout the rest of 1997, with much of the discussion repeating party analyses of issues that had been presented at the Brooke-Mayhew talks, Sinn Féin excepted, together with an identification of the principles and requirements that each believed were necessary for a solution.[55] Dominating proceedings at this stage and lending them an air of unreality was the UUP's refusal to engage directly with Sinn Féin, not only on the grounds that it still objected to Sinn Féin's presence, but also because Sinn Féin had not yet openly acknowledged the principle of consent, and hence had not acknowledged that Northern Ireland was part of the UK. Over Christmas, events on the outside again threatened the talks. Loyalist paramilitaries, some connected with the parties at the talks, targeted Catholics in a

series of random killings, while PIRA dissidents countered by murdering loyalists and by planting bombs in predominantly Protestant towns.[56] Within the
talks, these events led to the temporary expulsion of the UDP, and then, when
the PIRA was identified as being involved in the murder of two alleged drug
dealers, of Sinn Féin, further delaying progress.[57] Notwithstanding the gravity
of the events that had precipitated these expulsions, the SDLP had grave reservations about the manner in which the indictments were drawn up and the
evidence on which they were based, which the party felt to be more supposition
and media reports than hard evidence.[58] The SDLP criticized the amount of
time being devoted to presenting the indictments, and the negative effects that
these proceedings were having on the atmosphere within the talks. The two
governments insisted, however, that the indictments proceed.

When the parties eventually presented their proposals for new institutions,
significant differences emerged between the SDLP, Sinn Féin and the UUP,
notably in Strands 1 and 2. Harking back to the Brooke-Mayhew talks and earlier,
the UUP initially argued for a committee-style government, whereas the SDLP
argued for the kind of cabinet-style executive that was eventually agreed. In
Strand 2, the UUP strongly resisted SDLP proposals that a North-South body
should have executive, rather than purely advisory and consultative powers, and
also recommended that such a body should operate within the framework, and
under the authority, of a council of the (British) Isles. For the SDLP, a North-
South body lacking executive authority over a range of agreed functions would
lack credibility, and would be seen simply as a talking shop, while the proposed
Unionist format would diminish the all-Ireland dimension. Together with the
Irish government, the party pressed for meaningful economic, cultural and social
functions to be part of a new North-South council's remit, and ultimately this
was successful. The SDLP and the Irish government both supported the proposal
for a British-Irish council linking the UK, its devolved regions and Ireland in a
British-Irish council, but completely rejected the UUP proposal that a North-
South body in Ireland should be part of it.

SDLP V. SINN FÉIN

The SDLP's differences with Sinn Féin stemmed from the latter's very hardline
Nationalist approach. Arguing that partition was wrong, Sinn Féin declined to
make separate submissions to Strands 1 and 2 until almost the final week of nego-

tiations. Instead, the party clung to the view that 'the right of the Irish people, as a whole, to national self-determination is supported by universally recognized principles of international law',[59] refusing to also acknowledge the international consensus, shared by all other participants, that the principle of consent should apply to resolving disputes over self-determination. Sinn Féin's submissions referred, on the one hand, to the evils of partition, to Britain's malign role in Ireland and to Unionist discrimination, and, on the other hand, to the great benefits they claimed would follow from the establishment of an independent united Ireland. No reference was made to the effects of the PIRA campaign on relationships between the communities – it was almost as if that campaign had not happened. Indeed, a feature of Sinn Féin's approach to Unionists was Gerry Adams' habit of lecturing them about their 'Irish' identity and their 'failure' to emulate the late eighteenth-century, mainly Protestant, United Irishmen, and Martin McGuinness' practice of reminding delegates of how he had, allegedly, experienced discrimination when seeking work as a young man in Derry.[60] To the SDLP, this approach was patronizing, recriminatory and unhelpful and displayed a poor understanding of unionism. The party strongly criticized Sinn Féin's one-sided approach to violations of human rights, arguing that 'the abuses of Unionist governments are well documented ... added to those abuses are the pain and tragedy of the past three decades which Sinn Féin does not highlight'.[61] On the issue of identity, the party argued that Unionists' were entitled to describe themselves as British and to have that identity respected, just as Nationalists were entitled to have their Irish identity respected.

As a result of its approach, Sinn Féin had considerable difficulty with the very concept of an assembly for the North, saying that it would be impossible to 'sell' to their supporters because it 'acknowledged' partition, and would be Unionist dominated.[62] Instead, they proposed a set of regional councils, but whether for the whole of Ireland or just for the North was never made clear. The proposal ignored the fact that some such councils would also be Unionist dominated, and failed to clarify under what authority they would operate. To deal with all-Ireland matters, Sinn Féin unrealistically proposed a free-standing council, but how composed and with what links with Dublin and Belfast was also never made clear. Faced with the SDLP's proposals for an assembly with firm safeguards against abuses from whatever source, together with an executive representative of both sides of the community, Sinn Féin accused the party of pursuing a purely 'internal' settlement.[63] This allegation was patently untrue, given the SDLP's insistence on an all-Ireland context and its proposals for a

North-Ssouth council. With little to contribute on new institutional arrangements, Sinn Féin became preoccupied with matters of more immediate concern
to its paramilitary colleagues – prisoner releases, decommissioning and demili-
tarization – and, in effect, left the institutional arrangements to be negotiated
by others.

AGREEMENT IN SIGHT

In January, the two governments presented participants with a 'heads of agreement' document.[64] It proposed amendments to Articles 2 and 3 of the South's
constitution, and the repeal of the 1920 Government of Ireland Act; a new
Northern Ireland assembly; a North-South council with executive responsibilities; and a British-Irish council accountable to the Oireachtas and the assembly.
Other proposals included the provision of new measures to protect human
rights and equality, the early release of paramilitary prisoners, decommissioning
and policing. From then on, the negotiations increasingly focused on detailing
the various proposals.

The UUP, with some support from the British government, resisted, for a
time, proposals for an executive-type government because, in all likelihood, it
would mean the inclusion of Sinn Féin ministers, and the UUP again pressed
its committee proposal. The SDLP replied that an inclusive executive would
oblige ministers to work together, and so demonstrate partnership at the highest
political level. An inclusive executive would also ensure cross-party support, not
just for all of the new political institutions but, critically, also for the anticipated
policing, judicial and human rights reforms. Eventually, it was the SDLP's
proposals that were accepted. It was likewise with the party's approach to the
North-South council. The SDLP argued that the council have executive
responsibility for a number of functions, that it be answerable to the Oireachtas
and to the new Northern Ireland assembly, and that its decisions should require
unanimity between the ministers involved.

The final two weeks of negotiations were conducted under a firm direction
from George Mitchell that they end on 9 April, with or without agreement. To
focus minds, Mitchell published a draft agreement for discussion by participants.[65] The draft contained proposals for a much stronger North-South
council than Unionists were willing to accept and, for a time, it appeared that
the negotiations might end without agreement.[66] To achieve agreement, it was

necessary for the Irish government and the SDLP to agree to a reduced range of council functions. Last-minute difficulties also arose over the wording on decommissioning, over terms for the early release of paramilitary prisoners, and over linkages between these issues and the overall implementation of an agreement. To achieve Sinn Féin's agreement, the governments adopted dangerously vague language on decommissioning,[67] agreed that the completion of prisoner releases would be within two years instead of three, and that no linkages would exist between these issues. These concessions caused huge last-minute problems for the UUP, and would become a Damocles sword hanging over the agreement, threatening early attempts at its implementation.

GOOD FRIDAY AGREEMENT

After several long days and late nights of negotiations in which Prime Minister Blair and Taoiseach Ahern were fully engaged, agreement was finally reached early on Good Friday morning, 10 April. But, while the other parties and both governments greeted the news with a sense of relief mixed with joy and exhaustion, a further twelve hours elapsed while UUP delegates agonized as to whether they would accept what was already becoming known as the Good Friday Agreement. Eventually they did, but not before several of their negotiators had withdrawn because of their unwillingness to accept the terms for decommissioning and prisoner releases.[68] Within the SDLP, the agreement was seen as the ultimate vindication of the party's stand for democratic principles, and for the creation of political institutions in which the people of Ireland, North and South, could work and build a future together on the basis of equality and mutual respect (pl. 25).

Overjoyed that agreement had at last been reached, an agreement very much along lines long promoted by the SDLP, John Hume emphasized its historic significance, saying

> only once in a generation does an opportunity like this come along, an opportunity to resolve our deep and tragic conflict. No one should diminish the difficulties we face. No one should deny the tough decisions that have been made and tough choices that have to be made. We must draw reassurance that our agreement today reflects the firmest wish of all our people.[69]

It was an agreement for which a great price had been paid, a price that the party believed had been totally unnecessary. Indeed, in many respects, the agreement bore striking similarities to that achieved in 1973. Both agreements provided for an assembly and a power-sharing executive, and both provided for the establishment of a North-South council, together with a parliamentary forum. In several other respects the 1998 agreement was much more comprehensive, with its provision for constitutional change in the South, for commissions on policing and judicial reform, for human rights and equality commissions, for decommissioning, and for prisoner releases, none of which were as specifically provided for in 1973. The 1973 agreements had provided an opportunity to build and develop on similar principles, however, and might well have come to include similar features to that of 1998. The differences between the two hardly merited the huge loss of life, the injuries and the destruction suffered in the decades in between, and, of course, it was not because of what was not in the 1973 agreement that the campaigns of violence had been waged. Reflecting on that suffering and on so many lost opportunities since then, Séamus Mallon ruefully summed up many people's feelings when he described the Good Friday Agreement as 'Sunningdale for slow learners'.

Just as in 1973, reaching agreement was only a first step in building a better future. Implementing the agreement would be the real test, and a severe test it would prove to be.

Chapter 19

Jumping first

SDLP members experienced a great sense of satisfaction when the agreement was accepted by all participants late on Good Friday afternoon. Satisfaction and relief were also expressed when the agreement was subsequently endorsed by the UUP's executive, and later at a special Sinn Féin ard fheis.[1] For the SDLP itself, ratification was a mere formality, since the agreement met all of the necessary criteria specified by the party. The immediate challenge now was two-fold: ensure that the agreement was endorsed in the North at the referendum scheduled for 22 May; and if endorsed, mount the strongest possible campaign for the assembly elections that would follow at the end of June.

VICTORY CAMPAIGNS

While the SDLP approached the referendum full of confidence, the same was not true for the UUP. Despite the safe UUP executive vote in favour of the agreement, there was grave concern that the anti-agreement campaign being mounted by the DUP and the UKUP, assisted by the Orange Order and some within the UUP, could attract sufficient support to achieve a majority within unionism. As a result, there was uncertainty as to what kind of a campaign David Trimble and his supporters would mount. Consequently, for the first time in the history of the North, the leading party from the Nationalist community and its Unionist counterpart joined forces at one of the feature events of the campaign, a concert by the world famous Irish group, U2, accompanied by local group Ash.[2] Organized by the SDLP and targeted at a young audience, it was decided that John Hume and David Trimble would attend. When invited on stage by U2's lead singer, Bono, the party leaders were presented to the audience as 'two men who are taking a leap of faith out of the past into the future' (pl. 26).[3] This image of the two leaders together assisted in off-setting some of the negativity within the UUP and the wider Unionist community, and in no small way contributed to the agreement being endorsed by almost 72 per cent of the electorate in the highest ever turnout for any poll in Northern Ireland.[4] It was an overwhelming endorsement that suggested considerable support for pro-agreement parties in the assembly elections that were to follow four weeks later.

The SDLP's referendum manifesto spelled out the party's belief that the agreement had provided 'the means of resolving the relationships ruptured by our conflict: relationships between Unionists and Nationalists; relationships between North and South; relationships between Ireland and Britain'.[5] For the SDLP, the agreement had achieved its primary objective, an agreed Ireland 'in which the consent of Nationalists and Unionists would be secured for a partnership within agreed political institutions based on the highest standards of human rights'.[6] The party urged support for what it called 'a new covenant between the two main traditions in Ireland, a covenant wherein each will not only recognize the legitimacy of the other, but the future of all will be dependent on the equal legitimacy of both'.[7] Conscious of the tragic and terrible price that had been paid, the manifesto acknowledged the violent deaths of over 3,000 men, women and children, and the injuries suffered by over 30,000 more, and hoped that 'their tragedies and their wounds must never be forgotten or ignored, as we chart the healing process of which the Good Friday Agreement has marked but the first step'.[8] The party strongly urged that the 'gun' be removed from Irish politics in accordance with the approach laid down in the agreement. On this critical issue, the SDLP believed that 'decommissioning should not be made a precondition', but that 'it is now the responsibility of those with influence in this area to cooperate to ensure that decommissioning does actually take place'.[9]

The referendum over, the SDLP prepared for the assembly election, for which it nominated thirty-eight candidates. The widely acknowledged role of the party in shaping the Good Friday Agreement meant that SDLP hopes were high that the party's vote would be close to, and possibly even exceed the 1997 Westminster level. Pre-election polls suggested that the party would win 26 per cent of the votes. In the event, the party gained only 22 per cent. Although receiving more votes (177,963) than any other party, due to the vagaries of the PR voting system, the SDLP won four fewer seats than the UUP (172,225 votes; 28 seats). The results also showed that the gap within the Nationalist community between support for the SDLP and Sinn Féin had widened slightly in the SDLP's favour compared with the 1997 Westminster elections. The overall performance marked another triumph for the party, and was a tribute to the SDLP's stand for partnership, for human rights and for a comprehensive settlement within a British-Irish framework.

DISRUPTION THREATENS

As so frequently in Northern Ireland, political progress was overshadowed by a darker message. The total pro-agreement vote returned seventy members to the assembly, with twenty-eight anti-agreement members. But, just as in the 1973 assembly elections, Unionists were almost evenly split between both. The DUP and the UKUP won twenty-five between them, but counting three dissident UUP members, the anti-agreement numbers equalled the twenty-eight seats held by UUP. Only the two PUP members gave pro-agreement Unionists a slight majority. With the reliability of some of his UUP members uncertain, the combined anti-agreement block would gradually constrain David Trimble's room for manoeuvre. Recognizing the divisions within unionism, Trimble signalled that his approach to the agreement's implementation would be gradual, and that the transition period to full implementation would extend beyond the specified 31 October deadline.[10] In an attempt to reassure supporters, the UUP manifesto declared that its members would not sit in government with 'unreconstructed terrorists' (meaning Sinn Féin), while decommissioning had not commenced, punishment beatings continued, and the PIRA's military structures remained in place.[11] It was not an empty threat.

Following the elections, the new assembly met for the first time on 1 July.[12] The initial presiding officer, John Alderdice, who had been selected by the secretary of state, retained the office unchallenged, and when members had signed the roll, called for nominations for the offices of first and deputy first minister (designate). In a motion moved by John Taylor, seconded by John Hume, David Trimble and Séamus Mallon were jointly proposed for the posts and elected unopposed. In accepting his nomination for the deputy first minister's post, Séamus Mallon committed himself and the SDLP to upholding every aspect of the agreement, including decommissioning, which he said unequivocally he wanted to happen.[13] The assembly then recessed to allow the parties agree procedures, committee structures and ministerial portfolios.

OUTRAGES AT BALLYMONEY AND OMAGH

Over the following weeks, Unionist divisions created uncertainty about the agreement's implementation and, adding to the uncertainty, street politics exploded once more. Protests over Orange Order parades and ongoing sectarian violence resulted in several deaths, the most horrendous being the deaths of three young Catholic boys, the Quinn brothers, when their home in Ballymoney, Co. Antrim, was fire-bombed on 12 July. The deaths caused widespread revulsion and, in a display of solidarity and cross-community condemnation, David Trimble and Séamus Mallon together attended the boys' funeral mass.[14] But the Ballymoney deaths were soon overtaken in scale when the single most devastating act of violence of the Troubles took place in the centre of Omagh, Co. Tyrone, a month later. There, on 15 August, another busy Saturday afternoon, the dissident group, the Real IRA, exploded a bomb that murdered twenty-nine people and two unborn babies. Although that organization quickly admitted responsibility, and Sinn Féin leaders condemned the outrage, the incident was a reminder of just how tenuous the peace could be. While the outrage strongly reinforced the case for some moves towards decommissioning, none was forthcoming, and uncertainty grew as to the agreement's implementation.

Against this background, it was no surprise that inter-party negotiations made slow progress on agreeing ministerial portfolios and the remit of the North-South council. In the assembly, Séamus Mallon bluntly admitted that this 'is the price we are paying for the deadlock on decommissioning, and it is a very high price', and pointedly asserted that 'the will of the people has been denied'.[15] The PIRA ignored the implied accusation, and while Sinn Féin continued to insist that no prior decommissioning was required before it made nominations to the executive, that did not preclude indications being given that decommissioning would eventually take place. Indeed, if no preparatory moves were being made, how else were other parties to be convinced that decommissioning would be completed within the agreement's two-year timeframe? The SDLP regarded some such moves as essential in order to demonstrate the 'good faith' also required by the agreement.[16] But Sinn Féin's answer was to insist that its only obligation was to use its influence to try to persuade the PIRA and other paramilitaries to decommission, but that it could not guarantee that they would.

READY FOR DEVOLUTION

Negotiations on arrangements for devolution continued throughout the autumn and early winter of 1998. On the number of government departments,

Unionists proposed, on grounds of efficiency and economy, that there be no more than seven, while the SDLP proposed that there should be ten. The SDLP believed that an executive of ten would be more inclusive and would oblige parties to fully commit to all aspects of the agreement, in particular to decommissioning, and to new policing and justice arrangements. A second reason was that ten departments would allow a greater scrutiny of services that seldom came to public attention in larger departments. But the party had to face criticism that creating ten departments simply meant more ministerial posts, and that it had the effect of separating services, such as those in education, which had long been delivered jointly.[17] Among the recommendations for ministerial portfolios, the SDLP resisted strong pressure, especially from Sinn Féin, for a separate department charged with responsibility for the very sensitive equality issues. Instead, the party successfully argued that responsibility for this important cross-departmental issue should be placed with the first and deputy first ministers' office, because, as the party's spokesperson, Seán Farren, said, 'placing this responsibility at the heart of government symbolizes, in a powerfully effective way, a joint commitment by the leading ministers of both communities to have such (equality) principles upheld throughout the administration'.[18]

The SDLP pressed hard to obtain a meaningful set of implementation bodies under the control of the new North-South Ministerial Council. The party's approach was to have bodies established with the potential to influence economic development in both parts of Ireland, and cited wide support within the business sector for such an emphasis.[19] The party's main proposal was that a single all-Ireland authority be responsible for attracting overseas investment and for business development generally.[20] In all, the SDLP proposed eight bodies, including a single authority for tourism, and one for agriculture, an all-island strategic transportation authority, a languages body to promote Irish language and culture, and a body to coordinate cross-border European programmes. However, faced with strong resistance from the UUP to all-Ireland authorities for investment, for tourism and for transport, and with no strong support from the Irish government for some of these proposals,[21] an impasse developed in early December, which, despite the intervention of Tony Blair, risked derailing negotiations.[22] Eventually, compromises were struck. Instead of the single investment authority, a body eventually named Intertrade Ireland was agreed, with a remit to promote commercial links between North and South, and to remove barriers to such trade. The final set of North-South bodies included four with an economic development role: Intertrade Ireland; Waterways Ireland with responsibility for developing the recreational and tourist potential of the island's navigable lakes and rivers; Tourism Ireland, a limited company with responsibility for the overseas marketing of Ireland as a tourist destination; aquaculture and marine, a body that later took responsibility for managing and developing Carlingford Lough and Lough Foyle. The other implementation bodies agreed were: the Languages Body, to be responsible for promoting Irish and Ulster-Scots; the Food Safety Agency; and the EU Programmes Body. The agreement also included six areas for cooperation through existing agencies: transport, agriculture, education, health, environment and tourism. By mid-December, agreement was also reached on the SDLP's proposals for ten departments, as well as on the portfolios to be controlled by each.[23]

With these agreements, the preparatory work for devolution was complete, and all of the new institutions were ready to become fully operational. But the UUP refused to allow devolution to happen. The continuing release of paramilitary prisoners and on-going paramilitary punishment beatings, together with no move on decommissioning, all maintained pressure on Trimble not to agree the formation of the executive. Also, UUP members opposed to the agreement became increasingly outspoken, and allied themselves with the main opposition to the agreement led by Paisley and McCartney, reducing Trimble's assured majority among Unionists in the assembly.

SDLP THREATENS

Meantime, in an expectant spirit reminiscent of the 1973 conference, the SDLP gathered for its annual conference in Newry, in the heart of Séamus Mallon's constituency. It was another celebratory occasion. John Hume and David Trimble had just been proclaimed 1998 recipients of the Nobel peace prize for leading their parties and most of the community to the Good Friday Agreement (pl. 29). The announcement was a worldwide tribute to what Hume and the SDLP stood for and, addressing conference, Hume traced the journey made since he began talking with Gerry Adams and others in the Sinn Féin leadership, saying 'Unionists and Nationalists have at last taken their future in their hands, have seized control of their history rather than letting history hold them all in thrall'.[24] Anticipating the party's role in government, many conference motions amounted to a comprehensive agenda of initiatives in health and education, for promoting economic development, for supervising the conduct of parades and for enhancing equality and the role of women in the new assembly, as well as for reforming policing and the judicial system.[25]

On the critical issue of decommissioning, the conference was notable for two statements, one from Séamus Mallon, the second from John Hume, both stressing the urgent need for progress on the agreement's requirements. Hume declared that while the agreement did not require prior decommissioning for executive membership, the clear wish of the people of Ireland was that it take place and, therefore, the PIRA should concede to that wish. But it was Mallon's two-fold guarantee to Unionists and to Sinn Féin that made the bigger impact.[26] Acknowledging that both had genuine fears regarding the other, Mallon pledged that if decommissioning had not been completed within the two specified years, the SDLP 'would rigorously enforce the terms of the agreement and remove from office those who had so blatantly dishonoured their obligations'. Mallon based his proposal on the agreement's statement that 'those who hold office should use only democratic, non-violent means, and those who do not should be excluded or removed from office'.[27] To Sinn Féin, he pledged that the SDLP would not tolerate any failure by Unionists to live up to their obligations and would take similar action against them if they did.

Mallon's proposal was a dramatic attempt to break the logjam. In effect, he was offering the SDLP as a guarantor of the agreement. To Unionists, he was guaranteeing that Sinn Féin would not be permitted to remain in ministerial office if PIRA decommissioning did not happen within the two years the agreement specified. To Sinn Féin, he was saying that the SDLP accepted its right to unconditional nominations to the executive, and that the only condition related to its ministers remaining in office, provided commitments were met, a condition that applied to every party.

The offer was a gamble aimed particularly at persuading Trimble that he should allow an executive to be formed. But whether it could achieve its objective was problematic. The two parties for whom the offer was intended to provide reassurance promptly dismissed it. The UUP reiterated that its members would not sit with Sinn Féin in an executive without prior decommissioning, while Sinn Féin simply repeated that the agreement imposed no precondition on its right to nominate executive ministers.[28] Significantly, there was no comment from either government, though privately the Irish government was understood not to be pleased with the proposal. At this stage, the Irish view was closer to Sinn Féin's literal interpretation of the agreement; that parties only had 'to use any influence they may have, to achieve decommissioning of all paramilitary arms within two years'. In other words, Sinn Féin might try to persuade the PIRA to decommission but should not be punished if persuasion did not succeed. It was a view that would change over the next few months.

NOBEL VISIONS

The conferring of the Nobel prize on Hume and Trimble provided a unique international stage on which to spell out their visions for the new era made possible by the Good Friday Agreement.[29] John Hume's vision owed much to civil rights leaders like Martin Luther King, whose inspiration he had frequently acknowledged over the years, and to the founders of the European Union, 'the best example in the history of the world of conflict resolution', on whose polit- ical institutions the SDLP had modelled several of its own proposals for the agreement. Hume expressed deep appreciation of the international support for the peace process, and acknowledged the pain of those who had suffered bereavement, injury or loss of any kind as a result of the violence. Trimble also spoke of a new beginning, but emphasized the need to move ahead cautiously and steadily. His inspiration was Edmund Burke and the politics of the possible. He acknowledged that Northern Ireland, in many respects, had proved 'a cold house' for Nationalists, but like Hume, he hoped that the two communities could now work together for the mutual benefit of all. In other remarks at Oslo, Trimble stated that his emphasis on decommissioning arose from an under- standable wish to know that the PIRA's war was over,[30] and that a credible start to disarmament, not total decommissioning, was what the UUP required to allow the executive be formed. But the day after the conferring, the PIRA rejected any suggestion that it should decommission at all.[31] The statement was a direct rebuff to Trimble, as well as to Mallon's conference offer, and left the former with increasingly less room to manoeuvre.

MOVING DEADLINES

Following the failure to meet the October deadline, a new date, 10 March, was set for the devolution of powers to a Northern Ireland executive and assembly.[32] In their report to the assembly on 18 January, David Trimble and Séamus Mallon outlined what had been agreed regarding departmental portfolios and all-Ireland bodies, together with other matters related to preparing for devolution. In doing so, Trimble again made clear that progress would have to be achieved on decommissioning and so, no matter how much preparation was made otherwise, this requirement remained to be fulfilled. Without it, Trimble indicated that the UUP would not nominate ministers. In his stand, he was supported by Taoiseach Ahern, who stated, contrary to the Irish government's view up to then, that Sinn Féin's participation in the executive would not be possible 'without at least commencement of decommissioning'.[33] Despite Ahern's statement, when the assembly voted on the Trimble-Mallon Report, the same number of Unionists, twenty-nine, voted for the report as voted against it, revealing just how deeply and evenly divided Unionists were. With all of the other parties voting in favour, the report had a comfortable majority of forty-three.[34] With its adoption, full implementation was now formally possible, and, on 8 March, the two governments signed the necessary treaties providing the legal frameworks allowing it to happen. But, given the impasse over decommissioning, the British government announced that devolution would not take place until 2 April, a date that also came and went without a resolution.

In yet another bid to break the logjam, the two governments convened further talks at Hillsborough at the end of March and early April, with only one item on the agenda, namely decommissioning of PIRA weaponry. At their conclusion, Blair and Ahern issued a joint declaration, in which they acknowledged that all of the parties accepted that while decommissioning was not a precondition, it was an obligation deriving from the agreement, a significant move by the Sinn Féin leadership, who, up until then, had only accepted the 'best influence' obligation.[35] The two governments proposed that nominations to the executive should proceed, and that, within a month, 'a collective act of reconciliation will take place. This will see some arms put beyond use on a voluntary basis, in a manner which will be verified by the Independent International Commission on Decommissioning (IICD)'.[36] As an assurance against these steps not being taken, the declaration indicated, in what would have amounted to an amendment to the agreement, that the assembly would not then confirm ministerial nominations.[37] For a time, it appeared that these proposals would be accepted. Sinn Féin negotiators seemed attracted, and said they would consult within their movement. However, within twenty-four hours, the PIRA stated bluntly that it would not be 'forced into a surrender masquerading as decommissioning', and that there would be no decommissioning of its weapons.[38] Twelve days later, Sinn Féin formally rejected the declaration, throwing doubt on what it understood by decommissioning being an 'obligation'. Rather than resolving the impasse, the latest initiative had only deepened it.

PIRA IMPERVIOUS

The weeks that followed the Hillsborough talks were filled with claims and counter-claims about the future of the agreement. Pro-agreement Unionists continued to demand some indication that decommissioning would happen, while their anti-agreement rivals demanded full decommissioning, and castigated the former for 'betraying' democratic principles. The PIRA remained impervious to any demand for an indication that it was even considering decommissioning. The SDLP claimed that Unionist demands and PIRA intransigence were effectively 'vandalizing' the agreement, and called on the UUP and Sinn Féin to compromise on their positions, or risk 'bringing the agreement to an end'.[39] Another attempt by the SDLP to break the impasse was made when Hume proposed that Sinn Féin should enter into an undertaking that would have it automatically face expulsion from the executive if there were to be any return to violence by the PIRA.[40] Hume's proposal was a variation on the guarantee that Séamus Mallon had advanced at the party's conference. However, since it did not address the central issue of concern to Unionists, namely decommissioning, it had no appeal to the UUP.

In mid-May, at the Prime Minister's residence in Downing Street, yet another plan to achieve devolution by 30 June was agreed. According to it, parties would engage with the decommissioning body and, subject to a positive report from its chair, General John de Chastelain, an executive would be formed.[41] However, David Trimble was unable to persuade all of his colleagues to accept the plan because, unlike the Hillsborough declaration, it did not explicitly require actual decommissioning to be part of de Chastelain's report.[42] Nonetheless, more in hope than in expectation, the British government announced that 30 June would be the new deadline by which the executive should be formed.

HUME AGAIN TRIUMPHANT

Meantime, the SDLP had to prepare for yet another European election, for which John Hume had already been chosen as a candidate. On this occasion,

Hume was contesting not just on his European record, but also as Nobel peace prize winner, as well as on his role in achieving the Good Friday Agreement. It was a formidable record, and the party had every expectation that he would once again be elected without any difficulty. Indeed, in light of his record, there was considerable hope within the party that Hume would outpoll Paisley and give the whole pro-agreement constituency a morale boost.

Hume's fifth victory saw him just 2,000 votes behind Paisley, who was elected with 192,762 votes against Hume's 190,731. Compared with the referendum results of the previous year, 68 per cent of the overall electorate voted for pro-agreement parties, a drop of 3 per cent. This was significant because it was interpreted as declining Unionist support for the accord. In terms of the SDLP's battle with Sinn Féin, the results signalled that a large gap still existed between the two parties. Twenty-eight per cent of the total votes were cast for the SDLP, against 17 per cent for Sinn Féin, though, as ever, the caveat of Hume receiving a strong personal vote, including many votes that would normally be cast for the APNI, qualified this margin. So, while the party rejoiced in another victory that confirmed its dominance within the Nationalist community, as elections in the new millennium would show, it was to be its last such victory.

SHAM EXECUTIVE

The election over, the two governments once again set about trying to break the impasse on forming an executive before the 30 June deadline. By now, both were expressing a high degree of frustration at the lack of progress. For the SDLP, Séamus Mallon summed up that frustration when he bitterly decried the 'unilateral letters of comfort, together with secret deals and understandings', a reference to the various efforts by Downing Street over the previous year to provide support for David Trimble.[43] Mallon called on the two governments to 'recognize that their role and responsibility go far beyond that of honest broker'. By implication, he was saying that the agreement belonged to the people, not any particular party, that it was losing credibility and, therefore, that there should be no resiling from the June deadline. At the same time, Mallon reiterated his conference proposal that Sinn Féin would be expelled from the executive if PIRA decommissioning had not happened by May 2000. Significantly, in discussions with Blair and Ahern, his proposal was refined to suggest that the two governments, as guarantors of the agreement, as well as the SDLP and the UUP, would also support the expulsion of Sinn Féin.[44] However, in negotiations at the end of June, this proposal was replaced by a British commitment to legislate, not for expulsion but, instead, for the total suspension of the political institutions, a move that would affect all parties, not just the party in default.

After five days of negotiations with the pro-agreement parties, on 2 July, the two governments announced proposals for breaking the impasse in a document entitled *The way forward*.[45] The proposals set out a schedule for decommissioning, which would be completed by May 2000, and on which progress would be regularly reported by de Chastelain; a commitment by the British to introduce legislation on sanctions for failure to comply with requirements; and a date for establishing the executive, 18 July. The SDLP supported these proposals, as did Sinn Féin, but the UUP delayed its decision, and then, expressing dissatisfaction with the 'sanctions' legislation, declined to accept the package.[46]

It now appeared as if the UUP would never be satisfied, and that the real problem was its unwillingness to have the agreement implemented at all, because it would mean participating in an executive along with Sinn Féin. The SDLP concluded that matters had to be brought to a head, forcing a review of the operation of the agreement. The manner in which this was done produced two of the most dramatic and bizarre events of this phase of the process. The first occurred when Mo Mowlam acceded to SDLP and Irish government demands that she allow the nominations of executive ministers to proceed on 15 July. The UUP decided not to nominate, and its members absented themselves from the assembly the day that nominations were called for. The DUP and the APNI also declined to nominate, creating the almost comical situation of only SDLP and Sinn Féin nominations being made. John Hume proceeded to nominate six of the party's assembly members to ministerial posts,[47] only for their nominations and those of Sinn Féin to be declared null and void immediately, because they obviously did not meet the agreement's cross-community requirement.[48] The nomination procedure was followed by the second, even more dramatic event, the resignation of Séamus Mallon as deputy first minister (designate).

MALLON RESIGNS

In his resignation speech to the assembly, Mallon accused the UUP of rejecting all attempts to break the decommissioning impasse by insisting on prior decommissioning, saying that they were 'dishonouring this agreement; they are insulting its principles'.[49] He went to state that 'the two governments will have to initiate a review under the terms of this agreement ... that review is now the future of the political process'. This is precisely what the two governments did, and they invited George Mitchell to conduct the review.[50] Mallon's resignation was also intended to force the resignation of David Trimble, but despite initial expectations that he would be obliged to, Trimble did not resign, claiming that under the transition arrangements this was not required.[51]

Once again, uncertainty in the political process created a vacuum in which violence loomed as an ever-present threat. As if to confirm Unionist fears that decommissioning would never happen, three self-confessed members of the PIRA were arrested in Florida and accused of attempting to smuggle guns to Ireland. Then, in Gerry Adams' West Belfast constituency, an alleged informer, Charles Bennett, was found murdered near a local GAA club, and the finger of suspicion pointed to the PIRA. While not regarded by the governments as technical breaches of the ceasefire, these events suggested that achieving progress in the Mitchell review would not be easy.

POLICING COMMISSION PROGRESS

If progress in establishing the political institutions was faltering, the same was not the case with progress by the commission on policing headed by former NIO minister and until recently Governor of Hong Kong, Christopher Patten. Police reform was an issue on which the SDLP was determined to make a significant impact, and the party prepared a very detailed submission based on its recently approved conference paper.[52] When Patten's commission published its report in September 1999, the SDLP expressed general satisfaction with its recommendations.[53] The 175 recommendations included such long-standing party demands as a change of name to the Police Service of Northern Ireland (PSNI); the provision of a transition quota for Catholics to achieve a communally balanced service; the creation of a communally balanced policing board with overall responsibility for the service, along with the creation of local policing partnerships to strengthen relationships with local communities; an end to displaying the Union flag at stations on a daily basis; a strong oversight and complaints office in the form of a police ombudsman; enhanced cooperation and exchanges between the PSNI and the Garda Síochána; and the development of a human rights ethos to inform all aspects of policing. What was recommended amounted to a comprehensive overhaul of policing and the development of what would be effectively an entirely new service. According to Séamus Mallon, who had led the party's campaign for police reform

> The report, taken in totality, and implemented faithfully and speedily, contains the basis for the objectives of the Good Friday Agreement to be attained in terms of achieving a police service which can attract and sustain the whole community's support.[54]

While the uncertainties surrounding the agreement's implementation meant that it would be several years before all of the parties, especially Sinn Féin, would sign up to the new arrangements, preparations for implementing the Patten Report commenced almost immediately after its publication, and the new service replaced the RUC in November 2001. From then on, the police had the full support of the SDLP.

MITCHELL REVIEW

George Mitchell's review commenced in earnest in September 1999 and, while there was considerable scepticism about the possibility of success, Mitchell was determined to achieve a positive outcome. Given earlier efforts to break the impasse, the actual gap to be bridged was not huge. By now, Sinn Féin had publicly accepted that decommissioning had to happen, and that the obligation was not simply doing one's best to influence the PIRA that it should decommission.[55] As for Trimble, anxious as he was to secure devolution, he knew that the price was Sinn Féin's participation in the executive. He also knew that, however desirable, actual decommissioning would not coincide with the nomination of the executive. He accepted that some engagement by the PIRA with de Chastelain and his colleagues in the IICD would have to take place first, in order to make practical arrangements for decommissioning, but he did expect that decommissioning in some verifiable manner would commence soon thereafter. The issues were when and under what conditions would both processes start – the nomination of the executive and decommissioning. Trimble and Adams had talked about 'jumping together' when they had met in Washington in March, and the challenge to George Mitchell was to bring them to the 'jump-off' point together.

The focus of Mitchell's review was on closing the gap between the UUP and Sinn Féin. It was not a process to which the SDLP had much to contribute directly. The party had already made its offer in the form of Séamus Mallon's pledge, and it was almost unthinkable, having achieved the agreement and its endorsement, that a deal would not be completed. The party's role was essentially to encourage both the UUP and Sinn Féin to close the gap, and allow for the full implementation of the agreement. In the party's view, the greater onus lay with the provisional movement, which had to convince not just Unionists, but the whole community, that its 'war' was over, and that by decommissioning it was now fully committed to democracy. As Joe Hendron put it, the PIRA held the 'ace card',[56] and if they undertook to decommission in a credible and verifiable manner, the UUP could have no further excuses to delay the agreement's implementation.

SDLP UNCERTAINTIES

The party met for its annual conference amid much media speculation that it had peaked in popularity and was unlikely to withstand the growing challenge from Sinn Féin[57] Party spokespersons rejected this view, pointing to recent election results and their belief that the party would prove a very effective presence in the now eagerly anticipated power-sharing executive. Emphasizing the SDLP's anxiety to create a meaningful partnership government, Séamus Mallon appealed to Unionists to grasp the opportunity

> We know each other. Together we can deliver this. Together we can make it work. Together we can give the next generation, your children and mine, hope and real prospects. We belong together. We sink or swim together.[58]

It was a message that went to the core of the SDLP's approach. A practical example of that approach was presented to the conference in the policy document, *Innovation, investment and social justice: a framework of economic development.*[59] Included among the detailed proposals were: a lowering of corporation tax; enhanced training and research; extensive use of the new North-South Ministerial Council to increase trade and attract new investment; and the creation of synergies in the delivery of public services. Mindful of the party's social democratic roots, the document also stressed continued commitment to fairness and equity in the workplace, through enhanced fair employment mechanisms and the minimum wage. The party's anxiety to be in government, and to begin implementing its policies, was also reflected in John Hume's address, his first public appearance since again being hospitalized in August.[60] Hume expressed his hope that, in a new and more hopeful climate, 'the party will come into its own. When politics ceases to be about guns and bombs it can start to concern itself with health, education, employment and other issues which bear upon the welfare of the community'.[61] The first opportunities to do so were to present themselves within the following three weeks.

UUP JUMPS FIRST

As the Mitchell review moved towards a resolution, all eyes were on the UUP's response to the latest proposal that a representative from the PIRA be nominated to liaise with the IICD with a view to determining the practicalities of disarmament, with the understanding that actual decommissioning would soon follow. Trimble indicated that if the nomination was made, the UUP would allow the executive to be formed. It was a proposal for the two sides to 'jump together', and George Mitchell was now confident enough to conclude his review. Before formally doing so, he awaited a series of public statements from General de Chastelain, the political parties, the PIRA and the two governments, indicating a willingness to move along the lines he had recommended. When these statements were made as requested, Mitchell expressed himself satisfied that

> pro-agreement parties and the governments share the view that devolution should occur and the institutions should be established at the earliest possible date. It is also common ground that decommissioning should occur as quickly as possible and that the commission should play a central role in achieving this under the terms of the agreement.[62]

A few days later, the prime minister announced that the Northern Ireland Assembly would meet on 29 November to nominate executive ministers and that full powers would be devolved on 2 December.[63] Blair was careful to add that, in the event of a failure to decommission, or to fully operate all of the institutions, the governments would move to suspend all of the institutions. In the meantime, the 800-strong UUC met on 27 November to consider Trimble's proposal to allow the executive to be formed. The meeting was reminiscent of the one in January 1974, at which Faulkner lost the vote on the Sunningdale Agreement. The difference on this occasion was that the leader of the UUP obtained the endorsement he sought. A healthy majority, 480–349, supported Trimble and, at his press conference afterwards, he challenged Sinn Féin, saying 'We have done our bit. Mr Adams, it's over to you. We've jumped, you follow'.[64] The next two months were to show that the invitation to reciprocate would not be responded to as hoped.

SDLP TAKES OFFICE

With the final obstacles to devolution apparently overcome, the SDLP met to prepare for office and to consider how Séamus Mallon would be reinstated as deputy first minister. Mallon's position posed a procedural conundrum, given that he had been elected jointly with David Trimble, but Trimble had not resigned. Were he to do so now, and then stand jointly with Mallon for re-election, the divisions within unionism were such that a cross-community vote might not attain the prescribed threshold which required a majority from each of the assembly's two groups – Nationalists and Unionists.[65] In the event, the resolution to the 'Mallon' problem was something of a sleight of hand. When the assembly met on 29 November it agreed that it had not accepted his six-month old resignation. In other words, technically, the assembly stated that Mallon had not resigned and, then proceeded to vote, 71–28, to confirm him in the office of deputy first minister.[66]

There then followed the long-awaited nomination of executive ministers. John Hume named Mark Durkan as minister for finance and personnel, Seán Farren as minister for higher and further education, training and employment, and Bríd Rodgers as minister for agriculture and rural development. The team would later be completed when Denis Haughey was nominated as a junior minister in the office of the first and deputy first ministers. Formal devolution followed on 2 December and, along with their UUP, DUP and Sinn Féin colleagues, the SDLP ministers now began to address the 'bread and butter' issues they had so frequently wished they could address. On the same day, the PIRA announced that it had appointed a representative to meet with General de Chastelain and his colleagues, thus taking what appeared to be the first step towards meeting the decommissioning requirement.

The new executive was ushered into office, and the world applauded as Northern Ireland seemed to be entering a new era of peaceful self-government after thirty years of political instability and conflict (pl. 31). But, as so often in the past, that prospect would be severely challenged on several occasions, though in this instance, the framework put in place by the Good Friday Agreement would show itself to be more robust than its predecessors.

The executive was in office for only ten weeks when it and the other institutions established by the agreement suffered the first of four suspensions. The nomination of a PIRA representative to the IICD did not lead to any progress on actual decommissioning. In the words of John de Chastelain, the 'representative sat and took tea', but gave 'no information from the IRA as to when decommissioning will start'.[67] Peter Mandelson, who had replaced Mo Mowlam as secretary of state, then suspended the executive and restored direct rule. The executive was reinstated at the end of May 2000, after the PIRA agreed to open its arms dumps to inspection by two international figures, Cyril Ramaphosa from South Africa and Martti Ahtisaari from Finland. Trimble had accepted this as reassurance that the arms were out of use, a first move towards their total decommissioning, and agreed that the executive could be restored. However, keeping arms secure did not amount to decommissioning, and the PIRA's refusal to progress to complete disarmament remained a threat to the institutions. On two further occasions in 2001, the institutions were suspended, although on these occasions the suspensions were essentially technical and lasted only twenty-four hours, but each was caused when the UUP threatened to withdraw from the executive because of little or no progress on decommissioning. Finally, in October 2002, Secretary of State John Reid, who had replaced Mandelson, suspended the executive and assembly indefinitely when UUP ministers again threatened to resign because decommissioning was not being progressed. The institutions remained suspended until May 2007. Then, following the completion of PIRA decommissioning and Sinn Féin's eventual agreement to accept and support the new policing arrangements, full restoration was possible. On this occasion, however, the leading parties were not the

SDLP and the UUP. Since the 2003 assembly elections, these parties had been replaced by Sinn Féin and the DUP, a situation confirmed in 2007 elections.[68]

This reversal of fortune could not, however, take from the SDLP's contribution to politics over the preceding thirty years. The party's commitment to democratic nationalism was beyond question. It had stood resolutely against violence, particularly violence in pursuit of Irish unity, and had pioneered the way to a settlement eventually taken by unionism and militant nationalism. The template for the Good Friday Agreement owed much to SDLP's policies and to the party's determination to create a framework within which Ireland's two main political traditions, unionism and nationalism, could begin working together instead of working apart. Ireland's future, North and South, will be shaped by the manner in which the opportunities provided by that framework are exploited.

Epilogue

Reflecting on more than thirty years of violence and instability, it is difficult to understand how a society such as Northern Ireland's allowed itself to endure for so long the trauma that its people suffered, a trauma that affected not just those people, but society in Ireland as a whole, in Britain and beyond. The death-toll in that period, nearly 3,700, together with the toll of thousands more injured, of properties and businesses destroyed, have left a legacy of loss, pain and bitterness that may never be completely healed.

Most people in Northern Ireland were quite well educated, the majority claimed to profess religious beliefs whose moral and ethical codes shared very similar roots, and the majority did not condone the kind of violence witnessed over that period. Most people were not directly involved in any of the campaigns of violence, most condemned them and most supported political parties that did not have recourse to violence in order to promote their cause. Yet, when small unrepresentative groups decided to have recourse to violence, they seemed in some way to hold the rest of society to ransom. Their violence took a firm hold in some communities and was sustained despite strong evidence that the goals towards which it was directed were, from the outset, unattainable by violent means. Neither government policies nor aggressive security measures proved capable of suppressing that violence. Indeed, on many occasions, those policies and measures served only to exacerbate the situation.

The violence was contained and, ultimately, it was not allowed to triumph because of the resolute determination of men and women in political parties and in civic society who sustained democracy throughout those years. The men and women who served the SDLP over this period realized the utter futility of politically motivated violence and pledged themselves to a process of conflict-resolution based on respect for fundamental human and civil rights. As democratic Nationalists, they were determined to ensure that those Nationalists who espoused violence would not have their approval or support, and would not become their community's dominant political voice. Not only did they condemn the violence of the PIRA, of the INLA and of all their various offshoots, but they offered a positive alternative, a message of partnership, equality, respect and reconciliation directed at Unionists, together with practical policies for improving the social and economic lives of the whole of society.

The SDLP they joined was never a well-resourced party. There were few rewards, but the party's brand of social democratic nationalism has deep roots in constitutional nationalism and in the wider Irish labour movement. It was from those roots that the SDLP drew much of its strength and inspiration. Without a role in government throughout most of the period covered in this study, the SDLP was only able to use its political influence indirectly to effect changes in the social and economic spheres. Indirect as that influence was, it had significant effects on much of the human and civil rights legislation of those years and in promoting such economic investment as was possible, in equality legislation, and in the development of health, education and social services. Inevitably, most of the SDLP's focus was on creating the political and constitutional frameworks which would give peace and stability to the North. In this task, of course, the SDLP did not and could not work alone. To achieve these objectives, the party needed to establish links with Unionists who shared the same goals of peace and stability, and it needed to work with the Irish and British governments towards the same ends.

The party deeply regretted the collapse, after only five months in 1974, of the first product of such efforts, and regretted even more that twenty-five years passed before the Good Friday Agreement made possible the establishment of a second power-sharing executive, together with a North-South Ministerial Council. In the volatile and highly charged situations that paved the way towards Good Friday 1998, the SDLP's judgments, like those of other parties, may not always have been the most effective, or the most appropriate. However, the SDLP never wavered from its fundamental principles and is immensely proud of the leadership that it provided; a leadership that in all probability helped ensure that Northern Ireland did not experience the even greater trauma of a Balkan-type cataclysm.

After 2000, the implementation of the Good Friday Agreement did not prove any easier than it had been during its first year-and-a-half. The issue was the PIRA's continuing failure to decommission. But, eventually, the sword conceded to democracy's imperatives, and the organization that had been responsible for so much death and destruction over thirty years, complied with the agreement and disarmed.

Ironically, those years also witnessed a serious decline in support for the

SDLP, a decline that had many contributing factors. But the story of that decline must await another study. Those years also saw the departure from public life of two of the giants of Irish politics, John Hume and Séamus Mallon, together with several others who had served in the leadership of party from its early years – Bríd Rodgers, Denis Haughey and Seán Farren. Under the leadership first of Mark Durkan (2001–10) and now of Margaret Ritchie, the party faces a challenging future as it determines its contribution to the second decade of the twenty-first century and beyond. In meeting those challenges, the party has a record, as this study has attempted to show, that is, in many respects, unrivalled in its commitment to the deepest democratic values. It is a record that will inspire another generation of party activists.

Notes

CHAPTER 1

1. *Irish Times*, 1 Jan. 1970. The more important reforms included the civilianization of the Royal Ulster Constabulary (RUC), the replacement of the notorious police reserve known as the B-Specials by a locally recruited army unit, the Ulster Defence Regiment (UDR), the establishment of the Housing Executive to take public housing out of local control, and a commission to reform local government including the introduction of one person, one vote for local elections – all demands of the civil rights campaign.   **2.** The 'siege' occurred when police attempted to control crowds protesting at the annual Apprentice Boys' parade in the city. The crowds retreated into the Bogside area and conducted a two-day battle with the police, who were eventually replaced by British troops.   **3.** Eighteen people died through violence in 1969, and by the end of 1970 another twenty-eight had been killed.   **4.** Variously referred to as the Unionist Party, the Official Unionist Party and the Ulster Unionist Party (UUP), the preferred title in this study.   **5.** The CDU monitored civil rights abuses in Northern Ireland and was supported by over a hundred mainly Labour MPs and councillors.   **6.** Official Sinn Féin first adopted the title Republican Clubs, later Sinn Féin – the Workers Party and then the Workers Party; Provisional Sinn Féin was linked to the Provisional IRA and both were referred to collectively as the Provisionals/Provos or the 'provisional movement'.   **7.** Michael McKeown, *Greening of a Nationalist* (Dublin, 1986), p. 17.   **8.** Austin Currie, *All hell will break loose* (Dublin, 2002), pp 54–5.   **9.** The Lockwood Committee (1965) recommended Coleraine as the location, a choice that precipitated a large protest movement in Derry.   **10.** *Irish Times*, 19 May 1964.   **11.** The EEC became the EC (European Community), then the EU (European Union).   **12.** *Irish News*, 8 Feb. 1965.   **13.** Ibid.   **14.** John Hume, *Election manifesto* (1969). Copy in Linenhall Library, Belfast.   **15.** Ibid.   **16.** Ibid.   **17.** Ivan Cooper, interview, 2 July 2009.   **18.** *Irish Times*, 22 Jan. 1970.   **19.** NIHC, *Debates*, 30 June 1970.   **20.** Currie, *All hell will break loose*, pp 157–8.   **21.** *Irish Times*, 2 Mar. 1970.   **22.** The three-day curfew affected approximately fifty streets in the Lower Falls area of Belfast and was imposed by the British army to enable troops conduct house-to-house searches for weapons.   **23.** Interview with Austin Currie, 6 Dec. 2008.   **24.** Ibid.   **25.** *Irish Times*, 22 Aug. 1970.   **26.** Ibid. Stormont, in east Belfast, was the location of the Northern Ireland parliament and now of the Northern Ireland Assembly.   **27.** Ibid.   **28.** Garret FitzGerald (*Irish Times*, 27 Sept. 1997) claimed that both Fine Gael and Labour had endorsed the principle in 1969, but not formally. For Fianna Fáil, formal acceptance did not happen until the Good Friday Agreement, though in practice it had accepted the principle long before then.   **29.** *Irish News*, 22 Aug. 1970.   **30.** Ibid.   **31.** Ibid.   **32.** *Irish Times*, 3 Sept. 1970.   **33.** *Irish Times*, 30 Sept. 1970.   **34.** Ibid.   **35.** *Irish Times*, 23 Sept. 1970.   **36.** *Irish Press*, 1 Sept. 1970.   **37.** *Belfast Telegraph*, 27 Aug. 1970.   **38.** Among the early members of the office staff was Gerry Campbell (later Cosgrove), who went on to become general-secretary of the party and who, at the time of writing (2010), is still in post.   **39.** *Irish News*, 11 Sept. 1970.   **40.** Ibid.   **41.** Interview with Denis Haughey, 10 Dec. 2009.   **42.** *Irish News*, 15 Oct. 1970.   **43.** The council had a very short existence and never amounted to anything effective. SDLP relationships with Irish Labour developed through their common left-of-centre policies and through links with sister parties in Europe.   **44.** *Irish Times*, 24 Sept. 1970.   **45.** Thousands of Catholics fleeing disturbances went to the South to be accommodated in Irish army camps, hostels and in private homes.   **46.** Geoffrey Bing, *Irish Times*, 7 Jan. 1970.   **47.** *Review body on local government in Northern Ireland* (Macrory Report) (1970).   **48.** NIHC, *Debates*, 21 Jan. 1971.   **49.** NIHC, *Debates*, 5 Nov. 1970.   **50.** Protestant mobs burned down Catholic owned houses in Conway Street and Brookfield Street in Belfast, 14–16 Aug. 1969.   **51.** D/3072/7/3/1–3, PRONI.   **52.** *Irish News*, 26 Apr. 1971.   **53.** HC, *Debates*, 3 Feb. 1971.   **54.** *Irish Times*, 12 Feb. 1971.   **55.** *Irish Times*, 2 Mar. 1971.   **56.** *Irish Times*, 15 Mar. 1971.   **57.** NIHC, *Debates*, 23 Mar. 1971.   **58.** NIHC, *Debates*, 22 June 1971.   **59.** *Irish Times*, 2 Feb. 1971.   **60.** NIHC, *Debates*, 22 June 1971.   **61.** Ibid.   **62.** Ibid.   **63.** Ibid.   **64.** Ibid.   **65.** Ibid.   **66.** *Irish News*, 12 July 1971.   **67.** Chris Ryder, *Fighting Fitt* (Belfast, 2006), p. 178.   **68.** Paddy Devlin, *Straight left: an autobiography* (Belfast, 1993), p. 155.   **69.** *Irish Times*, 17 July 1971.   **70.**

Irish News, 6 Oct. 1971. **71.** Interview with Ivan Cooper, 2 July 2009. **72.** HC, *Debates*, 6 Aug. 1971.
73. During the IRA's 1956–62 campaign, internment was introduced both North and South. **74.** *Irish Times*, 12 Aug. 1971. **75.** There is no evidence that the consequences of calling a rent and rates strike were fully considered. Some SDLP leaders, notably Cooper, Hume, Denis Haughey and Hugh Logue, suggested that payments be lodged in a special fund in local credit unions, from which householders could draw to pay arrears whenever the strike would be called off. The extent to which this advice was heeded is difficult to determine. Interviews with Denis Haughey (17 June), Ivan Cooper (2 July) and Hugh Logue (31 Oct. 2009). **76.** Currie, *All hell will break loose*, p. 177. Following the *Hunt Report* (1969), Currie and Hume had called for support for the UDR when it was established as part of a reform programme for the RUC. **77.** *Irish Times*, 19 Aug. 1971. Soon afterwards, retrospective legislation hastily enacted at Westminster removed the impediment to the British army's powers of arrest. **78.** Currie, *All hell will break loose*, p. 179. **79.** *Irish News*, 1 Sept. 1971. **80.** Danny Kennelly and Eric Preston, *Belfast, August 1971: a case to be answered* (Belfast, 1971). **81.** *Irish Times*, 23 Aug. 1971. **82.** *Irish News*, 20 Aug. 1971.

CHAPTER 2
1. From 9 to 31 Aug., 35 people were killed by violence in Northern Ireland. **2.** The ill-treatment consisted of 'noise' disorientation while hooded, making detainees jump from helicopters hovering just above ground but under the impression that they were higher, standing for long hours etc. **3.** *Irish Times*, 1 Oct. 1971. **4.** *Irish Times*, 25 Oct. 1971. **5.** SDLP, *Agenda first annual conference* (1971). **6.** Ibid. **7.** *Irish News*, 25 Oct. 1971. **8.** Interview with Eddie McGrady, 14 Oct. 2009. **9.** *Irish News*, 27 Oct. 1971. **10.** Ibid.
11. 2002/19/394, NAI. **12.** D/3072/1/30/1, PRONI. **13.** Minutes of the Executive of the Assembly of the Northern Irish People, 10 Mar. 1972, D/3072/6/15/2, PRONI. **14.** The fourteenth victim died later from wounds inflicted. **15.** *Irish Times*, 24 Jan. 1972. **16.** *Irish Times*, 4 Jan. 1972. **17.** *Irish Times*, 26 Jan. 1972. **18.** *Irish Times*, 27 Jan. 1972. **19.** *Irish Times*, 28 Jan. 1972. **20.** *Irish Times*, 31 Jan. 1972. Although invited by NICRA to be among the speakers at the march, Hume did not participate. Ivan Cooper did and played a leading role in the march. **21.** HC, *Debates*, 2 Feb. 1972. **22.** *Irish Times*, 1 Feb. 1972. **23.** HC, *Debates*, 25 Nov. 1971. **24.** *Irish Times*, 6 Feb. 1972. **25.** D/3072/1/30/1, PRONI. **26.** D/3072/1/30/1, PRONI. **27.** Ibid. **28.** Speech to Bloomfield Association of Unionist Party, *Irish Times*, 11 Feb. 1972. **29.** *Irish Times*, 17 Feb. 1972. **30.** *News Letter*, 9 Feb. 1972. **31.** *Irish Times*, 6 Mar. 1972. **32.** *Irish News*, 27 Mar. 1972. **33.** Ibid. **34.** *Sunday Press*, 12 Mar. 1972. **35.** *Irish Times*, 1 Apr. 1972. **36.** *Irish Times*, 10 Apr. 1972. **37.** Lord Widgery, *Report of the Tribunal appointed to inquire into the events on Sunday 30 January 1972, which led to the losss of life in connection with the procession in Londonderry on that day* (London, 1972). **38.** *Irish News*, 19 Apr. 1972. **39.** Message to Whitelaw, 7 June 1972, Prem 15/1009, NAUK. **40.** *Irish Times*, 27 May 1972. **41.** Ibid. **42.** Ibid. **43.** Ibid. **44.** *Irish News*, 30 Apr. 1972. **45.** *Irish Times*, 3 June 1972. **46.** Note from British ambassador in Dublin, Sir John Peck, on SDLP request to the Secretary of State that he meet representatives of the Provisional IRA, FCO 87/74, NAUK. **47.** *Irish Times*, 15 June 1972. Instead of formal 'political status', Whitelaw granted 'special category' status, allowing internees to wear their own clothes, to receive extra visits and extra food parcels and to be housed in compounds. **48.** *Irish Times*, 24 July 1972. **49.** *Irish Times*, 27 July 1972. **50.** Ibid. **51.** *Irish Times*, 1 Aug. 1972. **52.** Ibid. **53.** Ibid. **54.** *Irish Times*, 2 Aug. 1972. **55.** Ibid. **56.** D/30721/30/1, PRONI. **57.** Note of meeting between the SDLP and Heath, 12 Sept. 1972, FCO 87/80, NAUK. **58.** *Irish Times*, 13 Sept. 1972. **59.** *Irish Times*, 11 Aug. 1972. **60.** SDLP, *Towards a new Ireland* (1972), p. 2. **61.** Ibid. **62.** The origin of these proposals within the party can be found in two documents, one authored by Ben Caraher, the other by Ivan Cooper, SDLP files 3072/1/30/6, PRONI. Devlin mentions that two outsiders, Paddy Lane, a Belfast surgeon, and Desmond Fennell, political commentator from the South, had advised the party on the condominium concept, Devlin, *Straight left*, p. 185. **63.** Currie, *All hell will break loose*, p. 228. **64.** Note by British ambassador in Dublin on conversation with Garret FitzGerald about SDLP, 5 Feb. 1973, FCO 33/1080, NAUK. **65.** Note on meeting between Frank Steele of the NIO and John Hume, 4 Oct. 1972, FCO 87/83, NAUK. **66.** *Irish Times*, 22 Sept. 1972. **67.** *Irish Times*, 6 Oct. 1972. **68.** Ibid. **69.** An edited transcript of the debate appeared in *This Week*, 16 Nov. 1972. Copy in Linenhall Library. **70.** The commission chaired by Lord Diplock recommended the establishment of so called non-jury Diplock courts. **71.** The Darlington conference was attended by the UUP, the APNI and the NILP.

CHAPTER 3
1. *The future of Northern Ireland* (Belfast, 1972). **2.** Ibid., para. 79. **3.** Ibid., paras 76–8. **4.** Ibid., para. 74. **5.** Ibid., para. 41. **6.** Following the 1968–9 disturbances, a reform programme had been introduced implementing recommendations from the Hunt Inquiry. **7.** Report of meeting between the Taoiseach and

the British prime minister, 6 Sept. 1971, department of external affairs, 2003/17/30, NAI. **8.** *Irish Times*, 1 Nov. 1972. **9.** Ibid. **10.** HC, *Debates*, 13 Nov. 1972. **11.** *Irish Times*, 8 Nov. 1972. **12.** *Irish Times*, 4 Nov. 1972. **13.** See notes from ambassador Donal O'Sullivan, 2007/110/13, NAI. **14.** *Irish Times*, 25 Nov. 1972. **15.** Ibid. **16.** SDLP, *Agenda second annual conference* (1972). **17.** *Irish Independent*, 24 Oct. 1972. **18.** *Irish Times*, 25 Nov. 1972. **19.** *Irish News*, 7 Dec. 1972. **20.** *Irish Times*, 14 Dec. 1972. **21.** *Irish Times*, 25 Jan. 1973. **22.** *Irish Times*, 2 Feb. 1973. **23.** 591,820 voted for the Union 6,463 voted for unity with the Republic. **24.** *Irish Times*, 14 Feb. 1973. **25.** *Irish News* and *News Letter*, 6 Mar. 1973. **26.** Ibid. **27.** *Northern Ireland constitutional proposals* (Belfast, 1973), section 3. **28.** SDLP, *Northern Ireland constitutional proposals: a critique by the Social Democratic and Labour Party*, 22 Mar. 1973. **29.** *Irish News*, 7 June 1973. **30.** *Irish News*, 7 May 1973. **31.** *Irish News*, 11 May 1973. **32.** SDLP, *New North: new Ireland* (1973). **33.** Ibid. **34.** Ibid. **35.** *Irish Times*, 11 June 1973. **36.** *Irish Times*, 18 June 1973. **37.** D/3072/3/1/39, PRONI. **38.** *Financial Times*, 24 Sept. 1973. **39.** The dossier was presented to William Van Straubenzee, minister of state at the NIO, on 24 Oct. 1973. *Irish Times*, 25 Oct. 1973. **40.** Minutes of the SDLP assembly party, 6 July; cited in Bew and Patterson, *The British state and the Ulster crisis* (London, 1985), p. 72, fn. 81. **41.** Minutes of meeting between Taoiseach, cabinet ministers and SDLP delegation, 2004/21/670, NAI. **42.** *Irish Times*, 13 July 1973. **43.** *Irish Times*, 15 Sept. 1973. **44.** 2003/13/18, NAI. **45.** 2007/58/24, NAI. **46.** According to Seán Donlon of the department of foreign affairs, the Irish government envisaged three strands in police control, the first of which would be the Council of Ireland through a police authority; meeting with NIO, 20 Nov. 1973, CJ 4/488, NAUK. **47.** 2003/13/1, NAI. **48.** *Irish Times*, 27 Sept. 1973. **49.** Note on opening session of the talks, 5 Oct., CJ 4/330, NAUK. **50.** The SDLP negotiators led by Fitt were Ivan Cooper, Austin Currie, Paddy Devlin, John Hume and Eddie McGrady. **51.** Agreement was reached within the sub-committee addressing the issues on 19 Oct. 1973, CJ 4/332, NAUK. **52.** A leading Faulkner supporter, Peter McLachlan, commented to NIO officials that 'the Unionists felt little hope about the forthcoming talks … the constituency parties were recoiling from power-sharing with people whom they regarded as republicans (i.e. SDLP)', CJ 4/330, NAUK. **53.** John Hume quoted in note on inter-party talks, 30 Oct. 1973, CJ 4/332, NAUK. **54.** Note of meeting of inter-party talks 21 Nov. 1973, CJ 4/332, NAUK. **55.** CJ4/488, NAUK. **56.** *Irish Times*, 24 Oct. 1973. **57.** *Irish Times*, 22 Nov. 1973. **58.** HC, *Debates*, 22 Nov. 1973. **59.** *Irish Times*, 12 Nov. 1973. **60.** *Irish Times*, 3 Dec. 1973. **61.** Ibid. **62.** Ibid. **63.** Ibid. **64.** Kadar Asmal was prominent in the Irish Anti-Apartheid movement, later elected to the first post-apartheid parliament in South Africa in which he became a minister. **65.** *Irish Times*, 7 Dec. 1973. **66.** Ibid. **67.** Garret FitzGerald, *All in a life* (Dublin, 1991), pp 214–16. **68.** *Irish Times*, 11 Dec. 1973. **69.** Ibid. **70.** Ibid. **71.** Ibid. **72.** Ibid. **73.** *Irish Times*, 10 Dec. 1973. **74.** *Irish Times*, 11 Dec. 1973. **75.** Ibid. **76.** *Irish News*, 29 Dec. 1973. **77.** Brian Faulkner, *Memoirs of a statesman* (London, 1978), pp 236–7. **78.** *News Letter*, 11 Dec. 1973. **79.** *Irish Times*, 11 Dec. 1973. **80.** Report of speech delivered at Portrush, *Irish Times*, 11 Dec. 1973. **81.** *News Letter*, 13 Dec. 1973.

CHAPTER 4

1. *Irish News*, 3 Jan. 1973. **2.** NIA, *Debates*, 24 Jan. 1974. **3.** *Irish News*, 31 Dec. 1973. **4.** Several members of the party's executive, among them Seán Hollywood, Gemma Loughran, Des O'Donnell and Eamon Scally, were involved (*Irish News*, 19 Jan. 1973). Motion Number 1 referred to the anti-internment motion passed at the party's 1973 conference. **5.** The Northern Ireland Executive, Statement of Economic and Social Aims, in *Steps to a better tomorrow* (Belfast, Jan. 1974). **6.** Ryder, *Fighting Fitt*, p. 264. **7.** 'Hume means business in US', *Guardian*, 26 Apr. 1974. **8.** Hans Niedermayer was abducted in Dec. 1973 and murdered some time later. His remains were not found until Mar. 1976. **9.** Merlyn Rees, *Northern Ireland: a personal perspective* (London, 1985), p. 57. **10.** Currie, *All hell will break loose*, pp 246–7. **11.** *Irish News*, 15 Jan. 1974. **12.** Currie, *All hell will break loose*, pp 246–7. **13.** *Belfast Telegraph*, 6 May 1974. **14.** Devlin, *Straight left*, pp 247–50. **15.** Note on inter-party talks, 8 Oct. 1973, CJ 4/330, NAUK. **16.** NIA, *Debates*, 3 Apr. 1974, col. 95. **17.** Maurice Hayes, *Minority verdict* (Belfast, 1995), pp 180–1. **18.** Interview with Ivan Cooper, 2 July 2009. **19.** NIA, *Debates*, 8 May 1974. **20.** NIA, *Debates*, 5 Feb. 1974, col. 502. **21.** Hayes, *Minority verdict*, p. 173. **22.** SDLP, *Another step forward with SDLP* (1974), p. 1. **23.** Ibid., p. 2. **24.** Ibid., p. 3. **25.** Brian Faulkner advised Unionists to abstain in constituencies where there was no pro-agreement Unionist candidate, advice that signalled a lack of unity within the executive. **26.** Dolours and Marian Price had been jailed for their part in planting bombs in London in Mar. 1973. **27.** *Belfast Telegraph*, 23 Jan. 1974. **28.** *Sunday News*, 20 Jan. 1974. **29.** HC, *Debates*, 1 Apr. 1974. **30.** *Irish Times*, 18 Jan. 1974. **31.** Note on meeting between Secretary of State and the Northern Ireland Executive, 25 Mar. 1974, CJ 4/512, NAUK. **32.** Faulkner, *Memoirs of a statesman*, p. 253. **33.** The commission recommended, as a way of circumventing the problem of trying to have fugitives extradited, that both jurisdictions become a common law enforcement area, so that fugitives could be tried wherever apprehended on the island. Such a law was eventually introduced, and would be used successfully in the South.   **34.** *Irish News,* 19 Mar. 1974. **35.** Interview with Eddie McGrady, 27 Nov. 2009.   **36.** The working group was appointed at the executive meeting on 7 May 1974, EO/2/19, PRONI.   **37.** The working group's ideas were discussed at the executive meeting on 13 May 1974, EO/2/21, PRONI.   **38.** *Irish Times,* 25 May 1973.   **39.** Ian McAllister, *The Northern Ireland Social Democratic and Labour Party* (London, 1977), p. 144.   **40.** *Irish Times,* 23 May 1974. **41.** CJ 4/512, NAUK.   **42.** The original motion was moved in the assembly on 19 Mar. and the debate ended on 14 May.   **43.** The UWC consisted of, at first, a co-ordinating committee led by assembly member Glen Barr along with leading figures from loyalist paramilitary organizations like Andy Tyrie (UDA) and Ken Gibson (UVF). When the strike spread, anti-agreement politicians like Craig, Paisley and West became openly associated with it.   **44.** *Belfast Telegraph,* 10 May 1974.   **45.** No one was ever brought to trial for these atrocities. A telephone call to the press claimed responsibility on behalf of a hitherto unknown organization, the 'Red Hand Brigade' and threatened more bombings until 'something was done about the Sunningdale Agreement' (*Irish Times,* 18 May 1974).   **46.** Report of meeting between the prime minister, secretary of state for Northern Ireland, secretary of state for defence, the attorney-general, Brian Faulkner, Gerry Fitt and Oliver Napier at Chequers. CAB129/177, NAUK.   **47.** Ibid.   **48.** At a meeting of executive ministers and leaders of both sides of industry, 23 May 1974, Faulkner opposed such talks, saying that 'talking with the perpetrators would only give them recognition', Cent/1/3/38, PRONI.

CHAPTER 5

1. *The Northern Ireland Constitution* (Belfast, 1974).   **2.** *Irish Times,* 1 June 1974.   **3.** *Irish Times,* 20 June 1974.   **4.** *News Letter,* 20 June 1974.   **5.** *Guardian,* 2 Aug. 1974.   **6.** Ironically, in view of the party's unsuccessful demand during the power-sharing executive that internment be ended, Rees announced in July that it would be gradually phased out.   **7.** Fitt, in particular, was strongly in favour of the RUC, though he did not publicly say so at this time. He was also of the view that the council of Ireland was of less significance than others in the leadership thought. See Ryder, *Fitting Fitt,* passim.   **8.** *Irish Times,* 26 June 1974, reported a meeting between Craig, Paisley and West with Merlyn Rees at which the Unionist leaders had spoken of a third force being established and at the 12 July celebrations, John Taylor told the Belfast demonstration that an 'Ulster Home Guard' would have to be formed.   **9.** Notes on meeting with an SDLP delegation, 20 Aug. 1974, 2008/74/3161, NAI.   **10.** Notes on briefing at SDLP meeting, Bunbeg, Co. Donegal, 2008/79/3161, NAI.   **11.** *Joint executive and assembly party statement,* 3 Sept. 1974, D3072/2/14/5, PRONI.   **12.** Ibid.   **13.** Ibid.   **14.** The talks took place in Dec. at Feakle, Co. Clare, and involved PIRA leaders and a group of Protestant clergy that included Bishop Arthur Butler, Revd Jack Weir, Revd Eric Gallagher and Revd William Arlow. Once again the PIRA's position was that a British declaration to withdraw from Northern Ireland would be required as the condition for a ceasefire.   **15.** SDLP, *One strong voice* (1974), para. 2.3.   **16.** Ibid., paras 3.2–3.5.   **17.** Ibid., para. 1.2.   **18.** Internal SDLP review on strategy for convention election, D3072/1B/63, PRONI.   **19.** UUP, *Manifesto for the convention* (1974). Copy in 2006/131/1432, NAI.   **20.** 2005/7/617, meeting with SDLP delegation, 22 Nov. 1974, NAI.   **21.** *Irish Times,* 14 June 1974.   **22.** Irish government meeting with SDLP, 2008/79/316, NAI.   **23.** 2005/7/617, report of meeting with SDLP delegation, 22 Nov. 1974, NAI.   **24.** The truce led to the establishment of 'incident centres' where PIRA members could liaise with British army officers ostensibly to prevent situations becoming inflamed and for a while gave credence to the possibility that the British would negotiate withdrawal with the PIRA.   **25.** Statement by Merlyn Rees to House of Commons, 11 Feb. 1975.   **26.** HC, *Debates,* 15 Feb. 1975, *Belfast Telegraph,* 14 Feb. 1975.   **27.** Between Aug. 1971 and Dec. 1975 when internment without trial ended, 1,981 people were interned.   **28.** *Irish Times,* 18 Jan. 1975.   **29.** Ibid.   **30.** SDLP, *Agenda fourth annual conference* (1975).   **31.** *News Letter,* 17 Jan. 1975.   **32.** *Irish News,* Jan. 1975.   **33.** *Irish Times,* 13 Jan. 1975.   **34.** SDLP, *Education: the need for reform* (1975).   **35.** Ibid.   **36.** *Education Times,* 23 Jan. 1975, p. 3.   **37.** Former assembly member, Paddy Duffy (Mid-Ulster), proposed that the party seek a pre-election agreement with Faulkner's UPNI and the APNI, that they would form an executive provided there would be, among other commitments, a meaningful Irish dimension, an end to internment, and policing reform. There is no evidence that any attempt to reach such an agreement was made. D3072/2/14/5, PRONI.   **38.** *The government of Northern Ireland: a society divided* (1975).   **39.** SDLP, *Speak with strength* (1975).   **40.** *The Social Democrat,* an election newspaper published by the SDLP in Derry, 1976.   **41.** *Irish Times,* 3 May 1975.   **42.** Interview with Conor Cruise O'Brien, RTÉ, 4 May 1975.   **43.** *Irish News,* 5 May 1975.   **44.** An SDLP delegation met with Foreign Affairs Minister Garret FitzGerald and colleagues on 2 Aug., after which John Hume expressed satisfaction with the Dublin government's approach. See FitzGerald, *All in a life,* pp 248–9. **45.** *The Northern Ireland Constitution* (London, 1974).   **46.** *Northern Ireland Convention Report,* July 1975.

47. Ibid.   **48.** Ibid.   **49.** 'Outline SDLP Proposals', reproduced in *Northern Ireland Constitutional Convention, report to Parliament*, London, HMSOO, 1975, p. 57.   **50.** 'UUUC Policy Document', reproduced in *Northern Ireland Constitutional Convention, report*, London, HMSOO, 1975, pp 56–7.   **51.** 'Comments of the SDLP on the UUUC Policy Document', *Northern Ireland Constitutional Convention, report*, London, HMSOO, 1975, pp 67–8.   **52.** *Belfast Telegraph*, 9 Sept. 1975.   **53.** The idea of a voluntary coalition is said to have been first suggested to Craig by Lord Chief Justice Robert Lowry, and initially had the support of Austin Ardill and William Beattie, his UUUC co-negotiators. See article by Conor O'Clery, *Irish Times*, 11 Sept. 1975.   **54.** SDLP, '*Proposals for government in Northern Ireland: report to parliament*', Nov. 1975.   **55.** Ibid.   **56.** *Northern Ireland Constitutional Convention, report to parliament* (1975).   **57.** Statement issued by Councillor Tom Donnelly, 22 Oct. 1975, copy in CJ4/1749, NAUK.   **58.** *Irish Times*, 1 Dec. 1975.   **59.** Ryder, *Fighting Fitt*, p. 320.   **60.** *News Letter*, 4 Feb. 1976.   **61.** Speech by Michael Kennedy TD, 13 Oct. 1975.   **62.** *Irish Times*, 2 Nov. 1975.   **63.** Ibid.   **64.** *Social Democrat*, Jan. 1976.   **65.** *Political outlook in Northern Ireland*, note by NIO official, 1 May 1976, CJ4/1389, NAUK.   **66.** *Irish Times*, 5 June 1976.   **67.** *Irish Times*, 24 July 1976.   **68.** Copy of statement in D/3072/ID/3, PRONI; *Irish Times*, 9 Sept. 1976.   **69.** Using a cover name, Republican Action Force, the PIRA claimed the killings were in retaliation for the murder of Catholics in Armagh and East Tyrone.

CHAPTER 6

1. Some went back to their former employment as teachers, lawyers and doctors, others found new employment – Paddy Devlin became a trade union official, John Hume became an adviser to Irish European Commissioner Dick Burke, and Hugh Logue joined the South's Combat Poverty agency – but others, like Austin Currie, Frank Feely and Séamus Mallon, did not find it easy to obtain full-time employment. A few gradually drifted away from active politics.   **2.** Interview with Austin Currie, 6 Dec. 2008.   **3.** *Irish Times*, 31 May 1976. See also Paddy Devlin, 'Why I'd back independence', *Sunday News*, 6 June 1976.   **4.** *Hibernia*, 4 June 1976.   **5.** *Irish Independent*, 11 June 1976.   **6.** Ibid.   **7.** *Irish Times*, 14 June 1976.   **8.** *Irish News*, 16 Sept. 1976.   **9.** Ibid.   **10.** Ibid.   **11.** Ibid.   **12.** *Irish News*, 9 Aug. 1976.   **13.** The Peace People movement was formed in Aug. 1976 when, after a PIRA gunman's getaway car killed two children, their aunt, Mairéad Corrigan, led a protest in West Belfast demanding peace. Initially the movement evoked a huge response across both communities for its demand that violence cease but, apart from a number of large peace demonstrations, the movement achieved little.   **14.** Mason's predecessor, Merlyn Rees, had taken significant steps towards a policy of police primacy in the campaign against terrorism. RUC numbers were increased and the RUC Reserve given responsibility for anti-terrorist measures; 'special category' status was withdrawn for prisoners convicted of terrorist incidents committed after internment without trial ended in Dec. 1975.   **15.** The 1975 annual conference had passed a motion prohibiting memberships of local security and police liaison committees. In Newry and Mourne, and Craigavon, a number of councillors remained members of the local security committee.   **16.** CJ4/1766, NAUK, contains reports of such meetings together with memoranda discussing how the SDLP might be encouraged to participate in local security committees.   **17.** Under the umbrella of the United Unionist Action Council, Paisley and colleague Ernest Baird unsuccessfully attempted to organize a general strike in May.   **18.** Note on meeting with Seán Donlon, DFA, 9 June 1977, CJ4/1869, NAUK.   **19.** *Irish News*, 16 May 1977.   **20.** See note on conversation between Paddy Devlin and NIO official J.N. Allen, 13 Aug. 1974, FCO 87/347, NAUK.   **21.** *Irish Times*, 14 June 1977.   **22.** US sports car manufacturer John De Lorean built a plant in 1978 at Dunmurry outside Belfast; it collapsed in a welter of suspicions about fraud and at great cost to the taxpayer.   **23.** Letter to Gerry Fit, 22 Nov. 1977, D/3072/1/24/1, PRONI. The SDLP rejected the invitation to talks on the grounds that there was no likelihood of success; see statement by constituency representatives, 17 Dec. 1977.   **24.** CJ 4/1927, NAUK.   **25.** HC, 13 Dec. 1976.   **26.** SDLP submission to the Standing Advisory Commission on Human Rights, *Irish News*, 14 May 1976. The Commission's report recommended that no action be taken to devise a separate Bill of Rights for Northern Ireland.   **27.** *Fair Employment (Northern Ireland) Bill*, 1976 proposed the establishment of the Fair Employment Agency to investigate complaints and to monitor employment practices.   **28.** Tip O'Neill was a congressman and Speaker of the House, Ted Kennedy and Patrick Moynihan were senators and Hugh Carey was Governor of New York.   **29.** *Irish Times*, 17 Mar. 1977. Several other leading Irish-American politicians joined the group in making the statement.   **30.** O'Neill's influence was particularly instrumental in President Carter making his first statement on Northern Ireland, 30 Aug. 1977, pledging support for power-sharing, and promising US investment.   **31.** A House of Commons select committee recommended three seats, but Unionists opposed the use of any electoral system in Northern Ireland different to that in the rest of the UK. Eventually, the government decided that PR would be used and that Northern Ireland would be a single constituency. See note in CJ4/1428, NAUK.   **32.** SDLP, *Agenda sixth annual* *conference* (1976), p. 24. **33.** See report by DFA official Seán Donlon, 2008/79/3069, NAI. **34.** Séamus Mallon, *Future strategy – a personal view*, a paper for internal SDLP discussion, 12 Sept. 1976. **35.** One of many loyalist paramilitary groups involved in sectarian killings. McKeague was said to have been among its founders. **36.** *Irish News*, 24 Nov. 1976. **37.** *Irish News*, 6 Dec. 1976 (copy in authors possession). **38.** Mallon, *Future strategy*. **39.** SDLP, *Partnership in Ireland*, policy document adopted by the sixth annual conference, Nov. 1976. **40.** Ibid. **41.** Note on SDLP conference in FCO 87/553, NAUK. **42.** Note in CJ4/1427, Sept. 1976, NAUK. **43.** NIO report on SDLP conference, 17 Dec. 1976, FCO 87/353, NAUK. **44.** Note on conversation with Garret FitzGerald, CJ 4/1907, NAUK. **45.** Discussion paper prepared by John Hume for constituency representatives, 5 Mar. 1977, D/3972/1/2/24/2, PRONI. **46.** *Irish News*, 9 Mar. 1977. **47.** HC, *Debates*, 30 June 1977. **48.** *Social Democrat*, Nov. 1977. **49.** *Irish Times*, 7 Nov. 1977. **50.** Amnesty International (1978), claimed that people held at Castlereagh detention centre had been ill-treated. **51.** Judge H. G. Bennett, *Report of the committee of inquiry into police interrogation procedures in Northern Ireland* (1979). The committee found that several suspects had sustained injuries in police custody which were not self-inflicted. The committee recommended that close circuit television be installed in police interview rooms and that suspects have access to a solicitor after forty-eight hours. **52.** Dan McAreavy had joined the SDLP's staff in 1973 as party organizer and when John Duffy resigned in Feb. 1975 succeeded him as Secretary General, a post he occupied until his death in 1981. The party established an annual award, the Dan McAreavy Trophy, in his honour to be granted for outstanding service to an individual, branch or other organ of the party. **53.** SDLP, *Know where you stand* (1977). **54.** Republican Clubs and other Nationalists won twelve seats. **55.** In a statement to the House of Commons, 24 Nov. 1977, Mason invited parties to talks on an interim form of devolution in which committees of an assembly might have a consultative role on such functions as planning, housing, health and education. Inter-party talks never took place. **56.** Proposals outlined to the SDLP at a meeting on 21 Nov. 1977, FCO 87/651, NAUK. **57.** SDLP executive paper, 11 June 1977, by Paddy Devlin and Denis Haughey. CJ4/1869, NAUK. **58.** In a speech to the executive committee of the UUC in early Sept., Party leader Harry West made it clear that power-sharing with the SDLP was still unacceptable. Copy in CJ4/1869, NAUK. **59.** Notes from the British embassy in Dublin, FCO 87/651, NAUK. **60.** The SDLP did benefit: John Hume, Séamus Mallon, Eddie McGrady and Joe Hendron would all become MPs as a result of the extra seats. **61.** SDLP, *Facing reality* (1977). **62.** *Irish News*, 26 Aug. 1977. **63.** *Irish Times*, 9 Aug. 1977. **64.** Social Democrat, Sept. 1977. **65.** Ibid. **66.** Devlin's expulsion took place at the Sept. meeting of the party's executive. **67.** Following the convention elections Devlin had lost his previous position as chief whip to Austin Currie and although then elected chair of the constituency representatives group, it was clear that his standing within the group was not as high as previously. Currie, *All hell will break loose*, p. 302. **68.** Devlin, *Straight left*, p. 283. **69.** Record of meeting with SDLP on 22 Sept. 1977, 2007/116/754, NAI. **70.** Record of meeting with SDLP, Nov. 1977, 2007/116/754, NAI. **71.** *Irish Times*, 7 Nov. 1977. **72.** Opening address to the SDLP's annual conference, *Irish News*, 5 Nov. 1977. **73.** *Irish Times*, 23 Nov. 1977. **74.** *Irish Times*, 30 Dec. 1977.

CHAPTER 7

1. *Irish Times*, 1 Feb. 1978. **2.** *Irish Times*, 9 Jan. 1978. **3.** *Irish Times*, 17 Jan. 1978. **4.** Referring to these statements, Séamus Mallon claimed that the SDLP was becoming 'peripheral', constituency representatives group, 17 Jan. 1978, D/3072/1/24/1, PRONI. **5.** The ECHR report was issued on 18 Jan. 1978. **6.** *Irish Times*, 7 Jan. 1978. **7.** *Irish Times*, 9 June 1978. **8.** *Irish Times*, 28 June 1978. **9.** *Daily Mirror*, 14 Aug. 1978. **10.** SDLP, *Agenda eighth annual conference* (1978). **11.** British officials' reports on the conference underlined the use of 'disengagement' saying it was deliberately chosen to suggest a long-term rather than an immediate process, FCO 87/770, NAUK. **12.** *Irish Times*, 8 Nov. 1978. **13.** Alan Huckle, *Report on the SDLP conference*, 7 Nov. 1978, Cent/1/7/20, PRONI. **14.** SDLP, *Report of sub-committee on conference motions 70 & 89*, Jan. 1979; D/3072/1/24/4, PRONI. **15.** The New Ireland Forum would be established to achieve a consensus approach to Northern Ireland among the main constitutional Nationalist parties, North and South. See ch. 10. **16.** *Irish News*, 11 Sept. 1978. **17.** Statement issued by the SDLP, 22 Sept. 1978. **18.** Paper by Denis Haughey and Seán Farren, *For and against emergency status*, 5 Dec. 1978, D/3072/1/24/4. **19** HC, *Debates*, 28 Mar. 1978. **20** *Report of the Committee of Inquiry into police interrogation techniques in Northern Ireland*, chairman Judge HC Bennett (1979). **21** Minutes of a special executive meeting, 21 Apr. 1979, D/3072/1/24/4, PRONI. **22** Ernest Baird of the United Ulster Unionist Party and Richard Ferguson of the UUP. **23** D3072/1/24/4, PRONI. party and Richard Ferguson of the UUP. **24** Currie, *All hell will break loose*, p. 312. **25** The Irish Independence Party (IIP) had been founded in Oct. 1977 by several former members of the Nationalist Party. A leading member was former SDLP North Antrim convention member, John Turnley, who was subsequently murdered by loyalists in June 1980. The anticipated threat to the SDLP never materialized and the party had a short-lived existence. **26** SDLP, *Strengthen your voice*, 1979. **27** Ibid. **28** The SDLP recorded 18% of the overall vote against 22% in Oct. 1974. **29** John Hume's election leaflet for the European parliamentary election, June 1979, copy in Linenhall Library, Belfast. **30** McAliskey was supported by the IIP and received almost 34,000 first preferences. The PIRA urged a boycott. **31** Simone Martin, *Report on Northern Ireland to the European Parliament* (Brussels, 1981). **32** Airey Neave was assassinated by an INLA (Irish National Liberation Army) car-bomb at the House of Commons on 30 Mar. 1979. The INLA was a splinter PIRA group infamous for the brutality of its killings. **33** *Irish Times*, 29 June 1979. **34** Policy review paper prepared by Paddy Duffy, Seán Farren and Séamus Mallon, D/3072/1/24/4, PRONI. **35** Ibid. **36** Ibid. **37** *Irish Times*, 17 Sept. 1979. **38** *Irish News*, 3 Oct. 1979. **39** *Irish Times*, 3 Oct. 1979. **40** *Irish Times*, 4 Oct. 1979. **41** Ibid. **42** *Irish News*, 26 Oct. 1979. **43** SDLP, *Towards a new Ireland: a policy review*, policy document adopted at the ninth annual conference, SDLP, 1979. **44** *Irish News*, 5 Nov. 1979. **45** *Irish News*, 21 Nov. 1979. **46** Minutes of a joint meeting of the party's executive and constituency representatives, D/3072/1/24/6, PRONI. **47** Note in Prem 19/83, NAUK, Nov. 1979. **48** *Irish Times*, 22 Nov. 1979. **49** *Irish News*, 20 Nov. 1978. **50** Currie, *All hell will break loose*, pp 315–6. **51** SDLP, *Agenda ninth annual conference* (1979). **52** Press statement from the SDLP, 15 Dec. 1979; *Irish Times*, 17 Dec. 1979. **53** *Irish Times*, 17 Dec. 1979.

CHAPTER 8

1. SDLP submission to the secretary of state's conference, Jan. 1979. D/3072/1/24/5, PRONI. **2.** *Irish Times*, 29 Feb. 1980. **3.** Ibid. **4.** Haughey succeeded Jack Lynch, who resigned on 5 Dec. 1979. His leadership marked a renewal of tensions within Fianna Fáil, particularly over how Haughey would deal with Northern Ireland issues. **5.** Haughey was arrested and tried but acquitted of involvement in the attempt to smuggle arms for use in the North. **6.** One difficulty was his attempt to remove the Irish ambassador to the US, Seán Donlon, who had been supportive of Hume's efforts to cultivate Irish-American politicians. Haughey's move against Donlon provoked the anger of those politicians, as well as John Hume, all of whom lobbied successfully to have Donlon retained at Washington. **7.** Report to meeting of constituency representatives, 14 May 1980, D/3072/1/24/6, PRONI. **8.** Paul Bew and Gordon Gillespie, *Northern Ireland: a chronology of the Troubles* (Dublin, 1999), p. 141. **9.** Statement issued by Taoiseach Haughey and Prime Minister Thatcher, 21 May 1980 (*Irish Times*, 22 May 1980). **10.** *The Government of Northern Ireland: proposals for further discussion* (1980). **11.** SDLP, *Poverty in an age of affluence and other papers*, proceedings of a conference (1980). **12.** Higher Education Review Group, *Report on the future of teacher education in Northern Ireland* (1980). **13.** SDLP, *Response to the Higher Education Review Group's recommendations for the future of teacher education in Northern Ireland* (1980) (copy in author's possession). **14.** *Irish Times*, 8 Mar. 1980. **15.** Special category had been retained for those convicted of terrorist offences committed before 1976. The new decision meant that persons convicted of crimes before that date would be treated the same as every other person jailed for a terrorist offence. **16.** D/3072/1/24/5, PRONI. **17.** A case against the British government alleging inhuman and degrading treatment had been taken to the Commission by four prisoners who had engaged in the 'dirty' protest. **18.** HC, *Debates*, 15 Dec. 1980. **19.** By then, the original seven strikers had been joined by many others and although *they* ended their strike, many of those on the dirty protest did not (*Irish Times*, 29 Dec. 1980). **20.** Among other concessions, the agreement allowed the prisoners to wear civilian clothes, to have greater freedom of association and to receive more frequent visits. But when the concessions were judged to be less than expected, a second round of hunger strikes commenced in Mar. 1981. **21.** SDLP, *Strategy for peace* (1980). Copy in the Linenhall Library, Belfast. **22.** SDLP, *Anglo-Irish relations: a discussion paper*, SDLP (1980) (copy in author's possession). **23.** *Irish Times*, 10 Nov. 1980. **24.** John Hume, 'Irish question, a British problem', *Sunday Times*, 12 Dec. 1980. **25.** Thatcher was accompanied by Foreign Secretary Geoffrey Howe and Northern Ireland Secretary Humphrey Atkins, while Haughey was accompanied by the ministers for foreign affairs and for justice. **26.** Communiqué issued following the meeting between the Taoiseach, the British Prime Minister and other Irish and British ministers, *Irish Times*, 9 Dec. 1980. **27.** *Irish Times*, 9 Dec. 1980. **28.** *Irish Times*, 13 Dec. 1980. **29.** Report of an interview with Brian Lenihan on BBC Northern Ireland by Barry Cowan, *Irish Times*, 16 Mar. 1981. **30.** *Irish Times*, 7 Feb. 1981. **31.** Ibid. **32.** Bishop Daly condemned the hunger strike as unjustified, and also what he termed the 'glorification … of violence', *Irish Times*, 2 Mar. 1981. **33.** 27-year-old Bobby Sands from Belfast was serving a 14-year sentence on an arms charge when he commenced his strike. **34.** *Irish Times*, 23 Apr. 1981. **35.** Currie, *All hell will break loose*, p. 320. **36.** Sands stood as an 'Anti-H-Block/Armagh' candidate; H-Block was the shape of the cell block at the Maze Prison, and Armagh Jail was where women prisoners were held. **37.** Murray's action was disowned by the party, and his later nomination for the district council elections was not ratified. When he stood as an independent candidate, he lost his seat. **38.** *Irish Times*, 2 Apr. 1981. **39.** Currie, *All hell will break loose*, pp 320–1. **40.** *Irish Times*, 3 Apr. 1981. **41.** *Irish Times*, 1 Apr. 1981. **42.** Paul Routledge, *John Hume: a biography* (London, 1997), p. 177. **43.** *Irish Times*, 6 Apr. 1981. **44.** The party won 104 seats, a loss of 9 compared with 1977, but the defection of several councillors like Fitt and Devlin meant that the party had entered the elections with fewer than 113 councillors. **45.** Address to SDLP local councillors, Dungannon, 8 June 1981. Copy in D3072/7/8/2, PRONI. **46.** Routledge, *John Hume*, pp 175–6. **47.** *Irish Times*, 6 Aug. 1981. **48.** *Irish Times*, 5 Aug. 1981. **49.** *Irish Times*, 8 Aug. 1981. **50.** Currie was not willing to nominate and while several other prominent SDLP members had been suggested, including John Hume and Hugh Logue, no name was submitted to the convention. **51.** *Irish Times*, 25 Aug. 1981. **52.** Carron received 31,278 votes, Maginnis 29,048. **53.** A phrase based on a remark by Sinn Féin member Danny Morrison at the party's 1981 conference. **54.** Fr Faul convened meetings of hunger strikers' families to discuss how to end the strikes. **55.** *Irish Times*, 18 Sept. 1981. **56.** A member of the Irish Commission for Justice and Peace, former SDLP convention member Hugh Logue was part of the delegation that brokered a deal in June, only to have it vetoed by Margaret Thatcher. **57.** A composite paper prepared by party chair Seán Farren and executive member Ben Caraher, *Political developments since the Atkins Talks*, provided the basis for discussion on the political way forward, the effects of the prison crisis and party organization. Copy in D3072/2/14/10. **58.** Ibid. **59.** Séamus Mallon and John McAvoy, chair of the Newry and Mourne Council, met two leading Sinn Féin members to discuss the hunger strike crisis in Dec. 1980. Hume met Jimmy Drumm and Eamon McCrory of Sinn Féin to discuss the same crisis in July 1981. **60.** *Irish Times*, 25 Aug. 1981. **61.** Molyneaux circulated members of the Socialist Group with a dossier designed to portray Hume as unsuitable for the role of vice-president because of his alleged involvement with Sinn Féin-PIRA. **62.** *Anglo-Irish joint studies, reports presented to both houses of the Oireachtas* by the Taoiseach Dr Garret FitzGerald TD, 11 Nov. 1981. **63.** Routledge, *John Hume*, p. 180. **64.** *News Letter*, 3 Sept. 1981. **65.** *News Letter*, 24 Nov. 1981. **66.** John Hume, 'Address of SDLP party leader to the 1981 annual conference' (Belfast, 1981) (copy in author's possession). **67.** David McKittrick, Seamus Kelters, Brian Feeney and Chris Thornton, *Lost lives* (Edinburgh, 1999), pp 1, 476.

CHAPTER 9

1. The conference was held on 19 Dec. and was attended by John Hume, Gerry Fitt, Jim Kilfedder (UPUP), John Dunlop (UUUC) and, in a personal capacity, John Taylor (UUP). Neither the DUP nor the UUP officially attended, *Irish Times*, 20 Dec. 1981. **2.** Early reports suggested that an executive might consist of members from a new assembly, UK MPs and possibly some of the NIO junior ministers, presided over by the Secretary of State. *Irish Times*, 14 Jan. 1982. **3.** *Irish Times*, 18 Jan. 1982. **4.** *Address by John Hume*, St Anne's Cathedral, Belfast, 2 Mar. 1982 (copy in author's possession). **5.** Ibid. **6.** *Irish Times*, 2 Feb. 1982. **7.** *Northern Ireland: a framework for devolution* (Belfast, 1982); central to Prior's proposal was 'cross-community' support for devolution, the measure being approximately seventy percent support in the proposed assembly. **8.** Paisley's welcome did not suggest acceptance of power-sharing arrangement or any North-South arrangements. **9.** *Mr Prior's white paper: a framework for devolution*, statement by John Hume, 26 Apr. 1982 (copy in author's possession). **10.** Ibid. **11.** Denis Haughey, interview 18 Dec. 2009. **12.** Statement by John Hume, 26 Apr. 1982. **13.** James Prior, *A balance of power* (London, 1986), p. 197. There is a strong suspicion that Thatcher removed the section because of the exaggerated claims made by Dublin ministers following the summit in Dec. 1980. **14.** *Irish Times*, 23 Mar. 1982. **15.** Séamus Mallon was appointed along with John Robb, a well known Co. Antrim doctor, a Protestant with liberal-Nationalist views. **16.** A special meeting of the party's executive on 19 May welcomed Mallon's appointment. **17.** In 1981, the general secretary of the Irish Labour Party had complained to the SDLP about remarks Mallon had made regarding his preference for a Fianna Fáil government, D3972/2/8/11, PRONI. **18.** *The Northern Ireland Assembly Disqualification Act* (1975) precluded members of a foreign legislature also being members of the Northern Ireland Assembly. **19.** Lord Hylton unsuccessfully tabled an amendment to remove the legal barrier in the House of Lords in July 1982. **20.** Led by several members including Henry Grattan MP, the exclusively Protestant Irish Parliament asserted independence from the British Parliament in 1782. Grattan campaigned for full constitutional independence for the parliament as well as for an end to penal laws directed mainly against Catholics. **21.** The speakers were Revd John Barkley, former principal of Union Theological College, Dr Martin Mansergh, special adviser to Taoiseach Charles Haughey, Dr Eric Gallagher, former President of the Methodist Church, Dr Garret FitzGerald, leader of Fine Gael, Senators John Robb and Séamus Mallon and SDLP leader John Hume. The papers presented were published in *Options for a new Ireland* (Belfast, 1981). **22.** At the outset the Irish supported the British position, but following the sinking of Argentina's battleship *General Belgrano*, the government accused the British of also being an aggressor. **23.**

Bew and Gillespie, *Northern Ireland*, pp 165–6. **24.** Among those who voted in favour of contesting the elections were John Hume, Austin Currie, Eddie McGrady, Paddy O'Hanlon, Joe Hendron, Seán Farren and Frank Feely; among those against were Séamus Mallon, Paddy Duffy, Hugh Logue and Michael Canavan. Canavan and Duffy, two founding members of the party, subsequently declared that they would not be candidates so convinced were they that Prior's proposals were doomed to failure. **25.** Currie, *All hell will break loose*, p. 325. **26.** SDLP, *Stand firm: manifesto for the assembly elections* (1982). **27.** Mansergh stressed British responsibility for the crisis while FitzGerald emphasized the role of the communities in the North. **28.** The UUP and DUP's manifestoes stressed that devolution could only be based on majority rule with no Irish dimension. **29.** John Hume, *Message from the party leader to the electorate* (1982) (copy in author's possession). **30.** A BBC's *Spotlight* opinion poll claimed that approximately 40% of SDLP supporters did not agree with the assembly boycott policy (*Irish Times*, 16 Oct. 1982). **31.** Sinn Féin required each of its candidates to support the PIRA's campaign. **32.** *Irish News*, 16 Oct. 1982. **33.** Currie, *All hell will break loose*, p. 325. **34.** *Irish Times*, 19 Nov. 1982. **35.** *Irish Times*, 13 Dec. 1982. **36.** The Droppin' Well was a public house in Ballykelly, Co. Derry, a village close to a British army base. **37.** Several suspected terrorists were killed at roadblocks, and at arms dumps, by RUC undercover squads. Contrary to RUC claims some of those killed were unarmed and entirely innocent of terrorist involvement. See John Bowyer Bell, *The Irish Troubles* (Dublin, 1993), pp 652–6. **38.** An election petition was heard at Armagh court on 16 Dec. In the subsequent by-election which the SDLP did not contest, the seat was won by a Unionist, Jim Speers. **39.** *Irish Times*, 29 Jan. 1983. **40.** *Irish Times*, 31 Jan. 1983. **41.** Ibid. **42.** Ibid. **43.** In his autobiography, *Straight left: a journey in politics* (Dublin, 2005), Quinn relates that he gave the endorsement on behalf of the Labour Party without consulting with his party leader, Dick Spring TD. However, Spring, having already called for a cross-party consensus on the North, had no difficulty supporting Quinn's commitment. **44** FitzGerald, *All in a life*, p. 462. **45.** In opposition, Haughey emphasized that such a declaration should be given prior to negotiations and that a constitutional conference would be the first step towards achieving withdrawal, see address to Fianna Fáil conference, *Irish Times*, 28 Feb. 1982. **46.** *Irish Times*, 12 Mar. 1983. **47.** By constitutional was meant all parties with no connection to paramilitary organizations such as the PIRA and who also were represented in either the Oireachtas or the Assembly of Northern Ireland. **48.** The SDLP delegation consisted of John Hume, Séamus Mallon, Joe Hendron, Austin Currie, Eddie McGrady, with, as alternates: Hugh Logue, Seán Farren, Paddy O'Donoghue, Frank Feely and Pascal O'Hare. Denis Haughey served as secretary to the delegation. **49.** D3972/2/12/5, PRONI. **50.** Denis Haughey, 'The Anglo-Irish dimension of the forum', D3072/12/5, PRONI. **51.** Seán Farren, 'Forum for a New Ireland: constitutional issues', other papers addressed British-Irish relations, and an all-Ireland approach to economic development. D3072/2/12/5, PRONI. **52.** SDLP, *The fundamental problems*, 10 Aug. 1983, D3072/12/5, PRONI. **53.** *New Ireland Forum, vol. 2, proceedings*, public session, 30 May 1983, p. 22. **54.** Ibid. **55.** Ibid., pp 7–15. **56.** *Irish News*, 30 Apr. 1983. **57.** HC, *Debates*, 28 June 1983. **58.** *New Ireland Forum, vol. 1, reports*. **59.** *New Ireland Forum, vol. 2, proceedings*. **60.** The Church's delegation consisted of Dr Cahal Daly, Bishop of Down and Connor, Dr Joseph Cassidy, Bishop of Clonfert, Dr Edward Daly, Bishop of Derry, and Dr Dermot O'Mahony, Auxiliary of Dublin, assisted by future president, then Professor Mary McAleese. **61.** *New Ireland Forum, vol. 2, proceedings*, 9 Feb. 1984. **62.** Ibid., p. 11. **63.** Ibid. **64.** Séamus Mallon, speech to the SDLP annual conference, Jan. 1984. **65.** *Irish Times*, 1 May 1984. **66.** The wording was: 'other views which may contribute to political development' and the clear intention was to leave the way open for negotiations on other models. *Report of the New Ireland Forum, vol. 1 reports*, ch. 5, para. 5.10. **67.** *New Ireland Forum, vol. 1, reports*, ch. 4.15. **68.** In 1986, she supported removing the constitutional prohibition on divorce, and was in favour of the pro-life amendment in 1983. **69.** A Constable Robinson was acquitted, despite the fact that he changed his statement several times and had been instructed by senior officers in what evidence to give and despite the fact that it was proven the deceased had been unarmed and had not displayed any aggression towards the police when his vehicle was obliged to stop. **70.** Seanad Éireann, *Debates*, 9 May 1984.

CHAPTER 10

1. *Irish Times*, 2 May 1984. **2.** *New Ireland Forum, vol. 2, public session*, 2 May 1984. While Hume expressed the views of the majority of the SDLP's delegation, some, like Séamus Mallon, inclined towards Haughey's emphasis on a unitary state, see *Irish Times*, 12 May 1984. **3.** *Irish Times*, 4 May 1984. **4.** DUP, *The Unionist case: the forum report answered* (1984). **5.** *Irish Times*, 3 May 1984. **6.** Ibid. **7.** *Irish Times*, 25 May 1984. **8.** *Irish Times*, 23 May 1984. **9.** *Irish Times*, 22 May 1984. **10.** The report, initiated by Hume argued that Northern Ireland was not solely a UK matter, and that the EC could assist the two governments. **11.** The report was debated and passed in the European Parliament, 29 Mar. 1984. *Irish Times*, 30 Mar. 1984.

12. Ulster Unionist Assembly Party, *The way forward* (1984). **13.** HC, *Debates*, 2 July 1984. **14.** Ibid. **15.** British Labour Party spokesperson on Northern Ireland, Peter Archer, HC, *Debates*, 2 July 1984. **16.** HC, *Debates*, 2 July 1984. **17.** Interview with the Secretary of State, *Irish News*, 26 July 1984. **18.** Statements by Peter Barry, minister for foreign affairs, *Irish Times*, 5 July 1984 and *Irish Times*, 19 Sept. 1984. **19.** Address to the National Marketing Conference, *Irish Times*, 4 Oct. 1984. **20.** *Irish Times*, 29 Sept. 1984. **21.** *Irish News*, 12 Oct. 1984. **22.** Garret FitzGerald's address to Fine Gael annual conference, *Irish Times*, 8 Oct. 1984. **23.** *Irish Times*, 16 Oct. 1984. **24.** *Irish Times*, 13 Oct. 1984. **25.** *Irish Times*, 7 Nov. 1984. **26.** Ibid. **27.** FitzGerald, *All in a life*, pp 499–523, details the negotiations that took place between the two governments from June to Nov. 1984, during which the British government seemed willing to move towards some form of joint authority but, in the end, resiled from it. **28.** Ibid., p. 518. **29.** David McKittrick, *Irish Times*, 12 Nov. 1984. **30.** *Irish Times*, 21 Nov. 1984. **31.** *Irish Times*, 22 Nov. 1984. **32.** FitzGerald, *All in a life*, ch. 16. **33.** *Irish Times*, 23 Nov. 1984. Like Haughey, O'Hare had argued that the forum should adopt one agreed option. See memorandum circulated to party colleagues (copy in author's possession). **34.** *Irish Times*, 20 Nov. 1984. **35.** *Irish Times*, 23 Nov. 1984. **36.** *Irish Times*, 29 Nov. 1984. **37.** *Irish Times*, 5 Dec. 1984. **38.** FitzGerald, *All in a life*, ch. 16. **39.** *Irish Times*, 3 Dec. 1984. **40.** Copy in author's possession. **41.** *Irish Times*, 17 Jan. 1985. **42.** Routledge, *John Hume*, p. 201. **43.** *Irish Times*, 25 Jan. 1984. **44.** Chairman's address to conference (copy in author's possession); *Irish Times*, 25 Jan. 1985. **45.** A letter from the UUP had indicated that James Molyneaux was 'anxious to open a dialogue with Nationalists on the 'realities and perceptions' about Northern Ireland (*Irish Times*, 27 Jan. 1985). **46.** *Irish News*, 27 Jan. 1985. **47.** Ibid. **48.** Among the issues on which the Irish government sought a formal consultative role was the administration of justice, and policing. **49.** The Irish government had put the future of the UDR on the agenda. Despite intentions to keep it above inter-communal tensions, the UDR had become a focus of strong Nationalist opposition, almost akin to the hated B-Specials it had replaced. Calls for its disbandment mounted as regiment members were charged with terrorist-related offences and membership of loyalist paramilitaries. **50.** Fionnuala O'Connor, Conference sketch, *Irish Times*, 27 Jan. 1985. Ferguson was a leading Unionist on Fermanagh District Council. **51.** *Irish Times*, 4 Feb. 1985. **52.** *Irish Times*, 5 Feb. 1985. **53.** Statement from the Republican Press Centre, *Irish Times*, 2 Feb. 1985. **54.** James Molyneaux, *Irish Times*, 26 Feb. 1985. **55.** Ibid. **56.** SDLP, *Manifesto for the district council elections* (1985). **57.** *Irish Times*, 6 June 1985. **58.** *Irish Times*, 1 Apr. 1985. **59.** FitzGerald, *All in a life*, pp 536–7. **60.** Currie, *All hell will break loose*, pp 346–7. **61.** FitzGerald, *All in a life*, pp 535–6; this proposal encountered severe opposition from the Northern Ireland judiciary led by Lord Chief Justice Robert Lowry and was never adopted. **62.** SDLP, *Justice in Northern Ireland* (1985). **63.** Single-judge courts had been introduced in the 1970s to address the problem of jury intimidation, which had resulted in 'not guilty' verdicts, where the evidence suggested otherwise. **64.** Jeffrey Donaldson, *Irish Times*, 26 Sept. 1985. **65.** *Irish Times*, 7 Oct. 1985. **66.** *Irish Times*, 6 Oct. 1985. **67.** *Irish Times*, 15 Oct. 1985. **68.** His main contacts were those with whom he had developed close relations over the preceding decade, Tip O'Neill, Ted Kennedy and Patrick Moynihan. **69.** *Irish Times*, 11 Nov. 1985. **70.** Ibid.

CHAPTER 11

1. NIA, *Debates*, 16 Nov. 1985. **2.** HC, *Debates*, 18 Nov. 1985. **3.** HC, *Debates*, 19 Nov. 1985. **4.** In the three months following the agreement, the PIRA murdered ten members of the RUC and UDR. **5.** *Irish Times*, 16 Nov. 1985. **6.** Statement from Charles J. Haughey, leader of Fianna Fáil, *Irish Times*, 20 Nov. 1985. **7.** Dáil Éireann, *Debates*, 21 Nov. 1985. **8.** *Anglo-Irish Agreement*, Article 2(a), 1985. **9.** Spokespersons were allocated roles that matched government departments with responsibilities for matters mentioned in the agreement. **10.** Adrian Colton was a young barrister who came from Dromore, Co. Tyrone. **11.** Jim Cusack, 'Northern notebook', *Irish Times*, 19 Jan. 1986. **12.** SDLP pre-election press conference, *Irish Times*, 21 Jan. 1986. **13.** Sinn Féin's share of the Nationalist vote declined from 42% to 35%. Eddie McGrady's vote was 1,100 below Powell's in an electorate that had a combined Nationalist majority, a sign that the seat was winnable, as indeed turned out to be the case at the next general election. **14.** HC, *Debates*, 20 Feb. 1986. **15.** There was a marked increase in the number of Catholics murdered by loyalists in the years following the Ango-Irish Agreement. See 'Statistics' section of McKittrick, Kelters, Feeney and Thornton, *Lost lives*, pp 1473–93. **16.** *Irish Times*, 16 Nov. 1985. Haughey never legally tested the agreement. When UUP members, Michael and Chris McGimpsey, brought a case to the Irish Supreme Court in 1988, the agreement was found not in breach of the constitution. **17.** Author's notes. **18.** *Irish News*, 4 Jan. 1986. **19.** The Fianna Fáil MEP was Paddy Lalor, a vice-president of the parliament (*Irish Times*, 12 Dec. 1985). **20.** *Irish Times*, 13 Dec. 1985. **21.** Following pledges from the governments of the US, Canada and New Zealand, an agreement to establish the International Fund for Ireland was signed in Dublin in Sept. 1986. The fund amounted to over $120 million for its first three years and its aim was 'to promote the economic and social development of those parts of Ireland which have suffered most severely from the consequences of the instability of recent years ...' (Article 10(a), *Anglo-Irish Agreement*). **22.** *Irish Times*, 16 Nov. 1985. **23.** Address by party chair Seán Farren to Irish Association, Dec. 1987 (copy in author's possession). **24.** *Irish Times*, 16 Jan. 1986. **25.** King replaced Hurd in Sept. 1985. **26.** *Belfast Telegraph*, 17 Dec. 1985. Article 2(b) gave the Irish government the right to put forward views and proposals on matters relating to Northern Ireland and obliged both governments to resolve any differences. **27.** *Irish Times*, 4 Dec. 1985; pressure from the Irish government forced an early retraction, but not before Fianna Fáil and Sinn Féin had felt vindicated in their opposition to the agreement. **28.** Peter Robinson, NIA, *Debates*, 4 Jan. 1986. **29.** On 5 Aug. the PIRA threatened to kill civilians who supplied goods or services to the security forces. While not a new threat, the statement was deliberately issued to heighten inter-community tensions (*Irish News*, 6 Aug. 1986). **30.** *Irish Times*, 5 Aug. 1986. **31.** *Irish Times*, 5 Aug. 1986. **32.** The referendum took place on 26 June; the results were 935,842 against and 538,729 for the amendment. **33.** *Irish Times*, 28 June 1986. **34.** This 1954 legislation protected the display of the Union flag and was the basis upon which the tricolour could be prohibited if its display might cause a breach of the peace. Nationalists regarded the Act as discriminatory. **35.** Despite considerable pressure from the Irish government, Lord Hailsham, British Lord Chancellor, announced on 9 Oct. that there would be no change to the composition of the Diplock courts. **36.** Address to Social Studies Summer School, *Irish Times*, 5 Aug. 1986. **37.** Based at Maryfield, close to Hollywood in Co. Down, the Anglo-Irish secretariat was frequently picketed by anti-agreement protestors. **38.** The secretariat also provided a very useful contact with the Irish government for individuals and groups in civic society. **39.** Ken Maginnis MP, address to the MacGill Summer School, *Irish Times*, 25 Aug. 1986. **40.** Ray McSharry TD, address to MacGill Summer School, *Irish Times*, 20 Aug. 1986. **41.** *Irish Times*, 28 Aug. 1986. **42.** *Irish Times*, 14 Oct. 1986. **43.** SDLP, *Agenda, sixteenth annual conference* (1986). **44.** *Irish Times*, 24 Nov. 1986. **45.** Ibid. **46.** The Charter group included Harry West, Austin Ardill and Belfast lawyer, Peter Smyth. **47.** *Irish Times*, 19 Sept. 1986. **48.** *Irish Times*, 6 Sept. 1986. **49.** *Irish Times*, 11 Nov. 1986. **50.** *Irish News*, 1 Dec. 1986. **51.** New Ulster Political Research Group, *Common sense* (1987). **52.** *Irish News*, 6 Feb. 1987. **53.** *Irish News*, 7 Feb. 1987. **54.** *Irish Times*, 24 Feb. 1987. **55.** The proposal came from the Ulster Clubs another Unionist umbrella group which organized opposition to the re-routing of traditional loyalist parades and to the agreement. The main spokespersons were Alan Wright and future UUP leader David Trimble. **56.** The task-force consisted of Frank Millar (UUP), Harold McCusker (UUP) and Peter Robinson (DUP). **57.** Without the Irish government's continued support for the agreement, President Reagan would not have been able to sign the legislation allowing the fund to operate. **58.** *Irish Times*, 9 Apr. 1987. **59.** Haughey nominated two northerners, serving senator John Robb and playwright Brian Friel. **60.** Interview with Brian Lenihan, *Irish Times*, 11 May 1987. **61.** Ibid. **62.** The overall SDLP vote was 154,087 (137,012) compared with the Sinn Féin vote of 83,389 (102,701). 1983 figures in brackets. **63.** Ed Moloney, *Voices from the grave* (London, 2010), pp 272–4.

CHAPTER 12

1. *News Letter*, 20 Apr. 1987. **2.** Spiecker had ecumenical relationships with Northern Ireland and had played a mediation role during the hunger strikes. **3.** *An end to drift*, reproduced in *Irish Times*, 3 July 1987. **4.** Address to University College Dublin Summer School, *Irish Times*, 4 July 1987. **5.** Frank Millar, one of the report's authors, resigned his post with the UUP in Oct. and Peter Robinson resigned as deputy leader of the DUP at the same time, though resumed it three months later. **6.** Paisley moved quite quickly to distance himself from the task-force report calling for the complete suspension of the agreement before any inter-party talks. *Irish Times*, 17 Aug. 1987. **7.** *Irish Times*, 24 Jan. 1988. **8.** SDLP, *Equal and just opportunities for employment* (1986). **9.** Named after the retired southern politician, former IRA leader and human rights activist, Seán McBride, the principles consisted of a set of obligations to be adopted by employers to ensure fairness and equity in the workplace. Among those endorsing the principles were West Belfast priests Des Wilson and Brian Brady, trade unionist Inez McCormack, and Senator John Robb. **10.** Article by John Hume, *Irish Times*, 24 Sept. 1987. **11.** Letter to *Belfast Telegraph*, 14 May 1987, copy in SDLP file D3072/7/8/5. PRONI. **12.** *Fair Employment (Northern Ireland) Act* (1989). **13.** The Labour Party's Northern Ireland spokesperson, Kevin McNamara, was particularly active on the issue and worked very closely with the SDLP at Westminster to ensure the new legislation was effective. **14.** The Birmingham Six were Irishmen imprisoned when found guilty of planting bombs in the city in Nov. 1974 which caused the deaths of 21 people. Though innocent, the men spent 17 years in jail, finally being released when their convictions were declared 'unsound' in 1991. The Guildford Four and the Maguire Seven were also wrongly convicted of planting bombs. Their convictions were eventually quashed but not until many had served several years imprisonment and, one, Giuseppe Conlon had died in prison. **15.** Among those killed were PIRA members Gervais McKerr, Seán Burns and Eugene Toman, who were killed by the RUC at a check-point near Lurgan, and INLA members Roddy Carroll and Séamus Grew, who were shot dead at a check-point near Armagh. **16.** Stalker claimed that he was replaced because he had discovered incriminating evidence pointing to an attempt by senior RUC officers to pervert the course of justice. See John Stalker, *Stalker* (London, 1988). **17.** Aidan McAnespie was shot in the back by a soldier in an army observation post as he walked towards the local GAA ground on 21 Feb. Undercover agents shot the three PIRA members who were apparently on a bombing mission targeting British troops as they walked through Gibraltar on 7 Mar. 1988. **18.** *Irish Times*, 2 Feb. 1988. **19.** *Irish Times*, 9 Nov. 1987. **20.** *Irish Times*, 19 Nov. 1988. **21.** Speech to Unionist party meeting Banbridge, *Irish Times*, 8 Feb. 1988. **22.** *Irish Times*, 20 Feb. 1988. **23.** *Irish Times*, 27 Feb. 1988. **24.** The figure is based on statistics contained in McKittrick, Kelters, Feeney and Thornton, *Lost lives*, Table 1, p. 1453. **25.** Interview with Gerry Adams, *Hot Press*, Nov. 1987. **26.** General Sir James Glover, *Irish Times*, 1 Mar. 1988. **27.** *Scenario for peace* described the PIRA's campaign as a struggle against British colonialism; it claimed Unionists would have their rights respected in a united Ireland and offered to 'repatriate' any who would not accept that new situation. **28.** *Hot Press*, Nov. 1987. **29.** McGrory legally represented many members of the PIRA and was an outspoken human rights advocate. **30.** Fr Reid, who had already written to Hume in May 1986 to advocate that Nationalist parties North and South should cooperate to resolve the crisis, was a member of the Clonard community of Redemptorists in Belfast. Over the next fifteen years, he was to play a significant intermediary role in what became known as the 'peace process'. **31.** The SDLP participants were John Hume, Séamus Mallon, Austin Currie and Seán Farren; those from Sinn Féin were Gerry Adams, Danny Morrison, Mitchell McLaughlin and Tom Hartley. The larger group met on three occasions. **32.** Currie, *All hell will break loose*, pp 364–70, provides a detailed account of the meetings. **33.** The main measure was the electoral strength of Sinn Féin, which, North and South, indicated that support for violence in pursuit of a British withdrawal was very low. **34.** Sinn Féin, *Towards a strategy for peace*, paper presented to the SDLP-Sinn Féin talks, Mar. 1988 (copy in author's possession). **35.** Statement issued at the conclusion of the SDLP-Sinn Féin talks, *Irish Times*, 6 Sept. 1988. John Hume put his arguments in a letter to Gerry Adams, written after their first meeting and discussed at the Mar. meeting. Sinn Féin also tabled two further documents, *Sinn Féin and national self-determination and a proposal for joint action on fair pmployment*, and *Persuading the British: a joint call*. The SDLP prepared a *Commentary on Sinn Féin documents* for internal discussion (copies of documents in author's possession). **36.** Meeting of the constituency representatives group, Cookstown, 23 Jan. 1988. *Irish Times*, 25 Jan. 1988. **37.** *Irish Times*, 21 Mar. 1988. **38.** *Irish Times*, 4 July 1988. **39.** *Irish Times*, 12 Jan. 1988. **40.** Ibid. **41.** *Irish Times*, 13 Apr. 1988. **42.** Article in *Sunday Independent*, 17 Sept. 1988. **43.** The period was marked by several notorious incidents in which civilians with no security force or government connections were either killed or seriously injured. **44.** Sinn Féin, *Sinn Fein and national self-determination and a proposal on joint action on fair employment* (1988). **45.** Sinn Féin, *Persuading the British: a joint call* (1988). **46.** Seán Farren, address to North Belfast branch of the SDLP, 24 Apr. 1988 (copy in author's possession). **47.** Barry White, *Belfast Telegraph*, 8 Sept. 1988. **48.** *Irish Independent*, 18 Apr. 1988. **49.** *Irish Times*, 28 Mar. 1988. **50.** The working group consisted of Séamus Mallon, Austin Currie and Seán Farren (*Irish Times*, 27 Feb. 1988). **51.** *Irish Times*, 6 June 1988. **52.** The other parties were represented by Jack Allen (UUP), Peter Robinson (DUP), and Gordon Mawhinney of Alliance. Fr Alec Reid was also present. A fuller account of the encounter is contained in Currie, *All hell will break loose*, ch. 24. Details of the meeting were made public several months later (*Irish Times*, 3, 4 Feb. 1989). **53.** Currie, *All hell will break loose*, p. 356. **54.** According to Currie's account, a document purporting to be a report of the discussion contained an embellished account of what had been agreed and was presented to both governments, allegedly by Gordon Mawhinney. **55.** *Possible scenarios*, a document prepared by UUP's Jack Allen and Peter Robinson (DUP), both participants at the Duisbug meeting in Oct., was passed to John Hume in Dec. 1988 (copy in author's possession). **56.** *SDLP response to possible scenarios proposals* (copy in author's possession). Both the Unionist and SDLP documents were made public early in the New Year when details of the Duisberg meeting also became public (*Irish Times*, 4 Feb. 1989). **57.** The working party consisted of Eddie McGrady, Michael Boyd, Ben Caraher, Austin Currie, Mark Durkan, Seán Farren and Bríd Rodgers. **58.** *Outline of a basis for negotiations: a discussion paper*, Dec. 1989 (copy in author's possession). **59.** Ibid. **60.** SDLP, *Submission on the review of the Anglo-Irish Agreement* (1988) (copy in author's possession). **61.** The so-called 'I-voters' were those who were only permitted to vote in 'imperial' elections and not in local or assembly elections. The measure had been primarily directed against Republic of Ireland citizens. **62.** The Department of Education had proposed new regulations regarding the choice of a 'foreign' language which would have restricted the take-up of Irish at secondary level. **63.** The agenda for meetings of the Anglo-Irish

Conference indicate a gradual expansion in the range of issues discussed. In 1987, for example, controversial proposals for curriculum reform at secondary level in Northern Ireland threatened the teaching of Irish and, as result of strong lobbying by the SDLP and language organizations, the issue was addressed at several meetings of the conference. **64.** *Speech by John Hume to the SDLP's eighteenth annual conference* (1988) (copy in author's possession).

CHAPTER 13

1. The meeting on 1 Feb. was to express the leaders' joint concerns about privatization and to seek reassurances about jobs. **2.** *Irish Times*, 13 Jan., 14 Feb. 1989. **3.** *Irish Times*, interview with Frank Millar, 13 Jan. 1989. **4.** Ibid. **5.** *Irish Times*, interview with Frank Millar, 14 Feb. 1989. **6.** Ibid. **8.** *Irish Times*, 3 Apr. 1989. **9.** *Sunday Independent*, 2 Apr. 1989. **10.** SDLP, *Make a difference* (1989). **11.** The manifesto pointed to the fact that the Unionist majority on Belfast City Council denied SDLP councillors any representation to sixty-four external bodies. **12.** Led by former SDLP Mayor Raymond McClean, links had been established with the Ethiopian capital following Derry's contributions to relief efforts during the 1982 famine in that country. **13.** In 1985, Sinn Féin won more seats than the SDLP in Belfast, Cookstown, Fermanagh and Omagh; in 1989 the situation was reversed, except in Belfast, where both parties won eight seats. **14.** Among the councils to adopt forms of power-sharing were Derry, Downpatrick, Fermanagh, Moyle, Newry and Mourne, and Omagh. **15.** *The Anglo-Irish Agreement: review of the working of the conference* (1989). **16.** Earlier in the year, the SDLP had submitted a detailed regeneration plan for West Belfast to the Secretary of State. **17.** Ibid., para. 23. **18.** Ibid., para. 24. The SDLP submitted to both governments a policy paper entitled *The Anglo-Irish Agreement and the completion of the single market* (July 1989), which outlined how North-South cooperation should be directed to ensure the whole island benefitted most from the Single Market (copy in author's possession). **19.** John Hume quoted in the *Irish Times*, 27 May 1989. Currie won a seat in June 1989 and subsequently served as a TD until 2002. He was also Fine Gael's presidential candidate in 1990. For further details on his departure from the SDLP and subsequent career, see Currie, *All hell will break loose*, chs 26–8. **20.** *Irish Times*, 1 June 1989. **21.** SDLP, *Manifesto for the European elections* (1989). **22.** SDLP, *The form and doubling of the European structural funds: a new opportunity for the economy of Northern Ireland* (1988), and *The implications of the single market for Northern Ireland* (1988) (copies in author's possession). **23.** Sinn Féin and the DUP were still totally opposed to EC membership with the former advocating 'negotiated withdrawal'. The UUP's position was more nuanced, but was publicly negative. **24.** *Irish Times*, 29 June 1989. **25.** *Irish Times*, 13 July 1989. **26.** At a press conference at which he attempted to demonstrate a flexible approach to the agreement he misquoted Art. 29 of the agreement to suggest that it was to open to an alternative when all it stated was that 'changes in the scope and nature of the Conference ...' could be considered. **27.** John Hume, 'The Irish question in a changed world' in a supplement to the *Irish Times*, 14 Aug. 1989. **28.** Address to the conference *Northern Ireland into the nineties: what kind of society*, Corrymeela, 6–8 Oct. 1989 (copy in author's possession). **29.** *Irish News*, 12 Sept. 1989. **30.** Article 7, *Anglo-Irish Agreement* (1985). **31.** *Joint British and Irish governments statement following meeting of Anglo-Irish Conference*, Irish Times, 19 Oct. 1989. **32.** *Irish Times*, 9 Oct. 1989. **33.** Ibid. *Irish Times*, 23 Oct. 1989. **34.** *Irish Times*, 23 Oct. 1989. **35.** *Irish Times*, 6 Nov. 1989. **36.** Ibid. **37.** *Irish Times*, 22 Dec. 1989. **38.** *Irish Times*, 25 Jan. 1989. **39.** Speech by Peter Brooke to the Bangor Chamber of Commerce, Jan. 9 1989, reproduced in *Irish Times*, 10 Jan. 1989. **40.** An amendment bill on extradition requiring prima-facie evidence of a case before someone could be extradited from the Republic of Ireland was passed in the Dáil in Nov. 1987. **41.** The court ruled against the extradition of the two escapees on the grounds that their safety could not be assured should they be returned to the North. **42.** *Irish Times*, 20 Apr. 1990. **43.** Draft Unionist document outlining proposals for a new British-Irish agreement, *Irish Times*, 27 Feb. 1990. **44.** In an interview with Pádraig O'Malley reported in *Ireland: the uncivil wars* (Belfast, 1983), James Molyneaux had expressed this view in its most traditional form, saying that 'I could only talk to Dublin when we have the basis of a devolved administration here in Northern Ireland and when I would be negotiating on the part of Northern Ireland for matters of mutual interest which the assembly in Northern Ireland agreed we should talk to Dublin about'. In other words, not until there was a fully functioning assembly and administration in Northern Ireland would Unionists consent to talk to the Irish government. **45.** The draft was reproduced in the *Irish Times*, 22 Nov. 1990. **46.** Ibid. **47.** Brooke's draft repeatedly referred to the United Kingdom (seven times) and to Northern Ireland as part of the United Kingdom, used the phrase HMG (Her Majesty's Government) and displayed no balanced appreciation of the Nationalist position. **48.** For a detailed account of these negotiations and the whole Brooke initiative, see David Bloomfield, *Political dialogue in Northern Ireland: the Brooke Initiative, 1989–92* (London, 1998). **49.** Hume's draft also appeared in the *Irish Times*, 22 Nov. 1990 (copy in author's possession). **50.** The SDLP was represented by Denis Haughey and Seán Farren, the UUP by Reg Empey and Drew Nelson, the DUP by Peter Robinson and Gregory Campbell. **51.** *A Northern Ireland centre in Brussels: a feasibility study*, Centre for the Study of Conflict, University of Ulster (n.d.). **52.** Ibid. The inaugural meeting of the Northern Ireland Centre in Europe (NICE) brought together academics from the University of Ulster, and politicians, and a working party of the Law Society which had also been considering a similar initiative. For a number of years, NICE was an important link between Northern Ireland and the European Commission. **53.** SDLP, *Proposed agenda for talks* (1990) (copy in author's possession). **54.** Ibid. The *Report of the New Ireland Forum*, ch. 4, employs almost identical language to identify the issues to be resolved in an acceptable settlement. **55.** Ibid. **56.** Ibid. **57.** Ibid. **58.** *Irish Times*, 2 Oct. 1990. **59.** *Irish News*, 8 Oct. 1990. **60.** Only in this context could the SDLP see changes to Articles 2 and 3 of the South's constitution being effected. **61.** Address to SDLP annual conference, *Irish Times*, 19 Nov. 1990. **62.** Unionists attacked the SDLP's emphasis on the all-Ireland context, accusing the party of being opposed to devolution on whatever basis. **63.** Address to SDLP annual conference, *Irish Times*, 19 Nov. 1990. **64.** SDLP, *Proposals for cross-border cooperation* (1990), a policy document presented to the twentieth annual conference (SDLP, Nov. 1990). **65.** Speech delivered by Peter Brooke in Ballymena, *Irish Times*, 8 Sept. 1990. **66.** Earlier in the year, the PIRA had indicated that while it would not declare a ceasefire prior to talks with the British government a ceasefire 'could be the first item on agenda' should talks take place. However, while welcoming any sign that the PIRA might want to end its campaign, the government had insisted that until Sinn Féin no longer endorsed terrorism it could not 'expect to be treated as any other political party' (*Guardian*, 20 Feb. 1990). It was clear, however, that a debate about future strategy was continuing within Sinn Féin and the PIRA and that the government was anxious to encourage that debate. **67.** Northern Ireland Office press release of speech by Peter Brooke delivered in his London constituency of Westminster North, 9 Nov. 1990. **68.** Sinn Féin, *Setting the record straight* (1994). **69.** Eamonn Mallie and David McKittrick, *The fight for peace* (London, 1996), pp 102, 253. **70.** *Irish News*, 16 Nov. 1990. **71.** Ibid. **72.** Ibid. **73.** Comments by Martin McGuinness at a Sinn Féin press conference on 13 Nov. 1989. **74.** The ousting of Thatcher as leader of the Conservative Party at the end of Nov. and her replacement by John Major saw Peter Brooke retain his NIO position and no change of policy. **75.** Bloomfield, *Dialogue in Northern Ireland*, p. 56. **76.** A suspicion confirmed when, in a statement on 4 Jan., Paisley reverted to the 'substantial' progress demand (*Irish Times*, 5 Jan. 1991). **77.** Copy of draft in author's possession. **78.** Press release from the Northern Ireland Information Service, 26 Mar. 1991. **79.** Ibid. **80.** Statement by Secretary of State Peter Brooke to the House of Commons 26 Mar. 1991, *Irish Times*, 27 Mar. 1991. **81.** Ibid. The actual gap was announced at an Anglo-Irish Conference meeting on 9 Apr. It was to last from 26 Apr. until the following conference meeting on 16 July. **82.** In several other attacks, the drivers either escaped in time, or the bombs did not explode.

CHAPTER 14

1. Brooke-Mayhew: when Peter Brooke was succeeded by Patrick Mayhew as secretary of state and he continued the talks. **2.** *Irish Times*, 12 Apr. 1991. **3.** *Irish Times*, 11 May 1991. **4.** Ibid. **5.** *Irish Times*, 6 June 1991. Former Governor General of Australia, Sir Ninian Stephen, would soon accept the joint British-Irish invitation to act as chair. **6.** At a rally to commemorate Bobby Sands, Gerry Adams condemned his party's exclusion, claiming its electoral mandate entitled the party to participation (*Irish News*, 5 May 1991). **7.** Among the attacks was one at a Cookstown estate on 26 May that damaged over 100 houses, and another on 9 June 1991 at Donacloney, where the PIRA alleged security force members resided. **8.** The SDLP delegates were John Hume, Séamus Mallon, Eddie McGrady, Joe Hendron, Denis Haughey, Seán Farren, Mark Durkan, Bríd Rodgers, Alban Maginness, Frank Feely and Donovan McClelland. **9.** *Speech of John Hume to the first plenary session of Strand 1 of the talks* (SDLP, June 1991). **10.** SDLP, *SDLP Analysis of the nature of the problem* (1991). **11.** Ibid., paras 25–32. **12.** Ibid., para. 3. **13.** Ibid., para. 15. **14.** *Submission by Dr Ian Paisley MP, MEP at plenary session of Strand 1 talks*, June 1990. **15.** Ibid., p. 4. **16.** Unionist Party Presentation to Strand 1 talks, June 1991. **17.** SDLP, *Requirements for new structures* (1991). **18.** SDLP press statement, 3 July 1991; *Irish News*, 4 July 1991. **19.** There was continued speculation throughout the autumn of 1991 and early months of 1992 about a Unionist Party deal with the Conservatives should the latter need support in the new parliament. **20.** Paisley was insistent on an entirely new set of ground rules including the complete suspension of the Anglo-Irish Secretariat, *Irish Times*, 17 July 1991. Molyneaux denounced Brooke's 'futile summitry' at his party's annual conference, and suggested reform of procedures for dealing with Northern Ireland at Westminster (*Irish Times*, 28–9 Oct.). **21.** In Dec. the Unionist leaders indicated that they would not give a prior commitment to participating in talks should Labour win the election, despite an assurance from Labour Spokesperson on Northern Ireland that his party would continue the process (Bloomfield, *Dialogue in Northern Ireland*, p. 155). **22.** Deaths from violence increased from 76 in 1990 to 94 in 1991, with several PIRA attacks taking place in Britain. **23.** Frank Millar, 'Unionists not solely to blame for end of talks', *Irish Times*, 4 July 1991. **24.** The SDLP was due to table its proposals for the government of Northern Ireland on Monday 1 July, but given the increasing likelihood of the talks ending within days, decided not to ('Back to the void', *Sunday Times*, 7 July 1991). **25.** *Irish Times*, 5 July 1991. **26.** Bloomfield, *Dialogue in Northern Ireland*, p. 154. **27.** *Sunday Tribune*, 24 Nov. 1991. **28.** SDLP, *Agenda, twenty-first annual conference*, p. 32. **29.** The premises acquired turned out to be far more extravagant and expensive than the party really needed and became a severe drain on finances. **30.** SDLP, *Agenda, twenty-first annual conference*, p. 28. **31.** Ibid., motion 3, p. 14. **32.** Ibid. **33.** Ibid., motion 68, p. 18. **34.** The by-elections were in Ballycastle, Belfast and Tyrone and, while not winning the seat in all three, the party's vote held up very well, especially in the first two. **35.** Speech by John Hume, SDLP party leader, to the twenty-first annual conference, SDLP (n.d.), p. 12. The party's proposals would draw heavily on the European framework and would prove highly controversial when revealed at the resumed talks in 1992. **36.** Ibid., p. 10. **37.** Ibid. **38.** *Irish News*, 3 Jan. 1992. **39.** Ibid. **40.** Bloomfield, *Dialogue in Northern Ireland*, pp 157–8. **41.** Statement issued by Prime Minister John Major following a meeting with the four party leaders in London on 11 Feb. 1992 (*The Times*, 12 Feb. 1992). **42.** Statement by the four party leaders following their meeting in Belfast (*Irish News*, 29 Feb. 1992). **43.** Bloomfield, *Dialogue in Northern Ireland*, p. 164. **44.** SDLP, *A new North, a new Ireland, a new Europe* (1992), p. 1. **45.** The Unionist vote was 6.7% down on the 1987 election, a strong indication that many Unionists had voted tactically for Hendron to deny Adams the seat. **46.** *Irish News*, 7 Feb. 1992. **47.** Ibid. **48.** Mary Holland, 'The danger of denying Sinn Féin a place at the table', *Irish Times*, 30 Apr. 1992. **49.** The announcement was made at a meeting of the Intergovernmental Conference in London on 27 Apr., at which the Irish government insisted the 1920 Government of Ireland Act be on the agenda, if Articles 2 and 3 of the Irish constitution were to be discussed. **50.** *Record of a plenary session held at Parliament Buildings on the morning of 29 Apr. 1992* (copy in author's possession). **51.** SDLP, *Agreeing new political structures*, submission to the Strand 1 talks, May 1992, para. 3. This submission was based on documents first drawn up for the party in May 1991 (copies in author's possession). **52.** Ibid., para. 7. **53.** Ibid., paras 16–17. **54.** SDLP memorandum, 25 May 1992 (copy in author's possession). **55.** Ibid., para. 4. **56.** Speaking notes for John Hume when presenting SDLP proposals (copy in author's possession). **57.** Ibid., para. 5. **58.** *Irish Times*, 26 May 1992. **59.** *Irish Times*, 14 May 1992. Taylor was speaking after the proposals had been leaked several days before their formal presentation at the talks. **60.** DUP, *Impediments to progress*, submission, 27 May 1992 (copy in author's possession). **61.** APNI, *An Alliance view of the Strand 1 problem*, submission, 27 May 1992 (copy in author's possession). **62.** *Irish News*, 4 Nov. 1992. **63.** Author's notes on Brooke-Mayhew talks. **64.** *Irish News*, 13 May 1992. **65.** *Sunday Times* reporter Liam Clarke quoted a 'senior' Dublin government source, 17 May 1992. **66.** *New political institutions in Northern Ireland: possible outline framework*, paper prepared by the secretary of state's talks team, 3 June 1992 (copy in author's possession). The SDLP was represented on the sub-committee, but the party's delegation did not endorse the compromise. **67.** Author's notes on talks, 2 June 1992. **68.** SDLP, *Progressing beyond Strand 1*, memorandum, June 1992 (copy in author's possession). **69.** *Irish Times*, 8 July 1992. **70.** *Secretary of State's statement to plenary*, 1 July 1992 (copy in author's possession). **71.** *Irish Times*, 8 July 1992. **72.** In exchanges on 16 July, Dessie O'Malley for the Irish government indicated that while the constitution needed to be revised it might be best to put amendments to a referendum as part of a package of proposals; notes from plenary session (copy in author's possession). **73.** *Report of a meeting of the Strand 2 committee*, 2 Sept. 1992, p. 2 (copy in author's possession). **74.** Ibid., p. 6. **75.** *Submission by the Irish government on constitutional issues to the Strand 2 talks*, Sept. 1992; reproduced in *Irish Times*, 15 Sept. 1992. **76.** SDLP, *North-South institutions*, proposals submitted, 29 Oct. 1992 (copy in author's possession). **77.** Ibid., para. 13. **78.** *Overcoming lack of adequate channels of communication and cooperation between North and South*, paper by HM's Government, Strand 2, 9 Sept. 1992; reproduced in *Irish Times*, 15 Sept. 1992. **79.** *Irish Times*, 28 Sept. 1992. New Consensus, consisting of a number of prominent public figures like Senator David Norris also advocated a similar commitment. However, another group styling itself the National Irish Congress, led by artist Robert Ballagh, strongly opposed any changes to Articles 2 and 3. **80.** *Strand 2: Issues arising from the discussion on possible institutional arrangement*, paper submitted to Strand 2 talks, 9 Oct. 1992 (copy in author's possession). **81.** The UUP proposed a Council of the British Isles consisting of representatives of the British, Irish and Northern Irish governments, which would contain an Inter-Irish Relations Committee to deal with North-South cooperation. *Submission by the Ulster Unionist Party to the Strand 2 Talks*, Oct. 1992. **82.** *Elements of a settlement*, paper prepared by the independent chairman, Nov. 1992 (copy in author's possession). **83.** Press statement, SDLP, 10 Nov. 1992. **84.** Former Minister Robert Molloy of the Progressive Democrats, Fianna Fáil's coalition partners and a talks delegate, accused Taoiseach Reynolds of 'hindering' the talks by his stand on the constitutional issue (*Irish Times*, 13 Nov. 1992). Paisley and APNI leader John Alderdice accused both Dublin and the SDLP for the breakdown (*Irish News*, 11 Nov. 1992).

CHAPTER 15

1. The conference took place over the weekend of 6–8 Nov., a few days before the formal closure of the Brooke-Mayhew talks. **2.** John Hume, *Address to the twenty-second annual conference* (Belfast, 1993). **3.** *Areas of agreement and disagreement*, paper submitted by the SDLP to Sir Ninian Stephen, Oct. 1992 (copy in author's possession). **4.** *Irish News*, 9 Nov. 1992. **5.** SDLP, 'Executive report' in *Agenda for twenty-second annual conference*. **6.** SDLP policy summaries, Oct. 1992 (copy in author's possession). **7.** *Irish News*, 24 Apr. 1993. **8.** *Irish Times*, 4 Mar. 1993. **9.** Mallie and McKittrick, *The fight for peace*, pp 371–80. **10.** Ibid., p. 7. **11.** A number of speeches by Sinn Féin leaders like Mitchel McLaughlin and Jim Gibney had begun to signal a possible shift in the party's thinking, e.g. to the effect that Unionists could not be coerced into a united Ireland. **12.** *Irish Times*, 26 Apr. 1993. **13.** Chris McGimpsey, 'Aspiring to the ideal of national unity minus the economic costs', *Irish Times*, 2 July 1993. **14.** Draft of a declaration which Sinn Féin suggests should be made jointly by the British and Irish governments, June 1992. Reproduced in Mallie and McKittrick, *The fight for peace*, pp 375–6. **15.** Author's note on meeting of the constituency representatives group, 27 Apr. 1993. **16.** Ibid., p. 119. **17.** Sammy Wilson, DUP press officer, *Irish Times*, 26 Apr. 1993. **18.** *Irish Times*, 26 Apr. 1993. **19.** *Irish Times*, 27 Apr. 1993. **20.** Quoted in Liam Clarke, 'Hume takes a direct hit in war of words', *Sunday Times*, 18 Apr. 1993. **21.** Quoted in *Phoenix*, 21 May 1993, p. 13. **22.** Timothy Parry's father Colin became a leading peace activist promoting reconciliation between Ireland and Britain. **23.** The attack was at the NatWest Tower in the city centre. **24.** *Irish News*, 19 Sept. 1993. **25.** *Irish News*, 21 Sept. 1993. **26.** Garret FitzGerald, 'Why John Hume was right to meet Gerry Adams', *Irish Times*, 17 Apr. 1993. **27.** *Irish Times*, 12 Apr. 1993. **28.** At the request of Fr Alec Reid, Taoiseach Albert Reynolds asked his adviser Martin Mansergh, to engage in further talks with Sinn Féin. A series of talks then began exploring similar issues to those being addressed in the Hume-Adams dialogue. **29.** *Irish Times*, 27 Apr. 1993. **30.** Editorial, *Irish Times*, 28 Apr. 1993. **31.** *Initiative '92*, was described as a citizens' inquiry. It was established by, among others, Robin Wilson, editor of *Fortnight*. Chaired by Norwegian international human rights lawyer, Torkel Opsahl, the commission took evidence in public and private from over 500 individuals and organizations and issued its findings 9 June 1993. **32.** Andy Pollak (ed.), *Initiative '92, a citizens' inquiry: the Opsahl Report on Northern Ireland* (Dublin, 1993), p. 49. **33.** Extract from June 1993 document drawn up by John Hume and reproduced in Mallie and McKittrick, *The fight for peace*, p. 379. **34.** Ibid., p. 3. **35.** SDLP, *Progress through partnership* (1993), p. 2. **36.** The narrow Conservative majority gave Unionists leverage over John Major that they were able to demonstrate in the vote on the Maastricht Treaty in July when UUP MPs pledged support for the government. **37.** *Sunday Independent*, 5 Sept. 1993. **38.** *Irish News*, 18 Sept. 1993. **39.** *Irish News*, 27 Sept. 1993. The joint statement was issued on Saturday 25 Sept. **40.** While an official from the Irish department of foreign affairs had met Hume a formal report had not been submitted. Hume eventually indicated that he would brief the Irish government on his return from the US. **41.** *Irish Times*, 28 Sept. 1993. **42.** Ibid. **43.** *Irish Times*, 27 Sept. 1993. **44.** Peter Robinson, *Irish Times*, 27 Sept. 1993. **45.** *Irish Times*, 27 Sept. 1993. **46.** Barry White interview with Sir Patrick Mayhew, *Belfast Telegraph*, 29 Sept. 1993. **47.** The most accessible version of the report is contained in an article by Geraldine Kennedy, *Irish Times*, 28 Oct. 1993. **48.** Mallie and McKittrick, *The fight for peace*, p. 193. **49.** HC, *Debates*, 22 Oct. 1993. **50.** *Irish Times*, 4 Nov. 1993. **51.** Editorial, *Independent*, 25 Oct. 1993. **52.** Dáil Éireann, *Debates*, 27 Oct. 1993. **53.** Ibid. **54.** Communiqué issued by Taoiseach Albert Reynolds and Prime Minister John Major following talks at Brussels, 29 Oct. 1993. **55.** Ibid. **56.** HC, *Debates*, 1 Nov. 1993. **57.** *Irish Times*, 5 Nov. 1993. **58.** *Sunday Independent*, Oct. 1993. **59.** *Guardian*, 10 Nov. 1993. **60.** *Sunday Tribune*, 31 Oct. 1993. **61.** *Irish Times*, 16 Nov. 1993. **62.** John Hume, *Speech to the SDLP's twenty-third annual conference* (1994). **63.** The correspondence covering the period from Feb. to Nov. 1993 was released by the British government on 29 Nov. 1993 and was reproduced, among other outlets, in the *Irish Times*, 30 Nov. 1993. **64.** Message from the leadership of the provisional movement, 22 July 1993. **65.** Message from British government to the Provisional PIRA, 5 Nov. 1993. **66.** Message from the British government to the provisional movement, 19 Mar. 1993. **67.** See the PIRA briefing paper *Totally unarmed strategy* issued in Apr. 1994, reproduced in Mallie and McKittrick, *The fight for peace*, p. 381. **68.** *Irish Times*, 3 Dec. 1993. **69.** Commonly referred to as the *Downing Street Declaration*, it was issued by both premiers on 17 Dec. 1993. **70.** Ibid., par 10. **71.** Ibid. **72.** Ibid., para. 11. **73.** HC, *Debates*, 15 Dec. 1993. **74.** *Irish News*, 16 Dec. 1993. **75.** Ibid. **76.** *Irish Times*, 16 Dec. 1993, report by Maol Mhuire Tynan on Sinn Féin reaction. **77.** *Irish Times*, 22 Dec. 1993, article by Dick Grogan entitled 'Adams seeks direct talks with government on declaration'. **78.** The survey was conducted for ITN (Independent Television News) and was reported in *Irish Times*, Dec. 1993.

CHAPTER 16

1. Mary Holland, *Irish Times*, 30 Dec. 1993. **2.** Deaglán de Bréadún, *Irish Times*, 5 Jan. 1994. **3.** John Hume, 'A new door opens for the people of Ireland', *Irish News*, 5 Jan. 1994. **4.** HC, *Debates*, 21 Jan. 1994. **5.** Ibid. **6.** Text of letter from Gerry Adams to John Major, 7 Jan. 1994, reproduced in *Irish Times*, 22 Jan. 1994. **7.** John Hume, 'New ways of coming together in peace', *Irish Times*, 31 Jan. 1994. **8.** Ibid. **9.** Address by Martin McGuinness to Sinn Féin conference, *Irish Times*, 28 Feb. 1994. **10.** The visit was highly controversial given British and US State Department's opposition to granting Adams a visa while leading Irish-American politicians and John Hume were in favour. **11.** On 9, 11 and 13 Mar., the PIRA launched several mortar-bombs at the airport, most of which did not explode. **12.** Report and notes of meeting of the SDLP's constituency representative group meeting held in the O'Neill Arms Hotel, Toomebridge, Sunday 6 Mar. 1994 (copy in author's possession). **13.** Among the councillors whose homes were attacked were Donovan McClelland (Antrim), party vice-chair Jonathan Stephenson, and his colleague Dorita Field (Belfast). **14.** John Fee was an outspoken critic of the PIRA and had severely criticized a mortar-bomb attack on the town's police station shortly before he himself was attacked. **15.** *Irish News*, 2 May 1994. **16.** Conor O'Clery, *Irish Times*, 17 Mar. 1994. **17.** Conor O'Clery, *Irish Times*, 19 Mar. 1994. **18.** SDLP, *Towards a new century* (1994). **19.** SDLP, *The implications of the single market* (1992). **20.** Party members like Denis Haughey, Bríd Rodgers and Seán Farren participated regularly in several PES working groups on such matters as the manifesto, gender issues and economic development. **21.** The Sinn Féin candidates were Tom Hartley, Dodie McGuinness and Francie Molloy. **22.** Text of Sinn Féin motions adopted at the party's special conference, *Irish Times*, 25 July 1994. **23.** Ibid. **24.** *Irish Times*, 25 July 1994. **25.** Ibid. **26.** Ibid. **27.** Statement from Downing Street, *Irish Times*, 26 July 1994. For several months Michael Ancram, NIO minister, held bilateral talks with the Unionist parties, Alliance and SDLP, while the two governments worked on a framework document drawing on discussions at the Brooke-Mayhew talks. **28.** In July, the PIRA murdered three people and attempted to assassinate DUP MP Revd William McCrea. **29.** Séamus Mallon, *End violence now or be removed from the peace process*, press statement, 18 Aug. 1994 (copy in author's possession). **30.** Mallie and McKittrick, *The fight for peace*, pp 320–2. **31.** While there was no formal guarantee, it was clear that Sinn Féin saw in the US government a form of external support that it could use to bolster its position in the political negotiations that would follow a ceasefire. **32.** *Irish News*, 29 Aug. 1994. **33.** Joint statement by John Hume and Gerry Adams issued 28 Aug. 1994. **34.** In an interview with Frank Millar, *Irish Times*, 21 Nov. 1994, Adams argued that while the SDLP proposal for dual referenda 'would not constitute self-determination for the Irish people', they would constitute 'a very worthwhile way of measuring agreement, on whatever had to be agreed'. **35.** Statement from the leadership of the PIRA 31 Aug. 1994. **36.** *Irish News*, 1 Sept. 1994. **37.** In Belfast on 21 Oct., Major also announced the lifting of exclusion from Britain orders on Adams and McGuinness, and that cross-border road-blocks would be removed. **38.** On 13 Oct., the Combined Loyalist Military Command (CLMC) declared an end to all loyalist paramilitary campaigns and expressed remorse to 'the loved ones of all innocent victims over the past twenty-five years' (*Irish News*, 14 Oct. 1994). **39.** *Irish Times*, 21 Sept. 1994. **40.** Conor O'Clery, *Irish Times*, 20 Sept. 1994. **41.** *Irish Times*, 1 Sept. 1994. **42.** European Parliament, *Proceedings of the European Parliament*, 29 Sept. 1994. **43.** In the following months, Hume received awards from, among others, the Pio Manzu International Centre, the International League for Human Rights and Dublin City University. **44.** *Irish Times*, 5 Oct. 1994. **45.** The three-person working party consisted of Hugh Logue, Howard McNally and Robert Ramsey, all from Northern Ireland and European Commission officials. **46.** *SDLP proposals to President Delors' NI task-force*, Oct. 1994 (copy in author's possession). **47.** *Irish Times*, 10 Dec. 1994. **48.** The SDLP delegation, including alternates, consisted of John Hume, Séamus Mallon, Eddie McGrady, Joe Hendron, Bríd Rodgers, Seán Farren, Denis Haughey, Mark Durkan, John Fee and Alex Attwood. **49.** *Proceedings of the Forum for peace and reconciliation*, vol. 1, 28 Oct. 1994. **50.** Paper presented by Eddie McGrady MP to the Forum for Peace and Reconciliation, 18 Nov. 1994 (copy in author's possession). **51.** SDLP, *Agenda for the twenty-fourth annual conference* (1994). **52.** *Irish News*, 19 Nov. 1994. **53.** *Irish Times*, 21 Nov. 1994. **54.** Ibid.

CHAPTER 17

1. *Belfast Telegraph*, 2 Sept. 1994. The 70–30 split suggests that most Unionists were sceptical of the ceasefire's permanence, and that most Nationalists viewed it positively. **2.** While acknowledging that its members were involved, the PIRA claimed the robbery and murder were unauthorized (*Irish News*, 11 Nov. 1994). **3.**

Irish Times, 1 Dec. 1994. **4.** *Irish News*, 15 Dec. 1994. A further sign of its gradualist approach was the Secretary of State's refusal to extend invitations to Sinn Féin to attend the investment conference, agreeing only to offer personal invitations to a number of councillors, which were declined. **5.** Interview with James Naughtie on the BBC's *Today* programme, 30 Dec. 1994. **6.** Interview with Taoiseach John Bruton, *Sunday Tribune*, 18 Dec. 1994. **7.** *Irish Times*, 13 Jan. 1995. **8.** For several months, officials from both governments had been drafting a document that would set out the constitutional and institutional parameters within which the parties would be invited to agree a form of government for Northern Ireland and arrangements for North-South cooperation. **9.** HC, *Debates*, 22 Feb. 1995. **10.** Ibid. **11.** Ibid. **12.** *Frameworks for the future*, published by the Irish and British governments, 22 Feb. 1995. **13.** Ibid., pt B, para. 13(b). **14.** *News Letter*, 11 Mar. 1995. **15.** Major's initial Conservative majority in the House of Commons (21) was slim and with growing dissension over European policies was reducing; the UUP MPs offered a margin on which Major became increasingly dependent. **16.** *Irish Times*, 23 Feb. 1995. **17.** *Irish Times*, 8 Mar. 1995. **18.** The meetings commenced on 13 Apr. when the SDLP held separate meetings with the UUP and the DUP. **19.** Mark Durkan in *Proceedings of the Forum for peace and reconciliation*, 9 June 1995. **20.** Forum for Peace and Reconciliation, *Paths to a settlement in Ireland: realities, principles and requirement* (1996). **21.** HC, *Debates*, 6 July 1995. The suggestion that an international arbitrator should be appointed was being made by several sources, notably the Irish government with the further suggestion that the arbitrator should be from the US. **22.** John Mayor was under such pressure from anti-EU Tories that he resigned to force a leadership election, which he won. **23.** At Drumcree, a stand-off developed when thousands of Orangemen congregated to support their local members who were being blocked from parading down the Garvaghy Road, a predominantly Catholic area. Elsewhere, Catholic church property and Orange halls were attacked and damaged. **24.** In early Sept., the Irish government cancelled a summit meeting between Major and Bruton when officials could not agree a compromise on decommissioning. **25.** *Irish Times*, 23 Sept. 1995. **26.** The SDLP's proposals were presented by Hume and Mallon at a press conference, 8 Nov. 1995 (*Irish Times*, 9 Nov. 1995). **27.** Prime Minister and Taoiseach, *Joint communiqué: the twin-track initiative*, Downing Street, 28 Nov. 1995. **28.** Ibid. **29.** *Irish Times*, 6 Dec. 1995. **30.** *Irish Times*, 8 Dec. 1995. **31.** *Irish News*, 5 Dec. 1995. **32.** Taoiseach John Bruton hoped all parties would adopt an open-minded approach to the proposal (*Irish Times*, 5 Dec. 1995). **33.** *Irish News*, 18 Nov. 1995. **34.** *Irish Times*, 20 Nov. 1995. **35.** Ibid. **36.** Ibid. **37.** *Report of the International Body on Decommissioning*, 22 Jan. 1996 (*Irish Times*, 23 Jan. 1996). **38.** Ibid., para. 25. **39.** Ibid., para. 20. **40.** Ibid., para. 56. **41.** HC, 24 Jan. 1996, cols 355, 359. **42.** Ibid. **43.** Peter Robinson offered to 'meet with Mr Hume to discuss how his fears of a democratically elected assembly might be overcome' (*Irish Times*, 25 Jan. 1996). **44.** *Belfast Telegraph*, 1 Feb. 1996. **45.** *Irish Times*, 25 Jan. 1996. **46.** *Independent*, 14 Feb. 1996. **47.** SDLP, *Discussion paper on the elective process*, 29 Mar. 1996 (copy in author's possession). **48.** Prime Minister and Taoiseach, *Anglo/Irish communiqué for summit*, Downing Street, 28 Feb. 1996. **49.** HC, *Debates*, 28 Feb. 1996. **50.** Gerry Adams, *An Irish voice: the quest for peace* (Dingle, 1997), pp 203–11. **51.** *Irish News*, 29 Feb. 1996. **52.** Ibid. **53.** HC, *Debates*, 28 Feb. 1996. **54.** British and Irish Government, *Ground rules for substantive all-party negotiations*, 15 Mar. 1996. **55.** Ibid., para. 6. **56.** Minutes of SDLP Central Council meeting, 30 Mar. 1996 (copy in author's possession). **57.** *Irish Times*, 1 Apr. 1996. **58.** British government, *The framework for a broadly acceptable elective process leading to all-party negotiations*, 21 Mar. 1996. **59.** *Irish News*, 2 Apr. 1996. **60.** Ibid. **61.** A barrister of considerable repute, McCartney was an MP for North Down who had previously been a member of the UUP. A notable recruit to the UKUP was Conor Cruise O'Brien, who now espoused the Unionist cause. **62.** SDLP statement at launch of election campaign, 20 May 1996 (copy in author's possession). **63.** Interview with Denis Haughey, 19 Dec. 2009.

CHAPTER 18

1. The DUP and UKUP were both obliged to do likewise when they rejoined the talks the next day. **2.** Other areas to experience confrontation over parades included Dunloy, Co. Antrim, Derry city, and the Ormeau Road and Ardoyne in Belfast. **3.** Gerry Moriarty, *Irish Times*, 12 July 1996. **4.** *Irish News*, 15 July 1996. Taken at a special meeting of executive and forum members, the decision to resign as opposed to a temporary withdrawal was agreed by one vote (author's notes). **5.** *Irish News*, 15 June 1997. **6.** Following police action that prevented an Orange Order parade at Dunloy, loyalists in Ballymena mounted a picket outside the Catholic church at Harryville during Saturday evening mass. The picket was maintained until May 1998. Other churches picketed for a time were at Bushmills and Dervock. **7.** PIRA attacks included two car-bombs inside Lisburn army barracks, which injured over thirty people, while loyalist paramilitaries murdered a taxi driver, Michael McGoldrick, at Portadown. **8.** Author's notes on talks, June–Dec. 1996. **9.** *Agenda for the remainder of the opening plenary session*, 15 Oct. 1997. **10.** *Draft record of the opening plenary* session of the multi-party talks, 22 Oct. 1996.   **11.** *Statement on decommissioning by the SDLP*, 28 Oct. 1996 (copy in author's possession).   **12.** Ibid.   **13.** *Draft record of the opening plenary of the multi-party talks*, 18 Dec. 1996.   **14.** *Draft record of the opening plenary of the multi-party talks*, 5 Mar. 1997; this report provides summary statements of the different party positions on the impasse.   **15.** Letter from John Major to John Hume, *Irish Times*, 29 Nov. 1996.   **16.** Statements from the Irish government and from the White House, *Irish Times*, 29 Nov. 1996.   **17.** *Irish Times*, 4 Jan. 1997.   **18.** *Irish Times*, 9 Nov. 1996.   **19.** *Irish News*, 11 Nov. 1996.   **20.** Motion 136 from the Balmoral branch, *Agenda for the twenty-sixth annual conference*.   **21.** A reference to the eighteenth-century secret and exclusively Catholic, agrarian, militant society.   **22.** *Irish Times*, 11 Nov. 1996.   **23.** *Irish Times*, 6 Jan. 1997.   **24.** *Irish News*, 20 Feb. 1997.   **25.** The Independent Commission on Parades chaired by Dr Peter North of Oxford University, was established in July to advise on the management of controversial parades.   **26.** SDLP submission to the independent commission on parades, Nov. 1996.   **27.** John Hume together with local business and community representatives initiated a dialogue with the leadership of the Apprentice Boys to defuse tensions and to ensure peaceful parades for the latter.   **28.** *The report of the Independent Review of parades and marches* (HMSO, 1997).   **29.** *Irish Times*, 25 Feb. 1997.   **30.** SDLP, *Real leadership, real peace* (1997).   **31.** David McKittrick, 'How balance of power shifted from Unionists', *Irish News*, 29 May 1997.   **32.** *Irish News*, 17 May 1997.   **33.** Ibid.   **34.** Programme for the workshop, *South Africa negotiations: lessons learned*, 30 May–2 June 1997. The workshop was organized by Prof. Pádraig O'Malley of the McCormack Institute, University of Massachusetts, and the government of South Africa.   **35.** The vote in favour of Maginness was 26, against 22 for his DUP rival; his supporters included some independent Unionist councillors.   **36.** *Irish Times*, 3 June 1997.   **37.** Following general elections earlier in June, there had been a change of government in Dublin; a Fianna Fáil-Progressive Democrats coalition led by Bertie Ahern had taken office.   **38.** HC, *Debates*, 25 June 1997.   **39.** Ibid.   **40.** Author's notes on meeting, 7 July 1997.   **41.** *Irish News*, 10 July 1997.   **42.** The Orange Order announced that parades along the Ormeau Road in Belfast would be cancelled, that the Derry parade would be switched to Limavady, and that other parades would be re-routed.   **43.** *Irish Times*, 17 July 1997.   **44.** In a letter to Sinn Féin dated 9 July, the British government had indicated that following a ceasefire the only requirement would be full compliance with the Mitchell principles. Letter released to media on 18 July.   **45.** *Draft Record of the opening plenary session of the multi-party talks*, 23 July 1997.   **46.** Borrowed from the South African negotiations, the term implied significant support from both Unionist and Nationalist parties.   **47.** Among those consulted were leading members of the Catholic Church. Generally, the advice from all sources was for the UUP to remain in the talks.   **48.** In an interview with the *Washington Post*, 5 Aug. 1997, Hume gave the impression that he was seriously considering the possibility.   **49.** *Irish News*, 8 Sept. 1997.   **50.** Following the summer recess, the UUP did not rejoin the plenary sessions until 23 Sept. 1997.   **51.** *Draft record of the opening plenary session of the multi-party talks*, 23 Sept. 1997.   **52.** *Draft record of the opening plenary session of the multi-party talks*, 24 Sept. 1997 and *Irish Times*, 25 Sept. 1997.   **53.** *Opening statement by John Hume at the launch of Strand 1*, and *Opening statement by Séamus Mallon at the launch of Strand 2*, 7 Oct. 1997.   **54.** *SDLP submissions to the multi-party talks 1997*, a compendium of key party documents (copy in author's possession).   **55.** Author's notes of plenary sessions during Nov. and Dec. 1997.   **56.** The year ended with a total of 22 violent deaths, and 1998 opened with 6 more in Jan.   **57.** The UDP was formally expelled on 26 Jan. and Sinn Féin on 20 Feb.   **58.** *Summary record of plenary session*, Dublin Castle, 10 Feb. 1998.   **59.** *Peace in Ireland*, a Sinn Féin submission to Strands 1 and 2 of the peace talks, 17 Oct. 1997.   **60.** Author's notes on inter-party talks.   **61.** Seán Farren, address to the Ballycastle branch, *Ireland on Sunday*, 8 Feb. 1998.   **62.** In an *Ireland on Sunday* article, 8 Mar. 1998, outlining Sinn Féin proposals, Gerry Adams made no mention of an assembly. At a meeting with the SDLP, Sinn Féin argued that it could not accept an assembly and urged their regional councils proposal (author's notes on meeting).   **63.** See article by Sinn Féin in *Irish News*, 2 Feb. and reply by John Hume, *Irish News*, 3 Feb. 1998.   **64.** *Propositions on heads of agreement*, paper from the British and Irish governments, 12 Jan. 1998 (copy in author's possession).   **65.** Draft paper for discussion, 6 Apr. 1998 (copy in author's possession).   **66.** The paper circulated on 7 Apr. was rejected by the UUP, one of whose negotiators, John Taylor, says he 'wouldn't touch it with a forty-foot barge pole'.   **67.** The agreement simply required parties (para. 3 Decommissioning) 'to use any influence they may have, to achieve the decommissioning of all paramilitary arms within two years following endorsement in referendums ... of the agreement ...', a formula which was far from stating the absolute requirement sought by the UUP.   **68.** Among those who withdrew was Jeffrey Donaldson, who became a prominent opponent of the agreement.   **69.** John Hume, 10 Apr. 1998, quoted in the SDLP manifesto for the referendum on the Good Friday Agreement.

CHAPTER 19
1. Although the UUP executive endorsed the agreement 55–23, two MPs, William Ross and William Thompson, were among those who strongly opposed it. At the special Sinn Féin ard fheis, a vote of over 96% of delegates did likewise.   **2.** Organized in record time, the concert was the brain-child of SDLP official, Tim Attwood. The artists gave their services free and tickets were widely distributed to schools and youth organizations.   **3.** Ronan McCay, 'A night to remember', in SDLP *News Review '98*.   **4.** 81% of the electorate voted. An estimated 55% of Unionists voted in favour while 96% of Nationalists did.   **5.** SDLP, *A positive approach* (1998), p. 1.   **6.** Ibid.   **7.** Ibid., p. 8.   **8.** Ibid., p. 9.   **9.** Ibid., p. 7.   **10.** According to the agreement, the transition period was to be completed by 31 Oct. 1998. At the launch of his party's manifesto, Trimble dismissed the possibility of meeting that deadline (*Irish Times*, 10 June 1998).   **11.** UUP, *Manifesto for the assembly elections* (1998).   **12.** The New Northern Ireland Assembly was its official title until devolution.   **13.** NIA, *Debates*, 1 July 1998, p. 30.   **14.** This was their second appearance together in such tragic circumstances. The previous March, both leaders had visited the families of two young men, a Catholic and a Protestant, shot dead by loyalist paramilitaries in a pub in Poynzpass, Co. Armagh.   **15.** NIA, *Debates*, 26 Oct. 1998.   **16.** Para. 3, 'Decommissioning' section of *The agreement reached in the multi-party negotiations*, 10 Apr. 1998.   **17.** The Department of Education was divided in two with the creation of the Department for Employment and Learning, which was given responsibility for higher education and training.   **18.** Seán Farren, NIA, *Debates*, 18 Jan. 1999.   **19.** Seán Farren, NIA, *Debates*, 15 Dec. 1998.   **20.** SDLP, *Proposals for areas of cooperation and implementation bodies*, Sept. 1998 (copy in author's possession).   **21.** It was understood, though never formally stated, that the South's Industrial Development Authority (IDA) was strongly opposed to the proposal.   **22.** *Irish Times*, 4 Dec. 1998.   **23.** *Irish News*, 19 Dec. 1998.   **24.** John Hume, *A future together*, address to the twenty-eighth annual conference, 14 Nov. 1998.   **25.** SDLP, *Agenda of the twenty-eighth annual conference* (1998).   **26.** Séamus Mallon, address to the SDLP's annual cnference, *Irish Times*, 14 Nov. 1998.   **27.** *The agreement reached in the multi-party negotiations*, 10 Apr. 1998, para. 25, Strand 1, pp 7–8.   **28.** *Irish Times*, 14 Nov. 1998.   **29.** The full text of both speeches was reproduced in the *Irish Times*, 11 Dec. 1998.   **30.** *Irish Times*, 11 Dec. 1998.   **31.** *Irish News*, 12 Dec. 1998.   **32.** New Northern Ireland Assembly, *Debates*, 18 Jan. 1999.   **33.** *Sunday Times*, 14 Feb. 1999.   **34.** NIA, *Debates*, 16 Feb. 1999.   **35.** *Joint declaration by the British and Irish governments*, Hillsborough, 1 Apr. 1999.   **36.** Ibid.   **37.** According to the original agreement, ministerial appointments did not require assembly approval.   **38.** *Irish News*, 1 Apr. 1999.   **39.** *Irish News*, 21 Apr. 1999.   **40.** Hume announced his proposal on the BBC's *Inside Politics* radio programme, 24 Apr. 1999.   **41.** *Irish Times*, 17 May 1999.   **42.** Dean Godson, *Himself alone: David Trimble* (London, 2004), ch. 27.   **43.** *Irish Times*, 12 June 1999.   **44.** *Irish Times*, 30 June 1999.   **45.** Statement by the British and Irish governments, 2 July 1999.   **46.** Godson, *Himself alone*, ch. 28.   **47.** The SDLP members nominated were Mark Durkan, Seán Farren, Bríd Rodgers, Denis Haughey, Joe Hendron and Alban Maginness. Eddie McGrady declined his nomination as minister.   **48.** NIA, *Debates*, 15 July 1999.   **49.** Ibid.   **50.** Mitchell was contacted that same day and agreed to conduct the review.   **51.** Godson, *Himself alone*, ch. 28.   **52.** SDLP, *Submission to the Commission on Policing* (1998).   **53.** The Independent Commission on Policing for Northern Ireland, *A new beginning: policing in Northern Ireland* (1999).   **54.** *Irish Times*, 10 Sept. 1999.   **55.** Leading Sinn Féin members Pat Doherty and Martin Ferris were reported, in separate comments made in the US, as suggesting that the governments would not dare suspend the institutions even if decommissioning did not happen, Godson, *Himself alone*, p. 522.   **56.** *Irish Times*, 21 Oct. 1999.   **57.** Frank McNally, *Irish Times*, 6 Nov. 1999.   **58.** *Irish Times*, 6 Nov. 1999.   **59.** SDLP, *Innovation, investment and social justice: a framework for economic development*, Nov. 1999.   **60.** Hume had been taken to hospital in Austria where he had been attending a conference and had been obliged to rest for several weeks.   **61.** *Irish News*, 8 Nov. 1999.   **62.** *Irish Times*, 16 Nov. 1999.   **63.** HC, *Debates*, 23 Nov. 1999.   **64.** Godson, *Himself alone*, p. 551.   **65.** See Strand 1, *Safeguards*, para. 5 (d) (ii), parallel consent: 'a majority of those members present and voting including a majority of the Unionist and Nationalist designation present and voting'.   **66.** NIA, *Debates*, 30 Nov. 1999.   **67.** *Report of the Independent International Commission on Decommissioning*, Feb. 2000.   **68.** In 2003, the SDLP won 18 seats, Sinn Féin 24, the DUP 30 and the UUP 27; in 2007 these parties won 16, 28, 36 and 18 respectively.

Bibliography

OFFICIAL PUBLICATIONS

Ireland

Anglo-Irish Agreement (Dublin, 1985).

Anglo-Irish Agreement: review of the working of the conference (Dublin, 1989).

Anglo- Fish joint studies: reports presented to both houses of the Oireachtas (Dublin, 1981).

Forum for Peace and Reconciliation, *Paths to a settlement in Ireland: realities, principles and requirements* (Dublin, 1996).

Frameworks for the future (Dublin, 1995).

New Ireland Forum, *Proceedings of the New Ireland Forum, 1983–4* (Dublin, 1984).

New Ireland Forum, *Report: studies and reports on specific matters* (Dublin, 1984).

New Ireland Forum, *The economic consequences of the division of Ireland since 1920* (Dublin, 1983).

Proceedings of the Forum for Peace and Reconciliation, vol. 1 (Dublin, 1994).

Report of the International Body on Decommissioning (Dublin, 1996).

Seanad Éireann, *Debates* (Dublin, 1984).

The Agreement (Dublin, 1998).

United Kingdom

A new beginning: policing in Northern Ireland, report of the independent commission on policing in Northern Ireland (Patten Report) (Belfast, 1999).

Fair Employment (Northern Ireland) Act (London, 1976).

Fair Employment (Northern Ireland) Act (London, 1989).

House of Commons, *Debates*, 1970–2000.

Northern Ireland: a framework for devolution (Belfast, 1982).

Northern Ireland Assembly, *Debates*, 1973–4.

Northern Ireland Assembly, *Debates*, 1998–9.

Northern Ireland Constitutional Convention, Report (Belfast, 1975).

Northern Ireland constitutional proposals (Belfast, 1973).

Northern Ireland House of Commons, *Debates*, 1970–2.

Public Order (Northern Ireland) Act (London, 1987).

Report of the committee of inquiry into police interrogation procedures in Northern Ireland (Bennett report) (Belfast, 1979).

Report of the independent review of parades and marches (North report) (Belfast, 1997).

Report of the tribunal appointed to inquire into the events on Sunday, 30 January 1972, which led to the loss of life in connection wit the procession in Londonderry on that day (Widgery report) (London, 1972).

Report on the Advisory Committee on Police in Northern Ireland (Hunt report) (Belfast, 1969).
Report on the future of teacher education in Northern Ireland (Belfast, 1980).
Review body on local government in Northern Ireland (Macrory report) (Belfast, 1970).
Steps to a better tomorrow (Belfast, 1974).
Sunningdale's twenty points to peace (Belfast, 1974).
The future of Northern Ireland: a paper for discussion (Belfast, 1972).
The government of Northern Ireland: a society divided (Belfast, 1975).
The government of Northern Ireland: proposals for further discussion (Belfast, 1980).
The Northern Ireland Assembly Disqualification Act (1975).
The Northern Ireland Constitution (Belfast, 1974).

POLITICAL PARTY PUBLICATIONS

SDLP
A new North, a new Ireland, a new Europe (1992).
Address of party leader John Hume to the 22nd annual conference (1992).
Agenda for annual conferences (1971–99).
An examination of land-use (1976).
Another step forward with SDLP (1974).
Economic analysis and strategy (1976).
Education: the need for reform (1975).
Equal and just opportunities for employment (1986).
Facing reality (1977).
Innovation, investment and social justice: a framework for economic development (1999).
Justice in Northern Ireland (1985).
Know where you stand, manifesto (1977).
Local government 1977 (1976).
Make a difference, manifesto (1989).
Manifesto for the District Council elections (1985).
Manifesto for the European elections (1989).
New North: new Ireland (1973).
Northern Ireland constitutional proposals: a critique by the Social Democratic and Labour Party (1973).
One strong voice (1974).
Opportunity for excellence (1976).
Options for a new Ireland, proceedings of the Grattan conference, 1982.
Partnership in Ireland (1976).
Poverty in an age of affluence and other papers, proceedings of a conference (1980).
Poverty in Northern Ireland (1976).
Progress through partnership, manifesto (1993).
Proposals for cross-border co-operation (1990).
Proposals for government in Northern Ireland: report to parliament (1975).
Putting people first, manifesto (1999).

Real leadership real peace, manifesto (1997).
Response to the Higher Education Review Group's recommendations for the future of teacher education in Northern Ireland (1980).
SDLP: a positive approach, manifesto (1998).
SDLP News Review '98 (1998).
SDLP response to possible scenarios (1989).
Social Democrat (an occasional SDLP newspaper).
Speak with strength (1975).
Speech by John Hume to the SDLP's 21st annual conference (1992).
Speech by John Hume to the SDLP's 18th annual conference (1988).
Stand firm (1982).
Strategy for peace (1980).
Strengthen your voice (1979).
Submission on the review of the Anglo-Irish Agreement (1988).
Submission to the Commission on Policing (1998).
The Anglo-Irish Agreement and the completion of the single market (1989).
The form and doubling of the European structural funds: a new opportunity for the economy of Northern Ireland (1988).
The implications of the single market (1992).
The implications of the single market for Northern Ireland (1988).
The SDLP analysis of the nature of the problem (1991).
Towards a new century, manifesto (1994).
Towards a new Ireland: a policy review (1979).
Towards a new Ireland (1972).

Sinn Féin
A scenario for peace (1987).
Persuading the British: a joint call (1988).
Setting the record straight (1994).
Sinn Féin and national self-determiniation and a proposal for joint action on fair employment (1988).
Towards a strategy for peace (1988).

Unionist parties
Democratic Unionist Party, *The Unionist case: the Forum Report answered* (1984).
New Ulster Political Research Group, *Common sense* (1987).
Ulster Loyalist Central Coordinating Committee, *Ulster can survive unfettered* (1976).
Ulster Unionist Assembly Party, *The way forward* (1984).
Ulster Unionist Party, *Manifesto for the assembly elections* (1998).
Ulster Unionist Party, *Manifesto for the convention* (1974).
Unionist Task-Force, *An end to drift* (1987).

NEWSPAPERS AND JOURNALS

Belfast Telegraph	*Irish Press*
Boston Globe	*Irish Times*
Daily Mirror	*News Letter*
Education Times	*Phoenix*
Financial Times	*Sunday Independent*
Guardian	*Sunday News*
Hibernia	*Sunday Press*
Hot Press	*Sunday Times*
Independent (London)	*Sunday Tribune*
Irish Independent	*The Times*
Irish News	*This Week*
Ireland on Sunday	

BOOKS

Adams, Gerry, *An Irish voice: the quest for peace* (Dingle, 1997).

Bew, Paul and Henry Patterson, *The British state and the Ulster crisis* (London, 1985).

Bew, Paul and Gordon Gillespie, *Northern Ireland: a chronology of the Troubles* (Dublin, 1999).

Bloomfield, David, *Political dialogue in Northern Ireland: the Brooke Initiative, 1989–92* (London, 1998).

Bowyer Bell, John, *The Irish Troubles* (Dublin, 1993).

Centre for the Study of Conflict, *A Northern Ireland centre in Brussels: a feasibility study* (Coleraine [n.d.]).

Currie, Austin, *All hell will break loose* (Dublin, 2002).

Devlin, Paddy, *Straight left: an autobiography* (Belfast, 1993).

Faulkner, Brian, *Memoirs of a statesman* (London, 1978).

FitzGerald, Garret, *All in a life* (Dublin, 1991).

FitzGerald, Garret, *Towards a new Ireland* (Dublin, 1972).

Godson, Dean, *Himself alone: David Trimble* (London, 2004).

Hayes, Maurice, *Minority verdict* (Belfast, 1995).

Kennelly, Danny and Eric Preston, *Belfast, August 1971: a case to be answered* (Belfast, 1971).

Mallie, Eamonn and David McKittrick, *The fight for peace: the secret story behind the Irish peace process* (London, 1996).

Martin, Simone, *Report on Northern Ireland to the European Parliament* (Brussels, 1981).

McAllister, Ian, *The Northern Ireland Social Democratic and Labour Party* (London, 1977).

McKeown, Michael, *Greening of a Nationalist* (Dublin, 1986).

McKittrick, David, Seamus Kelters, Brian Feeney and Chris Thornton, *Lost lives* (Edinburgh, 1999).

Moloney, Ed, *Voices from the grave* (London, 2010)

O'Malley, Pádraig, *Ireland: the uncivil wars* (Belfast, 1983).

Pollak, Andy (ed.), *Initiative '92, a citizens' inquiry: the Opsahl Report on Northern Ireland* (Dublin, 1993).

Prior, James, *A balance of power* (London, 1986).

Quinn, Ruairi, *Straight left: a journey in politics* (Dublin, 2005)

Rees, Merlyn, *Northern Ireland: a personal perspective* (London, 1985).

Routledge, Paul, *John Hume, a biography* (London, 1997).

Ryder, Chris, *Fighting Fitt* (Belfast, 2006).

Stalker, John, *Stalker* (London, 1988).

INDIVIDUALS

In the course of writing this book I spoke with many people, most but not all of whom are members of the SDLP. I am deeply appreciative of the help, advice and information afforded me by Alex Attwood, Ben Caraher, Ivan Cooper, Gerry Cosgrove, Austin Currie, Mark Durkan, John and Pat Hume, Joe Hendron, Hugh and Anne Logue, Eddie McGrady, Berna McIvor, Michael McKeown, Séamus Mallon, Bríd Rodgers and Séamus Scally.

Index